C0-AVW-100

808.02 Ste
Steiner.
Historical journals.

The Lorette Wilmot Library
Nazareth College of Rochester

HISTORICAL JOURNALS

HISTORICAL JOURNALS

A Handbook for Writers and Reviewers

Second Edition

by

Dale R. Steiner
Casey R. Phillips

McFarland & Company, Inc., Publishers
Jefferson, North Carolina, and London

WITHDRAWN
LORETTE WILMOT LIBRARY
NAZARETH COLLEGE

British Library Cataloguing-in-Publication data are available

Library of Congress Cataloguing-in-Publication Data

Steiner, Dale R.
    Historical journals : a handbook for writers and reviewers / by
Dale R. Steiner and Casey R. Phillips. — 2nd ed.
      p. cm.
    Incudes bibliographical references (p.) and index.
    ISBN 0-89950-801-4 (lib. bdg. : 50# alk. paper).
    ISBN 0-89950-901-0 (perfectbound : 50# alk. paper) ∞
    1. History — Periodicals — Directories. 2. History — Authorship —
Marketing — Directories. 3. Book reviewing. I. Phillips, Casey R.
II. Title
    Z6205.S73   1993
    [D10]
    808'.02 — dc20   92-51090
                                                 CIP

©1993 Dale R. Steiner and Casey R. Phillips. All rights reserved

Manufactured in the United States of America

McFarland & Company, Inc., Publishers
 Box 611, Jefferson, North Carolina 28640

808.02
5td

To our wives,
Karen Puccetti and Lisa Phillips-Phillips,
and children,
Rachel and Marc Steiner,
Tiffany Watts and Jarrod Phillips

Acknowledgments

We are indebted to all of the journal editors who cooperated with this project by furnishing information about their publications. No less appreciated were the advice and the expressions of encouragement offered by a considerable number of them. Several of our colleagues deserve thanks for providing assistance above and beyond the call of duty. Most notable in that regard are Teresa Loveless and Karolyn Thompson. A final note of appreciation is extended to the University of Southern Mississippi for providing a grant which made this research possible.

Contents

Acknowledgments — vii

Preface to the Second Edition — xi

Introduction — 1

Advice on Articles — 5
Writing an Article — 5
Selecting a Journal — 6
Preparing Your Manuscript — 8
Submitting Your Manuscript — 10
What Happens Next — 12
Acceptance and Rejection — 12
Other Possibilities — 14
For Additional Advice — 15

Advice on Book Reviewing — 17
Why Review? — 17
Becoming a Reviewer — 17
Writing a Review — 18
Points to Cover — 18
Review Form — 19
A Final Note — 19
For Additional Advice — 20

Directory of Journals — 21

Subject Index — 269

Preface to the Second Edition

The first edition of *Historical Journals: A Handbook for Writers and Reviewers* appeared in 1981. Since then, many of the periodicals it listed have changed editors, moved to different locations, or undergone other substantive alterations, reducing the utility of the book to scholars seeking publishers. In short, the original edition is now well out of date, necessitating publication of a second edition.

Although its format remains fundamentally unchanged from the original, the second edition has been substantially revised. The most obvious change is in the number of entries: about twice as many journals are listed in the second edition as in the first. This increase results from several factors: more journals were contacted, more editors responded, and the book's focus was broadened. Coverage has been extended to incorporate British journals, and more interdisciplinary journals in the humanities and social sciences are included as well.

At the same time, however, the book has become a bit less eclectic and assumed a more scholarly emphasis than in the first edition. This does not mean that the interests and needs of amateur historians and buffs are ignored. The second edition still contains a representative offering of local historical society publications. It also lists a handful of annuals, newsletters, and genealogical publications, but as a rule the authors have tended to omit those kinds of works.

The second edition contains a bit more information in its listings, including subscription prices and sources where journals are indexed or abstracted. As in the first edition, some of the listings are only partially complete because not all editors furnished all of the information requested of them. And despite a generally better rate of response from editors this time as compared to a dozen years ago, some chose to ignore repeated solicitations. In a few such instances in which the journal seemed too important to omit and some of the desired information was readily available from other sources, the authors supplied the data themselves.

Not only are the journal listings changed, but so are the advisory essays which precede them. Computers and word processors are now much more widely used for the production of manuscripts than they were when the first edition appeared; the advice offered in the second edition reflects that development. The bibliographies which follow "Advice on Articles" and "Advice on Book Reviewing" have also been updated and revised.

Introduction

The present volume is designed to help would-be authors publish their work in historical periodicals. It also seeks to assist editors by promoting the submission of manuscripts that are consistent with the needs and standards of their publications. The authors draw no distinction between amateur and professional historians, academics and buffs, but simply proceed from the premise that you the reader have researched and planned a historical article which you would like to publish. If you are uncertain how to accomplish that goal, the following pages can assist you in several ways. First, the book offers general suggestions on the preparation and submission of manuscripts. Second, it contains a directory which lists nearly 700 journals published in the United States, Canada, and Great Britain, and provides specific information on the editorial standards and publishing policies of each. These two tools should help you maximize the chances of having a manuscript accepted for publication.

Much of the information and advice on the following pages was furnished by journal editors, the men and women who ultimately determine what is published. There is, of course, no guarantee of success to writers, even if they follow all of the editor's suggestions to the letter. But common sense argues that taking that advice and utilizing that information are practices clearly in an author's best interest.

This book is not a comprehensive catalog of historical periodicals published in the United States, Canada, and Great Britain. Some editors chose not to respond to several appeals for information; others were, no doubt, mistakenly overlooked. But with almost 700 detailed entries covering a broad spectrum of fields, interests, and eras, and ranging from highly specialized scholarly journals to avowedly amateur local publications, the directory offers historians numerous outlets for their work.

An additional feature is a section which discusses the purposes and techniques of book reviewing. The directory section includes information on the reviewing needs and policies of individual journals.

The information in the directory section is the product of a questionnaire completed by editors of historical journals. The format of the listings reflects the content of the questionnaire. Although the listings are for the most part readily understandable, a few explanatory remarks follow.

Unless otherwise indicated, the subscription price which is listed for each journal is the domestic individual rate. Costs often are higher for foreign and institutional subscribers. Also, the prices given are only as current as the information available at press time.

The subheading "Indexed/Abstracted" refers to the publications in which the journal is indexed or abstracted. Only those indexes and abstracts in which history and interdisciplinary journals were most likely to be found were included. Abbreviations are used to indicate indexing and abstracting sources:

ABC	*America: History and Life* and *Historical Abstracts*
AHCI	*Arts and Humanities Citation Index*
AHI	*American Humanities Index*
BHI	*British Humanities Index*
BRD	*Book Review Digest*
BRI	*Book Review Index*
CCAH	*Current Contents: Arts and Humanities*
CCSB	*Current Contents: Social and Behavioral Sciences*
HI	*Humanities Index*
IMB	*International Medieval Bibliography*
MLA	*MLA Bibliography*
PAIS	*PAIS International in Print*
RG	*Reader's Guide to Periodical Literature*
SSCI	*Social Sciences Citation Index*
SSI	*Social Sciences Index*
WAH	*Writings on American History*

Under the heading "Manuscripts" are the subheadings "Query" and "Abstract." Journal editors were asked whether queries or abstracts were required before a publication decision could be reached. The negative answer means not that queries or abstracts are unwelcome but that an article submitted without an initial query or without a summarizing abstract would nevertheless be considered.

The directory also employs abbreviations to denote the various style guides used by journals:

Chicago	University of Chicago Press, *The Chicago Manual of Style* (13th edition)

MLA	Modern Language Association, *The MLA Style Manual* (3rd edition)
ModHum	Modern Humanities Research Association, *Style Book: Notes for Authors, Editors, and Writers of Dissertations* (4th edition)
Turabian	Kate L. Turabian, *A Manual for Writers of Term Papers, Theses, and Dissertations* (5th edition)

Individual directory entries note other style guides where appropriate.

The subheading "Notes" gave editors an opportunity to state their preference for the placement of notes in articles published in their journals. "Blind referee" indicates whether a journal conceals the identity of an article's author from the reviewers who comment on the suitability of the work for publication. "Foreign languages" indicates whether languages other than English are acceptable.

The directory of journals is organized alphabetically by journal title. Journals known by titles in more than one language are listed under the English title.

Advice on Articles

Writing an Article

WHAT EDITORS LOOK FOR

All prospective authors should be aware of the various factors that influence an editor to accept or reject a manuscript. These factors should be considered carefully throughout the composition of an article and especially when deciding which journal to submit it to. While the order of importance may vary from periodical to periodical, the most significant factors are an article's suitability to the journal's readership, its quality of presentation, and the degree to which it conforms to the journal's requirements of space and style.

Suitability means that the subject of a manuscript falls within the focus of the journal and that it is aimed at that journal's readership. The editor of a journal dealing with African history is unlikely to consider an article on American expansion across the Great Plains. Similarly, an extremely technical piece of great interest to professional historians might be unwelcome at a journal geared to enthusiasts or the general public. *Quality* refers to the accuracy and credibility of a manuscript as well as to the clarity with which it is presented. An article which is well written and easily understood stands a far better chance of acceptance than one that is not. The physical form of a manuscript is also important — it should be neat and clean. *Conformity* involves the amount of work an editor must perform to bring an article into alignment with the journal's particular needs and standards. Confronted by a manuscript a half dozen pages too long, an editor may understandably opt for a shorter piece in preference to reducing the longer manuscript himself. Likewise an article which observes the same rules of style, punctuation, and note form and placement as are used by the journal to which it is submitted is more likely to receive a favorable response from the editor.

SEEK CRITICISM

Before your article is in its final form, tighten it up as well as you can. This should by no means be a solitary process. Discuss your ideas with colleagues and knowledgeable friends and invite them to read your rough draft. If you belong to a historical society or club, arrange to present your ideas as a paper at a meeting. Academics should take advantage of existing speakers series, or organize their own colloquium if their department lacks such a program. The point is to test your premises, research, and conclusions on an objective audience. Nothing is lost in the process and the possible rewards include useful criticism, a better article, and improved chances of publication.

LITERARY STYLE

The proper medium for your article is clear, formal English (not stiff, merely correct). Avoid using slang at all costs; most editors detest it. Professional jargon is scarcely more welcome, unless you happen to be writing for a narrow, highly specialized readership. *The Elements of Style,* by William Strunk and E. B. White, is a good place to turn for assistance. Questions of proper spelling and word division may be settled by consulting *Webster's Third New International Dictionary,* a volume recommended by many editors.

INTRODUCTION/TITLE

Pay particular attention to the first few paragraphs; they persuade readers that the article is worth reading. Editors realize that readers often skim the opening paragraphs before deciding to read an article in its entirety, so they look for articles which have strong introductions. One editor observed that "Too many articles simply 'die' in the first paragraph through bad writing, or by taking the reader for granted, i.e. simply assuming the article is of as great interest to him as it is to the author." The introduction should indicate what your article is about and tell why that topic is important. This should be done in an explicit, rather than implicit, manner.

The title of your article is also important. It should be informative and, if possible, intriguing. It should also be short; lengthy titles sometimes create space problems for journals. Editors are grateful for any effort that your foresight spares them.

Selecting a Journal

WHAT TO CONSIDER

Submitting your manuscript to the right journal greatly enhances the possibility of publication. You should therefore exercise considerable care in choosing where to send it. Begin by making a list of the journals whose focus of interest coincides with that of your article. Then consider the descriptions of their readership. Narrow your list down to those periodicals whose readership is compatible with the level of ideas and language contained in your article. Other factors to weigh include the size of a journal's circulation, its rate of acceptance, the length of time needed to reach a decision, and whether any payment is made to contributors. For most journals listed herein, payment consists of a few offprints of your article or several copies of the issue in which your work appears. Only a handful offer monetary payment. Another consideration is prestige. Certainly acceptance by some journals represents more of a distinction than does publication by others. But as prestige is rather an intangible and subjective factor, this book can offer no direction on this point.

If a particular journal has previously published an article of yours, you should not assume that your chances of having a second article printed by the same journal are any greater. Indeed, the opposite may well be true; lightning rarely strikes twice in the same place. Furthermore, publication in more than one journal can strengthen your reputation as a writer by conveying an impression of breadth.

Your final decision on a journal should not be made until you have perused a copy or two of each of the journals to which you have narrowed your choice. Make certain that your assumptions are correct, that your article really *is* suited to those journals. Eliminating uncertainty on this point is worth the trip to the library.

QUERY

If any of the entries for the journals you are considering indicate a query is in order, send a letter. Describe the theme of your article, mention the major sources you consulted, discuss why you believe the article is suited to that particular periodical, and indicate whether it makes an original or unique contribution to the literature on the subject. Be sure to include a self-addressed, stamped envelope with your letter of inquiry. Although you should never submit your article to more than one journal at a time, there is no reason to limit your inquiries in such a manner. Waiting to send a second query until the first one is answered will only delay your quest for publication, should your initial query receive a negative response.

Before sending a query to an editor in another country you should read the sections on "Mailing/Postage" and "Foreign history journals."

STYLE GUIDES

If the journal in question publishes its own style sheet, it is imperative that you write for a copy (again, include a self-addressed, stamped envelope with your request). This may be done in conjunction with a query. In fact, even if the journal from which you request a style sheet does not demand a query, you might as well send one since you are writing the editor anyway. It may give you encouragement or spare you a later rejection.

Preparing Your Manuscript

TYPING/WORD PROCESSING

All manuscripts submitted to journals should be typed or machine printed. The majority of historian-authors now use computers or word processors to produce their manuscripts. This is not surprising, given the clear advantages of such machines over typewriters in terms of editing, correcting, and revising text. When used in conjunction with a laser printer they can create a finished product that is superior in appearance to a typed manuscript.

More is not always better, however. When you type your article on a computer you should resist the temptation to utilize all of its capabilities: if you justify the right margin, or divide words at the ends of lines, you will complicate the task of copy editors.

Print out your manuscript on a laser printer, a letter-quality daisy-wheel printer, or a 24-pin dot matrix printer. Avoid using a 9-pin dot matrix printer; despite claims that they offer "near letter quality" performance, 9-pin printers produce results that are inferior to those created by the other types of printers mentioned, and the pages may not photocopy well. If your printer has a ribbon, replace it before beginning. Print your article on standard white 8½ by 11 inch, high quality, 20 pound paper. Do not use erasable, onionskin, second-copy, or perforated "tractor-feed" paper.

If you are using a typewriter you should also use standard, high quality bond paper, avoiding the types of paper warned against above. Before beginning to type, clean the keys of your typewriter and replace the ribbon if it is at all worn. A pica typeface is preferable to either elite or script, each of which is more difficult to read.

Whether you use a typewriter or a computer, you should double space the entire manuscript, including footnotes and quotations. This format facilitates editing as well as typesetting. One or two brief handwritten corrections per page are acceptable, provided they are done legibly and in ink.

Neatness is extremely important throughout. Carelessly typed or otherwise messy manuscripts create unfavorable impressions and are less likely to be judged on the merits of the ideas they present or the contributions they make to knowledge.

If you show consideration toward editors, they may be more favorably disposed toward your work. This can be done not only by double spacing but also by providing generous margins, making room for editorial notations and corrections. The left margin should be at least 1½ inches wide; all others should be at least 1 inch.

Construct your paper in the editorial style of the journal to which you are submitting it. If no specific guide is listed, use either the thirteenth edition of the University of Chicago's *Manual of Style* (1982) or the third edition of *The MLA Style Manual* (1985).

ILLUSTRATIONS

All tables, graphs, charts, or maps which accompany your text should conform to the journal's standard format. Usually that means they should each be on a separate sheet of paper, labeled properly, with the source of the information they convey cited. Be certain to indicate the correct location of all such material in your manuscript. Pictorial illustrations, including photographs, should likewise be labeled and identified. Make sure that you have obtained permission from the copyright holders for the use of any such material that is not original with you.

PERMISSIONS

Copyright law permits the "fair use" of copyrighted material, but this concept is not defined very precisely. Generally speaking, fair use refers to the reproduction of material for purposes of news reporting, comment, criticism, teaching, research, or scholarship. Factors which help determine whether fair use is being made of someone else's material include the character of that use (e.g. whether it is commercial or nonprofit), the nature of the copyrighted material, the proportion of the copyrighted work being reproduced or used, and the impact of that use upon the commercial potential or value of the copyrighted material.

These considerations weigh less heavily upon the authors of scholarly articles than they do, for example, upon the writers of textbooks, given the nonprofit nature of the former and the pecuniary aspirations of the latter. Still, historians of all stripes are affected by recent court decisions which have held that unpublished diaries, letters, and the like may not be used without permission. Moreover, because the law offers no specific guidelines on how long a quotation may run before it exceeds fair use, it is difficult to know where you stand when you use published material. It may not be necessary for you to obtain permissions, but it is better to be safe than sorry. When in doubt, obtain releases.

Once your article has been accepted, write the holder of the copyright to the material you seek to use, identify the material thoroughly, and describe the manner in which you intend to employ it. Mention the journal where your article will appear. Be sure to maintain a record of your request and the response to it. The journal editor may be able to advise you in this process, but it is the author's responsibility to obtain permissions.

IDENTIFICATION

Reviewers who evaluate a manuscript for publication are called "referees." "Blind" referees are reviewers from whom the author's identity is concealed. The obvious advantage of this system is that the article in question is more likely to be judged on its own merits than by the name or reputation of the author. If you are sending your article to a journal which utilizes blind referees you should omit your name from the manuscript (including the title page).

Be certain, however, that your work is fully identifiable by including your name and your article's title in the accompanying cover letter (see "Cover Letter/Abstract"). Some of the journals listed as not using blind referees in fact do so, but their editors prefer to delete authors' names themselves before forwarding manuscripts for review.

Submitting Your Manuscript

SINGLE SUBMISSION

Multiple submissions (i.e. sending articles to more than one journal at a time) are unethical and can prove embarrassing should you be found out (many individuals referee manuscripts for more than one periodical), or if two journals accept the same article. More to the point, you might seriously damage your chances of future publication in some journals. Admittedly, sticking to a policy of single submission can be both frustrating and excessively time-consuming if your article is rejected a few times, but as noted before, considerate treatment of editors is in your best interest.

COPIES

Before the widespread use of word processors the standard policy was always to submit the original typescript of an article as a way of suggesting to editors that the manuscript was not also under consideration elsewhere. Advances in technology have obviously rendered such a procedure moot. Nonetheless, the original typescript or a newly printed computerized version of your article will make the best appearance. Generally, however, a good quality photocopy is acceptable. If more than one copy of your article is needed, more photocopies are in order. Carbon copies, unless specifically called for, should be avoided. Be sure to keep a copy for yourself.

COVER LETTER/ABSTRACT

A cover letter which introduces your article to an editor is always a good idea; it is particularly useful if you are not submitting an abstract. The letter should briefly explain what your article is about, why it is suited to that particular journal, and how it enlarges the understanding of history. If your manuscript was prepared on a word processor or a computer, be sure to include information on the operating system and word processing program which you used, as well as your disk size. Some journals may wish to use your disk to facilitate editing or publishing your article; its availability on disk might even promote your article's acceptance.

Only a small percentage of the journals listed in the directory require abstracts. An abstract is a brief (one or two page), concise summary which outlines your thesis, argument, and conclusion.

MAILING/POSTAGE

Do not fold your manuscript. Mail it flat in a sturdy envelope. Leave the pages loose; do not staple them or secure them with a paper clip or in a binder. Include a self-addressed envelope to facilitate the return of your manuscript if it is rejected or in need of revision. Include sufficient postage to guarantee return, but do not attach the stamps to the envelope; they may be returned if the article is accepted. Failure to include a return envelope and postage represents a real imposition and may adversely influence an editor. It may also result in your article being thrown out rather than returned.

Growing numbers of editors are willing to be flexible about return postage in an era of rising postal rates and decreasing duplication costs. The return postage for three copies of a thirty page article may run considerably more than the expense of photocopying them. In view of this, it may be advisable to forego including return postage, provided you carefully explain in your cover letter that you are submitting disposable copies for the convenience of all concerned.

This particularly makes sense if you send the article to a journal in another country, because the return postage must be of that country's issue. Foreign editors are frequently frustrated by well-intentioned authors in the United States who include return postage in United States stamps. A Canadian editor who was only half joking described this practice as "cultural imperialism, deliberate or not." The best way to handle this problem is to purchase and send International Reply Coupons, available at any post office in the United States. These can be exchanged by editors in other countries for the correct stamps at the rate of one coupon per ounce.

For journals within the United States mail your article first class; use air mail for those in Canada or Great Britain. If you wish verification of your manuscript's safe arrival, send it by certified mail within the United States, or by registered mail to Canada or Great Britain; in any case be certain to request a return receipt.

A faster (and more expensive) alternative is offered by overnight delivery services like Federal Express, Airborne, United Parcel Service, and others. Speed of delivery may not be your primary consideration, but it is important to remember that the longer your manuscript is in transit, the more hazards it is exposed to.

What Happens Next

REVIEW/DECISION

Describing the process by which articles are reviewed is difficult; policies vary from journal to journal. Generally speaking, when a manuscript is received it is screened by an editor or two, or perhaps by an editorial board. If the article is outside the focus of the journal, a negative decision is quickly reached and the manuscript returned. Sometimes, especially in the case of smaller journals oriented toward local amateur historians, or buffs, the editor decides without consulting anyone else whether to accept or reject submitted material. In other instances, as with many scholarly journals aimed at professional historians, editors enlist the services of reviewers or referees (one or two or more). The referees are selected for their expertise in the field in which the article is written. They evaluate the manuscript and make recommendations to the editor. After weighing the referees' remarks, the editor decides whether to publish the article.

TIME

Obviously, the more people this process involves the more drawn out it becomes. This seems to be especially true for scholarly periodicals. Referees are, after all, engaged in their own research and writing, meeting classes, or whatever, and despite their good intentions they sometimes take longer in their reviewing than intended. During the summer, decisions tend to come even more slowly because so many scholars employed as reviewers depart the campus. If three months pass without a decision (unless a longer period is listed as standard for the journal in question), you are certainly within your rights to send a polite letter of inquiry. If handled diplomatically, this should in no way affect the decision on your manuscript.

Acceptance and Rejection

ACCEPTANCE

If your article is accepted as is, you deserve congratulations. Sometimes articles are returned with their ultimate acceptance contingent upon certain revisions being made. In such cases complete the revisions as promptly as possible. Even after acceptance important work remains to be done. Galley proofs are sent to the author in many cases; it is your responsibility to read them quickly yet carefully, noting any errors. Since it is possible that your original manuscript will not be returned to you, it is imperative that you retain a copy against which you can check the galleys.

REJECTION

At least among the more prestigious journals, rejection of manuscripts is a considerably more common experience than acceptance. It does not hurt, therefore, to be prepared for it. Perhaps the most important thing to remember is not to be discouraged. Rejection of your manuscript does not necessarily mean that it is valueless or that you are a failure as a historian. Sometimes editors or their referees will explain why they decided against your article, but more frequently you are left in the frustrating position of not knowing what they found objectionable in your work. You are therefore on your own in deciding whether or not to revise it.

Simply because one or two editors decided against publication of your manuscript does not mean that it is unworthy of publication. Their opinions are subjective, after all, and may not be shared by the editors or reviewers at another journal. So reconsider your article carefully and honestly, and if you still believe it to be historically sound and well written, send it out again without revision. And send it without delay. The natural response to rejection is discouragement, but do not allow it to immobilize you. In fact, even as you send your manuscript off initially, you should have a second journal in mind in case it is rejected.

REVISION

If you would like to make some changes in your article without undertaking a full-scale revision, the most profitable course of action may be to rewrite the first paragraph or two. Even though you may have already given the introduction a great deal of attention, you should be able to strengthen it further. The importance of the introduction cannot be stressed enough.

While you should not be devastated by rejection, you ought not to disregard it either. It means that a person or people with some expertise in history detected what appeared to be flaws in your work. You must seriously consider the possibility that, in its existing form, your article is not very good. If that is indeed the case, you will have to undertake major revisions to improve it. If your manuscript was returned with negative comments, the logical way to begin is to address those criticisms. Without benefit of the reviewers' comments, you should seek out criticism in the fashion described earlier. One major change that might prove beneficial is shortening your manuscript. Just as lengthy titles can create space problems, long articles may pose a challenge to editors. Paring your manuscript down may make it more acceptable to an editor wrestling with a shortage of space.

RESUBMISSION

As a general rule it is unwise to resubmit your article to a journal which has already rejected it, unless the editor has urged you to do so. This is true even if you have revised it extensively along the lines suggested by the journal's referees.

Other Possibilities

UNITED STATES, CANADA, AND GREAT BRITAIN

History is the mother of many disciplines. It is not surprising, therefore, that there are hundreds of journals in the United States, Canada, and Great Britain that publish articles by historians, even though their primary orientation is in other directions. Literary reviews, for example, frequently have a broader scope; they not only publish poetry, fiction, and literary criticism, but are also often interested in the culture that produces those artistic forms. Contemporary affairs magazines accept historical articles as a means for broadening perceptions of current events. Publications on political science, economics, social science, and other fields are frequently receptive to articles by historians. Travel magazines, including those published by automobile clubs and airlines, represent another market which views historical articles with favor. Failure to find a listing that coincides with your particular interest is by no means cause for giving up.

OTHER FOREIGN HISTORY JOURNALS

History is appreciated, studied, and written about throughout the world, so another possibility to consider is publication in a foreign journal. English-language periodicals are published in many other countries, including some where English is not the official language. The following list gives only the barest indication of that outlet.

> *International Review of Social History* (the Netherlands)
> *Irish Historical Studies* (Ireland)
> *Journal of Asian History* (Germany)
> *The Journal of Pacific History* (Australia)
> *Journal of Southeast Asian Studies* (Singapore)

For those capable of producing their work in other languages, the possibilities are even more extensive.

Dealing with journals in other countries can involve a considerable expenditure of time and money, usually in inverse proportion. Saving time costs money and vice versa. Surface mail takes an inordinately long time. It would not be unusual, for instance, for a query or a manuscript to take two months to travel from the United States to Germany. It goes without saying that a reply could take just as long. While airmail is much quicker, the expense is substantially greater. International Reply Coupons are an absolute necessity for transacting business with an overseas journal (see "Mailing/Postage"). Before deciding to send your manuscript overseas, carefully weigh the importance of time and money spent in pursuit of publication.

For Additional Advice

Achtert, Walter S., and Gibaldi, Joseph. *The MLA Style Manual.* 3rd ed. New York: Modern Language Association of America, 1985.

Barzun, Jacques. *Simple and Direct: A Rhetoric for Writers.* Rev. ed. New York: Harper and Row, 1985.

————, and Graff, Henry F. *The Modern Researcher.* 4th ed. San Diego: Harcourt Brace Jovanovich, 1985.

Bernstein, Theodore M. *The Careful Writer: A Modern Guide to English Usage.* New York: Atheneum, 1977.

Cortada, James W. "Publishing American Scholarship in Europe." *Scholarly Publishing,* vol. 5, no. 2 (January 1974), 173–78.

Felt, Thomas E. *Researching, Writing, and Publishing Local History.* Nashville: American Association for State and Local History, 1981.

Forscher, Bernard K. "The Role of the Referee." *Scholarly Publishing,* vol. 11, no. 2 (January 1980), 165–69.

Gibaldi, Joseph, and Achtert, Walter S. *MLA Handbook for Writers of Research Papers.* New York: Modern Language Association of America, 1988.

Harman, Eleanor. "On Seeking Permission." *Scholarly Publishing,* vol. 1, no. 2 (January 1970).

Kent, Sherman. *Writing History.* 2nd ed. New York: Meredith, 1967.

Lottinville, Savoie. *The Rhetoric of History.* Norman: University of Oklahoma Press, 1976.

Luey, Beth. *Handbook for Academic Authors.* Rev. ed. New York: Cambridge University Press, 1990.

MacGregor, A. J. "Graphics Simplified: Choosing Illustrations." *Scholarly Publishing,* vol. 9, no. 3 (April 1978), 270–79.

Maney, A. S., and Smallwood, R. L., eds. *Style Book: Notes for Authors, Editors and Writers of Dissertations.* 4th ed. London: Modern Humanities Research Association, 1991.

Markland, Murray F. "Taking Criticism — and Using It." *Scholarly Publishing,* vol. 14, no. 2 (February 1983), 139–47.

Marston, Doris. *A Guide to Writing History.* Cincinnati: Writer's Digest, 1976.

Mitchell, John H. *Writing for Professional and Technical Journals.* New York: John Wiley and Sons, 1968.

Mullins, Carolyn J. *A Guide to Writing and Publishing in the Social and Behavioral Sciences.* Melbourne, Fla.: Krieger, 1983.

Reitt, Barbara B. "An Academic Author's Checklist." *Scholarly Publishing,* vol. 16, no. 1 (October 1984), 65–72.

Riggar, T. F., and Matkin, R. E. "Breaking into Academic Print." *Scholarly Publishing,* vol. 22, no. 1 (October 1990), 17–20.

Rodman, Hyman. "Some Practical Advice for Journal Contributors." *Scholarly Publishing,* vol. 9, no. 3 (April 1978), 235–41.

_____, and Mancini, Jay A. "Editors, Manuscripts, and Equal Treatment." *Research in Higher Education,* vol. 7 (1977), 369–74.

Skillin, Marjorie E., Gay, Robert M., and others. *Words into Type.* 3rd ed. Englewood Cliffs, N.J.: Prentice-Hall, 1986.

Strunk, William Jr., and White, E. B. *The Elements of Style.* 3rd ed. New York: Macmillan, 1979.

Turabian, Kate L. *A Manual for Writers of Term Papers, Theses, and Dissertations.* 5th ed. Chicago: University of Chicago Press, 1987.

United States Government Printing Office. *Style Manual.* Rev. ed. Washington, D.C.: United States Government Printing Office, 1984.

University of Chicago Press. *The Chicago Manual of Style.* 13th ed., revised. Chicago: University of Chicago Press, 1982.

van Leunen, Mary-Claire. *A Handbook for Scholars.* 2nd ed. New York: Oxford University Press, 1992.

Westwood, John. *Typing for Print.* London: Pitman, 1976.

Advice on Book Reviewing

Why Review?

Writing a book (or film or tape) review is, generally speaking, a more readily accomplished alternative to authoring an article. While some review essays attain the length of a full-sized manuscript, most book reviews run three pages or fewer. Obviously an 800-word composition represents a considerable savings in time and effort compared to one of 8,000 words. Instead of conducting research in a variety of sources, the book reviewer need only read and reflect upon one volume.

The relative ease with which a book review can be written is by no means the only reason for reviewing, but it is a significant one. The college instructor who is too burdened by classes, the demands of students, and committee assignments to research and write an article (let alone a book) can nonetheless demonstrate continuing intellectual activity by regularly writing reviews. Amateur historians can satisfy their creative needs in a similar manner without encroaching upon their other interests.

Reviewing books is also a means for expanding your personal library: Customarily volumes which are sent to an individual for review become that person's property. Some reviewers see their activity as a way of imposing discipline upon their reading habits. Without the obligation to read and report upon books, they fear becoming too busy to remain well-read.

Book reviews not only benefit their authors but also serve the interests of readers. Reviews assist readers in deciding whether to spend time or money on a book, and they provide a means for keeping abreast of the latest literature — an otherwise impossible task, considering the vast number of newly published books. What's more, a good review can be read and appreciated for its own sake by someone who has no intention of ever picking up the book in question. Such a review is, in its own way, as informative and valuable as a much longer article.

Becoming a Reviewer

Some journals only publish reviews written by members of their staffs, but many historical journals maintain files of reviewers to whom they

17

periodically assign books. As a quick look through the directory will indicate, many journals are constantly seeking to expand their reviewer files. Becoming part of a file is therefore quite easy. Simply consult the directory entry for the journal you are interested in to see whether a special information or application form is required. If so, address a letter to the book review editor, indicate your interest in reviewing for the journal, and request an information form. In most instances, though, no such form is needed; a letter will suffice. The directory indicates the information each journal seeks from prospective reviewers—be certain to provide what is called for. Some journals may never contact you, others may require your services immediately and often. Be sensible and selective in offering your services. Special interest journals which focus on specific subjects often only review books that deal with those subjects, so if you are not interested or competent in maritime history, you should not become a reviewer for a journal that concentrates on that subject.

Writing a Review

A good book review must be interesting. It is, after all, a creative composition. A review should be neither a transcription of the book's table of contents nor a thinly disguised summary of its dustcover remarks. The conscientious reviewer attempts, in a few brief paragraphs, to bring a much longer work into focus through the application of his understanding of the subject of the book. The result is informative, whether the review itself is critical or laudatory. Since informing readers is the principal purpose of a review, you should bear in mind their interests and level of expertise. They are more interested in a thoughtful evaluation of the book than they are in a display of the reviewer's cleverness, vitriol, or overstatement. Remember, too, as a reviewer you should be as accountable as the authors you comment upon—indicate the page numbers of passages you quote in your review.

Points to Cover

Describe the author's purpose in writing the book and indicate the extent to which it was fulfilled. Assess the book's strengths and weaknesses and note whether one overshadows the other. While a book can be analyzed merely on its own merits, placing it in the context of other works on the same subject helps to establish its significance (or lack thereof). Similarly, a few words about the author may be in order—what are her qualifications in the field? Has she written on the same subject before? How biased is she? Comment as well on the book's utility to the readership you represent.

If you are reviewing a new edition of a previously published work, discuss the extent to which the book has been revised from previous editions. Indicate whether the book is of continuing significance.

Spot-check the book for accuracy. Is the author correct on basic facts? Are quotations accurate and citations proper? If there is a bibliography, is it comprehensive, or were important sources overlooked? What about the physical appearance of the book? Is the editing sloppy? Are illustrations reproduced clearly?

Review Form

Book reviewers whose services are solicited are usually instructed by the journals they write for as to the form they should use for the heading and signature. Those who are not given directions and authors of unsolicited reviews should check a copy of the journal in question for the desired form. An example of a standard heading is:

AUTHOR NAME (capitalized). Title (underlined to denote italic in print). Place of publication: publisher, year. Number of pages. Price.

Some journals desire more information, requiring reviewers to mention any foreword, introduction, acknowledgments, notes, appendixes, bibliography, or indexes; list the type and number of illustrations; and note whether the book is cloth or paperback. To know exactly what is needed, look at reviews in the journal in question.

The reviewer's signature is even more standardized:

Institutional affiliation   REVIEWER'S NAME

A Final Note

Try to conform to the length limitation imposed by the journal. Equally important is the need to observe the deadline for submitting your review. Usually only a few weeks are allowed between receipt of a book and the due date for its review. It may seem hypocritical that journals which take months to consider articles permit only a few weeks for the review of books, but the timeliness of a book review often determines its value. Most journals strive to minimize the lag between the appearance of a book and the publication of its review. Since other factors are fixed, the logical way to save time is by pressuring reviewers. Grace under pressure is an admirable quality.

For Additional Advice

Becker, Carl. "The Reviewing of Historical Books." *Annual Report of the American Historical Association for the Year 1912.* Washington: 1914, 127–36.

Budd, John. "Book Reviewing Practices of Journals in the Humanities." *Scholarly Publishing,* vol. 13, no. 4 (July 1982), 363–71.

Clark, G. N. "Historical Reviewing." *Essays in History Presented to Reginald Lane Poole.* Edited by H. W. C. Davis. Freeport, N.Y.: Books for Libraries Press, 1967.

Hoge, James O., ed. *Literary Reviewing.* Charlottesville: University Press of Virginia, 1987.

_____, and West, James L. W., III. "Academic Book Reviewing: Some Problems and Suggestions." *Scholarly Publishing,* vol. 11, no. 1 (October 1979), 35–41.

Jones, Llewellyn. *How to Criticize Books.* New York: Norton, 1928.

Kamerman, Sylvia E., ed. *Book Reviewing: A Guide to Writing Book Reviews for Newspapers, Magazines, Radio, and Television.* Boston: Writer, 1978.

Klemp, P. J. "Reviewing Academic Books: Some Ideas for Beginners." *Scholarly Publishing,* vol. 12, no. 2 (January 1981), 135–39.

Lichtman, Allan J., and French, Valerie. *Historians and the Living Past.* Arlington Heights, Ill.: AHM, 1978, 244–48.

Lottinville, Savoie. *The Rhetoric of History.* Norman: University of Oklahoma Press, 1976, 169–82.

Luey, Beth. *Handbook for Academic Authors.* Rev. ed. New York: Cambridge University Press, 1990, 24–25.

Mullins, Carolyn J. *A Guide to Writing and Publishing in the Social and Behavioral Sciences.* Melbourne, Fla.: Krieger, 1983.

Walford, A. J., ed. *Reviews and Reviewing: A Guide.* Phoenix: Oryx Press, 1986.

Wolper, R. S. "'A Grass-Blade': On Academic Reviewing." *Scholarly Publishing,* vol. 10, no. 4 (July 1979), 325–28.

_____. "On Academic Reviewing: Ten Common Errors." *Scholarly Publishing,* vol. 16, no. 3 (April 1985), 269–75.

Woodcock, George. "The Critic as Mediator." *Scholarly Publishing,* vol. 4, no. 3 (April 1973), 201–9.

Directory of Journals

Acadiensis: Journal of the History of the Atlantic Region

History of Atlantic Canada, the North Atlantic, Northern New England, and the Gulf of St. Lawrence
Affiliation: University of New Brunswick
Ed: David Frank
  Campus House
  University of New Brunswick
  Fredericton, NB E3B 5A3
  Canada
Bk Rev Ed: same
2/yr, 250 pp; subs $21
Circ: 1,000
Readership: academics, general public
Indexed/Abstracted: ABC, AHCI, CCAH, WAH
• MANUSCRIPTS
Query: no; *Abstract:* no
Preferred length: 25–35 pp
Copies: 1
Notes: footnotes
Blind referee: yes
Acceptance rate: 3/10
Time to consider ms: 8–10 wks
Charts, pictures, tables, graphs, maps
Foreign languages accepted: French
• REVIEWS
Seeking reviewers: yes
Unsolicited reviews accepted: no
Materials reviewed: books, films
How to apply: letter

The Accounting Historians Journal

Accounting and tax history
Affiliation: Academy of Accounting Historians
Ed: Dale L. Flesher
  School of Accountancy
  University of Mississippi
  University, MS 38677
Bk Rev Ed: Patti A. Mills
  Dept of Accounting
  Indiana State University
  Terre Haute, IN 47809
2/yr, 180 pp; subs $32
Circ: 1,200
Readership: academics, general public
Indexed/Abstracted: ABC, WAH
• MANUSCRIPTS
Query: no; *Abstract:* yes
Style guide: Chicago
Preferred length: 10–30 pp
Copies: 3
Notes: endnotes
Blind referee: yes
Acceptance rate: 1/5
Time to consider ms: 3 mos.
Charts, pictures, tables, graphs, maps
Foreign languages accepted: no
• REVIEWS
Seeking reviewers: no
Unsolicited reviews accepted: no
Materials reviewed: books, films
Review length: 600 wds
How to apply: letter
Include in application: professional degrees, institutional affiliation, areas of expertise, published works, current research
• ADDITIONAL NOTES
See a recent issue for further style guidelines. There is a manuscript submission fee ($32 for non-

members and $15 for Academy members).

African Studies Review

African studies—social sciences, humanities, development
Affiliation: University of South Carolina
Ed: Mark W. DeLancey
  Gint
  University of South Carolina
  Columbia, SC 29208
Bk Rev Ed: same
3/yr, 170 pp; subs: membership in African Studies Association
Circ: 3,000
Indexed/Abstracted: ABC, MLA, SSI
• MANUSCRIPTS
Query: no; *Abstract:* yes
Style guide: Chicago
Preferred length: not defined
Copies: 3
Notes: endnotes
Blind referee: yes
Acceptance rate: 1/7
Time to consider ms: 3–4 mos
Charts, tables, graphs, maps
Foreign languages accepted: no
• REVIEWS
Seeking reviewers: yes
Unsolicited reviews accepted: no
Materials reviewed: books
Review length: 750 wds
How to apply: letter
Include in application: professional degrees, institutional affiliation, areas of expertise, published works, foreign languages, current research

Afrique Histoire U.S.

African history
Affiliation: The Association of African Historians
Ed: Amadou Niang
Bk Rev Ed: Turner Fair III
  P.O. Box 88622

Indianapolis, IN 46208-0622
4/yr, 32 pp; subs $14
Circ: 5,000
Readership: general public
• MANUSCRIPTS
Query: yes
Preferred length: 5–8 pp
Copies: 1 or 2
Notes: endnotes or footnotes
Blind referee: no
Charts, pictures, tables, graphs, maps
Foreign languages accepted: no
• REVIEWS
Seeking reviewers: no
Unsolicited reviews accepted: yes
Materials reviewed: books
How to apply: letter
Include in application: professional degrees, institutional affiliation, areas of expertise, published works, foreign languages

Afro-Americans in New York Life & History

Interdisciplinary study of New York Afro-Americans
Affiliation: Afro-American Historical Association of the Niagra Frontier
Ed: Monroe Fordham
Bk Rev Ed: Lillian Williams
  P.O. Box 1663
  Buffalo, NY 14216
2/yr, 90 pp; subs $8
Circ: 500
Readership: academics, general public
Indexed/Abstracted: ABC, WAH
• MANUSCRIPTS
Query: no; *Abstract:* no
Style guide: MLA or other standard format
Preferred length: 20–30 pp
Copies: 1
Notes: footnotes
Blind referee: yes
Acceptance rate: 3/4
Time to consider ms: 4 wks
Charts, tables, graphs
Foreign languages: no

- REVIEWS
Unsolicited reviews accepted: yes
Materials reviewed: books
Review length: 2–4 pp
How to apply: letter
Include in application: professional
degrees, areas of expertise

After the Battle

World War II battlefields explored
through photographs
Ed: Winston Ramsey
Church House
Church Street
London E15 3JA
U.K.
4/yr; 56 pp
Circ: 12,000
Readership: academics, general public
- MANUSCRIPTS
Query: no; *Abstract:* no
Style guide: any
Preferred length: varies
Copies: 1
Notes: none
Acceptance rate: 1/3
Time to consider ms: varies
Pictures, maps
Foreign languages accepted: no

Agricultural History

Any aspect of agricultural history
Affiliation: University of California,
Davis
Ed: Morton Rothstein
Agricultural History Center
UCD
Davis, CA 95616
Bk Rev Ed: same
4/yr; 120 pp; subs $30
Circ: 1,200
Readership: academics, general public
Indexed/Abstracted: ABC, AHCI,
CCAH, HI, IMB, WAH
- MANUSCRIPTS
Query: no; *Abstract:* no
Style guide: Chicago
Preferred length: 30 pp

Copies: 2
Notes: endnotes
Blind referee: yes
- REVIEWS
Seeking reviewers: no
Unsolicited reviews accepted: no

The Agricultural History Review

Historical agriculture, rural society,
rural economy
Affiliation: Institute of Agricultural
History, University of Reading
Ed: J. A. Chartres
School of Business and Economic
Studies
University of Leeds
Leeds LS2 9JT
U.K.
Bk Rev Ed: A. D. M. Phillips
Dept of Geography
University of Keele
Keele
Staffordshire ST5 5BG
U.K.
2/yr; 96 pp; subs £15
Circ: 1,100
Readership: academics, general public
Indexed/Abstracted: ABC, AHCI,
BHI, CCAH, IMB
- MANUSCRIPTS
Query: yes; *Abstract:* no
Style guide: own
Preferred length: 8,000 wds max
Copies: 2
Notes: endnotes
Blind referee: yes
Acceptance rate: 2/5
Time to consider ms: 2–3 mos
Charts, pictures, tables, graphs, maps
Foreign languages accepted: no
- REVIEWS
Seeking reviewers: yes
Unsolicited reviews accepted: no
Materials reviewed: books, pamphlets
Review length: 400–500 wds
How to apply: letter
Include in application: professional

degrees, institutional affiliation, areas of expertise, published works, foreign languages, current research

Alabama Heritage

The history, culture, and heritage of Alabama and the South
Affiliation: University of Alabama
Ed: Suzanne Wolfe
  Box 870342
  Tuscaloosa, AL 35487
4/yr, 52 pp; subs $16.95
Circ: 15,000
Readership: academics, general public
Indexed/Abstracted: ABC, WAH
• MANUSCRIPTS
Query: yes; *Abstract:* no
Preferred length: 3,000 to 5,000 wds
Copies: 1
Notes: none
Blind referee: no
Acceptance rate: varies
Time to consider ms: 3 months
Charts, pictures, tables, graphs, maps
Foreign languages accepted: no
• REVIEWS
Seeking reviewers: no
Unsolicited reviews accepted: no

Alabama Review

Alabama history and culture
Affiliation: University of Alabama
Ed: Sarah Woolfolk Wiggins
  Box 1209
  University of Alabama
  Tuscaloosa, AL 35486-1209
Bk Rev Ed: same
4/yr, 80 pp; subs $15
Circ: 2,000
Readership: academics, general public
Indexed/Abstracted: ABC, WAH
• MANUSCRIPTS
Query: no; *Abstract:* no
Style guide: Chicago
Preferred length: no specific length
Copies: 2
Notes: endnotes

Blind referee: yes
Acceptance rate: 1/5
Time to consider ms: 3–6 mos
Charts, pictures, maps
Foreign languages accepted: no
• REVIEWS
Seeking reviewers: yes
Unsolicited reviews accepted: no
Materials reviewed: books
Review length: varies
How to apply: letter
Include in application: professional degrees, institutional affiliation, areas of expertise, published works, current research

Alaska History

History of Alaska and related northern topics
Affiliation: Alaska Historical Society
Ed: James H. Ducker
  P.O. Box 100299
  Anchorage, AK 99510
Bk Rev Ed: Joan Antonson
2/yr, 80 pp; subs $10
Circ: 750
Readership: academics, general public
Indexed/Abstracted: ABC, WAH
• MANUSCRIPTS
Query: no; *Abstract:* no
Style guide: Chicago
Preferred length: 20 pp
Notes: endnotes
Blind referee: yes
Time to consider ms: 3 mos
Pictures, tables, graphs, maps
Foreign languages accepted: no
• REVIEWS
Seeking reviewers: yes
Unsolicited reviews accepted: no
Materials reviewed: books
Review length: 500 wds
How to apply: letter
Include in application: professional degrees, institutional affiliation, areas of expertise, published works, foreign languages, current research

Alberta History

History of Alberta
Affiliation: Historical Society of
Alberta
Ed: Hugh A. Dempsey
95 Holmwood Avenue, N.W.
Calgary, AB T2K 2G7
CANADA
Bk Rev Ed: same
4/yr, 28 pp; subs $20
Circ: 2,000
Readership: academics, general public
Indexed/Abstracted: ABC
• MANUSCRIPTS
Query: preferred; *Abstract:* no
Preferred length: 5,000–8,000 wds
Copies: 1
Notes: endnotes
Blind referee: yes
Acceptance rate: 1/4
Time to consider ms: 1–2 mos
Charts, pictures, tables, maps
Foreign languages accepted: no
• REVIEWS
Seeking reviewers: no
Unsolicited reviews accepted: no
Materials reviewed: bks

Albion

British history and culture; all
periods from Roman times to the
present
Affiliation: North American Con-
ference on British Studies
Ed: Michael J. Moore
Department of History
Appalachian State University
Boone, NC 28608
Bk Rev Ed: same
4/yr, 198 pp; subs $35
Circ: 1,768
Readership: academics
Indexed/Abstracted: ABC, AHCI,
CCAH
• MANUSCRIPTS
Query: no; *Abstract:* preferred
Style guide: Chicago
Preferred length: 10,000 wds

Copies: 2
Notes: endnotes
Blind referee: yes
Acceptance rate: 1/5
Time to consider ms: 3–4 mos
Pictures, tables, graphs
Foreign languages accepted: no
• REVIEWS
Seeking reviewers: yes
Unsolicited reviews accepted: no
Materials reviewed: books
Review length: 700–1,000 wds
How to apply: letter
Include in application: professional
degrees, institutional affiliation,
areas of expertise, published
works, current research

Ambix: The Journal of the Society for the History of Alchemy and Chemistry

All aspects of the history of alchemy
and chemistry
Ed: Gerrylynn K. Roberts
Department of History of
Science and Technology
The Open University
Milton Keynes MK7 6AA
U.K.
Bk Rev Ed: W. H. Brock
Department of History
University of Leicester
Leicester LE1 7RH
U.K.
4/yr, 48 pp; subs £18
Circ: 750
Readership: academics, general pub-
lic
Indexed/Abstracted: ABC, IMB
• MANUSCRIPTS
Query: preferred; *Abstract:* no
Style guide: own
Preferred length: 10,000 wds
Copies: 2
Notes: endnotes
Blind referee: yes
Time to consider ms: 3–4 mos

Charts, pictures, tables, graphs,
    maps, chemical formulae
Foreign languages accepted: no
• REVIEWS
Seeking reviewers: no
Unsolicited reviews accepted: no
Materials reviewed: books, journals,
    catalogs
Review length: 400 wds

Amerasia Journal

Asian American history, literature,
    and social sciences
Affiliation: UCLA Asian American
    Studies Center
Ed: Russell Leong
    Asian American Studies Center
    3230 Campbell Hall
    University of California, Los Angeles
    Los Angeles, CA 90024
Bk Rev Ed: Glenn Omatsu
3/yr, 180 pp; subs $15
Circ: 1,500
Readership: academics, general public
Indexed/Abstracted: ABC, AHCI,
    CCAH, WAH
• MANUSCRIPTS
Query: preferred; *Abstract:* no
Style guide: Chicago
Preferred length: 20–25 pp
Copies: 3
Notes: endnotes
Blind referee: yes
Acceptance rate: 1/2
Time to consider ms: 3–4 mos
All illustrations accepted
Foreign languages accepted: no
• REVIEWS
Seeking reviewers: yes
Unsolicited reviews accepted: yes
Materials reviewed: books, films
Review length: 2–4 pp
How to apply: letter
• ADDITIONAL NOTES
Historical focuses include labor, com-
    munity development, women,
    Asian Americans, popular culture,
    ethnography, and cultural criticism.

America's Civil War

All aspects of the Civil War
Affiliation: Empire Press
Ed: Roy Morris, Jr.
    602 S. King Street
    Suite 300
    Leesburg, VA 22075
Bk Rev Ed: varies
6/yr, 72 pp; subs $16.95
Circ: 130,000
Readership: academics, general public
Indexed/Abstracted: WAH
• MANUSCRIPTS
Query: yes; *Abstract:* no
Style guide: own
Copies: 1
Notes: endnotes
Blind referee: no
Acceptance rate: 1/10
Time to consider ms: 4–6 mos
Charts, pictures, tables, graphs, maps
Foreign languages accepted: no
• REVIEWS
Seeking reviewers: no
Unsolicited reviews accepted: no
Materials reviewed: books, films,
    audio cassettes
How to apply: letter
Include in application: institutional
    affiliation, areas of expertise

American Anthropologist

Integrative perspective in anthro-
    pology
Affiliation: University of Illinois,
    Urbana-Champaign
Ed: Janet Dixon Keller
    University of Illinois
    Anthropology
    109 Davenport Hall
    607 S. Matthews Avenue
    Urbana, IL 61801
Bk Rev Ed: same
4/yr, 260 pp
Circ: 10,000
Readership: academics
Indexed/Abstracted: ABC, AHCI,

BRI, CCSB, MLA, SSCI, SSI,
WAH
• MANUSCRIPTS
Query: no; *Abstract:* yes
Copies: 5
Notes: endnotes
Blind referee: yes
Acceptance rate: 1/5
Time to consider ms: 6 mos
Charts, tables, graphs, maps
• REVIEWS
Unsolicited reviews accepted: yes
Materials reviewed: books, films
Review length: 600 wds
How to apply: letter
Include in application: professional
degrees, institutional affiliation,
areas of expertise, published
works, foreign languages, current
research

American Antiquity

Archaeology of the New World and
archaeological method, theory, and
practice worldwide
Affiliation: Society for American
Archaeology
Ed: Michael W. Graves
Department of Anthropology
2424 Maile Way
University of Hawaii
Honolulu, HI 96822
Bk Rev Eds: Tom Jones, Charlotte
Beck
Department of Anthropology
Hamilton College
Clinton, NY 13323
4/yr, 192 pp; subs $75
Circ: 5,603
Readership: academics, general pub-
lic, avocational archaeologists, cul-
tural-resource managers
Indexed/Abstracted: ABC, AHCI,
BRI, CCAH, CCSB, HI, SSCI,
WAH
• MANUSCRIPTS
Query: no; *Abstract:* yes
Style guide: own

Preferred length: 40–50 pp
Copies: 5
Notes: endnotes
Blind referee: no
Acceptance rate: 3/10
Time to consider ms: 2–4 mos
Charts, pictures, tables, graphs, maps
Foreign languages accepted: Spanish
abstracts
• REVIEWS
Seeking reviewers: yes
Unsolicited reviews accepted: no
Materials reviewed: books, manu-
scripts
Review length: open
How to apply: letter
Include in application: professional
degrees, institutional affiliation,
areas of expertise, foreign lan-
guages, current research, telephone
and fax numbers

American Archivist

Trends and major issues in archival
theory and practice
Affiliation: Society of American
Archivists
Ed: Richard J. Cox
Society of American Archivists
600 S. Federal, Suite 504
Chicago, IL 60605
Bk Rev Ed: same
4/yr, 160 pp; subs $70
Circ: 4,600
Readership: academics, archivists,
librarians, manuscript curators,
records managers, historians
Indexed/Abstracted: ABC, AHCI,
BRI, CCAH, CCSB, SSCI, WAH
• MANUSCRIPTS
Query: no; *Abstract:* yes
Style guide: Chicago
Preferred length: variable
Copies: 3
Notes: footnotes
Time to consider ms: 3 mos
Charts, pictures, tables, graphs
Foreign languages accepted: no

• REVIEWS
Seeking reviewers: yes
Unsolicited reviews accepted: yes
Materials reviewed: books
Review length: 2–3 pp
How to apply: letter
Include in application: professional
   degrees, institutional affiliation,
   areas of expertise, published
   works, foreign languages

The American Benedictine Review

Religious history
Ed: Terrence Kardong
   Box A
   Assumption Abbey
   Richardton, ND 58562
4/yr, subs $15
Readership: academics, religious
   historians
Indexed/Abstracted: ABC, MLA,
   WAH
• MANUSCRIPTS
Query: no; *Abstract:* no
Style guide: MLA
Copies: 1
Notes: endnotes
Foreign languages accepted: no

American Heritage

American history
Affiliation: The Society of American
   Historians; The American Associa-
   tion for State and Local History
Ed: Richard F. Snow
   Forbes Building
   60 Fifth Avenue
   New York, NY 10011
8/yr, 120 pp; subs $29
Readership: general public
Indexed/Abstracted: ABC, AHCI,
   BRI, CCAH, RG, WAH

American Historical Review

History on all topics by scholars in
the U.S.

Affiliation: American Historical As-
   sociation
Ed: David L. Ransel
   American Historical Review
   914 Atwater
   Bloomington, IN 47401
Bk Rev Ed: William V. Bishel
5/yr, 400 pp; subs membership $25–
   $85
Circ: 17,000
Readership: academics
Indexed/Abstracted: ABC, AHCI,
   BRD, BRI, CCAH, CCSB, HI,
   IMB, SSCI, WAH
• MANUSCRIPTS
Query: no; *Abstract:* no
Style guide: Chicago
Preferred length: 30 pp
Copies: 4
Notes: endnotes
Blind referee: yes
Acceptance rate: 1/4
Time to consider ms: 4 mos
Charts, pictures, tables, graphs, maps
Foreign languages accepted: no
• REVIEWS
Seeking reviewers: yes
Unsolicited reviews accepted: no
Materials reviewed: books, films
Review length: 400–1,000 wds
How to apply: letter
Include in application: professional
   degrees, institutional affiliation,
   areas of expertise, published
   works, foreign languages, current
   research, vita

American History Illustrated

The American past; pre–Columbian
   era to recent past
Affiliation: none
Ed: Ed Holm
   P.O. Box 8200
   Harrisburg, PA 17105
Bk Rev Ed: Margaret Fortier
6/yr, 74 pp; subs $20
Circ: 140,000
Readership: academics, general public

Indexed/Abstracted: ABC, AHCI, CCAH, RG, WAH
- MANUSCRIPTS

Query: preferred; *Abstract:* no
Preferred length: 1,500 to 8,000 wds
Copies: 1
Notes: bibliography of sources
Blind referee: no
Acceptance rate: 1/10
Time to consider ms: 6–8 wks
Pictures, maps
Foreign languages accepted: no
- REVIEWS

Seeking reviewers: no
Unsolicited reviews accepted: no
Materials reviewed: books, videos, tapes
- ADDITIONAL NOTES

About ½ of the articles are assigned. The editors prepare their own reviews. *American History Illustrated* publishes narrative and biographical articles and portfolios on all aspects of social, political, cultural, and military history. Many of the stories relate to currently newsworthy topics, especially with regard to centennials and other significant anniversaries. Stories must be both authoritative and lively, meeting the theme of "the Adventure of the American Past."

American Indian Culture and Research Journal

American Indian history, culture, and contemporary issues
Affiliation: University of California, Los Angeles
Ed: Duane Champagne
American Indian Studies Center
UCLA
3220 Campbell Hall
405 Hilgard Avenue
Los Angeles, CA 90024-1548
Bk Rev Ed: Troy Johnson
4/yr, 200 pp; subs $20
Circ: 1,500

Readership: academics, general public, Indian communities
Indexed/Abstracted: ABC, AHI, WAH
- MANUSCRIPTS

Query: no; *Abstract:* no
Style guide: Chicago
Preferred length: 7,500 wds
Copies: 4
Notes: endnotes
Blind referee: yes
Acceptance rate: 2/5
Time to consider ms: 3 mos
Charts, pictures, tables, graphs, maps
Foreign languages accepted: no
- REVIEWS

Seeking reviewers: yes
Unsolicited reviews accepted: no
Materials reviewed: books
Review length: 1,200 to 1,500 wds
How to apply: letter
Include in application: professional degrees, institutional affiliation, areas of expertise, published works, current research, vita

American Indian Quarterly

Interdisciplinary—history, anthropology, literature, and the arts, related to American Indian studies
Affiliation: University of California, Berkeley
Ed: Robert Black
University of California
NAS/3415 Dwinelle Hall
Berkeley, CA 94720
Bk Rev Ed: same
4/yr, 145 pp; subs $25
Circ: 700
Readership: academics, general public
Indexed/Abstracted: ABC, HI, MLA
- MANUSCRIPTS

Query: preferred; *Abstract:* preferred
Style guide: Chicago
Preferred length: 25–30 pp
Copies: 2
Notes: endnotes
Blind referee: no

Acceptance rate: 1/5
Time to consider ms: 3 mos
Charts, pictures, tables, graphs, maps
Foreign languages accepted: no
• REVIEWS
Seeking reviewers: yes
Unsolicited reviews accepted: no
Materials reviewed: books, films
Review length: 2–3 pp
How to apply: letter
Include in application: professional
   degrees, institutional affiliation,
   areas of expertise

American Jewish Archives

Preservation and study of the Ameri-
   can Jewish experience
Affiliation: Hebrew Union College
Ed: Jacob Rader Marcus
   3101 Clifton Ave
   Cincinnati, OH 45220
Bk Rev Ed: same
Readership: academics, Jewish his-
   torians
Indexed/Abstracted: ABC, AHCI,
   CCAH
• MANUSCRIPTS
Query: no; *Abstract:* no
Style guide: modified Chicago
Notes: endnotes
• REVIEWS
Materials reviewed: books

American Jewish History

American Jewish history
Affiliation: American Jewish Histori-
   cal Society
Ed: Marc Lee Raphael
   American Jewish Historical
      Society
   2 Thornton Road
   Waltham, MA 02154
Bk Rev Ed: Dr. Hasia Diner
4/yr, subs $50
Circ: 3,800
Readership: academics, general public
Indexed/Abstracted: ABC, AHCI,
   CCAH, HI, WAH

• MANUSCRIPTS
Query: preferred; *Abstract:* no
Style guide: Chicago
Preferred length: 30 pp max
Copies: 1
Notes: footnotes
Blind referee: yes
Acceptance rate: 2/5
Time to consider ms: 1–2 mos
Charts, pictures, tables, graphs, maps
Foreign languages accepted: some
   Yiddish, Hebrew, and Ladino
• REVIEWS
Seeking reviewers: yes
Unsolicited reviews accepted: no
Materials reviewed: books, films,
   catalogs
Review length: varies, some essay
   reviews
How to apply: letter
Include in application: professional
   degrees, institutional affiliation,
   areas of expertise, published works,
   foreign languages, current research

American Journal of Ancient History

Ancient Greek and Roman history
   and related areas
Affiliation: none
Ed: E. Badian
   Robinson Hall
   Harvard University
   Cambridge, MA 02138
2/yr, 96 pp
Circ: 600
Readership: academics
• MANUSCRIPTS
Query: no; *Abstract:* no
Style guide: own
Copies: 2
Notes: endnotes
Blind referee: yes
Acceptance rate: varies
Time to consider ms: 2 mos
Charts, pictures, tables, graphs, maps
Foreign languages accepted: German,
   French

• ADDITIONAL NOTES
This journal does not publish reviews, but does occasionally publish major review-discussions.

American Journal of Islamic Social Sciences

Islamic critique of Western social sciences
Affiliation: International Institute of Islamic Thought and Association of Muslim Social Scientists
Ed: Sayyid M. Syeed
P.O. Box 669
555 Grove Street
Herndon, VA 22070
Bk Rev Ed: Anas Sheikh-Ali
IIIT—London Office
P.O. Box 126
Richmond, Surrey TW9 2UD
U.K.
4/yr, 160 pp; subs $30
Circ: 4,000
Readership: academics, general public
Indexed/Abstracted: ABC, PAIS
• MANUSCRIPTS
Query: no; *Abstract:* no
Style guide: Chicago
Preferred length: 20–25 pp
Copies: 2
Notes: footnotes or bibliography
Blind referee: yes
Acceptance rate: 1/2
Time to consider ms: 4–8 wks
Tables, graphs
Foreign languages accepted: no
• REVIEWS
Seeking reviewers: yes
Unsolicited reviews accepted: yes
Materials reviewed: books
Review length: 2–3 pp
How to apply: letter
Include in application: professional degrees, institutional affiliation, areas of expertise, published works, foreign languages, current research, resume

American Journal of Legal History

Legal history
Affiliation: Temple University School of Law
Ed: Diane C. Maleson
Temple University School of Law
1719 N. Broad Street
Philadelphia, PA 19122
Bk Rev Ed: Judith K. Schafer
Murphy Institute of Political Economy
Tulane University
108 Tilton Hall
New Orleans, LA 70118-5698
Bk Rev Ed: Henry J. Bourguignon
University of Toledo
College of Law
Toledo, OH 43606
4/yr, 120 pp; subs $20
Circ: 1,200
Readership: academics, general public
Indexed/Abstracted: ABC, AHCI, CCSB, IMB, SSCI, WAH
• MANUSCRIPTS
Query: no; *Abstract:* no
Style guide: Chicago or *A Uniform System of Citation*
Copies: 2
Notes: footnotes
Time to consider ms: 12 wks min
Charts, pictures, tables
Foreign languages accepted: no
• REVIEWS
How to apply: letter
Include in application: professional degrees, institutional affiliation, areas of expertise

American Literary History

The idea and development of an American national literature
Affiliation: Oxford University Press
Ed: Gordon Hunter
Department of English
University of Wisconsin, Madison
Madison, WI 53706
Bk Rev Ed: Arthur D. Casciato

Department of English
Miami University
Oxford, OH 45056
4/yr, subs $27
Readership: academics
Indexed/Abstracted: ABC, MLA,
   WAH
• MANUSCRIPTS
Query: no; *Abstract:* no
Style guide: MLA
Preferred length: open
Copies: 3
Notes: endnotes
Blind referee: by request
Charts, pictures, tables, graphs, maps
Foreign languages accepted: no
• REVIEWS
Materials reviewed: books
How to apply: letter
Include in application: professional
   degrees, institutional affiliation,
   areas of expertise, published
   works, foreign languages, current
   research

American Literature

American literary history, criticism,
   and bibliography
Affiliation: Duke University Press;
   Modern Language Association of
   America
Ed: Cathy N. Davidson
   304E Allen Building
   Duke University
   Durham, NC 27706
Bk Rev Ed: same
4/yr, subs $24
Readership: academics
Indexed/Abstracted: ABC, AHCI,
   BRD, BRI, CCAH, HI, MLA
• MANUSCRIPTS
Query: no; *Abstract:* no
Style guide: Chicago
Copies: 1
Notes: endnotes
Foreign languages accepted: no
• REVIEWS
Materials reviewed: books

The American Neptune

Maritime history
Affiliation: Peabody Museum of
   Salem
Ed: Timothy J. Runyan
   Department of History
   Cleveland State University
   Cleveland, OH 44115
Bk Rev Ed: Briton C. Busch
   Colgate University
   Hamilton, NY
4/yr, 75 pp; subs $32
Circ: 1,050
Readership: academics, general public
Indexed/Abstracted: ABC, AHCI,
   CCAH, WAH
• MANUSCRIPTS
Query: yes; *Abstract:* no
Style guide: Chicago
Preferred length: 45 pp
Copies: 2
Notes: footnotes
Blind referee: no
Acceptance rate: 9/10
Time to consider ms: 3–6 mos
Charts, pictures, tables, graphs, maps
Foreign languages accepted: no
• REVIEWS
Seeking reviewers: no
Unsolicited reviews accepted: no
Materials reviewed: books
Review length: 800 wds

American Presbyterians

American Presbyterian and Reformed
   history
Affiliation: Presbyterian Historical
   Society
Ed: James H. Smylie
   425 Lombard Street
   Philadelphia, PA 19147
Bk Rev Ed: same
4/yr, 90 pp; subs $15
Circ: 1,174
Readership: academics, general pub-
   lic, Presbyterians
Indexed/Abstracted: ABC, AHCI,
   CCAH, WAH

• MANUSCRIPTS
Query: no; *Abstract:* no
Style guide: Chicago
Preferred length: 25 pp
Copies: 2
Notes: endnotes
Blind referee: no
Time to consider ms: 2–3 mos
Pictures
Foreign languages accepted: no
• REVIEWS
Seeking reviewers: yes
Unsolicited reviews accepted: yes
Materials reviewed: books
Review length: 500 wds
How to apply: letter
Include in application: professional
degrees, institutional affiliation,
areas of expertise, current research

American Quarterly

Interdisciplinary studies of American
culture
Affiliation: American Studies Asso-
ciation
Ed: Gary Kulik
National Museum of American
History
Room 4601
Smithsonian Institution
Washington, DC 20560
Bk Rev Ed: George Lipsitz
Department of Ethnic Studies
9500 Gilman Drive
University of California, San
Diego
La Jolla, CA 92039-0414
4/yr, 208 pp; subs membership $15–
$60
Circ: 5,560
Readership: academics, museum di-
rectors, archivists, public officials,
administrators, critical theorists
Indexed/Abstracted: ABC, AHCI,
BRD, BRI, CCAH, HI, MLA,
WAH
• MANUSCRIPTS
Query: no; *Abstract:* no

Style guide: Chicago
Preferred length: 30–40 pp
Copies: 3
Notes: endnotes
Blind referee: yes
Acceptance rate: 1/20
Time to consider ms: 2–5 mos
Charts, pictures, tables, graphs, maps
Foreign languages accepted: no
• REVIEWS
Seeking reviewers: yes
Unsolicited reviews accepted: occa-
sionally
Materials reviewed: books, exhibitions
Review length: 10–15 pp
How to apply: letter
Include in application: professional
degrees, institutional affiliation,
areas of expertise, published
works, current research

American Review of Canadian Studies

Canadian studies
Affiliation: Association for Canadian
Studies in the United States
Ed: Lee Briscoe Thompson
Canadian Studies Program
University of Vermont
589 Main Street
Burlington, VT 05405-0114
Bk Rev Ed: Robert Thacker
Canadian Studies
St. Lawrence University
Canton, NY 13617
4/yr, 136 pp; subs $45
Circ: 1,500
Readership: academics
Indexed/Abstracted: ABC, PAIS
• MANUSCRIPTS
Query: no; *Abstract:* no
Style guide: Chicago
Preferred length: 15–20 pp
Copies: 3
Notes: endnotes
Blind referee: yes
Acceptance rate: 1/7
Time to consider ms: 5 mos (varies)

Charts, pictures, tables, graphs, maps
Foreign languages accepted: French
• REVIEWS
Seeking reviewers: yes
Unsolicited reviews accepted: no
Materials reviewed: books, journals
Review length: 3–4 pp
How to apply: letter
Include in application: professional degrees, institutional affiliation, areas of expertise, published works, current research
• ADDITIONAL NOTES
Canadian-American comparative topics are welcome. It is possible to propose review essays which cluster several related new books and discuss them in a linked way.

American Speech

Social, regional, and historical aspects of the English language in North America and the Caribbean and languages influencing or influenced by English
Affiliation: American Dialect Society
Ed: Ronald R. Butters
English Department
Duke University
Durham, NC 27706
Bk Rev Ed: same
4/yr, 112 pp; subs $25
Circ: 2,000
Readership: academics, general public
Indexed/Abstracted: ABC, AHCI, CCAH, HI, MLA
• MANUSCRIPTS
Query: no; *Abstract:* no
Style guide: MLA
Preferred length: 1 paragraph to 40 pp
Copies: 2
Notes: endnotes
Blind referee: yes
Acceptance rate: 1/7
Time to consider ms: 4–6 mos
Charts, tables, graphs, maps
Foreign languages accepted: no
• REVIEWS
Seeking reviewers: yes

Unsolicited reviews accepted: no
Materials reviewed: books
Review length: 4–6 pp
How to apply: letter
Include in application: professional degrees, institutional affiliation, areas of expertise, published works, foreign languages, current research, American Dialect Society membership preferred

American Studies

Interdisciplinary cultural studies, past and present
Affiliation: Mid-America American Studies Association and University of Kansas
Ed: David M. Katzman and Norman R. Yetman
American Studies
2120 Wescoe Hall
University of Kansas
Lawrence, KS 66045
Bk Rev Ed: same
2/yr, 136 pp; subs $15 individual; $25 institutional; $5 student
Circ: 1,500
Readership: academics
Indexed/Abstracted: ABC, HI, MLA
• MANUSCRIPTS
Query: no; *Abstract:* yes
Style guide: modified MLA
Preferred length: 20–30 pp
Copies: 3
Notes: endnotes
Blind referee: yes
Acceptance rate: 1/10
Time to consider ms: 4–6 mos
Charts, pictures, tables, graphs, maps
Foreign languages accepted: no
• REVIEWS
Seeking reviewers: yes
Unsolicited reviews accepted: no
Materials reviewed: books
Review length: 300–600 wds
How to apply: letter

American Studies International

American studies; history, culture, folklore, politics, religion, material culture, and literature of the U.S.A.
Affiliation: The George Washington University
Ed: Lisa Johnson Bedell
2108 G Street
Washington, DC 20052
Bk Rev Ed: Catherine Griggs
2/yr, 128 pp; subs $22
Circ: 1,250
Readership: academics
Indexed/Abstracted: ABC, AHCI, CCAH, HI
• MANUSCRIPTS
Query: preferred; *Abstract:* no
Style guide: Chicago
Preferred length: 20–30 pp
Copies: 1
Notes: endnotes
Blind referee: no
Charts, tables, graphs
Foreign languages accepted: no
• REVIEWS
Seeking reviewers: no
Unsolicited reviews accepted: no
Materials reviewed: books, films
• ADDITIONAL NOTES
The editors prefers to accept feature articles from overseas scholars. *American Studies International*'s bibliographical essays are commissioned.

American Visions

African-American history and culture
Ed: Joanne Harris
1538 9th Street, N.W.
Washington, DC 20001
Bk Rev Ed: same
6/yr, 64 pp; subs $18
Circ: 125,000
Readership: academics, general public
Indexed/Abstracted: ABC, RG
• MANUSCRIPTS
Query: yes; *Abstract:* preferred
Preferred length: 1,000–2,000 wds

Copies: 1
Blind referee: yes
Time to consider ms: 2–3 mos
Pictures, maps
Foreign languages accepted: no
• REVIEWS
Seeking reviewers: yes
Unsolicited reviews accepted: yes
Materials reviewed: books, films, recordings, art exhibits, theater productions, etc.
Review length: 1,000–1,500 wds
How to apply: letter
Include in application: professional degrees, institutional affiliation, areas of expertise, published works

The Americas

Inter-American cultural history
Affiliation: Academy of American Franciscan History
Ed: James D. Riley
B-17, Gibbons Hall
The Catholic University of America
Washington, DC 20064
Bk Rev Ed: Vincent C. Peloso
4/yr, 130 pp; subs $28
Circ: 1,100
Readership: academics
Indexed/Abstracted: ABC, AHCI, BRI, CCAH, HI, MLA
• MANUSCRIPTS
Query: no; *Abstract:* no
Copies: 2
Notes: endnotes or footnotes
Time to consider ms: 3 mos
Charts, pictures, tables, graphs, maps
Foreign languages accepted: Spanish, Portuguese
• REVIEWS
Seeking reviewers: yes
Unsolicited reviews accepted: no
Materials reviewed: books, films
Review length: 650 wds
How to apply: letter
Include in application: professional degrees, institutional affiliation,

areas of expertise, foreign
languages, current research

Anchor News

Great Lakes maritime history
Affiliation: Manitowoc Maritime
  Museum
    75 Maritime Drive
    Manitowoc, WI 54220
6/yr, 24 pp; subs $25
Circ: 1,600
Readership: museum members
Indexed/Abstracted: ABC
• MANUSCRIPTS
Query: preferred; *Abstract:* preferred
Preferred length: 10–15 pp
Copies: 2
Notes: endnotes
Blind referee: no
Acceptance rate: 1/2
Time to consider ms: 2–3 mos
Charts, pictures, maps
Foreign languages accepted: no
• REVIEWS
Seeking reviewers: no

Ancient Mesoamerica

Mesoamerican archaeology, art his-
  tory, ethnohistory, historical lin-
  guistics, etc.
Affiliation: Cambridge University
  Press
Eds: William R. Fowler, Jr., and
  Stephen D. Houston
    Vanderbilt University
    P.O. Box 6307-B
    Nashville, TN 37235
2/yr; subs $43
Readership: academics, general public
• MANUSCRIPTS
Query: preferred; *Abstract:* yes
Style guide: own
Preferred length: 15–30 pp
Copies: 5
Notes: endnotes
Blind referee: yes
Pictures, tables, line drawings
Foreign languages accepted: Spanish

Anglican and Episcopal History

Anglican and Episcopal church his-
  tory; English and Commonwealth
  church history
Affiliation: Historical Society of the
  Protestant Episcopal Church
Ed: John F. Woolverton
    P.O. Box 261
    Center Sandwich, NH 03227
Bk Rev Ed: J. Barrett Miller and
  James E. Bradley
    Fuller Theological Seminary
    P.O. Box L
    Pasadena, CA 91162
4/yr, 120 pp; subs $25
Circ: 1,326
Readership: academics, clergy, theo-
  logical students
Indexed/Abstracted: ABC, WAH
• MANUSCRIPTS
Query: no; *Abstract:* no
Style guide: Chicago
Preferred length: 30–40 pp
Copies: 2
Notes: endnotes or footnotes
Blind referee: yes
Acceptance rate: 3/5
Time to consider ms: 6 mos
Charts, pictures, tables, graphs, maps
Foreign languages accepted: Spanish,
  French
• REVIEWS
Seeking reviewers: yes
Unsolicited reviews accepted: rarely
Materials reviewed: books, films,
  church services
Review length: 3–4 pp
How to apply: letter
Include in application: areas of ex-
  pertise, published works, foreign
  languages, current research

The Annals of Iowa

History of Iowa and the Midwest
Affiliation: State Historical Society of
  Iowa
Ed: Marvin Bergman

State Historical Society of Iowa
402 Iowa Avenue
Iowa City, IA 52240
Bk Rev Ed: same
4/yr, 120 pp; subs $20
Circ: 1,000
Readership: academics, general public
Indexed/Abstracted: ABC, WAH
• MANUSCRIPTS
Query: preferred; *Abstract:* no
Style guide: Chicago
Preferred length: 25-35 pp
Copies: 2
Notes: endnotes
Blind referee: yes
Acceptance rate: 1/2
Time to consider ms: 3 mos
Charts, pictures, tables, graphs, maps
Foreign languages accepted: no
• REVIEWS
Seeking reviewers: yes
Unsolicited reviews accepted: no
Materials reviewed: books
Review length: 200-1,000 wds
How to apply: letter
Include in application: professional
degrees, institutional affiliation,
areas of expertise, published
works, current research

Annals of Science

History of science and technology
since the 13th century
Ed: G. L'E. Turner
Inst. Sci. Group
Imperial College
London SW7 2AZ
U.K.
Bk Rev Ed: same
6/yr, 100 pp; subs £240.00
Circ: 800
Readership: academics
Indexed/Abstracted: ABC, AHCI,
BHI, CCAH, CCSB, SSCI, WAH
• MANUSCRIPTS
Query: preferred; *Abstract:* yes
Style guide: ModHum
Preferred length: 10,000-20,000 wds

Copies: 2
Notes: endnotes or footnotes
Blind referee: yes
Acceptance rate: 2/5
Time to consider ms: 6 mos
Charts, pictures, tables, graphs, maps
Foreign languages accepted: French,
German
• REVIEWS
Seeking reviewers: yes
Unsolicited reviews accepted: no
Materials reviewed: books
Review length: 500-2,000 wds
How to apply: letter
Include in application: professional
degrees, institutional affiliation,
areas of expertise, published
works, foreign languages, current
research

Annals of Wyoming

Wyoming and Western history
Ed: Mark Junge
Historical Research & Publica-
tions
Parks & Cultural Resources
Department of Commerce
Barrett Building
Cheyenne, WY 82002
Bk Rev Ed: same
4/yr, 72 pp
Circ: 2,000
Readership: academics, general public
Indexed/Abstracted: ABC, WAH
• MANUSCRIPTS
Query: no; *Abstract:* no
Style guide: Chicago
Preferred length: varies
Copies: 2
Notes: footnotes
Blind referee: yes
Time to consider ms: 2-3 mos
Charts, pictures, tables, graphs, maps
Foreign languages accepted: no
• REVIEWS
Seeking reviewers: yes
Unsolicited reviews accepted: no
Materials reviewed: books, films,
videos

Review length: 600 wds
How to apply: letter, form, or telephone
Include in application: professional degrees, institutional affiliation, areas of expertise, published works

The Antioch Review

Non-fiction, fiction, poetry, book reviews
Affiliation: Antioch College
Ed: Robert S. Fogarty
   P.O. Box 148
   Yellow Springs, OH 45387
Bk Rev Eds: Jon Saari and Gary Bower
4/yr, 160 pp; subs $25
Circ: 5,000
Readership: academics, general public
Indexed/Abstracted: ABC, AHCI, AHI, BRD, BRI, CCAH, HI, MLA
• MANUSCRIPTS
Query: no; *Abstract:* no
Preferred length: 8,000 wds max
Copies: 1
Blind referee: no
Acceptance rate: 1/100
Time to consider ms: 4 wks
Foreign languages accepted: no
• REVIEWS
Seeking reviewers: no
Unsolicited reviews accepted: no

Apeiron: A Journal for Ancient Philosophy and Science

Historical and philosophical studies of ancient philosophy and science
Affiliation: University of Alberta
Ed: Roger A. Shiner
   4-108 Humanities Centre
   Department of Philosophy
   University of Alberta
   Edmonton, AB T6G 2E5
   CANADA
Bk Rev Ed: same
4/yr, 80 pp; subs $42

Circ: 350
Readership: academics
• MANUSCRIPTS
Query: no; *Abstract:* no
Copies: 2
Notes: endnotes
Blind referee: yes
Acceptance rate: 1/10
Time to consider ms: 3–4 mos
Charts, pictures, tables, graphs, maps
Foreign languages accepted: French
• REVIEWS
Seeking reviewers: no
Unsolicited reviews accepted: no
Materials reviewed: books

Appalachian Journal: A Regional Studies Review

Appalachian studies, cross-disciplinary
Affiliation: Appalachian State University
Ed: J. W. Williamson
   University Hall
   Appalachian State University
   Boone, NC 28608
Bk Rev Ed: same
4/yr, 112 pp; subs $18
Circ: 600
Readership: academics, general public
Indexed/Abstracted: ABC, AHCI, AHI, CCAH, MLA, WAH
• MANUSCRIPTS
Query: no; *Abstract:* no
Style guide: Chicago or MLA
Preferred length: open
Copies: 2
Notes: endnotes
Blind referee: yes
Acceptance rate: 1/4
Time to consider ms: 1 mo
Charts, pictures, tables, graphs, maps
Foreign languages accepted: no
• REVIEWS
Seeking reviewers: yes
Unsolicited reviews accepted: occasionally

Materials reviewed: books, films, television, motion pictures, pop culture
Review length: up to 20 pp
How to apply: letter
Include in application: professional degrees, institutional affiliation, areas of expertise, published works, current research

Arab Studies Quarterly

Arabic culture, history, politics, and economics
Affiliation: Association of Arab-American University Graduates, Inc. and the Institute of Arab Studies
Ed: Jamal R. Nassar
　　Department of Political Science
　　Illinois State University
　　Normal, IL 61761
Bk Rev Ed: Janice Terry
　　History Department
　　Eastern Michigan University
　　Ypsilanti, MI 48197
4/yr, 165 pp; subs $24
Circ: 3,000
Readership: academics, general public
Indexed/Abstracted: ABC, PAIS
● MANUSCRIPTS
Query: no; *Abstract:* no
Style guide: Chicago
Preferred length: 25-35 pp
Copies: 2
Notes: endnotes
Blind referee: yes
Acceptance rate: 1/7
Time to consider ms: 2-3 mos
Charts, tables, graphs, maps
Foreign languages accepted: no
● REVIEWS
Seeking reviewers: yes
Unsolicited reviews accepted: yes
Materials reviewed: books
Review length: 750 wds
How to apply: letter
Include in application: professional degrees, institutional affiliation, areas of expertise

Archives

Historical studies based on archival sources; archival issues
Affiliation: British Records Association
Ed: Jeremy Black
　　38 Elmfield Road
　　Newcastle NE3 4BB
　　U.K.
Bk Rev Ed: same
2/yr, 180 pp; subs £20
Circ: 1,200
Readership: academics, librarians, archivists
Indexed/Abstracted: ABC, BHI, IMB
● MANUSCRIPTS
Query: preferred; *Abstract:* no
Style guide: own
Preferred length: 6,000 wds
Copies: 2
Notes: endnotes
Blind referee: yes
Acceptance rate: 3/10
Time to consider ms: 4 wks
Charts, pictures, tables, graphs, maps
Foreign languages accepted: no
● REVIEWS
Seeking reviewers: no
Unsolicited reviews accepted: yes
Materials reviewed: books
Review length: 250 wds

Archives of Natural History

History and bibliography of natural history
Affiliation: Society for the History of Natural History
Ed: Alwyne Wheeler
　　Epping Forest Conservation Centre
　　High Beach, Loughton
　　Essex IG10 4AF
　　U.K.
Bk Rev Ed: E. C. Nelson
　　National Botanic Gardens
　　Glasnevia
　　Dublin 9
　　IRELAND

3/yr, 140 pp; subs £17
Circ: 800
Readership: academics, naturalists
Indexed/Abstracted: ABC
• MANUSCRIPTS
Query: no; *Abstract:* preferred
Preferred length: 50 pp max
Copies: 2
Notes: endnotes
Blind referee: yes
Acceptance rate: 3/4
Time to consider ms: 1-2 mos
Charts, pictures, tables, maps
Foreign languages accepted: no
• REVIEWS
Seeking reviewers: no
Unsolicited reviews accepted: no
Materials reviewed: books
Review length: 250-300 wds
How to apply: letter
Include in application: institutional
affiliation, areas of expertise, pub-
lished works

Arizona Quarterly

Theoretical, historical, and cultural
approaches to American literature
and film
Affiliation: University of Arizona
Ed: Edgar A. Dryden
Main Library
B-541
University of Arizona
Tucson, AZ 85721
4/yr; subs $12
Circ: 750
Readership: academics
Indexed/Abstracted: ABC, AHI,
MLA, WAH
• MANUSCRIPTS
Query: no; *Abstract:* no
Style guide: MLA
Copies: 2
Notes: endnotes
Pictures, other suitable illustra-
tions
Foreign languages accepted: no

Arkansas Historical Quarterly

Arkansas history
Affiliation: Arkansas Historical Asso-
ciation and the University of Ar-
kansas, Fayetteville
Ed: Jeannie M. Whayne
Arkansas Historical Association
Department of History
University of Arkansas
416 Old Main
Fayetteville, AR 72701
Bk Rev Ed: same
4/yr, 110 pp; subs $16
Circ: 1,600
Readership: academics, general public
Indexed/Abstracted: ABC, AHCI,
CCAH, WAH
• MANUSCRIPTS
Query: no; *Abstract:* no
Style guide: Chicago
Preferred length: 25-35 pp
Copies: 3
Notes: endnotes
Blind referee: yes
Acceptance rate: 1/2
Time to consider ms: 3-4 mos
Charts, pictures, tables, graphs, maps
Foreign languages accepted: no
• REVIEWS
Seeking reviewers: yes
Unsolicited reviews accepted: no
Materials reviewed: books, films
Review length: 500-750 wds
How to apply: letter
Include in application: professional
degrees, institutional affiliation,
areas of expertise, published
works, current research, vita

Art History

History of art, architecture, design,
material and visual culture
Affiliation: Association of Art His-
torians
Ed: Marcia Pointon
Department of History of Art
University of Manchester

Manchester M13 9PL
U.K.
Bk Rev Ed: Kathleen Adler
Department of Extramural
  Studies
Birkbeck College
University of London
26 Russell Square
London WC1B 5DQ
U.K.
4/yr, 250 pp; subs £41
Circ: 1001
Readership: academics, museum professionals
Indexed/Abstracted: ABC, AHCI, BHI, CCAH, HI, IMB
• MANUSCRIPTS
Query: no; *Abstract:* no
Style guide: own
Preferred length: 5,000 wds
Copies: 2
Notes: endnotes
Blind referee: yes
Acceptance rate: 9/20
Time to consider ms: 6–8 wks
Charts, pictures, tables, graphs, maps
Foreign languages accepted: exceptionally any
• REVIEWS
Seeking reviewers: no
Unsolicited reviews accepted: no
Materials reviewed: books, exhibition catalogues
Review length: 600–1,000 wds
How to apply: letter
Include in application: professional degrees, institutional affiliation, areas of expertise, published works, foreign languages, current research

Atlanta History: A Journal of Georgia and the South

Original research on Atlanta, its region, and the South, including art, architecture, religion, urban structure, politics, minorities, the Civil War, literature, famous people,

transportation, wars, and much more
Affiliation: Atlanta Historical Society, Inc.
Ed: Bradley R. Rice
Atlanta History Center
3101 Andrews Drive, N.W.
Atlanta, GA 30305
Bk Rev Ed: S. Fred Roach
History Department
Kennesaw State College
P.O. Box 444
Marietta, GA 30061
4/yr, 64 pp; subs $20
Circ: 5,500
Readership: academics, general public, society membership
Indexed/Abstracted: ABC, WAH
• MANUSCRIPTS
Query: no; *Abstract:* no
Style guide: Chicago
Preferred length: 30–75 pp
Copies: 2
Notes: endnotes
Blind referee: yes
Acceptance rate: 7/10
Time to consider ms: 12 wks
Charts, pictures, tables, graphs, maps
Foreign languages accepted: no
• REVIEWS
Seeking reviewers: yes
Unsolicited reviews accepted: no
Materials reviewed: books
Review length: 1,500 wds
How to apply: letter
Include in application: professional degrees, institutional affiliation, areas of expertise

Atlantis: A Women's Studies Journal/Revue d'Etudes sur les Femmes

Interdisciplinary women's studies, especially women in Canadian society
Affiliation: Institute for the Study of Women, Mount Saint Vincent University
Ed: Deborah C. Poff

Institute for the Study of Women
Mount Saint Vincent University
Halifax, NS B3M 2J6
CANADA
Bk Rev Ed: same
2/yr, 150 pp; subs $20
Circ: 1,000
Readership: academics
Indexed/Abstracted: A&C, MLA
• MANUSCRIPTS
Query: no; *Abstract:* yes
Style guide: MLA or *Publication
    Manual of the American Psycho-
    logical Association*
Preferred length: 10,000 wds
Copies: 4
Notes: endnotes
Blind referee: yes
Acceptance rate: 1/5
Time to consider ms: 6–8 mos
Charts, pictures, tables, graphs, maps
Foreign languages accepted: French
• REVIEWS
Seeking reviewers: yes
Unsolicited reviews accepted: yes
Materials reviewed: books
Review length: 1,000–1,500 wds max
How to apply: letter
Include in application: professional
    degrees, institutional affiliation,
    areas of expertise, published
    works, current research

Attakapas Gazette

History of several Louisiana parishes:
    St. Martin, Lafayette, Vermilion,
    St. Mary, Iberia, St. Landry,
    Acadia
Affiliation: The Attakapas Historical
    Association
Ed: Rebecca A. Batiste
    P.O. Box 43010
    University of Southwestern Loui-
        siana
    Lafayette, LA 70504
Bk Rev Ed: same
4/yr; subs $10
Readership: academics, general public

• MANUSCRIPTS
Query: no; *Abstract:* no
Copies: 1
Pictures, other suitable illustrations
• REVIEWS
Materials reviewed: books

Au Pays de Matane

Matane, Quebec
Affiliation: Société d'Histoire et
    Généalogie de Matane
Ed: editorial board
    Box 608
    Matane, PQ G4W 3P6
    CANADA
Bk Rev Ed: same
2/yr, 40 pp; subs $10
Circ: 1,000
Readership: general public, society
    members
• MANUSCRIPTS
Query: preferred; *Abstract:* preferred
Preferred length: 4–6 pp
Copies: 10
Notes: endnotes
Blind referee: yes
Acceptance rate: 1/2
Time to consider ms: 3 mos
Pictures, graphs, maps
Foreign languages accepted: French
• REVIEWS
Seeking reviewers: no
Unsolicited reviews accepted: yes
Materials reviewed: books
Include in application: institutional
    affiliation, published works

Augusta Historical Bulletin

Augusta County, Virginia history
Affiliation: Augusta County Histori-
    cal Society
Ed: Katherine G. Bushman
    12 Taylor Street
    Staunton, VA 24401
2/yr, 60 pp; subs membership or $4
    per issue
Circ: 575
Readership: general public

- MANUSCRIPTS
Query: no; *Abstract:* no
Preferred length: varies
Copies: 2
Notes: endnotes
Charts, pictures, tables, graphs, maps
Foreign languages accepted: no

Aviation

All aspects of flight, excluding space
travel
Affiliation: Empire Press
Ed: Arthur H. Sanfelici
602 S. King Street
Suite 300
Leesburg, VA 22075
Bk Rev Ed: varies
6/yr; subs $16.95
Circ: 92,000
Readership: academics, general public
- MANUSCRIPTS
Query: yes; *Abstract:* no
Style guide: own
Copies: 1
Notes: endnotes
Blind referee: no
Acceptance rate: 1/10
Time to consider ms: 4–6 mos
Charts, pictures, tables, graphs, maps
Foreign languages accepted: no
- REVIEWS
Seeking reviewers: no
Unsolicited reviews accepted: no
Materials reviewed: books, films
How to apply: letter
Include in application: institutional
affiliation, areas of expertise

BC Studies

Human history of British Columbia
Affiliation: The University of British
Columbia
Ed: Allan Smith
2029 West Mall
The University of British Co-
lumbia
Vancouver, BC V6T 1Z2
CANADA

Bk Rev Ed: same
4/yr, 130 pp; subs $25
Circ: 800
Readership: academics, general pub-
lic, teachers, students, business,
special interest groups
Indexed/Abstracted: ABC
- MANUSCRIPTS
Query: no; *Abstract:* no
Style guide: Chicago
Preferred length: 30 pp
Copies: 3
Notes: footnotes
Blind referee: yes
Acceptance rate: 3/4
Time to consider ms: 3 mos
Charts, pictures, tables, graphs, maps
- REVIEWS
Seeking reviewers: yes
Unsolicited reviews accepted: yes
Materials reviewed: books
Review length: 3–5 pp
How to apply: letter
Include in application: professional
degrees, institutional affiliation,
areas of expertise

Backwoodsman Magazine

Muzzleloading, fur trade, primitive
survival, how-to projects from yes-
teryear
Ed: Charlie Richie
P.O. Box 627
Westcliffe, CO 81252
6/yr, 64 pp; subs $14
Circ: 7,000
Readership: general public
- MANUSCRIPTS
Query: yes; *Abstract:* preferred
Preferred length: varies

Baptist History and Heritage

Baptist history
Affiliation: Southern Baptist Histori-
cal Commission
Ed: Lynn E. May, Jr.
901 Commerce Street
Suite 400
Nashville, TN 37206-3630

Bk Rev Ed: Carol Woodfin
4/yr, 64 pp; subs $10.95
Circ: 1,700
Readership: academics, Southern
    Baptists
Indexed/Abstracted: ABC, WAH
• MANUSCRIPTS
Query: preferred; *Abstract:* no
Style guide: Chicago
Preferred length: 16–20 pp or less
Copies: 3
Notes: endnotes
Blind referee: yes
Acceptance rate: 2–3 ms per yr
Time to consider ms: 3–6 mos
Charts, pictures, tables, graphs
Foreign languages accepted: no
• REVIEWS
Seeking reviewers: no
Unsolicited reviews accepted: no
Materials reviewed: books, films
Review length: 1–2 pp
How to apply: letter
Include in application: professional
    degrees, institutional affiliation,
    areas of expertise, published
    works, current research
• ADDITIONAL NOTES
Most articles are assigned; very few
    unsolicited articles are accepted.
    The editors are not actively seeking
    new reviewers but will consider
    well qualified and interested re-
    viewers.

The Baptist Quarterly

Baptist history and theology
Affiliation: The Baptist Historical So-
    ciety
Ed: John H. Y. Briggs
    Department of History
    University of Keele
    Newcastle under Lyme
    Staffs ST5 5BG
    U.K.
Bk Rev Ed: same
4/yr, 52 pp; subs £20
Circ: 650

Readership: academics, general public
Indexed/Abstracted: ABC
• MANUSCRIPTS
Preferred length: open
Notes: endnotes
Time to consider ms: 3–6 mos
Charts, pictures, tables, graphs, maps
Foreign languages accepted: no
• REVIEWS
Seeking reviewers: no
Materials reviewed: books

Baseball Research Journal

Baseball history
Affiliation: Society for American
    Baseball Research
Ed: Mark Alvarez
    P.O. Box 98183
    Cleveland, OH 44101
1/yr, 96 pp; subs $35
Circ: 6,500
Readership: baseball fans
Indexed/Abstracted: ABC
• MANUSCRIPTS
Query: preferred; *Abstract:* no
Notes: none
Blind referee: no
Foreign languages accepted: no
• REVIEWS
Seeking reviewers: no
Unsolicited reviews accepted: no

The Beaver: Exploring
Canada's History

Canadian history
Affiliation: Hudson's Bay Company
Ed: Christopher Dafoe
    450 Portage Avenue
    Winnipeg, MB R3C 0E7
    CANADA
Bk Rev Ed: same
6/yr, 64 pp; subs $21.50
Circ: 40,000
Readership: academics, general public
Indexed/Abstracted: ABC
• MANUSCRIPTS
Query: yes; *Abstract:* no
Preferred length: 3,000 wds max

Copies: 1
Notes: endnotes
Blind referee: no
Acceptance rate: 1/10
Time to consider ms: 4 mos
Charts, pictures, tables, graphs, maps
Foreign languages accepted: no
• REVIEWS
Seeking reviewers: no
Unsolicited reviews accepted: no
Materials reviewed: books
How to apply: letter

Bend of the River

Regional and local history
Ed: Lee Raizk
    P.O. Box 39
    Perrysburg, OH 43552
Bk Rev Ed: same
12/yr, 40 pp; subs $8.50
Circ: 3,500
Readership: senior citizens, local history buffs
• MANUSCRIPTS
Query: preferred; *Abstract:* no
Preferred length: 1,500
Copies: 1
Notes: none
Blind referee: no
Acceptance rate: 4/5
Time to consider ms: 6 wks
Pictures
Foreign languages accepted: no
• REVIEWS
Seeking reviewers: no
Unsolicited reviews accepted: yes
Materials reviewed: books
Review length: 850 wds max

Biography

A multidisciplinary forum for all scholarly articles dealing with life writing, including biographical theory, aesthetics, historiography, and epistemology
Affiliation: Biographical Research Center, University of Hawaii at Manoa
Ed: George Simson
    Center for Biographical Research
    Varsity Cottage
    University of Hawaii
    Honolulu, HI 96822
Bk Rev Ed: Marie-Jose Fassiotto
    Department of European Languages and Literature
    Moore Hall
    1890 East-West Road
    University of Hawaii
    Honolulu, HI 96822
4/yr, 112 pp; subs $22
Circ: 500
Readership: academics, general public
Indexed/Abstracted: ABC, AHCI, BRI, CCAH, MLA, WAH
• MANUSCRIPTS
Query: no; *Abstract:* no
Style guide: Chicago
Preferred length: 2,500 to 7,500 wds
Copies: 2
Notes: endnotes
Blind referee: yes
Acceptance rate: 1/4
Time to consider ms: 3 mos
Charts, pictures, tables, graphs, maps
Foreign languages accepted: no, unless germane to text and translated
• REVIEWS
Seeking reviewers: yes
Unsolicited reviews accepted: yes
Materials reviewed: books, films
Review length: 500–1,000 wds
How to apply: letter
Include in application: areas of expertise, sample of previous reviews
• ADDITIONAL NOTES
Books reviewed should be about biography (historiography, theory, aesthetics, etc.)

The Black Scholar

Black studies
Ed: Robert Chrisman
    P.O. Box 2869
    Oakland, CA 94609
Bk Rev Ed: same

4/yr, 72 pp; subs $30
Circ: 10,000
Readership: academics
Indexed/Abstracted: ABC, BRI,
  CCSB, SSCI, SSI, WAH
- MANUSCRIPTS
Query: preferred; *Abstract:* preferred
Style guide: Chicago
Preferred length: 10-15 pp
Copies: 1
Notes: endnotes
Blind referee: varies
Acceptance rate: 1/10
Time to consider ms: 3-6 mos
Charts, tables, graphs, maps
Foreign languages accepted: no
- REVIEWS
Seeking reviewers: yes
Unsolicited reviews accepted: yes
Materials reviewed: books
Review length: 2-5 pp
How to apply: letter
Include in application: professional
  degrees, institutional affiliation,
  areas of expertise, published
  works, current research

Borthwick Papers

History of Yorkshire and North of
  England; special reference to reli-
  gion
Affiliation: University of York
Ed: W. J. Sheils
  Borthwick Institute
  St. Anthony's Hall
  York YO1 5PY
  U.K.
2/yr, 36 pp; subs £3.50
Circ: 500
Readership: academics, local his-
  torians
Indexed/Abstracted: IMB
- MANUSCRIPTS
Abstract: yes
Preferred length: 12,000-14,000 wds
Copies: 2
Notes: endnotes
Blind referee: occasionally

Acceptance rate: 1/2
Time to consider ms: 6 wks
Charts, tables, graphs, maps
Foreign languages accepted: no

British Columbia Historical News

Local and provincial history of
  British Columbia
Affiliation: British Columbia Histori-
  cal Federation
Ed: Naomi Miller
  Box 105
  Wasa, BC V0B 2K0
  CANADA
Bk Rev Ed: Anne Yandle
  3450 West 20th Avenue
  Vancouver, BC V6S 1E4
  CANADA
4/yr, 36 pp; subs $10
Circ: 1,300
Readership: academics, general pub-
  lic, federation members
Indexed/Abstracted: IMB
- MANUSCRIPTS
Query: no; *Abstract:* no
Preferred length: 2,500 wds max
Copies: 1
Notes: endnotes or footnotes
Blind referee: no
Acceptance rate: 4/5
Time to consider ms: 2 wks
Charts, pictures, graphs, maps
Foreign languages accepted: no
- REVIEWS
Seeking reviewers: no
Unsolicited reviews accepted: yes
Materials reviewed: books
Review length: 2 pp max

British Heritage

The history and culture of Britain,
  with an emphasis on travel
Ed: Gail Huganir
  6405 Flank Drive
  Harrisburg, PA 17112
Bk Rev Ed: same
6/yr, 84 pp; subs $19.95

Circ: 100,000
Readership: general public
Indexed/Abstracted: ABC
• MANUSCRIPTS
Query: yes; *Abstract:* no
Preferred length: 1,000–2,000 wds
Copies: 2
Notes: none
Blind referee: no
Acceptance rate: 1/10
Time to consider ms: 8–12 wks
Pictures
Foreign languages accepted: no
• REVIEWS
Seeking reviewers: no
Unsolicited reviews accepted: no
Materials reviewed: books, films, videos
Review length: 300–400 wds
• ADDITIONAL NOTES
Use British grammar and spellings as per the Concise Oxford Dictionary. Include photocopies or transcripts of source material.

The British Journal for the History of Science

All aspects of the history of science
Affiliation: British Society for the History of Science
Ed: J. H. Brooke
Department of History
Furness College
University of Lancaster
Lancaster LA1 4YG
U.K.
Bk Rev Ed: John Henry
Science Studies Unit
University of Edinburgh
21 Buccleuch Place
Edinburgh EH8 9LN
U.K.
4/yr, 128 pp; subs £18.50
Circ: 1,800
Readership: academics, general public
Indexed/Abstracted: ABC, AHCI, BHI, CCAH, CCSB, HI, IMB, SSCI

• MANUSCRIPTS
Query: no; *Abstract:* yes
Style guide: own
Preferred length: 10,000 wds max
Copies: 2
Notes: endnotes
Blind referee: yes
Acceptance rate: 1/3
Time to consider ms: 2 mos
Charts, pictures, tables, graphs, maps
Foreign languages accepted: occasionally French
• REVIEWS
Seeking reviewers: no
Unsolicited reviews accepted: no
Materials reviewed: books
Review length: 500–800 wds
How to apply: letter
Include in application: professional degrees, institutional affiliation, areas of expertise, published works, current research

British Journal of Canadian Studies

Canadian studies
Affiliation: British Association of Canadian Studies
Ed: Colin Nicholson
Department of English Literature
David Hume Tower
University of Edinburgh
EH8 9JX
U.K.
Bk Rev Ed: Michael Burgess
Department of American Studies
University of Keele
Keele
Staffs ST5 5BG
U.K.
2/yr, 250 pp; subs £10
Circ: 1,200
Readership: academics, general public
Indexed/Abstracted: ABC
• MANUSCRIPTS
Query: yes; *Abstract:* no
Style guide: ModHum or MLA
Preferred length: 5,000–7,000 wds

Copies: 3
Notes: endnotes
Blind referee: yes
Acceptance rate: 2/5
Time to consider ms: 4 mos
Charts, pictures, tables, graphs, maps
Foreign languages accepted: French
• REVIEWS
Seeking reviewers: yes
Unsolicited reviews accepted: no
Materials reviewed: books
Review length: 400 wds
How to apply: letter
Include in application: professional
degrees, institutional affiliation,
areas of expertise

British Journal of Middle Eastern Studies

Middle East since the rise of Islam
Affiliation: British Society for Middle
Eastern Studies
Ed: P. G. Starkey
CMEIS
South End House
South Road
Durham DH1 3TG
U.K.
Bk Rev Ed: P. J. Sluglett
2/yr, 120 pp; subs £22
Circ: 300
Readership: academics, others in-
terested in the Middle East
• MANUSCRIPTS
Query: no; *Abstract:* no
Style guide: any
Preferred length: 25 pp
Copies: 1
Notes: endnotes or footnotes
Blind referee: usually
Acceptance rate: 3/5
Time to consider ms: 3 mos
Charts, tables, graphs, maps
Foreign languages accepted: occa-
sionally French
• REVIEWS
Seeking reviewers: yes
Unsolicited reviews accepted: no

Materials reviewed: books
Review length: varies
How to apply: letter
Include in application: professional
degrees, institutional affiliation,
areas of expertise, published
works, foreign languages, current
research

Bulletin du Regroupement des Chercheurs en Histoire des Travailleurs et Travailleuses du Quebec

Labour history
Ed: Jacques Rouillard
Departement d'histoire
Université de Montréal
C.P. 6128, Succ. A
Montreal, PQ H3C 3J7
CANADA
Bk Rev Ed: same
3/yr, 55 pp; subs $10
Circ: 100
Readership: academics
• MANUSCRIPTS
Query: no; *Abstract:* no
Preferred length: 20 pp
Copies: 1
Notes: endnotes
Acceptance rate: 4/5
Time to consider ms: 2 mos
Charts, pictures, tables, graphs, maps
Foreign languages accepted: French
• REVIEWS
Seeking reviewers: no
Unsolicited reviews accepted: yes
Materials reviewed: books
Review length: 4 pp
How to apply: letter
Include in application: professional
degrees, institutional affiliation,
areas of expertise

Bulletin of Bibliography

Highly specialized bibliographies
covering arts, humanities, and the
social sciences

Affiliation: Greenwood Publishing Group, Inc.
Ed: Bernard McTigue
   308 Library East
   University of Florida
   Gainesville, FL 32611
Bk Rev Ed: Willard Fox
   Department of English
   The University of Southwestern
   Louisiana
   P.O. Box 44691
   Lafayette, LA 70501-4691
4/yr, 72 pp; subs $95
Readership: academics
Indexed/Abstracted: ABC, MLA, WAH
• MANUSCRIPTS
Query: yes; *Abstract:* no
Style guide: any
Preferred length: 75 pp max
Copies: 2
Notes: endnotes
Blind referee: yes
Time to consider ms: 3 mos
Pictures
Foreign languages accepted: no
• REVIEWS
Seeking reviewers: no
Unsolicited reviews accepted: no
Materials reviewed: books
Review length: 300–500 wds
How to apply: letter
Include in application: professional degrees, institutional affiliation, areas of expertise, published works, foreign languages, current research

Bulletin of Concerned Asian Scholars

Modern and contemporary Asia, very occasional pieces on premodern times
Eds: Nancy and Bill Doub
   3239 9th Street
   Boulder, CO 80304-2112
Bk Rev Ed: Bill Doub

4/yr, 76 pp; subs $22 individuals; $55 institutions
Circ: 1,370
Readership: academics, general public
Indexed/Abstracted: ABC, AHCI, CCSB, SSCI
• MANUSCRIPTS
Query: preferred; *Abstract:* yes
Style guide: Chicago
Preferred length: 7,000 wds
Copies: 4
Notes: footnotes
Blind referee: yes
Acceptance rate: 1/5
Time to consider ms: 3 mos
Charts, pictures, tables, graphs, maps, drawings, cartoons
Foreign languages accepted: no
• REVIEWS
Seeking reviewers: yes
Unsolicited reviews accepted: rarely
Materials reviewed: books, films, videos, television
Review length: 3,000 wds
How to apply: letter
Include in application: professional degrees, institutional affiliation, areas of expertise, published works, foreign languages, current research
• ADDITIONAL NOTES
Review essays are strongly preferred over traditional book reviews.

Bulletin of Latin American Research

Social sciences and humanities issues in Latin America
Affiliation: Society of Latin American Studies
Eds: Brian Hamnett, Colin Clarke, Lewis Taylor
   Department of History
   University of Essex
   Wivenhoe Park
   Colchester CO4 3SQ
   U.K.
Bk Rev Ed: Lewis Taylor

Institute of Latin American
Studies
University of Liverpool
P.O. Box 147
Liverpool L69 3BX
U.K.
3/yr, 120 pp; subs $135 institutional
Readership: academics
Indexed/Abstracted: ABC, BHI,
PAIS
• MANUSCRIPTS
Query: no; *Abstract:* no
Style guide: own
Preferred length: 8,000 wds
Copies: 2
Notes: endnotes
Blind referee: yes
Acceptance rate: 13/20
Time to consider ms: 4 mos
Tables, graphs, maps
Foreign languages accepted: no
• REVIEWS
Seeking reviewers: yes
Materials reviewed: books
Review length: 2,000–3,000 wds
How to apply: letter
Include in application: professional
degrees, institutional affiliation,
areas of expertise, current research

Bulletin of the American Schools of Oriental Research

Near Eastern archaeology and
philology
Affiliation: American Schools of
Oriental Research
Ed: J. W. Flanagan
Department of Religion
Case Western Reserve University
Cleveland, OH 44106
Bk Rev Ed: W. Pitard
Program of Religious Studies
University of Illinois
3014 Foreign Language Building
707 South Mathews Avenue
Urbana, IL 61801
4/yr, 96 pp
Circ: 2,000

Readership: academics
Indexed/Abstracted: AHCI, CCAH,
IMB
• MANUSCRIPTS
Query: preferred; *Abstract:* yes
Style guide: own
Preferred length: 60 pp max
Copies: 1
Notes: endnotes
Blind referee: yes
Acceptance rate: 7/10
Time to consider ms: 3 mos
Charts, pictures, tables, graphs,
maps
Foreign languages accepted: no
• REVIEWS
Seeking reviewers: yes
Unsolicited reviews accepted: no
Materials reviewed: books
Review length: 600–2,500 wds
How to apply: letter
Include in application: professional
degrees, institutional affiliation,
areas of expertise, published
works, foreign languages, current
research

Bulletin of the Camden County Historical Society

History of Southern New Jersey and
Camden County
Affiliation: Camden County Histori-
cal Society
c/o Camden County Historical
Society
Park Boulevard and Euclid
Avenue
Camden, NJ 08103
irregular, about 1/yr, 15–25 pp; subs
$3
Circ: 1,000
Readership: academics, general pub-
lic
• MANUSCRIPTS
Query: preferred; *Abstract:* yes
• REVIEWS
Seeking reviewers: no

Bulletin of the Canadian Society for Mesopotamian Studies

Ancient history, languages, and archaeology of Mesopotamia
Affiliation: Universite Laval
Ed: Michel Fortin
Departement d'Histoire
Universite Laval
Quebec G1K 7P4
CANADA
Bk Rev Ed: same
2/yr, 60 pp; subs $20
Circ: 300
Readership: academics, general public
• MANUSCRIPTS
Query: preferred; *Abstract:* no
Preferred length: 10–20 pp
Copies: 1
Notes: footnotes
Blind referee: no
Acceptance rate: 9/10
Time to consider ms: 3–4 mos
Charts, pictures, tables, graphs, maps
Foreign languages accepted: French
• REVIEWS
Seeking reviewers: no
Unsolicited reviews accepted: yes
Materials reviewed: books
Review length: 1 pp
How to apply: letter
Include in application: professional degrees, institutional affiliation, areas of expertise, published works, current research

The Bulletin of the Fort Ticonderoga Museum

18th century military history of the Champlain Valley
Affiliation: Fort Ticonderoga
Ed: Nicholas Westbrook
Fort Ticonderoga
P.O. Box 390
Ticonderoga, NY 12883
Bk Rev Ed: same
1/yr, 80 pp; subs membership
Circ: 500

Readership: academics, general public, reenactors
• MANUSCRIPTS
Query: preferred; *Abstract:* no
Style guide: Chicago
Preferred length: 25 pp
Copies: 3
Notes: footnotes
Blind referee: yes
Acceptance rate: 3/5
Time to consider ms: 6 mos
Period graphics
• REVIEWS
Seeking reviewers: yes
Unsolicited reviews accepted: no
Materials reviewed: books, films, exhibits
Review length: 5 pp
How to apply: letter
Include in application: professional degrees, institutional affiliation, areas of expertise, published works, foreign languages, current research
• ADDITIONAL NOTES
Emphasis: (a) annotated primary documents dealing with the wars for empire and liberation on the New York Frontier; (b) interpretive essays on the French and Indian War and the American Revolution; (c) studies of 18th century military material culture; (d) essays on tourism to and preservation of colonial military sites during the 19th and 20th centuries.

Bulletin of the History of Dentistry

History of dentistry
Affiliation: American Academy of the History of Dentistry
Ed: Hannelore T. Loevy
5524 S. Harper
Chicago, IL 60637
Bk Rev Ed: same
3/yr, 58 pp; subs $35
Circ: 1,000
Readership: academics, dentists

• MANUSCRIPTS
Query: no; *Abstract:* yes
Style guide: Chicago
Preferred length: open
Copies: 3
Notes: endnotes
Blind referee: yes
Acceptance rate: 3/4
Time to consider ms: 3 mos
Charts, pictures, tables, graphs, maps
Foreign languages accepted: no
• REVIEWS
Seeking reviewers: no
Unsolicited reviews accepted: no
How to apply: by invitation

Bulletin of the History of Medicine

History of medicine
Affiliation: Johns Hopkins University and the American Association for the History of Medicine
Ed: Gert Brieger
    323 Welch Medical Library
    1900 E. Monument Street
    Baltimore, MD 20205
Bk Rev Ed: same
4/yr, 160 pp; subs $20
Circ: 2,500
Readership: medical and general historians, medical practitioners, association members
Indexed/Abstracted: ABC, AHCI, IMB, SSCI, WAH
• MANUSCRIPTS
Query: no; *Abstract:* no
Style guide: modified Chicago
Preferred length: 40 pp max
Copies: 2
Notes: endnotes
Blind referee: yes
Acceptance rate: 2/5
Time to consider ms: 3 mos
Charts, pictures, tables, graphs, maps
Foreign languages accepted: no
• REVIEWS
Seeking reviewers: no
Unsolicited reviews accepted: no

Bulletin of the Society for Spanish and Portuguese Historical Studies

Spanish and Portuguese history
Affiliation: Central Missouri State University and Millersville University (PA)
Ed: Daniel A. Crews
    Department of History
    Central Missouri State University
    Warrensburg, MO 64093
Bk Rev Ed: same
3/yr, 50 pp; subs $17
Circ: 400
Readership: academics
• MANUSCRIPTS
Foreign languages accepted: Spanish, Portuguese
• REVIEWS
Seeking reviewers: no
Unsolicited reviews accepted: no
Materials reviewed: books
Review length: any reasonable length
How to apply: letter

Bus History Magazine

Bus transportation history
Affiliation: Bus History Association
Ed: Loring M. Lawrence
    195 Lancelot Drive
    Manchester, NH 03104-1420
Bk Rev Ed: same
4/yr, 42 pp; subs $20
Circ: 400
Readership: general public, bus operators, bus associations
• MANUSCRIPTS
Query: preferred; *Abstract:* no
Preferred length: 3–15 pp
Copies: 1
Blind referee: no
Acceptance rate: 1/2
Time to consider ms: 1 mo
Charts, pictures, tables, maps
Foreign languages accepted: no
• REVIEWS
Seeking reviewers: no

Unsolicited reviews accepted: sometimes
Materials reviewed: books
Review length: 1 pp max
How to apply: letter
• ADDITIONAL NOTES
Subject matter includes current and historical topics relating to city and intercity bus transportation, corporate histories, regional histories, vehicles themselves, and related ephemera.

Business History

History of business
Ed: Charles Harvey
  Department of History
  Royal Holloway and Bedford
    New College
  Egham Hill, Egham
  Surrey TW20 0EX
  U.K.
Ed: Geoffrey Jones
  Department of Economics
  University of Reading
  P.O. Box 218
  Whiteknights
  Reading RG6 2AA
  U.K.
Bk Rev Ed: Mary Rose
  Department of Economics
  Gillow House
  University of Lancaster
  Lancaster LA1 4YX
  U.K.
4/yr, 200 pp; subs £25
Circ: 1,000
Readership: academics
Indexed/Abstracted: ABC, AHCI, BHI, CCSB, SSCI, WAH
• MANUSCRIPTS
Abstract: yes
Preferred length: 5,000–6,000 wds
Copies: 3
Notes: endnotes
Blind referee: yes
Time to consider ms: varies
Charts, pictures, tables, graphs, maps
Foreign languages accepted: no

• REVIEWS
Seeking reviewers: yes
Unsolicited reviews accepted: yes
Materials reviewed: books, journals
Review length: 1,000 wds
How to apply: letter
Include in application: professional degrees, institutional affiliation, areas of expertise, published works, foreign languages, current research

Business History Review

Business history
Affiliation: Harvard Business School
Ed: Steven W. Tolliday
  Baker Library 5A
  Harvard Business School
  Soldiers Field
  Boston, MA 02136
Bk Rev Ed: Paticia Denault
4/yr, 245 pp; subs $25
Circ: 2,100
Readership: academics, general public
Indexed/Abstracted: ABC, BRD, BRI, CCSB, PAIS, SSCI, WAH
• MANUSCRIPTS
Query: no; *Abstract:* yes
Style guide: Chicago
Preferred length: 25–60 pp
Copies: 3
Notes: endnotes
Blind referee: yes
Acceptance rate: 1/3
Time to consider ms: 4–12 wks
Charts, pictures, tables, graphs, maps
Foreign languages accepted: no
• REVIEWS
Seeking reviewers: yes
Unsolicited reviews accepted: no
Materials reviewed: books
Review length: 600–800 wds
How to apply: letter
Include in application: professional degrees, institutional affiliation, areas of expertise, published works, foreign languages, current research

LORETTE WILMOT LIBRARY
NAZARETH COLLEGE

Bygone Kent

All aspects of the history of the
county of Kent, England
Ed: Pat O'Driscoll
18 Dunoon Road
Forest Hill
London SE23 3TF
U.K.
Bk Rev Ed: same
12/yr, 64 pp; subs £26
Circ: 2,000
Readership: general public
• MANUSCRIPTS
Query: no; *Abstract:* no
Preferred length: 1,500 wds
Copies: 1
Notes: endnotes
Blind referee: no
Charts, pictures, tables, graphs, maps
Foreign languages accepted: no
• REVIEWS
Seeking reviewers: no
Unsolicited reviews accepted: no
Materials reviewed: books

Cahiers de la Société Historique Acadienne

Acadian studies
Ed: R.-Gilles LeBlanc
Centre d'Etudes Acadiennes
Université de Moncton
Moncton, NB E1A 3E9
CANADA
Bk Rev Ed: same
4/yr, 60 pp; subs $20
Circ: 550
Readership: academics, general public
• MANUSCRIPTS
Query: preferred; *Abstract:* no
Preferred length: 15–25 pp
Copies: 1
Notes: footnotes
Blind referee: no
Acceptance rate: 9/10
Time to consider ms: 1 mo
Charts, pictures, tables, graphs, maps
Foreign languages accepted: French
• REVIEWS

Seeking reviewers: yes
Unsolicited reviews accepted: yes
Materials reviewed: books
Review length: 2–3 pp
How to apply: letter
Include in application: professional
degrees, institutional affiliation,
areas of expertise, published
works, foreign languages, current
research

Cake and Cockhorse

History and archaeology of Banbury
and surrounding area
Affiliation: Banbury Historical Society
Ed: David Hitchcox
1 Dorchester Grove
Banbury OX16 0BD
U.K.
Bk Rev Ed: same
3/yr, 28 pp; subs £5
Circ: 200
Readership: general public, genealo-
gists
• MANUSCRIPTS
Abstract: no
Preferred length: 10,000 wds max
Copies: 1
Notes: endnotes or footnotes
Blind referee: no
Acceptance rate: 9/10
Time to consider ms: 1 mo
Charts, pictures, tables, graphs, maps
Foreign languages accepted: no
• REVIEWS
Seeking reviewers: no
Unsolicited reviews accepted: yes

California Historian

California history
Affiliation: Conference of California
Historical Societies
Ed: Mary Otis
112 Sierrawood Circle
Folsom, CA 95630
Bk Rev Ed: Lois McDonald
14609 Skyway
Magalia, CA 95954

4/yr, 38 pp; subs membership
Circ: 1,400
Readership: academics, historical
   societies
• MANUSCRIPTS
Query: preferred; *Abstract:* preferred
Preferred length: open
Copies: 1
Notes: footnotes and bibliography
Blind referee: yes
Acceptance rate: 3/4
Time to consider ms: 6 mos
Charts, pictures, maps
Foreign languages accepted: no
• REVIEWS
Seeking reviewers: no
Unsolicited reviews accepted: occa-
   sionally
Materials reviewed: books
Review length: concise
• ADDITIONAL NOTES
Manuscripts can be accompanied by
   an IBM compatible 3½″ disk in
   WordPerfect format.

California History

The history of California and the
   American West
Affiliation: California Historical
   Society
Ed: Richard Orsi
   Department of History
   California State University
   Hayward, CA 94542
Bk Rev Ed: James Rawls
   c/o California Historical Society
   2099 Pacific Avenue
   San Francisco, CA 94109
4/yr, 100 pp; subs $40
Circ: 5,300
Readership: academics, general pub-
   lic, CHS members
Indexed/Abstracted: ABC, AHCI,
   CCAH, WAH
• MANUSCRIPTS
Query: no; *Abstract:* no
Style guide: Chicago
Preferred length: 20–35 pp

Copies: 2
Notes: endnotes
Blind referee: yes
Acceptance rate: 1/4
Time to consider ms: 1–4 mos
Charts, pictures, tables, graphs, maps
Foreign languages accepted: no
• REVIEWS
Seeking reviewers: yes
Unsolicited reviews accepted: no
Materials reviewed: books
Review length: 400–700 wds
How to apply: letter
Include in application: professional
   degrees, institutional affiliation,
   areas of expertise, published works,
   foreign languages, current research

Cambridge Medieval Celtic Studies

Interdisciplinary studies of the Celtic
   countries in the Middle Ages
Ed: Patrick Sims-Williams
   St. John's College
   Cambridge CB2 1TP
   U.K.
Bk Rev Ed: same
2/yr; subs £10
Readership: academics
Indexed/Abstracted: AHCI, CCAH,
   IMB, MLA
• MANUSCRIPTS
Query: no; *Abstract:* no
Style guide: ModHum
Copies: 2
Notes: endnotes
• REVIEWS
Materials reviewed: books

Canadian Bulletin of Medical History

International and Canadian history
   of medicine; all periods
Affiliation: The University of Western
   Ontario
Ed: J. T. H. Connor
   Department of History of Medi-
   cine

The University of Western Ontario
London, ON N6A 5C1
CANADA
Bk Rev Ed (English): Faith Wallis
Osler Library
McGill University
Montreal, PQ H3G 1Y6
CANADA
Bk Rev Ed (French): Georges
Desrosiers
Faculty of Medicine
University of Montreal
Montreal, PQ H3C 3J7
CANADA
2/yr, 150 pp; subs $25
Circ: 400
Readership: academics, physicians
Indexed/Abstracted: ABC
• MANUSCRIPTS
Query: no; *Abstract:* yes
Style guide: own
Preferred length: 30–40 pp
Copies: 3
Notes: endnotes
Blind referee: yes
Acceptance rate: 3/4
Time to consider ms: 4–6 wks
Charts, pictures, tables, graphs
Foreign languages accepted: French,
German
• REVIEWS
Seeking reviewers: yes
Unsolicited reviews accepted: yes
Materials reviewed: books
Review length: 4–6 pp
How to apply: letter
Include in application: professional
degrees, institutional affiliation,
areas of expertise, foreign languages

Canadian Ethnic Studies/ Etudes Ethniques au Canada

Interdisciplinary study of ethnic relations and ethnicity
Affiliation: The University of Calgary
Eds: J. S. Frideres, A. W. Rasporich

Department of Sociology
The University of Calgary
2500 University Drive
Calgary, AB T2N 1N4
CANADA
Bk Rev Ed: same
3/yr, 180 pp; subs $30
Circ: 1,000
Readership: academics, general public, government officials
Indexed/Abstracted: ABC, MLA
• MANUSCRIPTS
Query: no; *Abstract:* yes
Style guide: any
Preferred length: 20–25 pp
Copies: 3
Notes: endnotes or footnotes
Blind referee: yes
Acceptance rate: 1/4
Time to consider ms: 6–8 wks
Charts, pictures, tables, graphs, maps
Foreign languages accepted: French
• REVIEWS
Seeking reviewers: yes
Unsolicited reviews accepted: yes
Materials reviewed: books, films,
conferences
Review length: 1–2 pp
How to apply: letter
Include in application: areas of expertise, published works, current
research

Canadian Historical Review

Canadian history
Affiliation: University of Toronto
Press
Eds: J. R. Miller, Susan Houston
10 St. Mary Street
Suite 700
Toronto, ON M4Y 2W8
CANADA
Bk Rev Ed: same
4/yr, 168 pp; subs $55
Circ: 2,600
Readership: academics
Indexed/Abstracted: ABC, AHCI,
BRD, BRI, CCAH, HI

• MANUSCRIPTS
Query: no; *Abstract:* preferred
Copies: 2
Notes: endnotes
Blind referee: yes
Time to consider ms: 4–6 mos
Charts, pictures, tables, graphs, maps
Foreign languages accepted: French
• REVIEWS
Seeking reviewers: no
Unsolicited reviews accepted: no
Materials reviewed: books
Review length: 500–1,000 wds
How to apply: letter
Include in application: professional
   degrees, institutional affiliation,
   areas of expertise

Canadian Journal of History/Annales Canadiennes d'Histoire

History of all countries and all
   periods
Affiliation: University of Saskatch-
   ewan
Ed: Brett Fairbairn
   707 Arts Building
   University of Saskatchewan
   Saskatoon, SK S7N 0W0
   CANADA
Bk Rev Ed: same
3/yr, 180 pp; subs $24
Circ: 725
Readership: academics
Indexed/Abstracted: ABC, HI, IMB,
   WAH
• MANUSCRIPTS
Query: no; *Abstract:* yes
Preferred length: 10,000 wds
Copies: 2
Notes: footnotes
Blind referee: yes
Acceptance rate: 3/10
Time to consider ms: 3–5 mos
Charts, tables, graphs, maps, cover
   illustrations
Foreign languages accepted: French

• REVIEWS
Seeking reviewers: no
Unsolicited reviews accepted: no
Materials reviewed: books
Review length: 600–1,000 wds
How to apply: form
Include in application: professional
   degrees, institutional affiliation,
   areas of expertise, published
   works, foreign languages
• ADDITIONAL NOTES
The editors particularly encourage
   submissions in women's, social,
   and comparative history.

Canadian Journal of Irish Studies

Irish culture
Affiliation: University of Saskatch-
   ewan
Ed: Ron Marken
   Department of English
   Arts Building
   University of Saskatchewan
   Saskatoon, SK S7N 0W0
   CANADA
Bk Rev Ed: Denis Sampson
   3511 Lorne Avenue
   Montreal, PQ H2X 2A4
   CANADA
2/yr, 125 pp; subs $13
Circ: 800
Readership: academics
Indexed/Abstracted: MLA
• MANUSCRIPTS
Query: no; *Abstract:* yes
Style guide: MLA
Preferred length: 6,000 wds max
Copies: 2
Notes: endnotes
Blind referee: yes
Acceptance rate: 2/5
Time to consider ms: 3 mos
Charts, pictures, tables, graphs, maps
Foreign languages accepted: French,
   Gaelic
• REVIEWS
Seeking reviewers: yes

Unsolicited reviews accepted: no
Materials reviewed: books
Review length: 1,500 wds
How to apply: letter
Include in application: professional
degrees, institutional affiliation,
areas of expertise, published
works, current research

Canadian Journal of Italian Studies

Italian literature, language, history,
philosophy, film, drama, history of
ideas, art history
Affiliation: McMaster University
Ed: Stelio Cro
Department of Modern Lan-
guages
McMaster University
Hamilton, ON L8S 4M2
CANADA
Bk Rev Ed: same
2/yr, 100 pp; subs $20
Circ: 350
Readership: academics
Indexed/Abstracted: MLA
• MANUSCRIPTS
Query: no; *Abstract:* yes
Style guide: MLA
Preferred length: 15–20 pp
Copies: 2
Notes: endnotes
Blind referee: yes
Acceptance rate: 2/5–1/2
Time to consider ms: 3–6 mos
Charts, pictures, tables, graphs,
maps, originals
Foreign languages accepted: Italian,
French, German, Spanish
• REVIEWS
Seeking reviewers: yes
Unsolicited reviews accepted: yes
Materials reviewed: books
Review length: 1,000 wds
How to apply: letter, send review
Include in application: institutional
affiliation

Canadian Journal of Netherlandic Studies

Dutch and Flemish languages, litera-
ture, art, history, etc.
Affiliation: Canadian Association for
the Advancement of Netherlandic
Studies
Ed: Basil D. Kingstone
Department of French
University of Windsor
Windsor, ON N9B 3P4
CANADA
Bk Rev Ed: same
2/yr, 64 pp; subs $15
Circ: 300
Readership: academics, general public
Indexed/Abstracted: ABC, MLA
• MANUSCRIPTS
Query: no; *Abstract:* no
Style guide: any
Preferred length: open
Copies: 1
Notes: endnotes
Blind referee: yes
Acceptance rate: 1/2
Time to consider ms: 3–6 mos
Charts, pictures, tables, graphs, maps
Foreign languages accepted: French,
Dutch
• REVIEWS
Seeking reviewers: yes
Unsolicited reviews accepted: yes
Materials reviewed: books, films
Review length: open
How to apply: letter
Include in application: professional
degrees, institutional affiliation,
areas of expertise, published works,
foreign languages, current research
• ADDITIONAL NOTES
The editors also welcome proposals
for special issues on suitable topics.
It is assumed that the proposer will
wish to edit the issue.

Canadian Quaker History Journal

History of Quakers in Canada

Affiliation: Canadian Friends Histori-
cal Association
Eds: Jane Zavitz, Kathleen Hertzberg
Canadian Friends Historical As-
sociation
Friends House
60, Lowther Avenue
Toronto, ON M5R 1C7
CANADA
Bk Rev Ed: same
2/yr, 35 pp; subs $15
Circ: 200
Readership: academics, association
members, Quakers
• MANUSCRIPTS
Query: yes; *Abstract:* yes
Preferred length: 4–6 pp
Copies: 2
Notes: footnotes
Blind referee: no
Acceptance rate: varies
Time to consider ms: 6 mos
Charts, pictures, maps
Foreign languages accepted: no
• REVIEWS
Seeking reviewers: no
Unsolicited reviews accepted: yes
Materials reviewed: books, magazine
articles
Review length: 1 pp
How to apply: letter

The Canadian Review
of American Studies

United States culture, past and present
Affiliation: Canadian Association for
American Studies; University of
Western Ontario; University of
Windsor
Eds: Roger Hall and Bruce Tucker
c/o Penelope Lister
Business Manager
The Canadian Review of Ameri-
can Studies
Social Science Centre 4433
University of Western Ontario
London, OH N6A 5C2
CANADA

Bk Rev Ed: Jean Matthews
3/yr; subs $35
Readership: academics
Indexed/Abstracted: ABC, AHCI,
CCAH, MLA, WAH
• MANUSCRIPTS
Query: no; *Abstract:* no
Style guide: Chicago or MLA
Copies: 2
Notes: endnotes
Foreign languages accepted: French
• REVIEWS
Materials reviewed: books

Canadian Review
of Studies in Nationalism

Nationalism, ethnic and nationality
issues
Affiliation: University of Prince Ed-
ward Island
Ed: Thomas Spira
History Department
University of Prince Edward
Island
Charlottetown, PE C1A 4P3
CANADA
Bk Rev Eds: Andrew Robb, Theo-
dore Veiter
1/yr, 350 pp; subs $13
Circ: 650
Readership: academics
Indexed/Abstracted: ABC, PAIS
• MANUSCRIPTS
Query: no; *Abstract:* yes
Style guide: Chicago
Preferred length: 25–35 pp
Copies: 2
Notes: endnotes
Blind referee: yes
Acceptance rate: 1/3
Time to consider ms: 60–90 days
Charts, tables, graphs, maps
Foreign languages accepted: German,
Spanish, French
• REVIEWS
Seeking reviewers: yes
Unsolicited reviews accepted: yes
Materials reviewed: books

Review length: 900 wds
How to apply: letter
Include in application: professional
  degrees, institutional affiliation,
  areas of expertise, published
  works, foreign languages, current
  research

Canadian Slavonic Papers/
Revue Canadienne des Slavistes

All aspects of central and eastern
  Europe and former USSR
Affiliation: Canadian Association of
  Slavists/Association Canadienne
  des Slavistes
Ed: E. Mozejko
  Department of Comparative Lit-
    erature
  347 Fine Arts Building
  University of Alberta
  Edmonton, AB T6G 2E6
  CANADA
Bk Rev Ed: O. S. Ilnytzkyj
4/yr, 126 pp; subs $40
Circ: 850
Readership: academics
Indexed/Abstracted: ABC, AHCI,
  CCAH, IMB, MLA, PAIS
• MANUSCRIPTS
Query: no; *Abstract:* no
Style guide: MLA
Preferred length: 25 pp
Copies: 3
Notes: footnotes
Blind referee: yes
Acceptance rate: 1/4
Time to consider ms: 3 mos
Charts, tables, graphs, maps
Foreign languages accepted: French
• REVIEWS
Seeking reviewers: yes
Unsolicited reviews accepted: no
Materials reviewed: books
Review length: 500 wds
How to apply: letter
Include in application: professional
  degrees, areas of expertise, current
  research

Canadian Social Studies:
The History and
Social Science Teacher

Comment and criticism on social
  education
Affiliation: University of Alberta
Ed: Joseph M. Kirman
  Publication Services
  4-116 Education North
  University of Alberta
  Edmonton, AB T6G 2G5
  CANADA
Bk Rev Ed: Robert Berard
  Department of Education
  Dalhousie University
  Halifax, NS B3H 3J5
  CANADA
4/yr, 48 pp; subs $19.50
Circ: 2,000
Readership: academics
Indexed/Abstracted: ABC
• MANUSCRIPTS
Query: no; *Abstract:* preferred
Style guide: Chicago
Preferred length: 750–1,800 wds
Copies: 4
Notes: endnotes
Blind referee: yes
Time to consider ms: 1 mo
Charts, pictures, tables, graphs, maps
Foreign languages accepted: no
• REVIEWS
Seeking reviewers: yes
Unsolicited reviews accepted: yes
Materials reviewed: books, films,
  software, etc.
How to apply: letter

Canadian West

History of Western Canada, pri-
  marily British Columbia, Alberta,
  and Yukon
Ed: G. Basque
  P.O. Box 3399
  Langley, BC V3A 4R7
  CANADA
Bk Rev Ed: same

4/yr, 48 pp; subs $13
Circ: 9,000
Readership: general public
Indexed/Abstracted: ABC
• MANUSCRIPTS
Query: no; *Abstract:* no
Style guide: own
Preferred length: 3,000 wds
Copies: 1
Notes: bibliography
Blind referee: no
Time to consider ms: 6–8 wks
Charts, pictures, graphs, maps
Foreign languages accepted: no
• REVIEWS
Seeking reviewers: no
Unsolicited reviews accepted: no
Materials reviewed: books

Canadiana Germanica

German-Canadian studies
Affiliation: German-Canadian Historical Association
Ed: Hartmut Froeschle
St. Michael's College
University of Toronto
81 St. Mary Street
Toronto, ON M5S 1J4
CANADA
Bk Rev Ed: same
4/yr, 50 pp; subs $12
Circ: 500
Readership: academics, general public
• MANUSCRIPTS
Query: preferred; *Abstract:* preferred
Preferred length: 20 pp max
Copies: 2
Notes: endnotes
Blind referee: no
Time to consider ms: 2 mos
Charts, tables, graphs, maps
Foreign languages accepted: German, French
• REVIEWS
Seeking reviewers: yes
Unsolicited reviews accepted: no
Materials reviewed: books
Review length: 2 pp

How to apply: letter
Include in application: professional degrees, areas of expertise, published works, foreign languages, current research

Catastrophism and Ancient History

To help support that there were great physical catastrophies and that the chronology of the ancient world can be interfaced with the Bible
Ed: Marvin Arnold Luckerman
3431 Club Drive, #7
Los Angeles, CA 90064
Bk Rev Ed: same
2/yr, 90 pp; subs $7.50
Circ: 2,000
Readership: academics, general public
• MANUSCRIPTS
Query: yes; *Abstract:* preferred
Preferred length: 30 pp
Copies: 2
Notes: footnotes
Blind referee: yes
Acceptance rate: 2/5
Time to consider ms: 1 yr
Charts, pictures, tables, graphs, maps
Foreign languages accepted: no
• REVIEWS
Seeking reviewers: yes
Unsolicited reviews accepted: yes
Materials reviewed: books, films
Review length: 2–4 pp
How to apply: letter
Include in application: institutional affiliation, areas of expertise, published works, current research

The Catholic Historical Review

History of Christianity, especially of the Catholic Church, from antiquity to the present in all parts of the world
Affiliation: The Catholic University of America
Ed: Robert Trisco
Mullen Memorial Library

Room 318
The Catholic University of
America
Washington, DC 20064
Bk Rev Ed: same
4/yr, 176 pp; subs $30
Circ: 2,083
Readership: academics, general public
Indexed/Abstracted: ABC, AHCI,
BRI, CCAH, HI, IMB, WAH
• MANUSCRIPTS
Query: no; *Abstract:* no
Style guide: Chicago
Preferred length: 30 pp max
Copies: 1
Notes: endnotes
Blind referee: yes
Acceptance rate: 1/4 to 1/3
Time to consider ms: 3 mos
Charts, pictures, tables, graphs, maps
Foreign languages accepted: no
• REVIEWS
Seeking reviewers: yes
Unsolicited reviews accepted: no
Materials reviewed: books
Review length: 500 wds
How to apply: letter and form
Include in application: professional
degrees, institutional affiliation,
areas of expertise, published
works, foreign languages, current
research

The Centennial Review

Interdisciplinary reflection on intellec-
tual work, particularly as set in the
University and its environment
Affiliation: The College of Arts and
Letters at Michigan State Univer-
sity
Ed: R. K. Meiners
Michigan State University
312 Linton Hall
East Lansing, MI 48824-1044
3/yr, 224 pp; subs $10
Circ: 1,000
Readership: academics
Indexed/Abstracted: ABC, AHCI,
AHI, CCAH, MLA

• MANUSCRIPTS
Query: no; *Abstract:* no
Style guide: Chicago preferred, MLA
accepted
Preferred length: 19 pp
Copies: 2
Notes: endnotes
Blind referee: no
Charts, pictures, tables, graphs, maps
Foreign languages accepted: no
• ADDITIONAL NOTES
This journal does not publish short
reviews of books. More indepth
analysis of a writer's body of work
would be considered.

Central European History

German language areas of central
Europe
Affiliation: University of California,
Riverside
Ed: Kenneth D. Barkin
Department of History
University of California, River-
side
Riverside, CA 92521-0204
Bk Rev Ed: same
4/yr, 120 pp; subs $29.95
Circ: 1,400
Readership: academics
Indexed/Abstracted: ABC, AHCI,
BRI, CCAH, HI, SSCI, WAH
• MANUSCRIPTS
Query: no; *Abstract:* no
Style guide: Chicago
Preferred length: 30–40 pp
Copies: 2
Notes: endnotes
Blind referee: yes
Acceptance rate: 1/4
Time to consider ms: 3 mos
Charts, tables, graphs, maps
Foreign languages accepted: German
• REVIEWS
Seeking reviewers: yes
Unsolicited reviews accepted: no
Materials reviewed: books, films
Review length: 750 wds

How to apply: letter
Include in application: professional degrees, institutional affiliation, areas of expertise, published works, current research

Chemung Historical Journal

Chemung County History
Affiliation: Chemung County Historical Society
Ed: Thomas E. Byrne
1448 W. Water Street
Elmira, NY 14905
Bk Rev Ed: same
4/yr, 24 pp; subs $8
Circ: 1,150
• MANUSCRIPTS
Query: yes; *Abstract:* no
Preferred length: 500–600 wds
Copies: 1
Acceptance rate: 1/4
Pictures
Foreign languages accepted: no
• REVIEWS
Seeking reviewers: no
Unsolicited reviews accepted: no
Materials reviewed: books
Review length: 100 wds
How to apply: letter

Cheshire History

History and archaeology of old and new Cheshire
Affiliation: Cheshire Community Council
Ed: Derek Nuttall
Langdale
Pulford Lane
Dodleston
Chester CH4 9NN
U.K.
Bk Rev Ed: same
2/yr, 44 pp; subs £6
Circ: 350
Readership: academics, general public
• MANUSCRIPTS
Query: preferred; *Abstract:* preferred
Style guide: own

Preferred length: 700–3,500 wds
Copies: 1
Notes: endnotes
Time to consider ms: 1 mo
Charts, pictures, tables, graphs, maps
Foreign languages accepted: no
• REVIEWS
Seeking reviewers: no
Unsolicited reviews accepted: no
Materials reviewed: books

Chicago History

History of Chicago
Affiliation: Chicago Historical Society
Ed: Russell Lewis
Publications Office
Chicago Historical Society
Clark at North Avenue
Chicago, IL 60614
Bk Rev Ed: Claudia Wood
3/yr, 72 pp; subs $30
Circ: 9,500
Readership: academics, general public
Indexed/Abstracted: ABC, WAH
• MANUSCRIPTS
Query: preferred; *Abstract:* no
Style guide: Chicago
Preferred length: 3,000–4,500 wds
Copies: 1
Notes: endnotes
Blind referee: no
Acceptance rate: 1/10
Time to consider ms: 4 mos
No illustrations accepted
Foreign languages accepted: no
• REVIEWS
Seeking reviewers: no
Unsolicited reviews accepted: no

The China Quarterly

All aspects of contemporary China since 1949
Affiliation: School of Oriental and African Studies, University of London
Ed: David Shambaugh
School of Oriental and African Studies

Thornhaugh Street
Russell Square
London WC1H 0XG
U.K.
4/yr; subs £24
Readership: academics
Indexed/Abstracted: ABC, AHCI,
CCSB, SSCI, SSI
• MANUSCRIPTS
Query: no; *Abstract:* no
Style guide: own
Preferred length: 8,000 wds max
Copies: 4
Notes: endnotes
Foreign languages accepted: no

Christian History

History of Christianity
Affiliation: Christianity Today, Inc.
Ed: Kevin A. Miller
465 Gundersen Drive
Carol Stream, IL 60188
Bk Rev Ed: Mark J. Galli
4/yr, 52 pp; subs $16
Circ: 42,000
Readership: academics, general public
Indexed/Abstracted: ABC
• MANUSCRIPTS
Query: yes; *Abstract:* no
Preferred length: 2,500 wds
Copies: 1
Notes: none
Blind referee: no
Acceptance rate: 8/10–9/10
Time to consider ms: 4 wks
Charts, pictures, tables, graphs, maps
Foreign languages accepted: no
• REVIEWS
Seeking reviewers: no
Unsolicited reviews accepted: no
• ADDITIONAL NOTES
Each issue focuses on a single person
or theme; thus, most articles are
assigned so as to prevent overlap
of material. Prospective contribu-
tors should send a letter describ-
ing their key areas of historical
study.

Chronicle: The Quarterly Magazine of the Historical Society of Michigan

Michigan's history
Affiliation: Historical Society of
Michigan
Ed: Thomas L. Jones
2117 Washtenaw Avenue
Ann Arbor, MI 48104
4/yr, 24 pp; subs $25
Circ: 4,000
Readership: members of the society
Indexed/Abstracted: ABC
• MANUSCRIPTS
Query: no; *Abstract:* no
Style guide: Chicago
Preferred length: 2,000 wds
Copies: 2
Notes: endnotes
Blind referee: no
Acceptance rate: 3/4
Time to consider ms: 2 mos
Charts, pictures, tables, graphs, maps
Foreign languages accepted: no

The Chronicles of Oklahoma

Oklahoma history
Affiliation: Oklahoma Historical So-
ciety
Ed: Bob L. Blackburn
Oklahoma Historical Society
2100 N. Lincoln Boulevard
Oklahoma City, OK 73105-4997
Bk Rev Ed: Mary Ann Blochowiak
4/yr, 112 pp; subs $15
Circ: 6,000
Readership: academics, general public
Indexed/Abstracted: ABC, WAH
• MANUSCRIPTS
Query: no; *Abstract:* no
Style guide: Chicago
Preferred length: 20–25 pp
Copies: 1
Notes: endnotes
Blind referee: yes
Acceptance rate: 3/4
Time to consider ms: 3–6 mos

Pictures, tables, maps
Foreign languages accepted: no
• REVIEWS
Seeking reviewers: no
Unsolicited reviews accepted: no
Materials reviewed: books
Review length: 450–640 wds
How to apply: letter
Include in application: professional
  degrees, institutional affiliation,
  areas of expertise, published
  works, current research

Church History

History of Christianity
Affiliation: American Society of
  Church History
Eds: Martin E. Marty and Jerald C.
  Brauer
  1025 E. 58th Street
  Chicago, IL 60637
Bk Rev Ed: Jerald C. Brauer
4/yr, 180 pp; subs $30
Circ: 3,043
Readership: academics, general public
Indexed/Abstracted: ABC, AHCI,
  BRI, CCAH, HI, IMB, WAH
• MANUSCRIPTS
Query: no; *Abstract:* no
Style guide: Chicago
Preferred length: 25 pp
Copies: 2
Notes: endnotes
Blind referee: yes
Acceptance rate: 1/4
Time to consider ms: 6–8 mos
No illustrations accepted
Foreign languages accepted: no
• REVIEWS
Seeking reviewers: yes
Unsolicited reviews accepted: no
Materials reviewed: books
Review length: 200–800 wds
How to apply: form
Include in application: professional
  degrees, institutional affiliation,
  areas of expertise, published works,
  foreign languages, current research

Civil War History: A Journal of the Middle Period

Civil War era, broadly defined
Affiliation: Kent State University
Ed: John T. Hubbell
  Kent State University Press
  Kent, OH 44242
Bk Rev Ed: same
4/yr, 96 pp
Circ: 1,700
Readership: academics, general public
Indexed/Abstracted: ABC, AHCI,
  CCAH, HI, WAH
• MANUSCRIPTS
Query: no; *Abstract:* no
Style guide: Chicago
Preferred length: 30 pp max
Copies: 2
Notes: footnotes
Blind referee: yes
Acceptance rate: 1/5
Time to consider ms: 6 wks
Graphs
Foreign languages accepted: no
• REVIEWS
Seeking reviewers: yes
Unsolicited reviews accepted: no
Materials reviewed: books
Review length: 500–750 wds
How to apply: letter
Include in application: professional
  degrees, institutional affiliation,
  areas of expertise, published
  works, current research

Civil War Times Illustrated

Popular history of the American
  Civil War
Ed: John E. Stanchak
  Cowles Magazines
  6405 Flank Drive
  Harrisburg, PA 17112
Bk Rev Ed: Carl Zebrowski
6/yr, 74 pp; subs $20
Circ: 165,000
Readership: general public
Indexed/Abstracted: ABC, WAH

- MANUSCRIPTS
Query: yes; *Abstract:* no
Preferred length: 2,000–4,000 wds
Copies: 1
Notes: informal, marginal source
   notes
Blind referee: no
Acceptance rate: 1/20
Time to consider ms: 12–16 wks
Charts, pictures, tables, graphs,
   maps, art transparencies
Foreign languages accepted: no
- REVIEWS
Seeking reviewers: no
Unsolicited reviews accepted: no
Materials reviewed: books, films,
   audio tapes
Review length: 150–300 wds
How to apply: editor's solicitation
   only
- ADDITIONAL NOTES
Articles written for *CWTI* should ap-
   peal to the broadest audience,
   assuming little knowledge of the
   American Civil War on the reader's
   part. Human interest elements
   should be strong in almost any
   submission. Though not a primary
   outlet for works showcasing
   original, academic research, it is
   often the first popular publication
   to share new Civil War history
   findings with the public.

Classical Antiquity

Ancient Greek and Roman civiliza-
   tion
Affiliation: University of California
   Press
Ed: Editorial Board
   c/o The Editor
   Classical Antiquity
   Department of Classics
   University of California
   Berkeley, CA 94720
Bk Rev Ed: Editorial Board
2/yr, 170 pp; subs $26
Readership: academics

Indexed/Abstracted: AHCI, CCAH,
   HI, MLA
- MANUSCRIPTS
Query: no; *Abstract:* no
Style guide: own
Copies: 2
Notes: endnotes
Blind referee: yes
Pictures, other suitable illustrations
Foreign languages accepted: no

The Classical Journal

History, literature, etc. of ancient
   Greece and Rome
Affiliation: Classical Association of
   the Middle West and South, Inc.
Ed: John F. Miller
   Department of Classics
   University of Virginia
   146 New Cabell
   Charlottesville, VA 22903
Bk Rev Ed: Jenny S. Clay
4/yr, 104 pp; subs $30
Circ: 2,700
Readership: academics, high school
   teachers
Indexed/Abstracted: AHCI, BRI,
   CCAH, MLA
- MANUSCRIPTS
Query: no; *Abstract:* no
Preferred length: 30 pp max
Copies: 2
Notes: endnotes
Blind referee: yes
Acceptance rate: 1/5
Time to consider ms: 6–8 wk
Charts, pictures, tables, graphs, maps
Foreign languages accepted: no
- REVIEWS
Seeking reviewers: yes
Unsolicited reviews accepted: no
Materials reviewed: books
Review length: varies
How to apply: letter
Include in application: areas of ex-
   pertise, published works, current
   research

Classical Philology

Languages, literatures, history and
life of classical antiquity
Affiliation: The University of Chicago
Ed: Richard Saller
   The Editory
   Classical Philology
   Box I
   Faculty Exchange
   The University of Chicago
   Chicago, IL 60637
Bk Rev Ed: same
4/yr; subs $34
Circ: 1,300
Readership: academics
Indexed/Abstracted: AHCI, CCAH,
   HI
• MANUSCRIPTS
Query: no; *Abstract:* no
Style guide: Chicago
Preferred length: 35 pp max
Copies: 3
Notes: endnotes
Blind referee: yes
Acceptance rate: 1/4
Time to consider ms: 2-3 mos
Tables
Foreign languages accepted: major
   European languages
• REVIEWS
Seeking reviewers: no
Unsolicited reviews accepted: no
Materials reviewed: books
Review length: 8 pp

Classical Views/Echoes du Monde Classique

Classical archaeology, Greek and
   Latin literature, ancient history
Affiliation: University of Victoria
Eds: D. R. Bradley, J. P. Oleson,
   S. G. Scully
   Classics
   Box 3045
   University of Victoria
   Victoria, BC V8W 3P4
   CANADA
Bk Rev Ed: same

3/yr, 400 pp; subs $15
Circ: 950
Readership: academics, general public
• MANUSCRIPTS
Query: preferred; *Abstract:* no
Style guide: any academic
Preferred length: 10,000 wds max
Copies: 2
Notes: endnotes or footnotes
Blind referee: yes
Acceptance rate: 1/3-1/2
Time to consider ms: 1-12 wks
Charts, pictures, tables, graphs, maps
Foreign languages accepted: French
• REVIEWS
Seeking reviewers: yes
Unsolicited reviews accepted: no
Materials reviewed: books
Review length: 1,000-2,000 wds
How to apply: letter
Include in application: professional
   degrees, institutional affiliation,
   areas of expertise, published
   works, foreign languages, current
   research

Clio: A Journal of Literature, History and the Philosophy of History

Literature as informed by historical
   understandings; historical writings
   considered as literature; philosophy
   of history, speculative and analytic
Affiliation: Indiana University—
   Purdue University at Fort Wayne
Ed: Henry Kozicki, Clark Butler
   Indiana University—Purdue Uni-
      versity at Fort Wayne
   Fort Wayne, IN 46805
Bk Rev Ed: Andrew McLean
4/yr, 108 pp; subs $15
Circ: 600
Readership: academics, students
Indexed/Abstracted: ABC, AHCI,
   BRI, CCAH, HI, MLA
• MANUSCRIPTS
Query: no; *Abstract:* no
Style guide: Chicago

Preferred length: 15–25 pp
Copies: 2
Notes: footnotes
Blind referee: yes
Acceptance rate: 1/4
Time to consider ms: 3 mos
No illustrations accepted
Foreign languages accepted: no
● REVIEWS
Seeking reviewers: yes
Unsolicited reviews accepted: no
Materials reviewed: books
Review length: 300–1,000 wds (more
if necessary)
How to apply: letter
Include in application: professional
degrees, institutional affiliation,
areas of expertise, published
works, foreign languages, current
research

Clwyd Historian/ Kanes Bro Clwyd

Local history of Clwyd and North-
east Wales
Affiliation: Clwyd Association for
Local History
Ed: R. K. Matthias and D. Pratt
Clwyd Record Office
46 Clwyd Street
Ruttin
Clwyd LL15 1HP
U.K.
2/yr, 34 pp; subs £2.50
Circ: 400
Readership: general public
● MANUSCRIPTS
Query: no; *Abstract:* no
Style guide: own
Preferred length: 1,500–2,000 wds
Copies: 1
Notes: endnotes
Blind referee: no
Acceptance rate: 3/4
Charts, pictures, tables, graphs,
maps
Foreign languages accepted: Welsh

Colorado Heritage

History of Colorado; popular, ideally
linking the past with the present
Affiliation: Colorado Historical So-
ciety
Ed: Clark Secrest
Colorado History Museum
1300 Broadway
Denver, Co 80203
Bk Rev Ed: David F. Halaas
4/yr, 48 pp; subs membership ranges
from $20 to $40
Circ: 8,500
Readership: academics, general public
Indexed/Abstracted: ABC, WAH
● MANUSCRIPTS
Query: no; *Abstract:* no
Preferred length: 20 pp
Copies: 1
Notes: footnotes and bibliography
Blind referee: yes
Acceptance rate: 1/5
Time to consider ms: 2 mos
Pictures, maps
Foreign languages accepted: no
● REVIEWS
Seeking reviewers: no
Unsolicited reviews accepted: no
Materials reviewed: books

Columbia: The Magazine of Northwest Territory

Pacific Northwest history, with an
emphasis on Washington state and
local history
Affiliation: Washington State Histori-
cal Society
Ed: David L. Nicandri
315 N. Stadium Way
Tacoma, WA 98403
Bk Rev Ed: Robert C. Carikker
History Department
Gonzaga University
Spokane, WA 99258
4/yr, 48 pp; subs $6 per issue
Circ: 3,000
Readership: academics, general pub-
lic, schools

• MANUSCRIPTS
Query: no; *Abstract:* no
Style guide: Chicago
Preferred length: 15 pp
Copies: 1
Notes: endnotes
Blind referee: no
Acceptance rate: 3/4
Time to consider ms: 2 wks
Charts, pictures, maps
Foreign languages accepted: no
• REVIEWS
Seeking reviewers: no
Unsolicited reviews accepted: no
Materials reviewed: books
Review length: 450 wds
How to apply: letter
Include in application: professional
  degrees, institutional affiliation,
  areas of expertise

Columbia Library Columns

Literature and history
Affiliation: Columbia University
Ed: Kenneth A. Lohf
  Columbia University
  535 West 114th Street
  New York, NY 10027
3/yr, 48 pp
Circ: 500
Readership: academics, friends of the
  Libraries
Indexed/Abstracted: MLA
• MANUSCRIPTS
Query: no; *Abstract:* no
Preferred length: 2,500 wds
Copies: 1
Notes: none
Blind referee: no
Time to consider ms: 3 mos
Pictures, maps
Foreign languages accepted: no
• ADDITIONAL NOTES
The articles are based on materials in
  the collections of the Columbia
  Libraries.

Comparative Studies in Society and History

Social history; interdisciplinary
Affiliation: Cambridge University
  Press
Ed: Raymond Grew
  102 Rackham Building
  University of Michigan
  Ann Arbor, MI 48109-1070
Bk Rev Eds: Nicholas B. Dirks,
  Diane Owen Hughes, James Turner
4/yr; subs $33
Readership: academics
Indexed/Abstracted: ABC, AHCI,
  CCAH, CCSB, HI, IMB, SSCI,
  WAH
• MANUSCRIPTS
Query: preferred; *Abstract:* no
Style guide: own
Copies: 2
Notes: endnotes
Any suitable illustrations accepted
Foreign languages accepted: no
• REVIEWS
Materials reviewed: books

Concordia Historical Institute Quarterly

History of Lutherans in America
Affiliation: Concordia Historical In-
  stitute
Ed: LeRoy E. Vogel
  Concordia Historical Institute
  801 DeMun Avenue
  St. Louis, MO 63105
Bk Rev Ed: Aug. R. Sueflow
4/yr, 48 pp; subs $20
Circ: 2,000
Readership: general public
Indexed/Abstracted: ABC, WAH
• MANUSCRIPTS
Query: no; *Abstract:* no
Preferred length: 5,000 wds
Copies: 1
Notes: endnotes
Blind referee: no
Acceptance rate: 3/5
Time to consider ms: varies

Charts, pictures, tables, graphs, maps
Foreign languages accepted: no
• REVIEWS
Seeking reviewers: yes
Unsolicited reviews accepted: yes
Materials reviewed: books
Review length: 500 wds max
How to apply: letter
Include in application: professional degrees, institutional affiliation, areas of expertise, published works, foreign languages, current research

Confederate Veteran

Civil War
Affiliation: Sons of Confederate Veterans
Ed: James N. Vogler, Jr.
    8506 Braesdale
    Houston, TX 77071
Bk Rev Ed: same
6/yr, 60 pp; subs $13
Circ: 17,000
Readership: general public
• MANUSCRIPTS
Query: no; *Abstract:* no
Preferred length: 3,600–4,000 wds
Copies: 1
Notes: none
Blind referee: no

Congress and the Presidency: A Journal of Capital Studies

Congress, the presidency, and the relations between them
Affiliation: Center for Congressional and Presidential Studies, The American University
Eds: Jeff Fishel, Susan Webb Hammond
    Center for Congressional and Presidential Studies
    School of Public Affairs
    The American University
    Washington, DC 20016
History Ed: Michael Les Benedict
    Department of History

106 Dulles Hall
230 West 17th Avenue
The Ohio State University
Columbus, OH 43210
Bk Rev Ed: Darrell West
    Department of Political Science
    Brown University
    Providence, RI 02912
subs $12
Readership: academics, general public
Indexed/Abstracted: ABC, CCSB, PAIS, SSCI, WAH
• MANUSCRIPTS
Query: no; *Abstract:* no
Style guide: own
Copies: 3
Notes: endnotes
Tables, other suitable illustrations
Foreign languages accepted: no
• REVIEWS
Materials reviewed: books

The Connecticut Historical Society Bulletin

Connecticut history; early New England history
Affiliation: The Connecticut Historical Society
Ed: Everett C. Wilkie, Jr.
    1 Elizabeth Street
    Hartford, CT 06105
Bk Rev Ed: same
2/yr, 124 pp; subs $12
Circ: 750
Readership: academics, general public
Indexed/Abstracted: WAH
• MANUSCRIPTS
Query: preferred; *Abstract:* no
Style guide: Chicago
Preferred length: open
Copies: 2
Notes: footnotes
Blind referee: yes
Acceptance rate: 3/5
Time to consider ms: 3–6 mos
Any illustrations accepted
Foreign languages accepted: no

- REVIEWS
Seeking reviewers: yes
Unsolicited reviews accepted: yes
Materials reviewed: books
Review length: open
Include in application: professional degrees, areas of expertise, published works

Connecticut History

History of Connecticut
Affiliation: The Association for the Study of Connecticut History
Ed: Barbara M. Tucker
  Center for Connecticut Studies
  Eastern Connecticut State University
  Willimantic, CT 06226
Bk Rev Ed: same
1/yr, 80 pp; subs $10
Readership: academics, general public
Indexed/Abstracted: ABC
- MANUSCRIPTS
Query: no; *Abstract:* no
Style guide: Chicago
Copies: 2
Notes: endnotes
Blind referee: yes
Foreign languages accepted: no
- REVIEWS
Materials reviewed: books

Contemporary French Civilization

Francophonic social and cultural studies
Affiliation: University of South Alabama and Montana State University
Ed: Bernard J. Quinn
  Department of Foreign Languages & Literatures
  University of South Alabama
  Mobile, AL 36688
Bk Rev Ed: Bernie Petit
  Department of Foreign Languages

SUNY – Brockport
  Brockport, NY 14420
2/yr, 140-160 pp; subs $15
Circ: 1,000
Readership: academics
Indexed/Abstracted: ABC
- MANUSCRIPTS
Query: preferred; *Abstract:* no
Style guide: MLA
Preferred length: 20 pp
Copies: 2
Notes: endnotes
Blind referee: no
Acceptance rate: 1/5
Time to consider ms: 2-3 mos
Any camera ready illustrations accepted, no color
Foreign languages accepted: French
- REVIEWS
Seeking reviewers: yes
Unsolicited reviews accepted: yes
Materials reviewed: books
Review length: 2-4 pp
How to apply: letter
Include in application: professional degrees, institutional affiliation, areas of expertise, published works, current research

Contemporary Record

British history since 1945; contemporary issues in historical context
Affiliation: Institute of Contemporary British History
Eds: Peter Catterall, Anthony Seldon, Brian Brivati
  Institute of Contemporary British History
  34 Tavistock Square
  London WC1H 9EZ
  U.K.
Bk Rev Ed: Nick Owen
  Christ Church
  Oxford OX1 1DP
  U.K.
3/yr, 200 pp; subs £25
Circ: 355

Readership: academics, civil servants, journalists, politicians
Indexed/Abstracted: ABC, BHI
• MANUSCRIPTS
Query: no; *Abstract:* yes
Style guide: own
Preferred length: 5,000–10,000 wds
Copies: 2
Notes: endnotes
Blind referee: yes
• REVIEWS
Materials reviewed: books

Continuity: A Journal of History

History; interpretive as well as specialized; articles that challenge the prevailing liberal tradition
Affiliation: Murray State University
Ed: Burton W. Folsom, Jr.
    Department of History
    Murray State University
    Murray, KY 42071
Bk Rev Ed: Hugh Ragsdale
    Department of History
    University of Alabama
    Tuscaloosa, AL 35487
2/yr, 125 pp; subs $12
Circ: 500
Readership: academics, general public
Indexed/Abstracted: ABC
• MANUSCRIPTS
Query: no; *Abstract:* no
Style guide: Chicago
Preferred length: 20–30 pp
Copies: 2
Notes: endnotes
Blind referee: yes
Acceptance rate: 1/5
Time to consider ms: 2 mos
Charts, tables, graphs
Foreign languages accepted: no
• REVIEWS
Seeking reviewers: yes
Unsolicited reviews accepted: no
Materials reviewed: books
Review length: 800 wds
How to apply: letter

Include in application: professional degrees, institutional affiliation, areas of expertise, published works

Continuity and Change

Legal, social and demographic history
Affiliation: Tulane University Law School; The Cambridge Group for the History of Population and Social Structure
Eds: Lloyd Bonfield and Richard Wall
    Tulane University Law School
    New Orleans, LA 70118
3/yr, 142 pp
Circ: 60
Readership: academics
Indexed/Abstracted: ABC, BHI, IMB, WAH
• MANUSCRIPTS
Query: no; *Abstract:* yes
Preferred length: 8,000 wds
Copies: 2
Notes: endnotes
Blind referee: yes
Acceptance rate: 1/2
Time to consider ms: 3 mos
Charts, tables, graphs, maps
Foreign languages accepted: no

County Historical Journal

Local history and biography
Affiliation: Bedford County Historical Society
Ed: Dick Poplin
    112 Lee Lane
    Shelbyville, TN 37160
Ed: Gilley Stephens
    301 Thompson Creek Road
    Shelbyville, TN 37160
Ed: Charles Woodruff
    1501 Lafayette Ar.
    Shelbyville, TN 37160
Bk Rev Ed: Dick Poplin
4/yr, 35 pp; subs $12.50
Circ: 300
Readership: general public

• MANUSCRIPTS
Query: yes; *Abstract:* no
Preferred length: open
Copies: 3
Notes: endnotes
Blind referee: no
Foreign languages accepted: no
• REVIEWS
Seeking reviewers: no
Unsolicited reviews accepted: occasionally
How to apply: letter
Include in application: areas of expertise, published works

Covered Bridge Topics

Covered bridges
Affiliation: National Society for the Preservation of Covered Bridges
Ed: Joseph Cohen
    130 Westfield Drive
    Holliston, MA 01746
Bk Rev Ed: same
1/yr, 16 pp; subs $15
Circ: 800
Readership: general public
• MANUSCRIPTS
Query: preferred; *Abstract:* no
Copies: 1
Notes: none
Blind referee: no
Acceptance rate: 19/20
Time to consider ms: 2 wks
Charts, pictures, tables, maps
Foreign languages accepted: no
• REVIEWS
Seeking reviewers: no
Unsolicited reviews accepted: no
Materials reviewed: books

Crossroads: An Interdisciplinary Journal of Southeast Asian Studies

History, culture, and politics in Southeast Asia
Affiliation: Center for Southeast Asian Studies, Northern Illinois University

Ed: Grant A. Olson
    Center for Southeast Asian Studies
    140 Carroll Avenue
    Northern Illinois University
    DeKalb, IL 60115
Bk Rev Ed: Harold Smith
2/yr, 130 pp; subs $14
Circ: 160
Readership: academics
Indexed/Abstracted: ABC
• MANUSCRIPTS
Query: preferred; *Abstract:* no
Style guide: Chicago
Preferred length: 30–60 pp
Copies: 3
Notes: footnotes
Blind referee: yes
Acceptance rate: 1/2
Time to consider ms: 3–4 mos
Charts, tables, graphs, maps, some scanned images
Foreign languages accepted: no
• REVIEWS
Seeking reviewers: yes
Unsolicited reviews accepted: no
Materials reviewed: books
Review length: 800 wds
How to apply: letter
Include in application: vita

Cultures du Canada Français

French Canadian Studies
Affiliation: Centre for Research on French Canadian Culture, University of Ottawa
Ed: editorial board
    CRCCF
    University of Ottawa
    145 Jean-Jacques Lussier Street
    Ottawa, ON K1N 6N5
    CANADA
1/yr, 100 pp; subs $9
Readership: academics, general public
Indexed/Abstracted: ABC
• MANUSCRIPTS
Query: no; *Abstract:* no
Preferred length: 15 pp

Copies: 1
Notes: endnotes
Blind referee: no
Charts, pictures, tables, graphs, maps
Foreign languages accepted: French
   only

Curator

Museums and museum-related
   research; history; conservation;
   storage
Affiliation: American Museum of
   Natural History
Ed: Samuel M. Taylor
   Exhibits
   American Museum of Natural
      History
   Central Park West at 79 Street
   New York, NY 10024
Bk Rev Ed: Nancy Creshkoff
   Special Publications
   American Museum of Natural
      History
   Central Park West at 79 Street
   New York, NY 10024
4/yr, 80 pp; subs $27.50
Circ: 1,500
Readership: academics, general pub-
   lic
Indexed/Abstracted: ABC
• MANUSCRIPTS
Query: no; *Abstract:* no
Preferred length: 10–15 pp
Copies: 6
Notes: endnotes or footnotes
Blind referee: yes
Acceptance rate: 4/5
Time to consider ms: 2–3 mos
Charts, pictures, tables, graphs, maps
Foreign languages accepted: no
• REVIEWS
Seeking reviewers: no
Unsolicited reviews accepted: yes
Materials reviewed: books, museum
   exhibits
Review length: 800–1,500 wds
How to apply: invitation

Current History

World affairs
Ed: William W. Finan, Jr.
   4225 Main Street
   Philadelphia, PA 19127
Bk Rev Ed: Debra Soled
9/yr, 48 pp; subs $31
Circ: 25,000
Readership: academics, general public
Indexed/Abstracted: ABC, AHCI,
   BRI, CCSB, PAIS, RG, SSCI,
   WAH
• MANUSCRIPTS
Query: yes; *Abstract:* no
Style guide: Chicago
Preferred length: 4,500 wds max
Copies: 1
Notes: endnotes
Blind referee: no
Acceptance rate: small
Time to consider ms: varies
Charts, tables, graphs, maps
Foreign languages accepted: no
• REVIEWS
Seeking reviewers: no
Unsolicited reviews accepted: no
• ADDITIONAL NOTES
Most articles are solicited.

Czechoslovak and Central European Journal

Things Czech and Slovak, mainly
   humanities and social sciences
Affiliation: Czechoslovak Society of
   Arts and Sciences
Ed: Paul I. Trensky
   Fordham University
   2 Fordham Hill Oval, 9G
   New York, NY 10468
Bk Rev Ed: same
2/yr, 140 pp; subs $23
Circ: 700
Readership: academics, general public
Indexed/Abstracted: ABC
• MANUSCRIPTS
Query: no; *Abstract:* no
Style guide: MLA
Preferred length: 5–30 pp

Copies: 1
Notes: endnotes
Blind referee: yes
Acceptance rate: 7/10
Foreign languages accepted: Czech,
    Slovak, German — will be translated
• REVIEWS
Seeking reviewers: yes
Unsolicited reviews accepted: yes
Materials reviewed: books
Review length: 1 pp min
How to apply: letter
Include in application: institutional
    affiliation, areas of expertise, for-
    eign languages, current research

Dalhousie Review

Interdisciplinary with emphasis on
    matters of interest to Canadian
    scholars
Affiliation: Dalhousie University
Ed: Alan R. Andrews
    Room 314 Sir James Dunn
    Building
    Halifax, NS B3H 3J5
    CANADA
Bk Rev Ed: same
4/yr, 132 pp; subs $19
Circ: 1,000
Readership: academics, general public
Indexed/Abstracted: ABC, AHCI,
    BRI, CCAH, HI, MLA
• MANUSCRIPTS
Query: no; *Abstract:* no
Style guide: modified MLA
Preferred length: 5,000 wds
Copies: 2
Notes: endnotes, works cited
Blind referee: yes
Acceptance rate: 1/2
Time to consider ms: 2–12 mos
Foreign languages accepted: no
• REVIEWS
Seeking reviewers: yes
Unsolicited reviews accepted: yes
Materials reviewed: books
Review length: 750 wds
How to apply: letter

Include in application: professional
    degrees, institutional affiliation,
    areas of expertise, published works

Dance Research

All aspects of dance, primarily his-
    torical
Affiliation: Society for Dance Re-
    search
Ed: Richard Ralph
    17 Duke's Road
    London WC1H 9AB
    U.K.
Bk Rev Ed: same
2/yr, 90 pp
Circ: 1,000
Readership: academics, dance
    scholars
Indexed/Abstracted: BHI
• MANUSCRIPTS
Query: no; *Abstract:* no
Style guide: any
Preferred length: 4,000 wds
Copies: 1
Notes: footnotes
Blind referee: yes
Time to consider ms: 3 mos
Charts, pictures, tables, graphs, maps
Foreign languages accepted: some-
    times
• REVIEWS
Seeking reviewers: yes
Unsolicited reviews accepted: yes
Materials reviewed: books, films,
    journals
Review length: 1,000–2,000 wds
How to apply: letter
Include in application: professional
    degrees, institutional affiliation,
    areas of expertise, published
    works, foreign languages, current
    research

Delaware History

History of the state of Delaware
Affiliation: Historical Society of
    Delaware
Ed: John A. Munroe

Historical Society of Delaware
505 Market Street
Wilmington, DE 19801
2/yr, 75 pp; subs $25
Circ: 1,500
Readership: academics, general public
Indexed/Abstracted: ABC, WAH
• MANUSCRIPTS
Query: no; *Abstract:* no
Style guide: Chicago
Preferred length: 30–50 pp
Copies: 1
Notes: endnotes
Blind referee: yes
Acceptance rate: 3/5
Time to consider ms: 3 mos
Charts, pictures, tables, graphs, maps
Foreign languages accepted: no

Devon and Cornwall Notes and Queries

Antiquities, archaeology, and history
  of the counties of Devon and
  Cornwall
Ed: M. M. Rowe
    21 Clyst Valley Road
    Clyst St. Mary
    Near Exeter
    Devon
    U.K.
Bk Rev Ed: same
2/yr, 40 pp; subs £5
Circ: 400
Readership: academics, general public
Indexed/Abstracted: IMB
• MANUSCRIPTS
Query: preferred; *Abstract:* no
Preferred length: 3,000 wds max
Copies: 1
Notes: endnotes
Blind referee: yes
Acceptance rate: 17/20
Time to consider ms: 6 wks
Charts, pictures, tables, graphs, maps
Foreign languages accepted: no
• REVIEWS
Seeking reviewers: no
Unsolicited reviews accepted: no

Materials reviewed: books, some
  periodicals
Review length: 500 wds max

The Devon Historian

Devon history
Affiliation: The Devon History So-
  ciety
Ed: Helen Harris
    Hirondelles
    22 Churchill Road
    Whitchurch
    Tavistock
    Devon PL19 9BU
    U.K.
Bk Rev Ed: Sheila Stirling
    Devon and Exeter Institution
    7 The Close
    Exeter
    Devon EX1 1EZ
    U.K.
2/yr, 40 pp; subs £5
Circ: 500
Readership: academics, general pub-
  lic, amateur historians
• MANUSCRIPTS
Query: preferred; *Abstract:* no
Preferred length: 2,000–2,500 wds
Copies: 1
Foreign languages accepted: no
• REVIEWS
Seeking reviewers: no
Unsolicited reviews accepted: no
Materials reviewed: books

Diggins

Local history of Butte County, Cali-
  fornia
Ed: Roberta R. Hammon
    P.O. Box 2195
    Oroville, CA 95965
4/yr, 28 pp; subs $15
Circ: 1,000
Readership: academics, general public
• MANUSCRIPTS
Query: no; *Abstract:* yes
Preferred length: varies
Copies: 1

Notes: endnotes or footnotes
Blind referee: no
Time to consider ms: 1 yr max
Pictures, maps
Foreign languages accepted: no
• REVIEWS
Seeking reviewers: no

Dimensions: A Journal of Holocaust Studies

The Holocaust and its repercussions in our world today
Affiliation: Anti-Defamation League
Ed: Dennis B. Klein
  Braun Center for Holocaust
    Studies
  Anti-Defamation League
  823 United Nations Plaza
  New York, NY 10017
Bk Rev Ed: same
3/yr; subs $15
Circ: 10,000
Readership: academics, general
  public, Jewish organizations
Indexed/Abstracted: ABC
• MANUSCRIPTS
Query: no; *Abstract:* no
Preferred length: 4,000 wds
Copies: 2
Notes: endnotes
Blind referee: yes
Acceptance rate: 1/10
Time to consider ms: 2 mos
Charts, pictures, tables, graphs, maps
Foreign languages accepted: no
• REVIEWS
Seeking reviewers: no
Unsolicited reviews accepted: yes
Materials reviewed: books, films,
  articles
Review length: 1,000 wds
How to apply: letter
Include in application: professional
  degrees, institutional affiliation,
  areas of expertise, published
  works, foreign languages, current
  research

Diplomacy and Statecraft

Diplomatic history
Eds: David Armstrong and Erik
  Goldstein
  Graduate School of International
    Studies
  University of Birmingham
  P.O. Box 363
  Birmingham B15 2TT
  U.K.
Bk Rev Ed: Geoffrey Warner
3/yr, 150 pp; subs £28
Circ: 350
Readership: academics
Indexed/Abstracted: ABC, IMB,
  PAIS
• MANUSCRIPTS
Abstract: no
Preferred length: 5,000–6,000 wds
Copies: 3
Notes: endnotes
Blind referee: yes
Time to consider ms: varies
Charts, pictures, tables, graphs, maps
Foreign languages accepted: no
• REVIEWS
Seeking reviewers: yes
Unsolicited reviews accepted: yes
Materials reviewed: books, journals
Review length: varies
How to apply: letter
Include in application: professional
  degrees, institutional affiliation,
  areas of expertise, published
  works, current research

Diplomatic History

History of American foreign policy
Affiliation: Society for Historians of
  American Foreign Relations
Ed: Michael J. Hogan
  Department of History
  The Ohio State University
  106 Dulles Hall
  230 West 17th Avenue
  Columbus, OH 43210
Bk Rev Ed: Peter L. Hahn
4/yr, 170 pp; subs $20

Circ: 2,200
Readership: academics
Indexed/Abstracted: ABC, AHCI,
    CCAH, HI, WAH
• MANUSCRIPTS
Query: no; *Abstract:* no
Style guide: Chicago
Preferred length: 25–30 pp
Copies: 3
Notes: endnotes
Blind referee: yes
Acceptance rate: 1/9
Time to consider ms: 3 mos
No illustrations accepted
Foreign languages accepted: no
• REVIEWS
Seeking reviewers: no
Unsolicited reviews accepted: no
Materials reviewed: books
Review length: 4–8 pp
How to apply: letter
Include in application: professional
    degrees, institutional affiliation,
    areas of expertise, published works

The Dukes County Intelligencer

History of Martha's Vineyard and the
    Elizabeth Islands
Affiliation: Dukes County Historical
    Society
Ed: Arthur R. Railton
    Box 827
    Edgartown, MA 02539
4/yr, 48 pp; subs $25
Circ: 1,300
Readership: society members
Indexed/Abstracted: ABC
• MANUSCRIPTS
Query: preferred; *Abstract:* no
Preferred length: 6,000 wds
Copies: 1
Notes: endnotes
Blind referee: no
Acceptance rate: 4/5
Time to consider ms: 2 wks
Pictures, maps
Foreign languages accepted: no

The Durham University Journal

Humanities
Affiliation: University of Durham
Ed: P. E. Lewis
    School of English
    Elvet Riverside
    New Elvet
    Durham DH1 3JT
    U.K.
Bk Rev Ed: same
2/yr, 160 pp; subs £22
Circ: 450
Readership: academics
Indexed/Abstracted: ABC, BHI,
    CCAH, IMB, MLA
• MANUSCRIPTS
Query: no; *Abstract:* preferred
Style guide: modified ModHum
Preferred length: open
Copies: 2
Notes: endnotes
Blind referee: yes
Time to consider ms: 3–4 mos
Charts, pictures, tables, graphs, maps
Foreign languages accepted: no
• REVIEWS
Seeking reviewers: yes
Unsolicited reviews accepted: yes
Materials reviewed: books
Review length: 750–1,000 wds
How to apply: letter
Include in application: professional
    degrees, institutional affiliation,
    areas of expertise, published works

ELH

The conditions affecting major works
    in English and American literature
Affiliation: The Johns Hopkins Uni-
    versity
Ed: Ronald Paulson
    Department of English
    The Johns Hopkins University
    Baltimore, MD 21218
Bk Rev Ed: same
4/yr, 256 pp; subs $19.50
Circ: 2,400

Readership: academics
Indexed/Abstracted: ABC, AHCI,
   CCAH, HI, IMB, MLA
• MANUSCRIPTS
Query: no; *Abstract:* no
Style guide: Chicago
Preferred length: 20–40 pp
Copies: 1
Notes: endnotes
Blind referee: no
Acceptance rate: 1/6
Time to consider ms: 1–3 mos
Charts, pictures, tables, graphs, maps
Foreign languages accepted: no
• REVIEWS
Seeking reviewers: no
Unsolicited reviews accepted: no

Early American Life

American social history reflecting the
   period 1600–1850
Ed: Frances Carnahan
   Box 8200
   Harrisburg, PA 17105
      or
   6405 Flank Drive
   Harrisburg, PA 17112
Bk Rev Ed: same
6/yr, 84 pp; subs $18
Circ: 150,000
Readership: general public
• MANUSCRIPTS
Query: preferred; *Abstract:* preferred
Style guide: New York Times Manual
   of Style and Usage
Preferred length: 1,500–3,000 wds
Copies: 1
Notes: none
Blind referee: no
Acceptance rate: 1/5
Time to consider ms: 2–8 wks
Charts, pictures, maps, plans
Foreign languages accepted: no
• REVIEWS
Seeking reviewers: no
Unsolicited reviews accepted: no
Materials reviewed: books
• ADDITIONAL NOTES
Early American Life does not publish

book reviews on a regular basis,
   perhaps once or twice a year only.

Early China

Cultural history of ancient China
   through the end of the Han dy-
   nasty (AD 220)
Affiliation: Institute of East Asian
   Studies, University of California,
   Berkeley
Ed: Edward L. Shaughnessy
   EALC/W301
   University of Chicago
   1050 E. 59th Street
   Chicago, IL 60637
Bk Rev Ed: same
1/yr, 320 pp; subs $30
Circ: 350
Readership: academics
• MANUSCRIPTS
Query: no; *Abstract:* yes
Preferred length: open
Copies: 3
Notes: endnotes or footnotes
Blind referee: yes
Acceptance rate: 2/5
Time to consider ms: 6–12 wks
Charts, pictures, tables, graphs, maps
Foreign languages accepted: no
• REVIEWS
Seeking reviewers: no
Unsolicited reviews accepted: yes
Materials reviewed: books
Review length: 12–20 pp

Early Music

History of music up to and including
   the early 19th century
Ed: Tess Knighton
   3 Park Road
   London NW1 6XN
   U.K.
Bk Rev Ed: David Fallows
   10 Chatham Road
   Manchester M16 0DR
   U.K.
Recording Rev Ed: Graham Sadler
   Department of Music

University of Hull
Kingston upon Hull
North Humberside HU6 7RX
U.K.
4/yr, 160 pp; subs £32
Readership: academics, general
public, instrument makers
Indexed/Abstracted: ABC, AHCI,
BHI, CCAH, HI
• MANUSCRIPTS
Abstract: preferred
Style guide: own
Preferred length: 6,000 wds max
Copies: 2
Notes: endnotes
Blind referee: yes
Acceptance rate: 1/2
Time to consider ms: 2 mos
Charts, pictures, tables, graphs,
maps, color illustrations, music
examples
Foreign languages accepted: no
• REVIEWS
Seeking reviewers: yes
Unsolicited reviews accepted: no
Materials reviewed: books, music,
recordings
Review length: 800–1,000 wds
How to apply: letter
Include in application: professional
degrees, institutional affiliation,
areas of expertise, published
works, current research, samples of
published reviews

Earth Sciences History

History of earth sciences
Affiliation: Brooklyn College and The
City University of New York
Ed: Gerald M. Friedman
P.O. Box 746
Troy, NY 12181-0746
Bk Rev Ed: Gretchen Wedke
U.S. Geological Survey
345 Middlefield Road
MS-999
Menlo Park, CA
2/yr, 80 pp; subs $30

Circ: 800
Readership: academics
Indexed/Abstracted: ABC
• MANUSCRIPTS
Query: no; *Abstract:* yes
Preferred length: open within reason
Copies: 3
Notes: none
Blind referee: yes
Acceptance rate: 7/10
Time to consider ms: 6 mos to 1 yr
Charts, pictures, tables, graphs, maps
Foreign languages accepted: no
• REVIEWS
Seeking reviewers: yes
Unsolicited reviews accepted: no
Materials reviewed: books
Review length: 1 pp
How to apply: letter
Include in application: professional
degrees, institutional affiliation,
areas of expertise, published
works, foreign languages, current
research

East European Quarterly

History, culture, and civilization of
Eastern Europe
Affiliation: University of Colorado
Ed: Stephen Fischer-Galati
Department of History
University of Colorado
Boulder, CO 80309-0234
Bk Rev Ed: same
4/yr, 128 pp; subs $12 individual; $15
institutional
Circ: 950
Readership: academics, students
Indexed/Abstracted: ABC, AHCI,
CCSB, PAIS, SSCI, SSI, WAH
• MANUSCRIPTS
Query: no; *Abstract:* no
Style guide: Chicago
Preferred length: 15–30 pp
Copies: 1
Notes: endnotes
Blind referee: yes
Acceptance rate: 3/4

Time to consider ms: 6 wks
Charts, pictures, tables, graphs, maps
Foreign languages accepted: French,
German, Italian
• REVIEWS
Seeking reviewers: no
Unsolicited reviews accepted: yes
Materials reviewed: books
Review length: 500–2,000 wds
How to apply: letter
Include in application: professional
degrees, areas of expertise, foreign
languages

East Texas Historical Journal

History of Texas, with emphasis on
East Texas
Affiliation: East Texas Historical As-
sociation and Stephen F. Austin
State University
Ed: Archie P. McDonald
Box 6223
Stephen F. Austin State Univer-
sity
Nacogdoches, TX 75962
Bk Rev Ed: same
2/yr, 96 pp; subs $15
Circ: 500
Readership: academics, general public
Indexed/Abstracted: ABC
• MANUSCRIPTS
Query: no; *Abstract:* no
Style guide: own
Preferred length: 20–30 pp
Copies: 1
Notes: endnotes
Blind referee: yes
Acceptance rate: 1/2
Time to consider ms: 1 mo
Charts, pictures, tables, graphs, maps
Foreign languages accepted: no
• REVIEWS
Seeking reviewers: yes
Unsolicited reviews accepted: no
Materials reviewed: books
Review length: 300 wds
How to apply: letter
Include in application: institutional
affiliation, areas of expertise

Economic History Review

Economic and social history
Affiliation: Economic History Society
Ed: Christopher Dyer
School of History
University of Birmingham
Edgbaston
Birmingham B15 2TT
U.K.
Bk Rev Ed: Peter Fearon
Department of Economic and
Social History
University of Leicester
Leicester LE1 7RH
U.K.
4/yr, 192 pp; subs £16
Circ: 5,000
Readership: academics
Indexed/Abstracted: ABC, AHCI,
BHI, CCAH, CCSB, IMB, SSCI,
SSI, WAH
• MANUSCRIPTS
Query: preferred; *Abstract:* yes
Style guide: own
Preferred length: 8,000 wds
Copies: 2
Notes: abbreviated footnotes and bib-
liography
Blind referee: yes
Acceptance rate: 1/4
Time to consider ms: 6 mos
Charts, tables, graphs, maps
Foreign languages accepted: no
• REVIEWS
Seeking reviewers: no
Unsolicited reviews accepted: no
Materials reviewed: books
Review length: 200–400 wds
How to apply: letter

The Eighteenth Century: Theory and Interpretation

Contemporary theoretical and interpretive approaches to American,
British, and European culture,
1660–1800
Affiliation: Texas Tech University

Eds: Bruce Clarke, Robert M. Markley, and Joel Reed
Department of English
Texas Tech University
Lubbock, TX 79409-3091
Bk Rev Ed: Robert M. Markley
Department of English
GN-30
University of Washington
Seattle, WA 98195
3/yr, 96 pp; subs $16
Circ: 750
Readership: academics
Indexed/Abstracted: ABC, AHCI, CCAH, MLA, WAH
• MANUSCRIPTS
Query: no; *Abstract:* no
Style guide: Chicago
Preferred length: 40 pp max
Copies: 2
Notes: endnotes
Blind referee: no
Acceptance rate: 1/5
Time to consider ms: 3–4 mos
Pictures, maps
Foreign languages accepted: no
• REVIEWS
Seeking reviewers: no
Unsolicited reviews accepted: no
Materials reviewed: books
Review length: 10–12 pp
How to apply: letter
Include in application: areas of expertise, current research

Eighteenth-Century Life

European and Eastern studies of all aspects of late 17th and 18th century culture
Affiliation: College of William and Mary; Johns Hopkins University Press
Ed: Robert P. Maccubbin
English Department
College of William and Mary
Williamsburg, VA 23185
Bk Rev Ed: same
3/yr, 144 pp; subs $19

Circ: 850
Readership: academics
Indexed/Abstracted: ABC, AHCI, CCAH, MLA
• MANUSCRIPTS
Query: no; *Abstract:* no
Style guide: Chicago
Preferred length: 45 pp max
Copies: 4
Notes: endnotes
Blind referee: yes
Acceptance rate: 1/7
Time to consider ms: 6 mos max
Charts, pictures, tables, graphs, maps
Foreign languages accepted: French
• REVIEWS
Seeking reviewers: yes
Unsolicited reviews accepted: yes
Materials reviewed: books, films, key journal articles
Review length: open
How to apply: letter
Include in application: professional degrees, institutional affiliation, areas of expertise, published works, foreign languages, current research

Eighteenth-Century Studies

Interdisciplinary 18th century culture
Affiliation: University of California, Davis
Ed: Arthur McGuinness
Department of English
University of California, Davis
Davis, CA 95616
Bk Rev Ed: same
4/yr, 115 pp; subs $52
Circ: 3,000
Readership: academics
Indexed/Abstracted: ABC, AHCI, BRI, CCAH, HI, MLA
• MANUSCRIPTS
Query: no; *Abstract:* no
Style guide: Chicago
Preferred length: 30 pp
Copies: 2
Notes: footnotes

Blind referee: yes
Time to consider ms: 6 wks
Charts, pictures, tables
Foreign languages accepted: no
• REVIEWS
Seeking reviewers: no
Unsolicited reviews accepted: no
Materials reviewed: books
How to apply: letter
Include in application: professional
degrees, institutional affiliation,
areas of expertise, published works

Eire-Ireland

Multidisciplinary Irish studies
Affiliation: Irish American Cultural
Institute
Ed: Thomas Dillon Redshaw
2115 Summit Avenue
University of St. Thomas (5026)
St. Paul, MN 55105
Bk Rev Ed: Robert Ward
Department of English
University of Western Kentucky
Bowling Green, KY 42101
4/yr, 144 pp; subs $35
Circ: 4,500
Readership: academics, general public
Indexed/Abstracted: ABC, AHCI,
AHI, CCAH, MLA, WAH
• MANUSCRIPTS
Query: no; *Abstract:* no
Style guide: Chicago or MLA, but
not "Works Cited" format
Preferred length: 15–20 pp
Copies: 3
Notes: footnotes
Blind referee: no
Acceptance rate: 2/5
Time to consider ms: 6 mos max
Charts, pictures, tables, graphs, maps
Foreign languages accepted: Irish
• REVIEWS
Seeking reviewers: yes
Unsolicited reviews accepted: no
Materials reviewed: books
Review length: 1,000 wds
How to apply: letter

Include in application: areas of expertise, current research

El Escribano *see under* Es...

Emblematica

Interdisciplinary emblem studies
Eds: Peter M. Daly
McGill University
Department of German
1001 Sherbrooke Street West
Montreal, PQ H3A 1G5
CANADA
or Daniel S. Russell
Department of French and Italian
University of Pittsburgh
Pittsburgh, PA 15260
Bk Rev Ed: same
2/yr; subs $30
Readership: academics, emblem col-
lectors and enthusiasts
Indexed/Abstracted: MLA
• MANUSCRIPTS
Query: no; *Abstract:* no
Style guide: MLA
Copies: 2
Notes: endnotes
Pictures, other suitable illustrations
• REVIEWS
Materials reviewed: books

English Historical Review

History of West and of the overseas
possessions of the Western powers
in the post-classical period
Ed: R. J. W. Evans
Brasenose College
Oxford OX1 4AJ
U.K.
Bk Rev Ed: J. R. Maddicott
Exeter College
Oxford OX1 3DP
U.K.
4/yr, 288 pp; subs £56
Circ: 2,500
Readership: academics
Indexed/Abstracted: ABC, AHCI,
BHI, BRD, BRI, CCAH, HI, IMB

- MANUSCRIPTS
Query: no; *Abstract:* no
Style guide: own
Preferred length: 10,000 wds
Copies: 2
Notes: endnotes
Blind referee: yes
Acceptance rate: 1/4
Time to consider ms: 6–8 wks
Charts, tables, graphs, maps
Foreign languages accepted: no
- REVIEWS
Seeking reviewers: no
Unsolicited reviews accepted: no
Materials reviewed: books, journals
Review length: 500–2,000 wds

Environmental History Review

Historical perspectives on the human
experience within the environment
Affiliation: New Jersey Institute of
Technology; The American Society
for Environmental History
Ed: John Opie
Center for Technology Studies
New Jersey Institute of Tech-
nology
Newark, NJ 07102
Bk Rev Ed: Hal Rothman
Department of History
Wichita State University
Box 45
Wichita, KS 67208
4/yr, 125 pp; subs $24
Circ: 825
Readership: academics
Indexed/Abstracted: ABC
- MANUSCRIPTS
Query: no; *Abstract:* no
Style guide: MLA or any social
science form
Preferred length: 20–30 pp
Copies: 3
Notes: endnotes
Blind referee: yes
Acceptance rate: 1/5
Time to consider ms: 3–6 mos
Charts, pictures, tables, graphs, maps
Foreign languages accepted: no

- REVIEWS
Seeking reviewers: no
Unsolicited reviews accepted: no
Materials reviewed: books, films
Review length: 500–750 wds
How to apply: letter
Include in application: professional
degrees, institutional affiliation,
areas of expertise, published
works, current research

Environments: A Journal of Interdisciplinary Studies

Comprehensive, interdisciplinary
study of the environment
Affiliation: University of Waterloo
Ed: H. S. Coblentz
Faculty of Environmental Studies
University of Waterloo
Waterloo, ON N2L 3G1
CANADA
Bk Rev Ed: Mary Ellen Tyler
School of Urban and Regional
Planning
University of Waterloo
Waterloo, ON N2L 3G1
CANADA
3/yr, 60 pp; subs $27
Circ: 500
Readership: academics, general pub-
lic, government agencies
Indexed/Abstracted: ABC
- MANUSCRIPTS
Query: preferred; *Abstract:* yes
Preferred length: 15 pp
Copies: 3
Notes: endnotes
Blind referee: yes
Acceptance rate: 2/3–3/4
Time to consider ms: 2–6 mos
Charts, pictures, tables, graphs, maps
Foreign languages accepted: French
- REVIEWS
Seeking reviewers: yes
Unsolicited reviews accepted: no
Materials reviewed: books, films,
articles
How to apply: letter

Include in application: professional degrees, areas of expertise, published works, foreign languages, current research, professional experience
• ADDITIONAL NOTES
The editors welcome short works in progress for their "Ideas" section.

El Escribano: The St. Augustine Journal of History

History of Northeast Florida
Affiliation: St. Augustine Historical Society
Ed: Jacqueline K. Fretwell
    685 Pope Road
    St. Augustine, FL 32084
Bk Rev Ed: same
1/yr, 130 pp; subs membership
Circ: 550
Readership: academics, general public
Indexed/Abstracted: ABC
• MANUSCRIPTS
Query: no; *Abstract:* no
Style guide: Chicago
Preferred length: 5,000 wds
Copies: 2
Notes: MLA
Blind referee: no
Time to consider ms: 2 mos
Charts, pictures, tables, graphs, maps
Foreign languages accepted: no
• REVIEWS
Seeking reviewers: no
Unsolicited reviews accepted: no
Materials reviewed: books
Review length: 500 wds
How to apply: letter
Include in application: professional degrees, institutional affiliation, areas of expertise, published works, current research

Essex Institute Historical Collections

History of Essex County, Massachusetts, or New England
Affiliation: Essex Institute

Ed: William T. LaMoy
    132 Essex Street
    Salem, MA 01970
Bk Rev Ed: same
4/yr, 80 pp; subs $25
Circ: 1,100
Readership: academics, general public, Institute members
Indexed/Abstracted: ABC, AHCI, CCAH, WAH
• MANUSCRIPTS
Query: no; *Abstract:* no
Style guide: Chicago
Preferred length: 2,000–8,000 wds
Copies: 2
Notes: endnotes
Blind referee: yes
Charts, pictures, tables, graphs, maps
Foreign languages accepted: no
• REVIEWS
Unsolicited reviews accepted: yes
Materials reviewed: books
How to apply: letter
Include in application: professional degrees, institutional affiliation, areas of expertise, published works, current research

Ethnohistory

Ethnohistory
Affiliation: American Society for Ethnohistory; Duke University Press
Ed: Shepard Krech III
    Department of Anthropology
    Box 1921
    Brown University
    Providence, RI 02912
Bk Rev Ed: Susan Schroeder
    Department of History
    Loyola University of Chicago
    820 N. Michigan Avenue
    Chicago, IL 60611
4/yr; subs $21
Readership: academics
Indexed/Abstracted: ABC, AHCI, CCAH, CCSB, SSCI, SSI, WAH

• MANUSCRIPTS
Query: no; *Abstract:* no
Style guide: Chicago
Copies: 4
Notes: endnotes
Blind referee: yes
Foreign languages accepted: no
• REVIEWS
Materials reviewed: books

Etudes/Inuit/Studies

Ethnic interests; Eskimo studies
Affiliation: GETIC; Inuksiutiit Kati-
   majiit Association, Université
   Laval
Ed: François Therien
      Pavillon Jean-Durand
      Université Laval
      Quebec G1K 7P4
      CANADA
Bk Rev Ed: Louis-Jacques Dorais
2/yr, 175 pp; subs $27
Circ: 800
Readership: academics
Indexed/Abstracted: ABC
• MANUSCRIPTS
Query: no; *Abstract:* yes
Style guide: any academic
Copies: 4
Notes: footnotes
Blind referee: yes
Acceptance rate: 7/10
Time to consider ms: 3 mos
Charts, pictures, tables, graphs, maps
Foreign languages accepted: French
• REVIEWS
Seeking reviewers: yes
Unsolicited reviews accepted: yes
Materials reviewed: books
How to apply: letter
Include in application: institutional
   affiliation, areas of expertise, pub-
   lished works

Etudes Internationales

International relations
Affiliation: Centre quebecois de rela-
   tions internationales
Ed: editorial board

Faculté des Sciences Sociales
Pavillon de Koninck
Université Laval
Quebec G1K 7P4
CANADA
Bk Rev Ed: Manon Tessier
4/yr, 220 pp; subs $40
Circ: 1,500
Readership: academics
Indexed/Abstracted: ABC
• MANUSCRIPTS
Query: no; *Abstract:* yes
Preferred length: 25 pp
Copies: 1
Notes: footnotes
Blind referee: yes
Acceptance rate: 1/2
Time to consider ms: 4 mos
Tables, graphs, maps
Foreign languages accepted: French
   only
• REVIEWS
Seeking reviewers: yes
Unsolicited reviews accepted: no
Materials reviewed: books
How to apply: letter

Europe-Asia Studies

Social, political, and economic affairs
   of the former Soviet Union and
   Eastern Europe and their successor
   states
Affiliation: University of Glasgow
Ed: Roger Clarke
      28/29 Bute Gardens
      Glasgow G12 8RS
      U.K.
Bk Rev Ed: D. J. I. Matko
6/yr, 180 pp; subs £40
Circ: 2,000
Readership: academics, decision
   makers
Indexed/Abstracted: ABC, AHCI,
   BHI, CCSB, PAIS, SSCI, SSI
• MANUSCRIPTS
Preferred length: 15,000–20,000 wds
Copies: 2
Notes: endnotes or footnotes

Blind referee: yes
Charts, tables, graphs, maps
Foreign languages accepted: no
• REVIEWS
Seeking reviewers: yes
Unsolicited reviews accepted: no
Materials reviewed: books
Review length: 500–700 wds
How to apply: letter
Include in application: professional
   degrees, areas of expertise, pub-
   lished works, current research

European History Quarterly

European history since the later mid-
   dle ages; social and political
   thought within an historical
   perspective
Ed: R. M. Blinkhorn
   Department of History
   University of Lancaster
   University House
   Lancaster LA1 4YW
   U.K.
Bk Rev Ed: Michael Mullett
   Department of History
   University of Lancaster
   Bailrigg
   Lancaster LA1 4YG
   U.K.
4/yr; subs £31
Readership: academics
Indexed/Abstracted: ABC, AHCI,
   CCAH, HI, IMB

European Studies Journal

European history; current European
   political, social, and economic
   movements; European cultural life,
   literature, and the arts
Ed: Rienhold K. Bubser
   Department of Modern Lan-
     guages
   University of Northern Iowa
   Cedar Falls, IA 50614-0504
Bk Rev Ed: Peter Suzuki
   Urban Studies Department

University of Nebraska, Omaha
   Omaha, NE 68182-0276
2/yr, 120 pp; subs $20
Circ: 200
Readership: academics, general public
Indexed/Abstracted: ABC, MLA
• MANUSCRIPTS
Query: no; *Abstract:* yes
Style guide: MLA
Preferred length: 10–20 pp
Copies: 4
Notes: endnotes
Blind referee: yes
Acceptance rate: 1/10
Time to consider ms: 2 mos
Charts, pictures, tables, graphs, maps
Foreign languages accepted: only in
   annotations
• REVIEWS
Seeking reviewers: yes
Unsolicited reviews accepted: no
Materials reviewed: books
Review length: 2–4 pp
How to apply: letter
Include in application: institutional
   affiliation, areas of expertise, pub-
   lished works, current research

Explorations in Economic History

Economic history
Ed: Larry Neal
   328 David Kinley Hall
   University of Illinois
   1407 West Gregory Drive
   Urbana, IL 61801
4/yr, 225 pp; subs $136
Readership: academics
Indexed/Abstracted: ABC, CCSB,
   SSCI, SSI, WAH
• MANUSCRIPTS
Query: no; *Abstract:* yes
Style guide: own
Preferred length: varies
Copies: 3
Notes: endnotes
Charts, tables, graphs
Foreign languages accepted: no

Feminist Studies

Analytical research, criticism of all
feminist issues
Ed: Claire G. Moses
 c/o Women Studies
 University of Maryland
 College Park, MD 20742
3/yr, 200 pp; subs $25
Circ: 10,000
Readership: academics
Indexed/Abstracted: ABC, AHCI,
 CCSB, IMB, MLA, SSCI, SSI,
 WAH
• MANUSCRIPTS
Query: no; *Abstract:* yes
Style guide: Chicago
Preferred length: 30 pp max
Copies: 3
Notes: endnotes
Blind referee: yes
Acceptance rate: 1/14
Time to consider ms: 3–4 mos
Charts, pictures, tables, graphs, maps
Foreign languages accepted: no
• ADDITIONAL NOTES
Feminist Studies publishes a few
 review essays. Query first.

Fides et Historia

The interaction of religion, politics
 and culture
Affiliation: Conference on Faith and
 History
Ed: Frank C. Roberts
 History Department
 Calvin College
 3201 Burton S.E.
 Grand Rapids, MI 49546
Bk Rev Ed: Daryl Hart
 Wheaton College
 Wheaton, IL 60187
3/yr, 128 pp; subs $15
Circ: 925
Readership: academics
Indexed/Abstracted: ABC, WAH
• MANUSCRIPTS
Query: no; *Abstract:* no
Style guide: Chicago

Preferred length: 25–40 pp
Copies: 2
Notes: footnotes
Blind referee: yes
Acceptance rate: 1/3
Time to consider ms: 6 mos max
Charts, pictures, tables, graphs, maps
Foreign languages accepted: no
• REVIEWS
Seeking reviewers: yes
Unsolicited reviews accepted: yes
Materials reviewed: books
Review length: 3–5 pp
How to apply: letter
Include in application: professional
 degrees, institutional affiliation,
 areas of expertise, foreign lan-
 guages
• ADDITIONAL NOTES
Review articles are also welcome.

Film and History

Film and history
Eds: Gregory Bush and John E.
 Connor
 P.O. Box 248107
 University of Miami
 Coral Gables, FL 33124
Bk Rev Ed: Kathy Fuller
 3013 N. Calvert Street
 Baltimore, MD 21218
4/yr, 30 pp; subs $12
Circ: 400
Readership: academics
Indexed/Abstracted: ABC, WAH
• MANUSCRIPTS
Query: no; *Abstract:* no
Preferred length: 12–20 pp
Copies: 2
Notes: endnotes
Blind referee: yes

The Filson Club Quarterly

History of Kentucky—political,
 social, cultural
Affiliation: The Filson Club Historical Society
Ed: Nelson L. Dawson

1310 South Third Street
Louisville, KY 40208
Bk Rev Ed: same
4/yr, 140 pp; subs $24
Circ: 3,300
Readership: academics, general public, Filson Club members
Indexed/Abstracted: ABC, WAH
• MANUSCRIPTS
Query: no; *Abstract:* no
Style guide: Chicago
Preferred length: 20-35 pp
Copies: 2
Notes: endnotes
Blind referee: yes
Acceptance rate: 1/2
Time to consider ms: 1-3 mos
Charts, pictures, tables, graphs, maps
Foreign languages accepted: no
• REVIEWS
Seeking reviewers: yes
Unsolicited reviews accepted: no
Materials reviewed: books
Review length: 400-600 wds
How to apply: letter
Include in application: professional degrees, institutional affiliation, areas of expertise, published works, current research

Flashback

Washington County (Arkansas) history
Affiliation: Washington County Historical Society
Ed: Keith Newhouse
118 East Dickson Street
Fayetteville, AR 72701
Bk Rev Ed: same
4/yr, 48 pp; subs $10
Circ: 900
Readership: academics, general public
• MANUSCRIPTS
Query: no; *Abstract:* no
Preferred length: open
Copies: 1
Blind referee: no
Acceptance rate: 3/4

Time to consider ms: 3 mos
Charts, pictures, tables, maps
Foreign languages accepted: no
• REVIEWS
Seeking reviewers: no
Unsolicited reviews accepted: yes

Florida Historical Quarterly

Florida history from the period of exploration and settlement to the present
Affiliation: University of Florida
Ed: Samuel Proctor
P.O. Box 14045
University Station
Gainesville, FL 32604-2045
Bk Rev Ed: same
4/yr, 130-150 pp
Circ: 2,500
Readership: academics, general public
Indexed/Abstracted: ABC, WAH
• MANUSCRIPTS
Query: no; *Abstract:* no
Style guide: Chicago
Preferred length: 25-30 pp
Copies: 1
Notes: endnotes
Blind referee: yes
Pictures, tables, graphs, maps
Foreign languages accepted: no
• REVIEWS
Seeking reviewers: yes
Unsolicited reviews accepted: no
Materials reviewed: books
Review length: 500-600 wds
How to apply: letter or form
Include in application: professional degrees, institutional affiliation, areas of expertise, published works, foreign languages, current research

Folklore

Personalized Saskatchewan history
Affiliation: Saskatchewan History and Folklore Society
Ed: Richard J. Wood
1860 Lorne Street

Regina, SK S4P 2L7
CANADA
Bk Rev Ed: same
4/yr, 24 pp; subs $16.10
Circ: 2,100
Readership: general public
• MANUSCRIPTS
Query: no; *Abstract:* no
Style guide: any
Preferred length: 500–3,000 wds
Copies: 1
Notes: endnotes are optional
Blind referee: no
Acceptance rate: 3/5
Time to consider ms: 4 mos max
Charts, pictures, maps
Foreign languages accepted: no
• REVIEWS
Seeking reviewers: no
Unsolicited reviews accepted: yes
Materials reviewed: books
Review length: 250–300 wds
Include in application: professional
degrees, institutional affiliation,
areas of expertise, published
works, foreign languages, current
research

Folklore Forum

Interdisciplinary material on folklore
and folklife
Affiliation: Indiana University
Eds: Charles Greg Kelley and Jill
Terry Rudy
504 North Fess
Bloomington, IN 47405
Bk Rev Eds: Clover Williams, Bar-
bara Hummel
2/yr, 60 pp; subs $8
Circ: 300
Readership: academics, folklorists
Indexed/Abstracted: ABC, MLA
• MANUSCRIPTS
Query: no; *Abstract:* no
Style guide: Chicago
Preferred length: 20–30 pp
Copies: 2
Notes: endnotes

Blind referee: yes
Time to consider ms: 3 mos
Foreign languages accepted: no
• REVIEWS
Seeking reviewers: yes
Unsolicited reviews accepted: no
Materials reviewed: books, films
Review length: 300–900 wds
How to apply: letter
Include in application: professional
degrees, institutional affiliation,
areas of expertise, published
works, foreign languages, current
research

Fort Concho and the South Plains Journal

Great Plains and Southwestern his-
tory
Affiliation: Fort Concho National
Historic Landmark
Ed: John C. Neilson
Fort Concho National Historic
Landmark
213 East Avenue D
San Angelo, TX 76903-7099
Bk Rev Ed: same
2/yr, 48 pp; subs $8
Circ: 1,000
Readership: academics, general public
Indexed/Abstracted: ABC
• MANUSCRIPTS
Query: no; *Abstract:* no
Style guide: Chicago
Preferred length: 30 pp max
Copies: 2
Notes: endnotes
Blind referee: yes
Acceptance rate: 3/4
Time to consider ms: 6–12 wks
Charts, pictures, tables, graphs,
maps
Foreign languages accepted: no
• REVIEWS
Seeking reviewers: no
Unsolicited reviews accepted: no
Materials reviewed: books

French Cultural Studies

Modern French culture
Affiliation: The University of Hull
Ed: Brian Rigby
    Department of French
    School of European Languages
        and Cultures
    The University of Hull
    Hull HU6 7RX
    U.K.
Bk Rev Ed: Nicholas Hewitt
    Department of French
    University of Nottingham
    Nottingham NG7 2RD
    U.K.
3/yr, 104 pp
Readership: academics
• MANUSCRIPTS
Query: no; *Abstract:* no
Preferred length: 7,000–8,000 wds
Copies: 3
Notes: footnotes
Blind referee: yes
Time to consider ms: 3–6 mos
Foreign languages accepted: French
• REVIEWS
Seeking reviewers: no
Unsolicited reviews accepted: yes
Materials reviewed: books, films,
    cultural events
Review length: 2,000–2,500 wds
How to apply: letter
Include in application: professional
    degrees, institutional affiliation,
    areas of expertise, published
    works, foreign languages, current
    research

French Historical Studies

French history
Affiliation: Purdue University
Eds: James R. Farr and John J.
    Contreni
    1358 University Hall
    Department of History
    Purdue University
    West Lafayette, IN 47907
2/yr, 300 pp; subs $20

Circ: 1,400
Readership: academics
Indexed/Abstracted: ABC, AHCI,
    CCAH, HI, IMB
• MANUSCRIPTS
Query: no; *Abstract:* yes
Style guide: Chicago
Preferred length: 30 pp
Copies: 2
Notes: endnotes
Blind referee: yes
Acceptance rate: 1/10
Time to consider ms: 2 mos
Charts, pictures, tables, graphs, maps
Foreign languages accepted: French

French History

French history from Gaul and Fran-
    cia through the Fifth Republic
Affiliation: Oxford University Press;
    Society for the Study of French
    History
Ed: Richard J. Bonney
    Department of History
    University of Leicester
    Leicester LE1 7RH
    U.K.
Bk Rev Ed: Alan Forrest
    Department of History
    University of York
    Hellington
    York YO1 5DD
    U.K.
4/yr, 125 pp; subs £54
Readership: academics
Indexed/Abstracted: ABC, IMB
• MANUSCRIPTS
Query: yes; *Abstract:* no
Style guide: own
Preferred length: 8,000–10,000 wds
Copies: 4
Notes: endnotes
Blind referee: yes
Acceptance rate: 1/2
Time to consider ms: 2–3 mos
Charts, pictures, tables, graphs, maps
Foreign languages accepted: French
• REVIEWS
Seeking reviewers: no

Unsolicited reviews accepted: no
Materials reviewed: books
Review length: 1,500 wds max
How to apply: letter
Include in application: professional degrees, institutional affiliation, areas of expertise, published works, foreign languages, current research

Frontiers: A Journal of Women Studies

Interdisciplinary women's studies
Affiliation: University of New Mexico
Ed: Louise Lamphere
    Mesa Vista Hall 2142
    University of New Mexico
    Albuquerque, NM 87131
Bk Rev Ed: same
3/yr, 200 pp; subs $20
Circ: 1,000
Readership: academics, general public
Indexed/Abstracted: ABC, AHCI, AHI, CCSB, MLA, SSCI
• MANUSCRIPTS
Query: no; *Abstract:* no
Style guide: Chicago
Preferred length: 30–35 pp
Copies: 3
Notes: endnotes
Blind referee: yes
Acceptance rate: 1/7
Time to consider ms: 3–6 mos
Charts, pictures, tables, graphs, maps
Foreign languages accepted: no
• REVIEWS
Seeking reviewers: no
Unsolicited reviews accepted: no
• ADDITIONAL NOTES
Frontiers considers lengthy multi-book review essays from a clear theoretical perspective. These are evaluated by the same process as other manuscript submissions.

Fulton County Images

Fulton County history, Potawatomi Indians

Affiliation: Fulton County Historical Society
Ed: Shirley Willard
    Rt. 2 Box 28
    Rochester, IN 46975
Bk Rev Ed: same
1/yr, 85 pp; subs $15
Circ: 700
Readership: general public
• MANUSCRIPTS
Query: preferred; *Abstract:* no
Preferred length: 100 pp max
Copies: 1
Notes: endnotes
Blind referee: no
Acceptance rate: 9/10
Time to consider ms: 6 mos
Charts, pictures, tables, graphs, maps
Foreign languages accepted: no
• REVIEWS
Seeking reviewers: no
Unsolicited reviews accepted: yes
Materials reviewed: books, films, other media
Review length: 5 pp max
How to apply: letter
Include in application: professional degrees, areas of expertise, published works

Garden History

Garden history
Affiliation: Garden History Society
Eds: Jane Crawley
    93 Castelnau
    London SW13 9EL
    U.K.
            or
    Elisabeth Whittle
    Meadow House
    Monmouth Road
    USK
    Gwent NP5 1RR
    U.K.
Bk Rev Ed: same
2/yr, 100 pp; subs £15
Circ: 2,000
Readership: academics, general public, society members

- MANUSCRIPTS
Query: no; *Abstract:* preferred
Style guide: own
Preferred length: 10,000 wds max
Copies: 2
Notes: endnotes
Acceptance rate: 1/4
Time to consider ms: 1–3 mos
Charts, pictures, tables, graphs, maps
Foreign languages accepted: no
- REVIEWS
Unsolicited reviews accepted: yes
Materials reviewed: books
Review length: 1,000 wds
How to apply: letter

Gateway Heritage

St. Louis and Missouri history;
    history of westward expansion and
    the fur trade
Affiliation: Missouri Historical So-
    ciety
Ed: Martha Kohl
    Missouri Historical Society
    P.O. Box 11940
    St. Louis, MO 63112-0940
Bk Rev Ed: same
4/yr, 76 pp; subs $20
Circ: 7,000
Readership: academics, general public
Indexed/Abstracted: ABC, WAH
- MANUSCRIPTS
Query: no; *Abstract:* no
Style guide: Chicago
Preferred length: 25 pp
Copies: 2
Notes: endnotes
Blind referee: yes
Acceptance rate: 1/2
Time to consider ms: 1–3 mos
Charts, pictures, tables, graphs, maps
Foreign languages accepted: no
- REVIEWS
Seeking reviewers: yes
Unsolicited reviews accepted: no
Materials reviewed: books, films
Review length: 600 wds
How to apply: letter

Include in application: professional
    degrees, institutional affiliation,
    areas of expertise, published
    works, current research

Gender and History

Historical gender studies
Affiliation: Blackwell Publishers
Ed: Leonore Davidoff
    Department of Sociology
    University of Essex
    Colchester CO4 3SQ
    U.K.
American Ed: Nancy Grey Osterud
    Radcliffe College
    10 Garden Street
    Cambridge, MA 02138
Bk Rev Ed: Jane Rendall
    Department of History
    University of York
    York YO1 5DD
    U.K.
3/yr, 100 pp; subs £21
Readership: academics
Indexed/Abstracted: ABC, WAH
- MANUSCRIPTS
Query: no; *Abstract:* yes
Style guide: own
Copies: 2
Notes: endnotes
Blind referee: yes
Tables, other suitable illustrations
Foreign languages accepted: no
- REVIEWS
Materials reviewed: books

Georgia Historical Quarterly

Georgia and Southern history
Affiliation: University of Georgia and
    Georgia Historical Society
Ed: John C. Inscoe
    203 LeConte Hall
    University of Georgia
    Athens, GA 30602
Bk Rev Ed: same
4/yr, 235 pp; subs $25
Circ: 2,600
Readership: academics, general public
Indexed/Abstracted: ABC, WAH

• MANUSCRIPTS
Query: no; *Abstract:* no
Style guide: Chicago
Preferred length: 20–30 pp
Copies: 2
Notes: endnotes
Blind referee: yes
Acceptance rate: 2/5–1/2
Time to consider ms: 6–8 wks
Charts, pictures, tables, maps
Foreign languages accepted: no
• REVIEWS
Seeking reviewers: no
Unsolicited reviews accepted: no
Materials reviewed: books
Review length: 600–900 wds
How to apply: letter
Include in application: professional
  degrees, institutional affiliation,
  areas of expertise, published
  works, current research

German History

All aspects and periods of German
  history
Affiliation: German History Society
Eds: Mary Fulbrook
  Department of German
  University College London
  Gower Street
  London WC1E 6BT
  U.K.
    or
  Jill Stephenson
  Department of History
  University of Edinburgh
  50 George Square
  Edinburgh EH8 9JY
  U.K.
Bk Rev Ed: Jeremy Noakes
  Department of History
  University of Exeter
  Exeter EX4 4QJ
  U.K.
3/yr, 140 pp
Circ: 1,000
Readership: academics
Indexed/Abstracted: ABC, IMB

• MANUSCRIPTS
Query: no; *Abstract:* no
Preferred length: 8,000 wds max
Copies: 2
Notes: endnotes
Blind referee: yes
• REVIEWS
Materials reviewed: books

German Studies Review

German and Austrian history, politi-
  cal science, and literature
Affiliation: German Studies Associa-
  tion
Ed: Gerald R. Kleinfeld
  Arizona State University
  Tempe, AZ 85287-4205
Bk Rev Ed: Wayne M. Senner
  Department of Foreign Lan-
  guages
  Arizona State University
  Tempe, AZ 85287-2201
3/yr, 200 pp; subs $25 individuals;
  $30 institutional
Circ: 1,700
Readership: academics
Indexed/Abstracted: ABC, AHCI,
  CCAH, MLA, WAH
• MANUSCRIPTS
Query: no; *Abstract:* no
Style guide: Chicago
Preferred length: 25 pp
Copies: 2
Notes: endnotes
Blind referee: yes
Time to consider ms: 90 days
Charts, pictures, tables, graphs, maps
Foreign languages accepted: German
• REVIEWS
Seeking reviewers: yes
Unsolicited reviews accepted: no
Materials reviewed: books
Review length: 450 wds
How to apply: letter and form
Include in application: professional
  degrees, institutional affiliation,
  areas of expertise, published works,
  foreign languages, current research

Germanic Notes and Reviews

Germanic studies
Ed: Richard K. Krummell
　　Rt. 7 Box 179 B2
　　Bemidji, MN 56601
Bk Rev Ed: same
2/yr, 48 pp; subs $10
Circ: 300
Readership: academics
Indexed/Abstracted: CCAH, MLA
* MANUSCRIPTS
Query: no; *Abstract:* no
Style guide: MLA
Preferred length: 8 pp
Copies: 2
Notes: endnotes or footnotes
Blind referee: yes
Acceptance rate: 3/5
Time to consider ms: 1–2 mos
Charts, pictures, tables
Foreign languages accepted: German
* REVIEWS
Seeking reviewers: yes
Unsolicited reviews accepted: yes
Materials reviewed: books
Review length: 3 pp
How to apply: letter
Include in application: professional
　degrees, institutional affiliation,
　areas of expertise, published works

Germantown Crier

History of Germantown, Penn-
　sylvania and the surrounding
　northwest Philadelphia neighbor-
　hoods
Affiliation: The Germantown Histori-
　cal Society
Ed: Lisabeth Holloway
　　Germantown Historical Society
　　5501 Germantown Avenue
　　Philadelphia, PA 19144
4/yr, 28 pp; subs $15
Circ: 650
Readership: academics, general public
Indexed/Abstracted: ABC
* MANUSCRIPTS
Query: preferred; *Abstract:* preferred

Preferred length: 10 pp max
Copies: 1
Notes: endnotes
Blind referee: no
Pictures
Foreign languages accepted: no

Gesta

History of medieval art
Affiliation: International Center of
　Medieval Art
Ed: Lucy Freeman Sandler
　　Department of Fine Arts
　　New York University
　　Main Building, Room 303
　　New York, NY 10003
2/yr, 72 pp; subs $35
Circ: 1,100
Readership: academics, museum staff,
　collectors, librarians
Indexed/Abstracted: AHCI, CCAH,
　IMB
* MANUSCRIPTS
Query: no; *Abstract:* yes
Style guide: MLA
Preferred length: 50 pp max
Copies: 3
Notes: endnotes
Blind referee: no
Acceptance rate: 1/7
Time to consider ms: 6 mos
Charts, pictures, tables, graphs, maps
Foreign languages accepted: all Euro-
　pean languages

The Glades Star

History of Garrett County, Maryland
Affiliation: The Garrett County His-
　torical Society
Ed: John A. Grant
　　115 N. Second Street
　　Oakland, MD 21550
Bk Rev Ed: same
4/yr, 32 pp; subs $10
Circ: 500
Readership: general public
* MANUSCRIPTS
Query: preferred; *Abstract:* no

Preferred length: 800–1,000 wds
Copies: 1
Notes: endnotes
Blind referee: no
Acceptance rate: majority
Time to consider ms: 3 wks
Pictures
Foreign languages accepted: no
• REVIEWS
Seeking reviewers: no
Unsolicited reviews accepted: no

Global Justice: Bulletin from the Center on Rights Development

Global human rights
Affiliation: University of Denver
Ed: Joy Sobrepena
    Graduate School of International
        Studies
    University of Denver
    University Park
    Denver, CO 80222
Bk Rev Ed: same
6/yr, 20 pp; subs $10
Circ: 300
Readership: academics, general public, activists, human rights advocates
Indexed/Abstracted: PAIS
• MANUSCRIPTS
Query: no; *Abstract:* no
Style guide: Turabian
Preferred length: 1,000 to 2,500 wds
Copies: 2
Notes: endnotes
Blind referee: yes
Acceptance rate: 1/2
Time to consider ms: 3–4 mos
Charts, tables, graphs
Foreign languages accepted: no
• REVIEWS
Seeking reviewers: yes
Unsolicited reviews accepted: yes
Materials reviewed: books
Review length: 500 wds
How to apply: letter
Include in application: professional

degrees, institutional affiliation, areas of expertise, published works, current research

Goldenseal: West Virginia Traditional Life

West Virginia folklife and popular history
Affiliation: West Virginia Division of Culture and History
Ed: Ken Sullivan
    Cultural Center
    Division of Culture and History
    Charleston, WV 25305
Bk Rev Ed: same
4/yr, 72 pp; subs $15
Circ: 32,000
Readership: general public
• MANUSCRIPTS
Query: preferred; *Abstract:* no
Preferred length: 3,000 wds
Copies: 1
Notes: none
Blind referee: no
Acceptance rate: 1/5
Time to consider ms: several wks
Illustrations accepted varies
Foreign languages accepted: no
• REVIEWS
Seeking reviewers: no
Unsolicited reviews accepted: no
Materials reviewed: books, films
Review length: 1,000 wds

The Goldfinch

Iowa history for children
Affiliation: State Historical Society of Iowa
Ed: Deborah Gore Ohrn
    402 Iowa Avenue
    Iowa City, IA 52240
4/yr, 32 pp; subs $10
Circ: 2,000
Readership: children in grades 5–8
• MANUSCRIPTS
Query: preferred; *Abstract:* no
Style guide: Chicago
Preferred length: 500–1,000 wds

Copies: 1
Notes: bibliography
Blind referee: no
Acceptance rate: 1/10
Time to consider ms: 2 wks
Charts, pictures, maps, games
Foreign languages accepted: no

Grand River Valley History

History of Grand River Valley area
in Western Michigan
Affiliation: Grand Rapids Historical
Society
Ed: Ellen Arlinsky
c/o Public Library
60 Library Plaza, N.E.
Grand Rapids, MI 49503
Bk Rev Ed: same
1/yr, 32 pp; subs $10
Circ: 500
Readership: general public
• MANUSCRIPTS
Query: no; *Abstract:* no
Preferred length: 5,000 wds max
Copies: 2
Notes: endnotes
Blind referee: no
Acceptance rate: 1/2
Time to consider ms: 6 mos
Charts, pictures, tables, graphs, maps
Foreign languages accepted: no
• REVIEWS
Seeking reviewers: no
Unsolicited reviews accepted: no
Materials reviewed: books, videos,
exhibits
Review length: 500 wds
How to apply: letter
Include in application: professional
degrees, institutional affiliation,
areas of expertise

Great Plains Journal

An interdisciplinary journal devoted
to the Great Plains of North
America
Affiliation: Institute of the Great
Plains

Ed: Steve Wilson
Museum of the Great Plains
P.O. Box 68
Lawton, OK 73502
1/yr, 96 pp; subs $15
Circ: 750
Readership: academics, general public
Indexed/Abstracted: ABC, WAH
• MANUSCRIPTS
Query: yes; *Abstract:* preferred
Style guide: Chicago
Preferred length: 5,000–10,000 wds
Copies: 1
Notes: endnotes
Blind referee: no
Pictures, maps
Foreign languages accepted: no

Great Plains Quarterly

Interdisciplinary studies of the Great
Plains
Affiliation: Center for Great Plains
Studies
Ed: Frances W. Kaye
1214 Oldfather Hall
University of Nebraska—Lincoln
Lincoln, NE 68588-0313
Bk Rev Ed: same
4/yr, 72 pp; subs $15
Circ: 700
Readership: academics, general public
Indexed/Abstracted: ABC, AHCI,
CCAH, MLA, WAH
• MANUSCRIPTS
Query: no; *Abstract:* no
Style guide: Chicago
Preferred length: 30 pp max
Copies: 3
Notes: endnotes
Blind referee: yes
Acceptance rate: 2/5
Time to consider ms: 2–9 mos
Charts, pictures, tables, graphs, maps
Foreign languages accepted: no
• REVIEWS
Seeking reviewers: yes
Unsolicited reviews accepted: yes
Materials reviewed: books

Review length: 400 wds
How to apply: letter
Include in application: professional
  degrees, institutional affiliation,
  areas of expertise, published works,
  foreign languages, current research

The Greek Orthodox Theological Review

Church history, theology, art, and
  scriptural studies
Affiliation: Holy Cross Greek Or-
  thodox School of Theology
Ed: Nomikos Michael Vaporis
     50 Goddard Avenue
     Brookline, MA 02146
Bk Rev Ed: same
4/yr, 110 pp; subs $22
Circ: 1,200
Readership: academics, general pub-
  lic, religious
• MANUSCRIPTS
Query: no
Style guide: Chicago
Preferred length: 25-30 pp
Copies: 2
Notes: footnotes
Blind referee: yes
Acceptance rate: 3/5
Time to consider ms: 1 mo
Foreign languages accepted: Greek
• REVIEWS
Seeking reviewers: yes
Unsolicited reviews accepted: yes
Materials reviewed: books
How to apply: letter
Include in application: areas of ex-
  pertise, published works

Greene County Historical Journal

History of people, places, and events
  of Greene County
Affiliation: Greene County Historical
  Society
Ed: Robert A. D'Agostino
     c/o Greene County Historical
     Society

RD #1
Coxsackie, NY 12051
4/yr, 10 pp; subs $12
Circ: 1,000
Readership: academics, society
  members
• MANUSCRIPTS
Query: preferred; *Abstract:* preferred
Preferred length: 2,500-5,000 wds
Copies: 1
Notes: endnotes
Blind referee: no
Acceptance rate: majority
Time to consider ms: 3 mos
Charts, pictures, tables, maps, others
  as applicable
Foreign languages accepted: no

Gulf Coast Historical Review

History of the United States Gulf
  Coast
Affiliation: University of South
  Alabama
Ed: Michael Thomason
     History Department
     Humanities 344
     University of South Alabama
     Mobile, AL 36688
Bk Rev Ed: James McSwain
     #37 Barron's Trailer Park
     Auburn, AL 36830
2/yr, 110 pp; subs $14
Circ: 500
Readership: academics, general public
Indexed/Abstracted: ABC
• MANUSCRIPTS
Query: preferred; *Abstract:* no
Style guide: Chicago
Preferred length: 40 pp max
Copies: 1
Notes: footnotes
Blind referee: yes
Time to consider ms: varies
Charts, pictures, tables, graphs, maps
Foreign languages accepted: no
• REVIEWS
Seeking reviewers: yes
Unsolicited reviews accepted: no

Materials reviewed: books
Review length: 1,000 wds
How to apply: letter
Include in application: professional
degrees, institutional affiliation,
areas of expertise

Hardin County Historical Quarterly

History of Hardin County, Tennessee
Affiliation: Hardin County Historical
Society
Ed: Ronney R. Brewington
Rt. 1 Box 220
Enville, TN 38332
Bk Rev Ed: same
4/yr, 50 pp; subs $12
Circ: 300
Readership: general public
• MANUSCRIPTS
Query: no; *Abstract:* no
Preferred length: open
Copies: 1
Blind referee: no
Acceptance rate: 3/4
Time to consider ms: 3 mos
Charts, pictures, tables, graphs, maps
Foreign languages accepted: no
• REVIEWS
Seeking reviewers: no
Unsolicited reviews accepted: yes

The Harvard Journal of Asiatic Studies

Interdisciplinary studies of pre-
modern China, Japan, Korea, and
Inner Asia (if related to China)
Affiliation: Harvard-Yenching Insti-
tute, Harvard University
Eds: Howard Hibbett and Joanna
Handlin Smith
2 Divinity Avenue
Cambridge, MA 02138
Bk Rev Ed: Milan Hejtmanek
2/yr, 350 pp; subs $30
Circ: 1,100
Readership: academics

Indexed/Abstracted: ABC, AHCI,
CCAH, HI, MLA
• MANUSCRIPTS
Query: no; *Abstract:* no
Style guide: own
Preferred length: open
Copies: 2
Notes: endnotes
Blind referee: yes
Acceptance rate: 1/5
Time to consider ms: 1 wk to 3 mos
Charts, pictures, tables, graphs, maps
Foreign languages accepted: no
• REVIEWS
Seeking reviewers: no
Unsolicited reviews accepted: no
Materials reviewed: books
Review length: varies
• ADDITIONAL NOTES
All manuscripts must be in English,
but authors may use Japanese,
Chinese, and Korean writing for
references and important terms.

Harvard Theological Review

Theology, ethics, history and philos-
ophy of religion, and cognate sub-
jects
Affiliation: Harvard Divinity School
Ed: Helmut Koester
45 Francis Avenue
Cambridge, MA 02138
4/yr, 125 pp; subs $25
Circ: 1,600
Readership: academics
Indexed/Abstracted: ABC, AHCI,
CCAH, HI, IMB, MLA, WAH
• MANUSCRIPTS
Query: no; *Abstract:* no
Style guide: own
Preferred length: 20–25 pp
Copies: 2
Notes: footnotes
Blind referee: yes
Acceptance rate: 1/4
Time to consider ms: 6–8 wks
Graphs, maps
Foreign languages accepted: query
before submitting

• ADDITIONAL NOTES

Although illustrations are accepted if they are integral to the text, it is unusual for this journal to publish them.

Harvard Ukrainian Studies

Ukrainian history, literature, linguistics, and related disciplines
Affiliation: Ukrainian Research Institute, Harvard University
Ed: George G. Grabowicz
    Harvard Ukrainian Research Institute
    1583 Massachusetts Avenue
    Cambridge, MA 02138
Bk Rev Ed: Lawrence Wolff
2/yr, 260 pp; subs $28
Circ: 400
Readership: academics, Ukrainian community
Indexed/Abstracted: ABC, MLA
• MANUSCRIPTS
Query: no; *Abstract:* no
Style guide: Chicago
Copies: 3
Notes: footnotes
Blind referee: no
Acceptance rate: 3/5–2/3
Time to consider ms: 3–6 mos
Charts, pictures, tables, graphs, maps
Foreign languages accepted: French, German
• REVIEWS
Seeking reviewers: yes
Unsolicited reviews accepted: yes
Materials reviewed: books
Review length: 1,000
How to apply: letter
Include in application: professional degrees, institutional affiliation, areas of expertise, published works, foreign languages, current research
• ADDITIONAL NOTES
Transliteration from Cyrillic may be in either the Library of Congress or International Standard System.

The Hawaiian Journal of History

History of Hawaii, Polynesia, and the Pacific area
Affiliation: The Hawaiian Historical Society
Ed: Helen G. Chapin
    c/o Hawaiian Historical Society
    560 Kawaiahao Street
    Honolulu, HI 96813
Bk Rev Ed: Nancy Morris
1/yr, 256 pp; subs $25
Circ: 1,600
Readership: academics, general public
Indexed/Abstracted: ABC, WAH
• MANUSCRIPTS
Query: no; *Abstract:* no
Style guide: MLA
Preferred length: 35 pp
Copies: 2
Notes: endnotes
Blind referee: no
Acceptance rate: less than 1/2
Charts, pictures, tables, graphs, maps
Foreign languages accepted: no
• REVIEWS
Seeking reviewers: yes
Unsolicited reviews accepted: no
Materials reviewed: books
Review length: 500–1,000 wds
How to apply: letter
Include in application: professional degrees, institutional affiliation, areas of expertise, published works

Hayes Historical Journal: A Journal of the Gilded Age

Movements, events, and people of the U.S., 1865–1917
Affiliation: Rutherford B. Hayes Presidential Center
Ed: Bruce Bowlus
    Hayes Presidential Center
    Spiegel Grove
    Fremont, OH 43420-2796
Bk Rev Ed: same
4/yr, 50 pp; subs $20
Circ: 800

Readership: academics, general public
Indexed/Abstracted: ABC, WAH
● MANUSCRIPTS
Query: no; *Abstract:* no
Style guide: own
Preferred length: 18–25 pp
Copies: 3
Notes: endnotes
Blind referee: yes
Acceptance rate: 1/3
Time to consider ms: several wks
Charts, pictures, tables, graphs, maps
● REVIEWS
Seeking reviewers: yes
Unsolicited reviews accepted: no
Materials reviewed: books, films
Review length: 3–5 pp
How to apply: letter
Include in application: professional degrees, institutional affiliation, areas of expertise, published works

The Hemingway Review

Interdisciplinary studies of Ernest Hemingway and his work
Affiliation: The Ernest Hemingway Foundation and the University of West Florida
Ed: Susan F. Beegel
180 Polpis Road
Nantucket, MA 02554
Bk Rev Ed: same
2/yr, 100 pp; subs $9
Circ: 1,000
Readership: academics
Indexed/Abstracted: ABC, HI, MLA
● MANUSCRIPTS
Query: no; *Abstract:* no
Style guide: MLA
Preferred length: 2–20 pp
Copies: 3
Notes: endnotes
Blind referee: yes
Acceptance rate: 1/6
Time to consider ms: 2 mos
Query before submission of illustrations
Foreign languages accepted: no

● REVIEWS
Seeking reviewers: yes
Unsolicited reviews accepted: yes
Materials reviewed: books
Review length: 2–5 pp
How to apply: letter
Include in application: professional degrees, institutional affiliation, areas of expertise, published works, current research

The Heritage

History of Vermilion County, Illinois
Affiliation: Vermilion County Museum Society
Ed: Donald G. Richter
RR #2 Box 3
Oakwood, IL 61832
4/yr, 16 pp; subs $10
Circ: 1,100
Readership: society members
● MANUSCRIPTS
Query: preferred; *Abstract:* no
Preferred length: open
Copies: 1
Notes: source list
Blind referee: no
Time to consider ms: 3 mos
Pictures, tables, maps
Foreign languages accepted: no

Hesperia: Journal of the American School of Classical Studies at Athens

Greek archaeology, architecture, art, history, and literature
Affiliation: American School of Classical Studies at Athens
Ed: Marion H. McAllister
American School of Classical Studies
c/o Institute for Advanced Study
Princeton, NJ 08540
4/yr, 132 pp; subs $40
Circ: 960
Readership: academics
Indexed/Abstracted: AHCI, CCAH, CCSB, SSCI

• MANUSCRIPTS
Query: preferred; *Abstract:* no
Style guide: own
Preferred length: 10–30 pp
Copies: 2
Notes: footnotes
Blind referee: yes
Acceptance rate: 3/4
Time to consider ms: 6 mos max
Charts, pictures, tables, graphs, maps
Foreign languages accepted: French, German, Spanish, Italian

• ADDITIONAL NOTES
Although the editors attempt to have papers reviewed blind, the field is so small that reviewers frequently guess the author. The journal exists to publish the work of the American School. Other manuscripts can more easily be anonymous. Their submission is encouraged, but their acceptance is not guaranteed, with or without revision.

Hispanic American Historical Review

Latin American history
Affiliation: Florida International University
Ed: Mark D. Szuchman
    Florida International University
    University Park
    Miami, FL 33199
Bk Rev Ed: same
4/yr, 236 pp; subs $36
Circ: 3,000
Readership: academics
Indexed/Abstracted: ABC, AHCI, BRI, CCAH, HI, IMB

• MANUSCRIPTS
Query: no; *Abstract:* no
Style guide: Chicago
Preferred length: 45 pp
Copies: 3
Notes: endnotes
Blind referee: yes
Acceptance rate: 2/10–3/10
Time to consider ms: 6 mos

Charts, tables, graphs, maps
Foreign languages accepted: Spanish

• REVIEWS
Seeking reviewers: no
Unsolicited reviews accepted: no
Materials reviewed: books
Review length: 450 wds
How to apply: letter
Include in application: areas of expertise, published works, foreign languages, current research

Historia Mathematica

History of mathematics
Affiliation: International Commission on the History of Mathematics
Managing Ed: David E. Rowe
    Department of Mathematics
    Pace University
    Pleasantville, NY 10570
Bk Rev Ed: Karen H. Parshall
    Department of History
    University of Virginia
    Randall Hall
    Charlottesville, VA 22903
4/yr, 124 pp
Readership: academics
Indexed/Abstracted: ABC

• MANUSCRIPTS
Query: no; *Abstract:* yes
Style guide: modified Chicago
Preferred length: varies
Copies: 4
Notes: endnotes
Blind referee: yes
Charts, pictures, tables, graphs, maps
Foreign languages accepted: any

• REVIEWS
Materials reviewed: books
How to apply: letter
Include in application: professional degrees, institutional affiliation, areas of expertise, published works, foreign languages, current research

The Historian

History of the Americas, Africa, Asia, and Europe that appeals to the general reader
Affiliation: Phi Alpha Theta
Ed: Roger Adelson
Department of History
Arizona State University
Tempe, AZ 85287-2501
Bk Rev Ed: Dean Phillip Thomas
Fairmount College of Arts & Sciences
Wichita State University
Wichita, KS 67208
4/yr, 200 pp; subs $20
Circ: 16,000
Readership: academics, general public
Indexed/Abstracted: ABC, AHCI, BRI, CCAH, HI, IMB, WAH
• MANUSCRIPTS
Query: no; *Abstract:* no
Style guide: Chicago
Preferred length: 6,000 wds
Copies: 2
Notes: footnotes
Blind referee: yes
Acceptance rate: 1/6
Time to consider ms: 2-4 mos
Charts, pictures, tables, graphs, maps, photo essays
Foreign languages accepted: no
• REVIEWS
Seeking reviewers: yes
Unsolicited reviews accepted: no
Materials reviewed: books
How to apply: letter
Include in application: vita
• ADDITIONAL NOTES
In the first fifty years of the journal's history, over 70% of the articles and book reviews focused on U.S. history. The Historian now globalizes its coverage and encourages the submission of manuscripts and books for review in the fields of Africa, Eurasian, and South American history that will interest a general reading audience.

Historic Kingston

History of Kingston, Ontario and the surrounding area
Affiliation: Kingston Historical Society
Ed: Donald A. Redmond
c/o Kingston Historical Society
Box 54
Kingston, OH K7L 4V6
CANADA
1/yr, 120 pp; subs $35
Circ: 280
Readership: academics, general public, society members
• MANUSCRIPTS
Query: yes; *Abstract:* no
Style guide: any
Preferred length: open
Copies: 1
Blind referee: no
Time to consider ms: 2 mos
Charts, pictures, tables, graphs, maps
Foreign languages accepted: no

Historic Preservation

Historic preservation
Affiliation: National Trust for Historic Preservation
Ed: Anne Elizabeth Powell
National Trust for Historic Preservation
1785 Massachusetts Avenue, N.W.
Washington, DC 20036
6/yr, 112 pp; subs $15
Readership: general public
Indexed/Abstracted: ABC, AHCI, CCAH

Historical Archaeology

Archaeology of historic period sites
Affiliation: Society for Historical Archaeology
Ed: Ronald L. Michael
Anthropology
California University of Pennsylvania
California, PA 15419

Bk Rev Ed: Roderick Sprague
  Laboratory of Anthropology
  University of Idaho
  Moscow, ID 83843
4/yr, 140 pp; subs $50
Circ: 2,400
Readership: academics, cultural re-
  source specialists, archaeologists
Indexed/Abstracted: ABC
* MANUSCRIPTS
Query: no; *Abstract:* yes
Style guide: own
Preferred length: 10–40 pp
Copies: 4
Notes: none
Blind referee: yes
Acceptance rate: 2/5
Time to consider ms: 45 days
Charts, pictures, tables, graphs, maps
Foreign languages accepted: Spanish
* REVIEWS
Seeking reviewers: yes
Unsolicited reviews accepted: no
Materials reviewed: books, films, re-
  ports
Review length: 3–5 pp
How to apply: letter
Include in application: institutional
  affiliation, areas of expertise, cur-
  rent research

The Historical Journal

European, British and American
  Commonwealth history, post–1500
Affiliation: University of Cambridge
Eds: J. S. Morrill and J. Steinberg
  Faculty of History
  West Road
  Cambridge CB3 9EF
  U.K.
Bk Rev Ed: same
4/yr, 256 pp; subs £46
Circ: 1,500
Readership: academics
Indexed/Abstracted: ABC, AHCI,
  BHI, CCAH, HI, WAH
* MANUSCRIPTS
Query: no; *Abstract:* yes

Style guide: own
Preferred length: 40 pp max
Copies: 2
Notes: endnotes
Blind referee: yes
Acceptance rate: 1/2
Charts, pictures, tables, graphs, maps
Foreign languages accepted: no
* REVIEWS
Seeking reviewers: no
Unsolicited reviews accepted: no
Materials reviewed: books
Review length: 1,000 wds
* ADDITIONAL NOTES
The editors encourage the submission
of articles by younger scholars.
Since *The Historical Journal*
publishes 6–8 articles per issue,
more space is available for first
scholarly articles than in most ma-
jor historical journals.

Historical Journal of Film, Radio and Television

History of film, radio and television
Affiliation: International Association
  for Audio-Visual Media in Histori-
  cal Research and Education
Ed: David Culbert
  Department of History
  Louisiana State University
  Baton Rouge, LA 70803
Bk Rev Ed: Denise Youngblood
  Department of History
  University of Vermont
  Wheeler House
  442 Main Street
  Burlington, VT 05405
4/yr, 112 pp
Circ: 500
Readership: academics, general pub-
  lic, media practitioners
Indexed/Abstracted: ABC, AHCI,
  CCAH, WAH
* MANUSCRIPTS
Query: no; *Abstract:* no
Style guide: own
Preferred length: 6,000–9,000 wds

Copies: 3
Notes: endnotes
Blind referee: yes
Acceptance rate: 1/10
Time to consider ms: 2 mos
Charts, pictures, tables, graphs,
  microfiche supplement
Foreign languages accepted: no
• REVIEWS
Seeking reviewers: yes
Unsolicited reviews accepted: usually
Materials reviewed: books, films
How to apply: letter

Historical Journal of Massachusetts

History of Massachusetts and the
  region, from the early colonial
  period to the present time
Affiliation: Westfield State College
Ed: Martin Kaufman
  Department of History
  Westfield State College
  Westfield, MA 01086
Bk Rev Ed: same
2/yr, 120 pp; subs $7
Circ: 1,200
Readership: academics, general public
Indexed/Abstracted: ABC, WAH
• MANUSCRIPTS
Query: no; *Abstract:* no
Style guide: own
Preferred length: 20 pp max
Copies: 1
Notes: endnotes
Blind referee: sometimes
Acceptance rate: 3/10
Time to consider ms: 6 mos
Charts, pictures, tables, graphs, maps
Foreign languages accepted: no
• REVIEWS
Seeking reviewers: no
Unsolicited reviews accepted: no
Materials reviewed: books
Review length: 300–500 wds
How to apply: letter
Include in application: professional
  degrees, institutional affiliation,

areas of expertise, published
  works, current research

Historical Methods

Methodologies in the interdisciplinary
  study of history
Ed: Myron P. Gutman
  Department of History
  The University of Texas at Austin
  Austin, TX 78712-1163
Bk Rev Ed: same
4/yr, 48 pp; subs $35
Circ: 567
Readership: academics
Indexed/Abstracted: ABC, AHCI,
  CCAH, WAH
• MANUSCRIPTS
Query: no; *Abstract:* no
Style guide: Chicago
Preferred length: varies
Copies: 3
Notes: endnotes
Time to consider ms: 60–90 days
Charts, tables, graphs
Foreign languages accepted: no
• REVIEWS
Seeking reviewers: no
Unsolicited reviews accepted: no
Materials reviewed: books
Review length: varies
How to apply: letter
Include in application: professional
  degrees, institutional affiliation,
  areas of expertise, published
  works, foreign languages, current
  research

Historical New Hampshire

New Hampshire history
Affiliation: New Hampshire Histori-
  cal Society
Eds: John L. Frisbee and Joan
  Desmarais
  New Hampshire Historical So-
  ciety
  30 Park Street
  Concord, NH 03301
Bk Rev Ed: same

4/yr, 64 pp; subs $30
Circ: 2,700
Readership: academics, general public
Indexed/Abstracted: ABC, WAH
• MANUSCRIPTS
Query: preferred; *Abstract:* preferred
Style guide: Chicago
Preferred length: 2,500–7,500
Copies: 2
Notes: footnotes
Blind referee: no
Acceptance rate: 1/10
Time to consider ms: 3 mos
Charts, pictures, tables, graphs, maps
Foreign languages accepted: no
• REVIEWS
Seeking reviewers: yes
Unsolicited reviews accepted: no
Materials reviewed: books
Review length: 500–750 wds
How to apply: letter
Include in application: professional degrees, institutional affiliation, areas of expertise, published works, current research

Historical Performance: The Journal of Early Music America

Performance of early music
Affiliation: Early Music America
Ed: Timothy Pfaff
171 Delmar
San Francisco, CA 94117
Bk Rev Ed: Julie Cumming
2/yr, 80 pp; subs $30
Readership: academics, musicians
• MANUSCRIPTS
Query: no; *Abstract:* no
Style guide: Chicago
Preferred length: 4,000–5,000 wds
Copies: 2
Notes: endnotes
Pictures, tables, music examples, other suitable illustrations

• REVIEWS
Materials reviewed: books, music, recordings, events
Review length: 3,000 wds max

Historical Reflections/ Réflexions Historiques

Intellectual-cultural history
Affiliation: Alfred University
Ed: Stuart L. Campbell
Department of History
Division of Human Studies
Alfred University
Alfred, NY 14802
3/yr, 125 pp; subs $42
Circ: 500
Readership: academics
Indexed/Abstracted: ABC, AHCI, CCAH, IMB
• MANUSCRIPTS
Query: no; *Abstract:* no
Style guide: Chicago
Preferred length: 30–35 pp
Copies: 3
Notes: endnotes or footnotes
Blind referee: yes
Acceptance rate: 1/8
Time to consider ms: 3 mos
Charts, pictures, tables, graphs, maps
Foreign languages accepted: French
• ADDITIONAL NOTES
Historical Reflections does not publish books reviews, but review essays are considered. The editors prefer manuscripts with innovative theoretical and methodological implications, especially those associated with the history of discourse and representation, and the history of art, literature, and the social sciences.

Historical Research

8th–20th century British and European history
Affiliation: University of London Institute of Historical Research
Ed: Patrick O'Brien

Institute of Historical Research
University of London
Senate House
London WC1E 7HU
U.K.
3/yr, 120 pp; subs £16
Circ: 1,200
Readership: academics
Indexed/Abstracted: ABC, AHCI,
BHI, CCAH, IMB
• MANUSCRIPTS
Query: no; *Abstract:* no
Style guide: own
Preferred length: 8,500 wds max
Copies: 1
Notes: endnotes
Blind referee: yes
Acceptance rate: 7/10
Time to consider ms: 2 mos
Charts, tables, graphs
Foreign languages accepted: French
• ADDITIONAL NOTES
Historical Research publishes the
work of established historians and
also aims to encourage and assist
young historians with the publica-
tion of their first research articles.

Historical Studies in the Physical and Biological Sciences

Intellectual and social history of the
physical sciences and experimental
biology since the 17th century
Affiliation: University of California
Press; Office for History of Science
and Technology, University of
California, Berkeley
Ed: J. L. Heilbron
Office for History of Science and
Technology
543 Stephens Hall
University of California
Berkeley, CA 94720
2/yr; subs $20
Readership: academics
Indexed/Abstracted: ABC
• MANUSCRIPTS
Query: no; *Abstract:* no

Style guide: own
Copies: 2
Notes: endnotes
Tables, equations

History

World history, primarily British,
European and American history
from early medieval to the present
Affiliation: The Historical Associa-
tion of Great Britain
Ed: H. T. Dickinson
History Department
University of Edinburgh
Edinburgh EH8 9JY
U.K.
Bk Rev Eds: Kenneth Feldon, Alan
Day, Tony Goodman
3/yr, 192 pp; subs £13.50
Circ: 4,000
Readership: academics, general pub-
lic, school teachers
Indexed/Abstracted: ABC, AHCI,
BHI, BRD, CCAH, CCSB, HI,
IMB, SSCI, WAH
• MANUSCRIPTS
Query: no; *Abstract:* no
Style guide: own
Preferred length: 6,000–8,000 wds
Copies: 2
Notes: endnotes
Blind referee: yes
Acceptance rate: 1/3
Time to consider ms: 2 mos
Charts, tables, graphs, maps
Foreign languages accepted: no
• REVIEWS
Seeking reviewers: no
Unsolicited reviews accepted: no
Materials reviewed: books
Review length: 400–500 wds
How to apply: letter
Include in application: professional
degrees, institutional affiliation,
published works, current research

History: Review of New Books

Reviews of books on a wide range of
historical subjects

Ed: Jerome J. Hanus
Heldref Publications
1319 Eighteenth Street, N.W.
Washington, D.C. 20036-1802
Bk Rev Ed: same
4/yr, 48 pp; subs $39
Circ: 495
Readership: academics, librarians
Indexed/Abstracted: ABC, BRI
• REVIEWS
Seeking reviewers: occasionally
Unsolicited reviews accepted: no
Materials reviewed: books
Review length: 400–450 wds
How to apply: letter
Include in application: professional
degrees, institutional affiliation,
areas of expertise, published
works, foreign languages, current
research

History and Computing

Use of computers by historians in
research and teaching
Affiliation: Association for History
and Computing
Ed: R. J. Morris
Department of Economic and
Social History
George Square
Edinburgh EH8 9JY
U.K.
Bk Rev Ed: Kevin Snurer
Cambridge Group for History of
Population
27 Trumpington Street
Cambridge CB2 1QA
U.K.
3/yr, 60 pp; subs £28
Circ: 984
Readership: academics, teachers,
archivists, computer advisors
Indexed/Abstracted: ABC
• MANUSCRIPTS
Query: no; *Abstract:* yes
Style guide: own
Preferred length: 5,000 wds
Copies: 2

Notes: endnotes
Blind referee: usually
Acceptance rate: 4/5
Time to consider ms: 3–6 mos
Charts, pictures, tables, graphs,
maps, screen dumps
Foreign languages accepted: abstracts
in French and German
• REVIEWS
Seeking reviewers: yes
Unsolicited reviews accepted: no
Materials reviewed: books, computer
related material
How to apply: letter
Include in application: professional
degrees, institutional affiliation,
areas of expertise, published
works, foreign languages, current
research

History and Philosophy of Logic

History and philosophy of logic
Ed: Ivor Grattan-Guinness
University of Middlesex
Enfield EN3 4SF
U.K.
Bk Rev Ed: same
2/yr, 130 pp; subs £60
Circ: 500
Readership: academics
Indexed/Abstracted: ABC, CCAH,
CCSB
• MANUSCRIPTS
Query: no; *Abstract:* yes
Style guide: ModHum
Preferred length: 15,000 wds
Copies: 2
Notes: footnotes
Blind referee: yes
Acceptance rate: 2/5
Time to consider ms: 4–8 mos
Charts, pictures, tables, graphs, maps
Foreign languages accepted: French,
German, Italian
• REVIEWS
Seeking reviewers: yes
Unsolicited reviews accepted: no

Materials reviewed: books
Review length: 500–2,000 wds
How to apply: letter
Include in application: professional
degrees, institutional affiliation,
areas of expertise, published
works, foreign languages, current
research

History and Theory: Studies in the Philosophy of History

Theories of history
Affiliation: Wesleyan University
Ed: Brian C. Fay
  Wesleyan Station
  Middletown, CT 06459-0507
Bk Rev Ed: Julia Perkins
4/yr, 125 pp; subs $25
Circ: 2,000
Readership: academics
Indexed/Abstracted: ABC, AHCI,
  BRI, CCAH, HI, WAH
• MANUSCRIPTS
Query: no; *Abstract:* yes
Style guide: own
Preferred length: 15–40 pp
Copies: 1
Notes: endnotes
Blind referee: no
Acceptance rate: 1/6–1/5
Time to consider ms: 2 mos
Charts, pictures, tables, graphs
Foreign languages accepted: French
• REVIEWS
Seeking reviewers: no
Unsolicited reviews accepted: no
Materials reviewed: books
Review length: 3,000 wds
Include in application: institutional
affiliation
• ADDITIONAL NOTES
The main focus areas of the journal
include Theories of history: law,
cause, explanation; Narrativism:
stylistics of historical writing, nar-
ration, rhetoric; Historical method:
interpretation, objectivity, social
and cultural implications of the

historian's method; Related disciplines: problems in historical
theory and practice compared to
those of sociology, economics, psychology, anthropology, and the
humanities.

History Microcomputer Review

Computer-assisted history education
  at the college level
Affiliation: Pittsburg State University
Ed: James B. M. Schick
  Department of History
  Pittsburg State University
  Pittsburg, KS 66762
Bk Rev Ed: Leslie Gene Hunter
  Department of History
  Texas A & I University
  Campus Box 166
  Kingsville, TX 78363
2/yr, 60 pp; subs $10
Circ: 150
Readership: academics
Indexed/Abstracted: ABC, WAH
• MANUSCRIPTS
Query: no; *Abstract:* yes
Style guide: open
Preferred length: open
Copies: 2
Notes: endnotes
Blind referee: yes
Acceptance rate: 3/4
Time to consider ms: 3–4 mos
Any illustrations accepted
Foreign languages accepted: no
• REVIEWS
Seeking reviewers: yes
Unsolicited reviews accepted: yes
Materials reviewed: books, software
Review length: 3 pp
How to apply: letter
Include in application: professional
degrees, institutional affiliation,
areas of expertise, published
works, current research, computer
systems used
• ADDITIONAL NOTES
The editors are always looking for ar-
ticles on the use of computers to

teach history. They focus on post-secondary education, but to not reject manuscripts on secondary history education.

History of Education

History of education
Affiliation: History of Education Society of U.K.
Ed: Roy Lowe
    School of Education
    University of Birmingham
    P.O. Box 363
    Birmingham B15 2TT
    U.K.
Bk Rev Ed: Harold Silver
    2 William Orchard Close
    Old Headquarters
    Oxford OX3 9DR
    U.K.
4/yr, 120 pp
Circ: 500
Readership: academics
Indexed/Abstracted: ABC, IMB
• MANUSCRIPTS
Query: no; *Abstract:* no
Style guide: own
Preferred length: 12,000 wds max
Copies: 2
Notes: footnotes
Blind referee: no
Acceptance rate: 2/5
Time to consider ms: 6 mos max
Charts, pictures, tables, graphs, maps
Foreign languages accepted: no
• REVIEWS
Seeking reviewers: no
Unsolicited reviews accepted: no
Materials reviewed: books

History of Education Quarterly

History of schooling, the family, and childhood covering all parts of the world
Affiliation: Indiana University; Indiana University, Northwest; and Cleveland State University
Ed: William J. Reese

School of Education
Indiana University
Bloomington, IN 47405
Bk Rev Ed: Ronald Cohen
    Department of History and Philosophy
    Indiana University, Northwest
    Gary, IN 46408
4/yr, 150 pp; subs $30
Circ: 1,550
Readership: academics
Indexed/Abstracted: ABC, AHCI, CCSB, IMB, SSCI, WAH
• MANUSCRIPTS
Query: no; *Abstract:* no
Style guide: Chicago
Preferred length: 25 pp
Copies: 2
Notes: endnotes
Blind referee: yes
Acceptance rate: 1/10
Time to consider ms: 6 wks
Charts, pictures, tables, graphs, maps
Foreign languages accepted: no
• REVIEWS
Seeking reviewers: yes
Unsolicited reviews accepted: no
Materials reviewed: books, films
Review length: 750 wds
How to apply: letter
Include in application: professional degrees, institutional affiliation, areas of expertise, published works, foreign languages, current research, vita

History of Nursing Society Journal

History of nursing
Affiliation: The Royal College of Nursing; History of Nursing Society
Ed: Monica E. Baly
    19 Royal Crescent
    Bath BA1 2LT
    U.K.
Bk Rev Ed: John Gibbin
    Flat 1

196 West Hill
Putney
London SW15 35J
U.K.

3/yr, 65 pp; subs £6
Readership: nurse historians, others
  interested in the history of health
  care
• MANUSCRIPTS
Query: no; *Abstract:* preferred
Preferred length: 3,000–4,000 wds
Notes: endnotes
Blind referee: no
Acceptance rate: 2/3
Time to consider ms: 2–3 wks
No illustrations accepted
Foreign languages accepted: no
• REVIEWS
Seeking reviewers: yes
Unsolicited reviews accepted: some-
  times
Materials reviewed: books
Review length: 500 wds
How to apply: letter
Include in application: professional
  degrees, institutional affiliation,
  areas of expertise, published
  works, current research

History of Philosophy Quarterly

All aspects of the history of
  philosophy
Affiliation: Philosophy Documenta-
  tion Center, Bowling Green State
  University; North American Philo-
  sophical Publications
Ed: Nicholas Rescher
  Department of Philosophy
  University of Pittsburgh
  Pittsburgh, PA 15260
4/yr; subs $32
Readership: academics
• MANUSCRIPTS
Query: no; *Abstract:* no
Style guide: own
Preferred length: 3,000–8,000 wds
Copies: 2

Notes: endnotes
Foreign languages accepted: no

History of Photography

History of photography
Ed: Mike Weaver
  Linacre College
  Oxford OX1 3JA
  U.K.
Bk Rev Ed: same
4/yr, 100 pp; subs $140 institutional
Circ: 800
Readership: academics, collectors
Indexed/Abstracted: AHCI, CCAH,
  WAH
• MANUSCRIPTS
Query: no; *Abstract:* no
Style guide: MLA
Preferred length: 3,000–8,000
Copies: 2
Notes: endnotes
Blind referee: no
Acceptance rate: 7/10
Time to consider ms: 1 mo
Charts, pictures, tables, graphs, maps
Foreign languages accepted: French,
  German, Italian, Spanish
• REVIEWS
Seeking reviewers: yes
Unsolicited reviews accepted: yes
Materials reviewed: books
Review length: 500–1,000 wds
How to apply: letter
Include in application: 30 wd bio

History of Political Economy

History of economic thought
Affiliation: Duke University Press
Ed: Craufurd D. W. Goodwin
  Department of Economics
  Duke University
  Durham, NC 27706
Bk Rev Ed: S. Todd Lowry
  Department of Economics
  Washington and Lee University
  Lexington, VA 24450
5/yr, 200 pp; subs $48
Circ: 1,500

Readership: academics
Indexed/Abstracted: ABC, AHCI, CCAH, CCSB, SSCI, SSI, WAH
• MANUSCRIPTS
Query: no; *Abstract:* yes, after acceptance
Style guide: Chicago
Preferred length: 50 pp max
Copies: 3
Notes: endnotes
Blind referee: yes
Acceptance rate: 1/4
Time to consider ms: 6 mos
Pictures, tables, graphs
Foreign languages accepted: no
• REVIEWS
Seeking reviewers: no
Unsolicited reviews accepted: occasionally
Materials reviewed: books, new journals
Review length: 3 pp
How to apply: letter

History of Political Thought

History of political ideas, antiquity to the present
Affiliation: London School of Economics and Political Science; Exeter University
Eds: Janet Coleman
    Government Department
    London School of Economics
    Houghton Street
    London WC2A 2AE
    U.K.
        or
    Iaian Hampsher-Monk
    Politics Department
    Exeter University
    Rennes Drive
    Exeter EX4 4RJ
    U.K.
Bk Rev Ed: same
4/yr, 200 pp; subs £26.50
Readership: academics, general public
Indexed/Abstracted: ABC, AHCI, CCAH, IMB, WAH

• MANUSCRIPTS
Query: no; *Abstract:* yes
Style guide: own
Preferred length: 20 pp
Copies: 3
Notes: endnotes or footnotes
Blind referee: yes
Time to consider ms: 3–4 mos
Charts, pictures, tables, graphs, maps
Foreign languages accepted: French, Italian, German
• REVIEWS
Seeking reviewers: yes
Unsolicited reviews accepted: rarely
Materials reviewed: books
Review length: 4–5 pp
How to apply: letter
Include in application: professional degrees, institutional affiliation, areas of expertise, published works, foreign languages, current research

History of Religions

Historical religious phenomena
Affiliation: The Divinity School, University of Chicago
Eds: J. Kitajawa, F. Reynolds, W. Doniger, G. Ebersole
    Swift 005
    1025 E. 58th Street
    Chicago, IL 60637
4/yr, 96 pp; subs $29
Circ: 1,850
Readership: academics
Indexed/Abstracted: ABC, AHCI, CCAH, HI
• MANUSCRIPTS
Query: no; *Abstract:* no
Preferred length: 40 pp
Copies: 3
Notes: endnotes
Time to consider ms: 3 mos
Charts, pictures, tables, maps
Foreign languages accepted: French, German

History of Science

Discussion of current and possible future work in history of science

Ed: Roy Porter
　Wellcome Institute for History of
　Medicine
　183 Euston Road
　London NW1 2BN
　U.K.
Bk Rev Ed: same
4/yr, 112 pp; subs £29
Circ: 750
Readership: academics
Indexed/Abstracted: ABC, AHCI,
　CCAH, CCSB, IMB, SSCI
● MANUSCRIPTS
Query: preferred; *Abstract:* no
Preferred length: 6,000–20,000 wds
Copies: 1
Notes: endnotes
Blind referee: no
Acceptance rate: 3/5
Time to consider ms: 3 mos
Charts, tables, graphs, maps
Foreign languages accepted: no
● REVIEWS
Seeking reviewers: no
Unsolicited reviews accepted: no
Materials reviewed: books

History of the Human Sciences

Intellectual history of the human
　sciences, including the social
　sciences, philosophy, art history,
　linguistics, and others
Eds: Arthur Still and Irving Velody
　University of Durham
　Centre for the History of the
　Human Sciences
　Elvet Riverside
　New Elvet
　Durham DH1 3JT
　U.K.
Bk Rev Ed: Robin Williams
4/yr, 160 pp; subs £24
Readership: academics
Indexed/Abstracted: ABC, BHI
● MANUSCRIPTS
Query: preferred; *Abstract:* no
Style guide: own
Preferred length: varies

Copies: 4
Foreign languages accepted: no
● REVIEWS
Materials reviewed: books
Review length: varies

The History Teacher

History teaching: craft of teaching,
　historiography, state of the profes-
　sion, general interest
Affiliation: American Historical Asso-
　ciation
Ed: Edward Gosselin
　History Department
　California State University, Long
　Beach
　1250 Bellflower Boulevard
　Long Beach, CA 90840-1601
Bk Rev Ed: Donald Schwartz
4/yr, 120 pp; subs $22
Circ: 1,300
Readership: academics, precollegiate
　teachers
Indexed/Abstracted: ABC
● MANUSCRIPTS
Query: no; *Abstract:* preferred
Style guide: Chicago
Preferred length: 20–25 pp
Copies: 3
Notes: endnotes
Blind referee: yes
Acceptance rate: 1/5
Time to consider ms: 3 mos
Charts, pictures, tables, graphs,
　maps
Foreign languages accepted: no
● REVIEWS
Seeking reviewers: yes
Unsolicited reviews accepted: no
Materials reviewed: books, films
Review length: 500–600 wds
How to apply: letter
Include in application: professional
　degrees, institutional affiliation,
　areas of expertise, published
　works, foreign languages, current
　research, vita

History Today

Contemporary history
Ed: Gordon Marsden
    83/84 Berwick Street
    London W1V 3PJ
    U.K.
Bk Rev Ed: same
12/yr, 64 pp; subs $49 U.S.A.
Circ: 30,000
Readership: academics, general public
Indexed/Abstracted: ABC, AHCI,
    BHI, BRD, BRI, CCAH, HI,
    IMB, RG, WAH
● MANUSCRIPTS
Query: yes; *Abstract:* yes
Copies: 1
Pictures, maps
Foreign languages accepted: no
● REVIEWS
Seeking reviewers: no
Unsolicited reviews accepted: no
Materials reviewed: books
How to apply: letter
Include in application: professional
    degrees, areas of expertise, pub-
    lished works, current research

History Workshop Journal: A Journal of Socialist and Feminist Historians

Any time or place in history; cross-
    disciplinary
Ed: editorial board
    c/o Barbara Bloomfield
    25 Havelock Road
    Brighton BN1 6GL
    U.K.
Bk Rev Ed: J. L. Nelson
    History Department
    Kings College
    Strand
    London WC2R 2LF
    U.K.
2/yr, 250 pp; subs £19
Circ: 1,400
Readership: academics, general pub-
    lic, adult education teachers and
    students, public historians

Indexed/Abstracted: ABC, AHCI,
    CCAH, CCSB, SSCI
● MANUSCRIPTS
Query: no; *Abstract:* preferred
Style guide: own
Preferred length: 10,000 wds max
Copies: 2
Notes: endnotes
Blind referee: no
Time to consider ms: 4–6 mos
Charts, pictures, tables, graphs, maps
Foreign languages accepted: French,
    Italian, German, Spanish
● REVIEWS
Seeking reviewers: yes
Unsolicited reviews accepted: some-
    times
Materials reviewed: books, exhibi-
    tions, films, performances, etc.
Review length: 800–1,500 wds
How to apply: letter
Include in application: professional
    degrees, institutional affiliation,
    areas of expertise, published
    works, foreign languages, current
    research, why interested in *History
    Workshop*

The Houston Review: History and Culture of the Gulf Coast

History of the Houston, Texas met-
    ropolitan region
Affiliation: Houston Public Library
Ed: Louis J. Marchiafava
    Houston Metropolitan Research
    Center
    Houston Public Library
    500 McKinney
    Houston, TX 77002
Bk Rev Ed: same
3/yr, 56 pp; subs $7.50
Circ: 750
Readership: academics, general public
Indexed/Abstracted: ABC
● MANUSCRIPTS
Query: preferred; *Abstract:* no
Style guide: Chicago
Preferred length: 15–25 pp

Copies: 1
Notes: endnotes
Blind referee: yes
Acceptance rate: 3/4
Time to consider ms: 6 wks
Charts, pictures, tables, maps
Foreign languages accepted: no
• REVIEWS
Seeking reviewers: yes
Unsolicited reviews accepted: no
Materials reviewed: books
Review length: 2–4 pp
How to apply: letter
Include in application: professional
   degrees, institutional affiliation,
   areas of expertise, published
   works, current research

Hudson Valley Regional Review

History of the Hudson Valley; comparative regionalism
Affiliation: Bard College
Eds: Richard Wiles and William
   Wilson
      Bard College
      Box 180
      Annandale-on-Hudson, NY 12504
Bk Rev Ed: same
2/yr, 100 pp; subs $8
Circ: 400
Readership: academics, general public
Indexed/Abstracted: ABC
• MANUSCRIPTS
Query: no; *Abstract:* no
Preferred length: 25–30 pp
Copies: 2
Notes: endnotes
Blind referee: yes
Acceptance rate: 4/5
Time to consider ms: 3 mos
Charts, pictures, tables, graphs, maps
Foreign languages accepted: no
• REVIEWS
Seeking reviewers: yes
Unsolicited reviews accepted: no
Materials reviewed: books
Review length: 4 pp

How to apply: letter
Include in application: professional
   degrees, institutional affiliation,
   areas of expertise, published
   works, current research

Human Rights Quarterly

Insight into complex human rights issues
Affiliation: University of Cincinnati
Ed: Bert Lochwood
      Urban Morgan Institute
      University of Cincinnati
      College of Law
      Cincinnati, OH 45221
Bk Rev Ed: same
4/yr, 145 pp; subs $23
Circ: 1,350
Readership: academics, lawyers, sociologists, policy makers, students
   of international affairs
Indexed/Abstracted: ABC, AHCI,
   CCSB, PAIS, SSCI, SSI
• MANUSCRIPTS
Query: no; *Abstract:* no
Style guide: Chicago
Preferred length: 5,000 wds
Copies: 1
Notes: footnotes
Blind referee: yes
Acceptance rate: 1/10
Time to consider ms: 3 mos
Charts, pictures, tables, graphs, maps
Foreign languages accepted: no
• REVIEWS
Seeking reviewers: yes
Unsolicited reviews accepted: yes
Materials reviewed: books
How to apply: letter
Include in application: professional
   degrees, institutional affiliation,
   areas of expertise, published
   works, current research

Hungarian Studies Review

History of Hungary and of Hungarians elsewhere; Hungarian studies
Affiliation: University of Toronto

Eds: G. Bisztray
    Hungarian Chair
    21 Sussex Avenue
    University of Toronto
    Toronto, ON M5S 1A1
    CANADA
    or
    N. Dreisziger
    Department of History
    Royal Military College
    Kingston, ON K7K 5L0
    CANADA
Bk Rev Ed: G. Bisztray
2/yr, 80 pp; subs $12
Circ: 400
Readership: academics, general public
Indexed/Abstracted: ABC, MLA
• MANUSCRIPTS
Query: preferred; *Abstract:* no
Style guide: Chicago
Preferred length: 5,000–10,000 wds
Copies: 2
Notes: endnotes
Blind referee: yes
Acceptance rate: 1/2
Time to consider ms: 3 mos
Charts, pictures, tables, graphs, maps
Foreign languages accepted: Hungarian, French
• REVIEWS
Seeking reviewers: yes
Unsolicited reviews accepted: yes
Materials reviewed: books
Review length: 500–1,500 wds
How to apply: letter
Include in application: institutional affiliation, published works, current research

Huntington Library Quarterly

16th–18th century British and American history, literature, and art; particularly related to materials in the Huntington Library collections
Affiliation: Huntington Library
Ed: Guilland Sutherland
    1151 Oxford Road
    San Marino, CA 91108

Bk Rev Ed: same
4/yr, 96–112 pp; subs $40
Circ: 1,050
Readership: academics
Indexed/Abstracted: ABC, AHCI, AHI, CCAH, HI, IMB, MLA, WAH
• MANUSCRIPTS
Query: no; *Abstract:* no
Style guide: Chicago
Preferred length: 10–30 pp
Copies: 2
Notes: endnotes
Blind referee: yes
Acceptance rate: 1/5
Time to consider ms: 2–3 mos
Charts, pictures, tables, graphs, maps
Foreign languages accepted: no
• REVIEWS
Seeking reviewers: no
Unsolicited reviews accepted: no
Materials reviewed: books

The Huntsville Historical Review

Madison County, Alabama and Huntsville history
Affiliation: Huntsville-Madison County Historical Society
Ed: Frances Roberts
    c/o Publications Committee
    P.O. Box 666
    Huntsville, AL 35804
Bk Rev Ed: same
2/yr, 40 pp; subs $10
Circ: 200
Readership: academics, general public
• MANUSCRIPTS
Query: preferred; *Abstract:* preferred
Style guide: any
Preferred length: 10–20 pp
Copies: 1
Notes: endnotes
Blind referee: yes
Charts, pictures, tables, graphs, maps
Foreign languages accepted: no
• REVIEWS
Seeking reviewers: yes

Unsolicited reviews accepted: no
Materials reviewed: books
Review length: 3-4 pp
How to apply: letter
Include in application: professional
degrees, institutional affiliation,
areas of expertise, published works

IA, The Journal of the Society for Industrial Archeology

Combines the insights of field works
and historical research to promote
understanding of the industrial age
by focusing on physical remains
Affiliation: National Museum of
American History, Smithsonian In-
stitution
Ed: David R. Starbuck
P.O. Box 147
Fort Edward, NY 12828
Bk Rev Ed: Donald C. Jackson
Department of History
Lafayette College
Easton, PA 18042
2/yr, 80 pp; subs $25
Circ: 1,700
Readership: academics, general public
Indexed/Abstracted: ABC
• MANUSCRIPTS
Query: preferred; *Abstract:* yes
Style guide: Chicago
Preferred length: 20-30 pp
Copies: 4
Notes: endnotes
Blind referee: yes
Acceptance rate: 1/2
Time to consider ms: 3 mos
Charts, pictures, tables, graphs, maps
Foreign languages accepted: no
• REVIEWS
Seeking reviewers: yes
Unsolicited reviews accepted: no
Materials reviewed: books
Review length: 3-5 pp
How to apply: letter
Include in application: professional
degrees, institutional affiliation,
areas of expertise

IEEE Annals of the History of Computing

History of computing and informa-
tion technology
Affiliation: IEEE Computer Society
Ed: J. A. N. Lee
Department of Computer Science
Virginia Tech
Blacksburg, VA 24061-0106
Bk Rev Ed: Paul Ceruzzi
National Air and Space Museum
Washington, DC 20560
4/yr, 80 pp; subs membership $16-
$39
Circ: 2,500
Readership: academics, computer his-
torians
Indexed/Abstracted: ABC, WAH
• MANUSCRIPTS
Query: preferred; *Abstract:* yes
Style guide: own
Preferred length: 40 pp max
Copies: 5
Notes: endnotes
Blind referee: no
Acceptance rate: 9/10
Time to consider ms: 6 mos
Charts, pictures, tables, graphs, maps
Foreign languages accepted: no
• REVIEWS
Seeking reviewers: yes
Unsolicited reviews accepted: yes
Materials reviewed: books, films,
articles
Review length: varies
How to apply: letter
Include in application: professional
degrees, institutional affiliation,
areas of expertise, published works

Iberian Studies

Spanish and Portuguese anthropology, economics, education,
geography, history, politics, and
sociology
Affiliation: Centre for Iberian Studies, University of Keele
Ed: John Naylon

Centre for Iberian Studies
University of Keele
Keele
Staffordshire ST5 5BG
U.K.
Bk Rev Ed: Andrew Dobson
2/yr, 80 pp; subs £12
Circ: 1,000
Readership: academics, general public
Indexed/Abstracted: ABC
* MANUSCRIPTS
Query: preferred; *Abstract:* preferred
Style guide: own
Preferred length: 10,000 wds max
Copies: 2
Notes: endnotes
Blind referee: yes
Acceptance rate: 1/2
Time to consider ms: 1 mo
Charts, pictures, tables, graphs, maps
Foreign languages accepted: no
* REVIEWS
Seeking reviewers: yes
Unsolicited reviews accepted: yes
Materials reviewed: books
Review length: 1,000–1,500 wds
How to apply: letter
Include in application: professional
   degrees, institutional affiliation,
   areas of expertise, published
   works, foreign languages, current
   research

Illinois Historical Journal

All facets of Illinois history including
Civil War related topics, Lincoln-
iana, biography
Affiliation: Illinois Historic Preserva-
tion Agency
Ed: E. Duane Elbert
   Illinois Historic Preservation
   Agency
   Old State Capitol
   Springfield, IL 62701
Bk Rev Ed: same
4/yr, 80 pp; subs $25
Circ: 3,000
Readership: academics, general pub-
lic, historical society members

Indexed/Abstracted: ABC, MLA,
   WAH
* MANUSCRIPTS
Query: no; *Abstract:* no
Style guide: MLA
Preferred length: 5,000–7,000 wds
Copies: 3
Notes: endnotes
Blind referee: yes
Acceptance rate: 1/4
Time to consider ms: 4 mos
Charts, pictures, tables, graphs, maps
Foreign languages accepted: no
* REVIEWS
Seeking reviewers: yes
Unsolicited reviews accepted: no
Materials reviewed: books
Review length: 500–700 wds
How to apply: letter
Include in application: professional
   degrees, institutional affiliation,
   areas of expertise, published
   works, current research

Imprint

American historical prints
Affiliation: American Historical Print
   Collectors Society
Ed: Rona Schneider
   12 Monroe Place
   Brooklyn Heights, NY 11201
Bk Rev Ed: Thomas Beckman
   Historical Society of Delaware
   505 Market Street Mall
   Wilmington, DE 19801
2/yr, 40 pp; subs $30
Circ: 500
Readership: academics, print collec-
tors & dealers, museums
Indexed/Abstracted: ABC
* MANUSCRIPTS
Query: yes; *Abstract:* preferred
Style guide: Chicago
Preferred length: 1,000–5,000 wds
Copies: 1
Notes: endnotes
Blind referee: yes
Acceptance rate: 4/5

Time to consider ms: 3 mos
Pictures
Foreign languages accepted: no
• REVIEWS
Seeking reviewers: yes
Unsolicited reviews accepted: no
Materials reviewed: books
Review length: 500–1,500 wds
How to apply: letter
Include in application: professional
degrees, institutional affiliation,
areas of expertise, published
works, current research

Indiana Magazine of History

Indiana and Midwestern history
Affiliation: Indiana University and
the Indiana Historical Society
Ed: James H. Madison
Ballantine Hall 742
Department of History
Indiana University
Bloomington, IN 47405
Bk Rev Ed: same
4/yr, 100 pp; subs $10
Circ: 10,100
Readership: academics, general public
Indexed/Abstracted: ABC, WAH
• MANUSCRIPTS
Query: no; *Abstract:* no
Style guide: MLA
Preferred length: 25 pp
Copies: 2
Notes: endnotes
Blind referee: yes
Acceptance rate: 1/4
Time to consider ms: 8–10 wks
Charts, pictures, tables, graphs, maps
Foreign languages accepted: no
• REVIEWS
Seeking reviewers: yes
Unsolicited reviews accepted: no
Materials reviewed: books
Review length: 400–800 wds
How to apply: letter
Include in application: professional
degrees, institutional affiliation,
areas of expertise, published
works, current research

Inland Seas

Great Lakes history
Affiliation: Great Lakes Historical
Society
Ed: William D. Ellis
27025 Knickerbocker Road
Cleveland, OH 44140
Bk Rev Ed: same
4/yr, 80 pp; subs $28
Circ: 3,000
Readership: academics, general
public, boaters
Indexed/Abstracted: ABC, WAH
• MANUSCRIPTS
Query: no; *Abstract:* no
Preferred length: 20 pp max
Copies: 1
Notes: endnotes
Blind referee: no
Acceptance rate: 4/5
Time to consider ms: 2 mos
All illustrations accepted
Foreign languages accepted: no
• REVIEWS
Seeking reviewers: no
Unsolicited reviews accepted: yes
Materials reviewed: books, films
Review length: 1 pp
• ADDITIONAL NOTES
Don't get too far from the water.

The Innes Review

Religious, social, cultural, and
political history of Scottish interest
from Celtic time to the present day
Affiliation: Scottish Catholic Histori-
cal Association
Eds: Dauvit Broun
Department of Scottish History
University of Glasgow
9 University Gardens
Glasgow G12 8QH
U.K.
or
Alasdair Roberts
Hilton Place
Aberdeen ABY 1FA
U.K.

Bk Rev Ed: same
2/yr, 80 pp; subs £14
Circ: 400
Readership: academics, general public, clergy
Indexed/Abstracted: ABC
• MANUSCRIPTS
Query: no; *Abstract:* no
Preferred length: open
Copies: 2
Notes: endnotes
Blind referee: yes
Acceptance rate: 7/10
Time to consider ms: 3 mos
Charts, pictures, tables, maps
Foreign languages accepted: no
• REVIEWS
Seeking reviewers: no
Unsolicited reviews accepted: no
Materials reviewed: books
Review length: 750 wds
How to apply: letter
Include in application: professional degrees, institutional affiliation, areas of expertise, published works, current research

Intelligence and National Security

History of intelligence and security matters; military and international history and politics
Eds: Christopher Andrew
    Corpus Christi College
    Cambridge CB2 1RH
    U.K.
        or
    Michael Handel
    Department of Strategy
    U.S. Naval War College
    Newport, RI 02841-5010
Bk Rev Eds: Richard Aldrich
    Department of Politics
    University of Nottingham
    University Park
    Nottingham NG7 2RD
    U.K.
        or

Wesley Wark
    Department of History
    University of Toronto
    Toronto, ON M5S 1A1
    CANADA
4/yr, 176 pp; subs £32
Readership: academics, general public
Indexed/Abstracted: ABC, BHI, WAH
• MANUSCRIPTS
Query: no; *Abstract:* no
Style guide: own
Preferred length: 10,000 wds
Copies: 2
Notes: endnotes
Blind referee: yes
Time to consider ms: 6 mos
Charts, tables, graphs, maps
Foreign languages accepted: no
• REVIEWS
Seeking reviewers: no
Unsolicited reviews accepted: no
Materials reviewed: books
Review length: 500–1,000 wds
How to apply: letter
Include in application: professional degrees, institutional affiliation, areas of expertise, published works

The International History Review

Relations between states throughout history
Affiliation: Simon Fraser University
Ed: Edward Ingram
    Simon Fraser University
    Burnaby, BC V5A 1S6
    CANADA
Bk Rev Ed: same
4/yr, 224 pp; subs $25
Readership: academics, general public
Indexed/Abstracted: ABC, AHCI, CCAH, IMB, WAH
• MANUSCRIPTS
Query: no; *Abstract:* no
Preferred length: 30–40 pp
Copies: 3
Notes: footnotes

Blind referee: yes
Acceptance rate: 1/10
Time to consider ms: 3 mos
Charts, tables, graphs, maps
Foreign languages accepted: no
• REVIEWS
Seeking reviewers: yes
Unsolicited reviews accepted: no
Materials reviewed: books
Review length: 750 wds
How to apply: letter or form
Include in application: professional
  degrees, institutional affiliation,
  areas of expertise, published
  works, foreign languages, current
  research

International Journal

Post–1945 international affairs; Cana-
dian foreign policy
Affiliation: Canadian Institute of In-
  ternational Affairs
Eds: Kim Richard Nossal, Stephen J.
  Randall
      c/o Canadian Institute of Inter-
      national Affairs
      15 King's College Circle
      Toronto, ON M5S 2V9
      CANADA
Bk Rev Ed: same
4/yr, 192 pp; subs $32.10
Circ: 2,000
Readership: academics, general pub-
  lic, bureaucrats
Indexed/Abstracted: ABC, CCSB,
  SSCI, WAH
• MANUSCRIPTS
Query: no; *Abstract:* no
Preferred length: 8,000 wds
Copies: 3
Notes: endnotes
Blind referee: yes
Acceptance rate: 1/6
Time to consider ms: 4–5 mos
Charts, tables, graphs, maps
Foreign languages accepted: French
• REVIEWS
Seeking reviewers: no

Unsolicited reviews accepted: no
Materials reviewed: books
Review length: 500 wds

International Journal of African Historical Studies

All aspects of the African past
Affiliation: Boston University
Ed: Norman R. Bennett
      African Studies Center
      Boston University
      270 Bay State Road
      Boston, MA 02215
Bk Rev Ed: same
3/yr, 240 pp; subs $30
Circ: 800
Readership: academics
Indexed/Abstracted: ABC, AHCI,
  CCAH, HI
• MANUSCRIPTS
Query: no; *Abstract:* no
Preferred length: 5,000–10,000 wds
Copies: 2
Notes: footnotes
Blind referee: yes
Acceptance rate: 1/4
Time to consider ms: 3–4 mos
Charts, pictures, tables, graphs, maps
Foreign languages accepted: French
• REVIEWS
Seeking reviewers: yes
Unsolicited reviews accepted: occa-
  sionally
Materials reviewed: books
Review length: 500–1,000 wds
How to apply: letter, form
Include in application: professional
  degrees, institutional affiliation,
  areas of expertise, published
  works, foreign languages, current
  research

International Journal of Middle East Studies

The Middle East from the 7th cen-
  tury to modern times
Affiliation: The Middle East Studies
  Association of North America

Ed: Leila Fawaz
   Cabot Intercultural Center
   The Fletcher School of Law and
      Diplomacy
   Tufts University
   Medford, MA 02155
Bk Rev Eds: Juan R. I. Cole, Aida
   A. Bamia, Mary-Jane Deeb, Mark
   A. Tessler
   contact the editor directly
4/yr; subs $60
Readership: academics
Indexed/Abstracted: ABC, AHCI,
   CCSB, MLA, SSCI, SSI
• MANUSCRIPTS
Query: no; *Abstract:* no
Style guide: Chicago
Preferred length: 40 pp max
Copies: 1
Notes: endnotes
Tables, figures, illustrations
Foreign languages accepted: no
• REVIEWS
Unsolicited reviews accepted: no
Materials reviewed: books

International Journal
of the History of Sport

History and development of sport all
   over the world with emphasis on
   social influences
Ed: J. A. Mangan
   Department of Education
   Jordanhill College
   Southbrae Drive
   Glasgow G11 1PP
   U.K.
U.K. Bk Rev Ed: same
North American Bd Rev Ed: Scott
   A. G. M. Crawford
   Physical Education Department
   Eastern Illinois University
   Charleston, IL 61920-3099
3/yr, 144 pp; subs £28
Readership: academics, general public
Indexed/Abstracted: ABC, BHI
• MANUSCRIPTS
Query: no; *Abstract:* no

Style guide: own
Preferred length: 8,000 wds max
Copies: 2
Notes: endnotes
Blind referee: yes
Time to consider ms: 6 mos
Charts, pictures, tables, graphs, maps
Foreign languages accepted: no
• REVIEWS
Seeking reviewers: no
Unsolicited reviews accepted: no
Materials reviewed: books
Review length: 500–1,000 wds
How to apply: letter
Include in application: professional
   degrees, institutional affiliation,
   areas of expertise, published works

International Journal
on World Peace

Interdisciplinary, international peace
   studies
Affiliation: Professors World Peace
   Academy
Ed: Panos D. Bardis
   University of Toledo
   Toledo, OH 43606
Bk Rev Ed: same
4/yr, 120 pp; subs $20
Circ: 10,000
Readership: academics, general public
Indexed/Abstracted: AHCI, CCSB,
   PAIS, SSCI
• MANUSCRIPTS
Query: no; *Abstract:* yes
Style guide: own
Preferred length: 10–40 pp
Copies: 2
Notes: endnotes
Blind referee: yes
Acceptance rate: 2/5
Time to consider ms: 1 mo
No illustrations accepted
Foreign languages accepted: no
• REVIEWS
Seeking reviewers: yes
Unsolicited reviews accepted: yes
Materials reviewed: books, computer
   software

Review length: 500–1,000 wds
How to apply: letter
Include in application: professional
degrees, institutional affiliation,
areas of expertise, published
works, current research

International Migration Review

Sociological, demographic, economic,
historical, and legislative aspects of
human migration and refugees
Affiliation: Center for Migration
Studies of New York, Inc.
Ed: S. M. Tomasi
209 Flagg Place
Staten Island, NY 10304
Bk Rev Ed: Eleanor M. Rogg
4/yr, 250 pp; subs $27.50
Circ: 2,200
Readership: academics
Indexed/Abstracted: ABC, AHCI,
CCSB, PAIS, SSCI, SSI, WAH
• MANUSCRIPTS
Query: no; *Abstract:* yes
Style guide: own
Preferred length: 30–35 pp
Copies: 4
Notes: endnotes
Blind referee: yes
Acceptance rate: 1/8
Time to consider ms: 2–3 mos
Charts, tables, graphs, maps
Foreign languages accepted: no
• REVIEWS
Seeking reviewers: yes
Unsolicited reviews accepted: no
Materials reviewed: books, con-
ferences
How to apply: letter
Include in application: professional
degrees, institutional affiliation,
areas of expertise

International Social Science Review

Interdisciplinary, international social
sciences
Affiliation: Pi Gamma Mu

Ed: Panos D. Bardis
University of Toledo
Toledo, OH 43606
Bk Rev Ed: same
4/yr, 48 pp; subs $10
Circ: 14,000
Readership: academics, general public
Indexed/Abstracted: ABC, PAIS
• MANUSCRIPTS
Query: no; *Abstract:* yes
Style guide: own
Preferred length: 10–30 pp
Copies: 2
Notes: endnotes
Blind referee: yes
Acceptance rate: 1/2
Time to consider ms: 1 mo
No illustrations accepted
Foreign languages accepted: no
• REVIEWS
Seeking reviewers: yes
Unsolicited reviews accepted: yes
Materials reviewed: books, computer
software
Review length: 300–900 wds
How to apply: letter
Include in application: professional
degrees, institutional affiliation,
areas of expertise, published
works, current research

International Studies Notes

Foreign policy, comparative politics,
area studies, international relations
Affiliation: American Graduate
School of International Manage-
ment
Ed: Llewellyn D. Howell
Department of International
Studies
American Graduate School of
International Management
Glendale, AZ 85306-6011
Bk Rev Ed: same
3/yr, 44 pp; subs $20
Circ: 3,000
Readership: academics, foreign policy
practitioners
Indexed/Abstracted: ABC

• MANUSCRIPTS
Query: preferred; *Abstract:* no
Style guide: Chicago
Preferred length: 15 pp
Copies: 4
Notes: endnotes
Blind referee: yes
Time to consider ms: 2 mos
Charts, tables, graphs, maps
Foreign languages accepted: Spanish, French (with English abstract)
• REVIEWS
Seeking reviewers: yes
Unsolicited reviews accepted: no
Materials reviewed: films, syllabi, simulations
Review length: 3-5 pp
How to apply: letter
Include in application: professional degrees, institutional affiliation, areas of expertise, published works, foreign languages, current research

International Studies Quarterly

Empirical and theoretical work in international relations and comparative politics
Affiliation: International Studies Association
Eds: Richard Herrmann, Brian Pollins, Goldie Shabad
   The Ohio State University
   Department of Political Science
   224 Neil Hall
   1634 Neil Avenue
   Columbus, OH 43210-1217
4/yr, 130 pp; subs $100
Circ: 6,500
Readership: academics
Indexed/Abstracted: ABC, BHI, CCSB, PAIS, SSCI, SSI
• MANUSCRIPTS
Query: no; *Abstract:* yes
Style guide: own
Preferred length: 35-40 pp
Copies: 5; 3 should be anonymized
Notes: endnotes

Blind referee: yes
Acceptance rate: 1/10
Time to consider ms: 3 mos
Charts, tables, graphs; (if camera ready)
Foreign languages accepted: no

Isis: An International Review Devoted to the History of Science and Its Cultural Influence

History of science, technology and medicine
Affiliation: History of Science Society
Ed: Ronald L. Numbers
   Isis Editorial Office
   University of Wisconsin
   Department of the History of Medicine
   1300 University Avenue
   Madison, WI 53706
Bk Rev Ed: Michael H. Shank
4/yr, 185 pp; subs $45
Circ: 4,000
Readership: academics
Indexed/Abstracted: ABC, AHCI, CCAH, CCSB, HI, SSCI, WAH
• MANUSCRIPTS
Query: no; *Abstract:* yes
Style guide: Chicago
Preferred length: 40 pp
Copies: 4
Notes: endnotes
Blind referee: yes
Acceptance rate: 1/7
Time to consider ms: 4-7 mos
Charts, pictures, tables, graphs, maps
Foreign languages accepted: French, German, Spanish
• REVIEWS
Seeking reviewers: yes
Unsolicited reviews accepted: no
Materials reviewed: books
Review length: 500-1,000 wds
How to apply: letter
Include in application: professional degrees, institutional affiliation, areas of expertise, published

works, foreign languages, current research

The Island Magazine

The human and natural heritage of Prince Edward Island
Affiliation: Prince Edward Island Museum and Heritage Foundation
Ed: Edward MacDonald
Prince Edward Island Museum and Heritage Foundation
Beaconsfield, 2 Kent Street
Charlottetown, PE C1A 1M6
CANADA
Bk Rev Ed: same
2/yr, 40 pp; subs $8.56
Circ: 2,500
Readership: academics, general public
Indexed/Abstracted: ABC
• MANUSCRIPTS
Query: preferred; *Abstract:* no
Preferred length: 1,000–7,000 wds
Copies: 1
Notes: endnotes
Blind referee: yes
Acceptance rate: 7/10
Time to consider ms: 6 mos
Charts, pictures, maps
Foreign languages accepted: no
• REVIEWS
Seeking reviewers: yes
Unsolicited reviews accepted: yes
Materials reviewed: books, films, sound recordings
Review length: 500–1,000 wds
How to apply: letter or telephone call
Include in application: professional degrees, institutional affiliation, areas of expertise, published works, current research
• ADDITIONAL NOTES
The Island Magazine attempts to combine good scholarship with readable texts. The editors use a magazine format and employ illustrations freely.

Italian Quarterly

Italian studies
Affiliation: Rutgers University
Ed: Guido Guarino
Rutgers University
Department of Italian
18 Seminary Place
New Brunswick, NJ 08853
Bk Rev Ed: Umberto Mariani
4/yr, 112 pp; subs $15
Circ: 1,050
Readership: academics, general public
Indexed/Abstracted: ABC, AHCI, IMB, MLA
• MANUSCRIPTS
Query: no; *Abstract:* no
Style guide: MLA
Preferred length: 20 pp
Copies: 2
Notes: endnotes or none
Blind referee: no
Charts, pictures, tables, graphs, maps
Foreign languages accepted: Italian
• REVIEWS
Seeking reviewers: yes
Unsolicited reviews accepted: yes
Materials reviewed: books
Review length: 5 pp
How to apply: letter
Include in application: areas of expertise

The Jewish Quarterly Review

Jewish and Near Eastern studies
Affiliation: Annenberg Institute
Eds: David M. Goldenberg and Leon Nemoy
Annenberg Institute
420 Walnut Street
Philadelphia, PA 19114
Bk Rev Ed: Bonnie L. Blankenship
4/yr, 98 pp; subs $35
Circ: 1,000
Readership: academics
Indexed/Abstracted: AHCI, CCAH, IMB
• MANUSCRIPTS

Query: preferred; *Abstract:* yes
Style guide: Chicago
Preferred length: 30–40 pp max
Copies: 2
Notes: footnotes
Blind referee: yes
Acceptance rate: 2/3
Time to consider ms: 6 mos
Pictures, tables, maps
Foreign languages accepted: French,
    German, Spanish
• REVIEWS
Seeking reviewers: yes
Unsolicited reviews accepted: no
Materials reviewed: books
Review length: 3 pp
How to apply: letter
Include in application: areas of ex-
    pertise, published works, foreign
    languages, current research

Jewish Social Studies

Contemporary and historical aspects
of Jewish life
Affiliation: Conference on Jewish
    Social Studies
Ed: Tobey B. Gitelle
    Conference on Jewish Social
        Studies
    Room 206
    2112 Broadway
    New York, NY 10023
Bk Rev Ed: Jane S. Gerber
4/yr; subs $40
Readership: academics, general pub-
    lic
Indexed/Abstracted: ABC, AHCI,
    SSCI
• MANUSCRIPTS
Query: no; *Abstract:* no
Style guide: own
Preferred length: varies
Copies: 3
Foreign languages accepted: no
• REVIEWS
Materials reviewed: books

Journal for the History of Astronomy

History of the science of astronomy
    since the earliest times; history in
    the service of astronomy
Ed: Michael Hoskin
    Churchill College
    Cambridge CB3 0DS
    U.K.
Bk Rev Ed: Owen Gingerich
    Harvard-Smithsonian Center for
        Astrophysics
    Cambridge, MA 02138
5/yr, 700 pp; subs £32
Circ: 700
Readership: academics
Indexed/Abstracted: ABC, IMB,
    WAH
• MANUSCRIPTS
Query: preferred; *Abstract:* no
Preferred length: 3,000–10,000 wds
Copies: 1
Notes: endnotes
Blind referee: no
Acceptance rate: 3/5
Time to consider ms: 1 mo
Charts, pictures, tables, graphs, maps
Foreign languages accepted: no
• REVIEWS
Seeking reviewers: no
Unsolicited reviews accepted: no
Materials reviewed: books

The Journal of African History

History of Africa
Affiliation: School of Oriental and
    African Studies, University of Lon-
    don
Eds: D. M. Anderson, R. C. C. Law,
    J. C. Miller, D. Robinson
    c/o D. M. Anderson
    History Department
    School of Oriental and African
        Studies
    University of London
    Russell Square

London WC1H 0XG
U.K.
Bk Rev Ed: D. M. Anderson
3/yr, 176 pp; subs £68
Circ: 2,000
Readership: academics
Indexed/Abstracted: ABC, AHCI, BHI, CCAH, CCSB, HI, IMB, SSCI

• MANUSCRIPTS
Query: no; *Abstract:* yes
Style guide: own
Preferred length: 8,000 wds max
Copies: 2
Notes: endnotes
Blind referee: yes
Acceptance rate: 1/5
Time to consider ms: 3–4 mos
Charts, pictures, tables, graphs, maps
Foreign languages accepted: French

• REVIEWS
Seeking reviewers: no
Unsolicited reviews accepted: no
Materials reviewed: books
Review length: varies

Journal of American Culture

All areas of American culture
Affiliation: American Culture Association and Bowling Green State University
Ed: Ray B. Browne
  Bowling Green State University
  Bowling Green, OH 43403
Bk Rev Ed: same
4/yr, 100 pp; subs $35
Circ: 1,000
Readership: academics
Indexed/Abstracted: ABC, AHCI, CCAH, HI

• MANUSCRIPTS
Query: no; *Abstract:* no
Style guide: Chicago or MLA
Preferred length: 15–20 pp
Notes: endnotes
Blind referee: yes
Acceptance rate: 1/10
Time to consider ms: 1 wk to 1 mo

Charts, pictures, tables, graphs, maps
Foreign languages accepted: no

• REVIEWS
Seeking reviewers: no
Unsolicited reviews accepted: yes
Materials reviewed: books
Review length: 200 wds
How to apply: letter
Include in application: areas of expertise

The Journal of American–East Asian Relations

American–East Asian relations
Affiliation: Committee on American–East Asian Relations
Ed: Michael A. Barnhart
  Department of History
  SUNY
  Stony Brook, NY 11794-4348
Bk Rev Ed: same
4/yr, 128 pp; subs $30
Readership: academics

• MANUSCRIPTS
Query: yes; *Abstract:* no
Style guide: Chicago
Preferred length: 30–40 pp
Copies: 5
Notes: endnotes
Blind referee: yes
Acceptance rate: 1/3
Time to consider ms: 40–100 days
Tables, graphs, maps
Foreign languages accepted: no

• REVIEWS
Seeking reviewers: yes
Unsolicited reviews accepted: no
Materials reviewed: books
Review length: 2–10 pp
How to apply: letter
Include in application: professional degrees, institutional affiliation, published works

Journal of American Ethnic History

The immigrant, ethnic and racial history of the North American people

Affiliation: Immigration History Society and Georgia Tech
Ed: Ronald H. Bayor
  School of History, Technology and Society
  Georgia Tech
  Atlanta, GA 30332
Bk Rev Ed: Elliott R. Barkan
  Department of History
  California State University
  San Bernadino, CA 92407
4/yr, 120 pp; subs $30
Circ: 1,200
Readership: academics, general public
Indexed/Abstracted: ABC, AHCI, CCAH, CCSB, HI, SSCI, WAH
• MANUSCRIPTS
Query: no; *Abstract:* no
Style guide: Chicago
Preferred length: 30–35 pp
Copies: 3
Notes: endnotes
Blind referee: yes
Acceptance rate: 1/4
Time to consider ms: 3 mos
Charts, pictures, tables, graphs, maps
Foreign languages accepted: no
• REVIEWS
Seeking reviewers: yes
Unsolicited reviews accepted: no
Materials reviewed: books, films, exhibits
Review length: 500–700 wds
How to apply: letter
Include in application: professional degrees, institutional affiliation, areas of expertise, published works, foreign languages, current research

Journal of American Folklore

International folklore and folklife
Affiliation: American Folklore Society
Ed: Burt Feintuch
  Center for the Humanities
  Murkland Hall
  University of New Hampshire
  Durham, NH 03284-3596

Bk Rev Ed: Amy Shuman
  Department of English
  Ohio State University
  Columbus, OH 43210-1370
4/yr, 144 pp; subs $50
Circ: 3,500
Readership: academics, general public
Indexed/Abstracted: ABC, AHCI, BRI, CCAH, HI, IMB, MLA, WAH
• MANUSCRIPTS
Query: no; *Abstract:* yes
Style guide: own, based on Chicago
Preferred length: varies
Copies: 3
Notes: endnotes
Blind referee: no
Acceptance rate: 1/11
Time to consider ms: 1–6 mos
Charts, pictures, tables, graphs, maps
Foreign languages accepted: no
• REVIEWS
Materials reviewed: books, films, sound recordings, exhibitions, events

Journal of American History

United States history
Affiliation: Organization of American Historians
Ed: David P. Thelen
  1125 Atwater
  Indiana University
  Bloomington, IN 47401-3701
Bk Rev Ed: Casey Nelson Blake
4/yr, 400 pp; subs membership ($30–$100)
Circ: 11,540
Readership: academics
Indexed/Abstracted: ABC, AHCI, BRD, BRI, CCAH, CCSB, HI, SSCI, WAH
• MANUSCRIPTS
Query: no; *Abstract:* no
Style guide: Chicago
Preferred length: 35–40 pp
Copies: 4
Notes: endnotes

Blind referee: yes
Acceptance rate: 1/14
Time to consider ms: 6 mos
Charts, pictures, tables, graphs, maps
Foreign languages accepted: no
• REVIEWS
Seeking reviewers: yes
Unsolicited reviews accepted: no
Materials reviewed: books, films,
  microforms, research and reference
  tools, textbooks, teaching aids,
  museum exhibitions
Review length: varies
How to apply: letter and form
Include in application: professional
  degrees, institutional affiliation,
  areas of expertise, published works,
  foreign languages, current research

Journal of American Studies

American culture, history, literature,
  politics, art, film, popular culture,
  etc.
Affiliation: British Association for
  American Studies
Ed: Michael Heale
  History Department
  Lancaster University
  Lancaster LA1 4YG
  U.K.
Bk Rev Ed: same
3/yr, 160 pp; subs $49 U.S.
Circ: 1,500
Readership: academics
Indexed/Abstracted: ABC, AHCI,
  BHI, BRI, CCAH, HI, MLA,
  WAH
• MANUSCRIPTS
Query: no; *Abstract:* preferred
Style guide: Chicago
Preferred length: 6,000–7,000 wds
Copies: 2
Notes: endnotes
Blind referee: yes
Acceptance rate: 1/7
Time to consider ms: 3 mos
Charts, pictures, tables, graphs, maps
Foreign languages accepted: no

• REVIEWS
Seeking reviewers: yes
Unsolicited reviews accepted: no
Materials reviewed: books
Review length: 400 wds
How to apply: form
Include in application: professional
  degrees, institutional affiliation,
  areas of expertise, published works,
  foreign languages, current research

The Journal of Arizona History

History of Arizona and the adjacent
  Southwest
Affiliation: Arizona Historical Society
Ed: Bruce J. Dinges
  949 E. Second Street
  Tucson, AZ 85719
Bk Rev Ed: same
4/yr, 120 pp; subs $25
Circ: 4,000
Readership: academics, general public
Indexed/Abstracted: ABC, WAH
• MANUSCRIPTS
Query: no; *Abstract:* no
Style guide: Chicago preferred
Preferred length: 18–24 pp
Copies: 2
Notes: endnotes
Blind referee: no
Pictures
Foreign languages accepted: no
• REVIEWS
Seeking reviewers: no
Unsolicited reviews accepted: no
Materials reviewed: books
Review length: 500 wds

Journal of Asian History

Historical research on any period and
  all the regions of Asia with the ex-
  ception of the Ancient Near East
Affiliation: Indiana University
Ed: Denis Sinor
  Goodbody Hall
  Indiana University
  Bloomington, IN 47405

Bk Rev Ed: Ruth I. Meserve
2/yr, 112 pp; subs $55
Circ: 900
Readership: academics, amateur historians
Indexed/Abstracted: ABC, AHCI, CCAH, HI, WAH
• MANUSCRIPTS
Query: preferred; *Abstract:* no
Style guide: open
Preferred length: 15-60 pp
Copies: 1
Notes: endnotes
Blind referee: yes
Acceptance rate: 1/2
Time to consider ms: 2-6 wks
Charts, pictures, tables, graphs, maps
Foreign languages accepted: French, German
• REVIEWS
Seeking reviewers: yes
Unsolicited reviews accepted: no
Materials reviewed: books
Review length: 500-1,000 wds
How to apply: letter
Include in application: areas of expertise, foreign languages

Journal of Asian Studies

Asian studies; emphasis on humanities and social sciences
Affiliation: Association for Asian Studies
Ed: David D. Buck
    390 Holton Hall
    Department of History
    University of Wisconsin-Milwaukee
    Milwaukee, WI 53201
Bk Rev Ed: several, contact editor
4/yr, 260 pp; subs $40
Circ: 8,600
Readership: academics
Indexed/Abstracted: ABC, AHCI, BRI, CCSB, HI, MLA, SSCI
• MANUSCRIPTS
Query: preferred; *Abstract:* no
Style guide: own

Preferred length: 10,000 wds
Copies: 4
Notes: endnotes
Blind referee: yes
Acceptance rate: 1/7
Time to consider ms: 2-3 mos
Charts, pictures, tables, graphs, maps
Foreign languages accepted: no
• REVIEWS
Seeking reviewers: yes
Unsolicited reviews accepted: no
Materials reviewed: books, films
Review length: 800 wds
How to apply: letter
Include in application: institutional affiliation, areas of expertise, published works, current research
• ADDITIONAL NOTES
Almost all articles have either significant fieldwork in Asia or use of Asian language texts as a basis. Also, English language scholarship is reviewed quite broadly, although special efforts are made to review important works in Asian and European languages.

Journal of Baltic Studies

Baltic states—Latvia, Estonia, Lithuania, Finland
Affiliation: Association for Advancement of Baltic Studies
Ed: William Urban
    Monmouth College
    Monmouth, IL 61462
        or
    Roger Noel
    Georgia College
    Milledgeville, GA 31061
Bk Rev Ed: William Urban
4/yr, 100 pp; subs $45
Circ: 1,300
Readership: academics, general public
Indexed/Abstracted: ABC, AHCI, CCAH, IMB, MLA
• MANUSCRIPTS
Query: no; *Abstract:* no
Style guide: MLA

Preferred length: 10-20 pp
Copies: 2
Notes: endnotes
Blind referee: yes
Acceptance rate: 1/2
Time to consider ms: 1-3 mos
Charts, pictures, tables, graphs, maps
Foreign languages accepted: German, French
• REVIEWS
Seeking reviewers: yes
Unsolicited reviews accepted: no
Materials reviewed: books
Review length: 600 wds
How to apply: letter
Include in application: professional degrees, institutional affiliation, areas of expertise, published works, foreign languages

Journal of Black Studies

Full inquiry into African phenomena
Affiliation: Temple University
Ed: Molefi Kete Asante
    African American Studies
    Temple University
    Philadelphia, PA 19122
Bk Rev Ed: Ella Forbes
4/yr, 120 pp
Circ: 3,500
Readership: academics
Indexed/Abstracted: ABC, AHCI, BRI, CCSB, PAIS, SSCI, WAH
• MANUSCRIPTS
Query: no; *Abstract:* no
Preferred length: 25 pp
Copies: 3
Blind referee: yes
• REVIEWS
Materials reviewed: books

Journal of British Studies

All periods and aspects of British studies
Affiliation: North American Conference on British Studies
Ed: Cynthia Herrup
    Department of History

Carr Building
Duke University
Durham, NC 27708
4/yr, 112 pp; subs $37
Readership: academics
Indexed/Abstracted: ABC, AHCI, CCAH, HI
• MANUSCRIPTS
Query: no; *Abstract:* no
Style guide: Chicago
Preferred length: 45-50 pp
Copies: 2
Notes: endnotes
Blind referee: yes
Time to consider ms: varies
Charts, pictures, tables, graphs, maps
Foreign languages accepted: no
• ADDITIONAL NOTES
The Journal of British Studies publishes review essays, but not reviews of individual books.

The Journal of Canadian Art History

Contemporary art, Inuit and Canadian art
Affiliation: Concordia University
Ed: Sanra Paikowsky
    1455 Boul. de Maisonneuve west
    VA-432
    Montreal, PQ J3G 1M8
    CANADA
Bk Rev Ed: same
2/yr, 120 pp; subs $20
Circ: 800
Readership: academics, general public
• MANUSCRIPTS
Query: no; *Abstract:* no
Style guide: Chicago
Preferred length: open
Copies: 1
Notes: footnotes
Blind referee: yes
Acceptance rate: 4/5
Time to consider ms: 5 mos
Charts, pictures, tables, graphs, maps, slides
Foreign languages accepted: French

● REVIEWS
Seeking reviewers: no
Unsolicited reviews accepted: yes
Materials reviewed: books
Review length: open

Journal of Canadian Studies/ Revue d'Etudes Canadiennes

Canadian studies
Affiliation: Trent University
Ed: Michael A. Peterman
   Trent University
   Peterborough, ON K9J 7B8
   CANADA
Bk Rev Ed: Robert Wright
4/yr, 176 pp; subs $25
Circ: 1,400
Readership: academics, diplomatic
   officials
Indexed/Abstracted: ABC, AHCI,
   CCAH, HI, MLA
● MANUSCRIPTS
Query: no; *Abstract:* yes
Style guide: MLA
Preferred length: 7,000–10,000 wds
Copies: 2
Notes: endnotes
Blind referee: yes
Time to consider ms: 6 mos
Tables, graphs, maps
Foreign languages accepted: French
● REVIEWS
Seeking reviewers: no
Unsolicited reviews accepted: no
Materials reviewed: books

Journal of Caribbean Studies

Caribbean studies
Affiliation: University of Kentucky
Ed: O. R. Dathorne
   P.O. Box 22202
   Lexington, KY 40502
Bk Rev Ed: Roland Bus
3/yr, 250 pp; subs $50
Circ: 1,000
Readership: academics
Indexed/Abstracted: ABC, MLA

● MANUSCRIPTS
Query: no; *Abstract:* no
Style guide: open
Preferred length: 20 pp
Copies: 3
Notes: endnotes
Blind referee: yes
Acceptance rate: 3/10
Charts, tables, graphs
Foreign languages accepted: Spanish,
   French
● REVIEWS
Seeking reviewers: no
Unsolicited reviews accepted: yes
Materials reviewed: books, films
How to apply: letter
Include in application: professional
   degrees, institutional affiliation,
   areas of expertise, published
   works, current research

Journal of Church and State

The critical examination of the in-
   teraction of religion and govern-
   ment worldwide
Affiliation: Baylor University
Ed: James E. Wood, Jr.
   Baylor University
   P.O. Box 97308
   Waco, TX 76798-7308
Bk Rev Ed: Charles M. Tolbert
4/yr, 200 pp; subs $20
Circ: 1,500
Readership: academics, general public,
   lawyers, jurists, religious leaders
Indexed/Abstracted: ABC, AHCI,
   BRI, CCAH, HI, PAIS, WAH
● MANUSCRIPTS
Query: no; *Abstract:* no
Style guide: Chicago
Preferred length: 30 pp
Copies: 3
Notes: endnotes or footnotes
Blind referee: yes
Acceptance rate: 3/10
Time to consider ms: 3–6 mos
Tables, graphs
Foreign languages accepted: no

• REVIEWS
Seeking reviewers: yes
Unsolicited reviews accepted: no
Materials reviewed: books
Review length: 300 wds
How to apply: letter
Include in application: professional
   degrees, institutional affiliation,
   areas of expertise

Journal of Confederate History

All aspects of Confederate history
Ed: John McGlone
   P.O. Box 1615
   Murfreesboro, TN 37133
Bk Rev Ed: Archie McDonald
   Department of History
   SFA Box 6223
   Stephen F. Austin State Univer-
   sity
   Nacogdoches, TX 75962
4/yr, 180 pp; subs $39.95
Readership: academics, general public
Indexed/Abstracted: ABC
• MANUSCRIPTS
Query: preferred; *Abstract:* preferred
Preferred length: 4,000–10,000 wds
Copies: 2
Notes: footnotes
Blind referee: yes
Foreign languages accepted: no
• REVIEWS
Materials reviewed: books
How to apply: letter
Include in application: professional
   degrees, institutional affiliation,
   areas of expertise, published
   works, current research

Journal of Conflict Resolution

Interdisciplinary research on peace
   and war
Affiliation: Yale University
Ed: Bruce Russett
   Political Science Department

   Box 3532 Yale Station
   New Haven, CT 06520
4/yr, 192 pp; subs $48
Circ: 2,400
Readership: academics
Indexed/Abstracted: ABC, CCSB,
   SSCI, SSI
• MANUSCRIPTS
Query: no; *Abstract:* yes
Style guide: Chicago
Preferred length: 35 pp
Copies: 4
Notes: endnotes
Blind referee: yes
Acceptance rate: 1/4
Time to consider ms: 2–3 mos
Charts, tables, graphs, maps
Foreign languages accepted: no

Journal of Contemporary History

The analysis and discussion of 20th
   century history: the people,
   periods, places and critical issues
Eds: Walter Laqueur and George L.
   Mosse
   4 Devonshire Street
   London W1N 2BH
   U.K.
4/yr, 280 pp; subs £31
Readership: academics
Indexed/Abstracted: ABC, AHCI,
   BHI, CCAH, HI, WAH
• MANUSCRIPTS
Query: no; *Abstract:* no
Style guide: own
Preferred length: 7,000 wds max
Copies: 2
Notes: endnotes
Charts, tables, graphs
Foreign languages accepted: no

Journal of Design History

History, theory and criticism of
   design
Affiliation: The Design History Society; University of Wolverhampton
Ed: Christopher Bailey

History of Art and Design
University of Wolverhampton
Dudley DY1 3HR
U.K.
Bk Rev Ed: Jonathan Woodham
Department of Art History
Brighton Polytechnic
Brighton BN2 2JY
U.K.
4/yr, 96 pp; subs £46
Circ: 1,000
Readership: academics, general public, professional designers, design managers
Indexed/Abstracted: ABC
• MANUSCRIPTS
Query: preferred; *Abstract:* preferred
Style guide: own
Preferred length: 5,000–10,000 wds
Copies: 1
Notes: endnotes
Blind referee: yes
Time to consider ms: 3 mos
Charts, pictures, tables, graphs, maps
Foreign languages accepted: no
• REVIEWS
Seeking reviewers: yes
Unsolicited reviews accepted: yes
Materials reviewed: books, films, exhibitions
Review length: 500–5,000 wds
How to apply: letter
Include in application: institutional affiliation, areas of expertise, current research

Journal of Developing Areas

Descriptive, theoretical, and comparative study of regional development, past and present
Affiliation: Western Illinois University
Ed: Nicholas C. Pano
232 Morgan Hall
Western Illinois University
Macomb, IL 61455
Bk Rev Ed: Ronald E. Nelson
4/yr, 150 pp; subs $20
Circ: 1,300

Readership: academics, government, business
Indexed/Abstracted: ABC, CCSB, PAIS, SSCI
• MANUSCRIPTS
Query: no; *Abstract:* no
Style guide: Chicago
Preferred length: 20–35 pp
Copies: 3
Notes: endnotes
Blind referee: yes
Acceptance rate: 1/12
Time to consider ms: 4–6 mos
Charts, tables, graphs, maps
Foreign languages accepted: no
• REVIEWS
Seeking reviewers: yes
Unsolicited reviews accepted: occasionally
Materials reviewed: books
Review length: 750–900 wds
How to apply: letter
Include in application: professional degrees, institutional affiliation, areas of expertise, published works, current research

Journal of Early Southern Decorative Arts

Material culture of the early South
Affiliation: Museum of Early Southern Decorative Arts and Old Salem, Inc.
Ed: Forsyth Alexander
Museum of Early Southern Decorative Arts
P.O. Box 10310
Winston-Salem, NC 27108
2/yr, 80–100 pp; subs $25
Circ: 1,200
Readership: academics
Indexed/Abstracted: ABC
• MANUSCRIPTS
Query: preferred; *Abstract:* preferred
Style guide: Chicago
Preferred length: 40–60 pp
Copies: 1
Notes: endnotes

Blind referee: no
Pictures, graphs, maps
Foreign languages accepted: no
• ADDITIONAL NOTES
The *Journal of Early Southern Decorative Arts* seeks manuscripts that treat virtually any facet of Southern decorative arts. The editors prefer the manuscripts to be accompanied by 8" × 10" black and white glossy photographs; they do not print in color.

The Journal of East Tennessee History

History of East Tennessee, Tennessee, Southern Appalachia, and the South
Affiliation: East Tennessee Historical Society
Ed: R. B. Rosenberg
    500 W. Church Avenue
    Knoxville, TN 37902
Bk Rev Ed: same
1/yr, 150 pp; subs $25
Circ: 2,500
Readership: academics, general public, society members
Indexed/Abstracted: ABC
• MANUSCRIPTS
Query: no; *Abstract:* no
Style guide: none
Preferred length: 25–30 pp
Copies: 1
Notes: footnotes
Blind referee: yes
Acceptance rate: 1/3
Time to consider ms: 3–4 mos
Charts, pictures, tables, graphs, maps
Foreign languages accepted: no
• REVIEWS
Seeking reviewers: no
Unsolicited reviews accepted: no
Materials reviewed: books
Review length: 400 wds
How to apply: letter

The Journal of Ecclesiastical History

Christian history
Affiliation: Cambridge University Press
Eds: B. Bradshaw and M. Brett
    St. John's College
    Cambridge CB2 1TP
    U.K.
Bk Rev Ed: same
4/yr, 190 pp; subs £42
Circ: 1,130
Readership: academics, general public
Indexed/Abstracted: ABC, AHCI, CCAH, HI, IMB
• MANUSCRIPTS
Abstract: no
Style guide: own
Preferred length: 20–25 pp
Copies: 2
Notes: endnotes
Blind referee: yes
Acceptance rate: 1/6
Time to consider ms: 2–5 mos
Tables, graphs, maps
Foreign languages accepted: French
• REVIEWS
Seeking reviewers: yes
Unsolicited reviews accepted: occasionally
Materials reviewed: books
Review length: 500–1,000 wds
How to apply: letter
Include in application: professional degrees, institutional affiliation, areas of expertise, foreign languages, current research

Journal of Economic History

Economic history of any and all nations
Affiliation: University of California, Davis
Ed: Peter Lindert
    Department of Economics
    University of California
    Davis, CA 95616
Bk Rev Ed: same

4/yr, 250 pp; subs $15 to $30 (by
    income)
Circ: 3,000
Readership: academics
Indexed/Abstracted: ABC, AHCI,
    BRI, CCAH, CCSB, SSCI, SSI,
    WAH
• MANUSCRIPTS
Query: no; *Abstract:* yes
Style guide: Chicago
Preferred length: 30 pp
Copies: 4
Notes: endnotes
Blind referee: yes
Acceptance rate: 1/8
Time to consider ms: 2 mos
Charts, tables, graphs, maps
Foreign languages accepted: no
• REVIEWS
Seeking reviewers: yes
Unsolicited reviews accepted: no
Materials reviewed: books
Review length: 500-750 wds
How to apply: letter
Include in application: professional
    degrees, institutional affiliation,
    areas of expertise, current research

Journal of Educational Administration and History

Educational history
Affiliation: School of Education,
    University of Leeds
Ed: J. Stuart Marriott
    Museum of the History of
        Education
    Parkinson Court
    University of Leeds
    Leeds LS2 9JT
    U.K.
Bk Rev Ed: W. B. Stephens
2/yr, 90 pp; subs £15
Circ: 400
Readership: academics
Indexed/Abstracted: ABC
• MANUSCRIPTS
Query: no; *Abstract:* no
Preferred length: 6,000 wds

Copies: 2
Notes: endnotes
Blind referee: no
Acceptance rate: 1/2
Time to consider ms: varies
Tables, graphs
Foreign languages accepted: no
• REVIEWS
Unsolicited reviews accepted: no
Materials reviewed: books
Review length: 350-400 wds
How to apply: letter

Journal of European Studies

European culture since the Renais-
    sance
Ed: J. E. Flower
    Department of French
    University of Exeter
    Exeter EX4 4QJ
    U.K.
Bk Rev Ed: A. G. Goss
    School of Slavonic Studies
    Sidgwick Avenue
    Cambridge
    U.K.
4/yr, 88 pp
Readership: academics
Indexed/Abstracted: ABC, AHCI,
    CCAH, HI, MLA
• MANUSCRIPTS
Query: no; *Abstract:* no
Style guide: own
Preferred length: open
Copies: 2
Notes: endnotes
Blind referee: yes
Acceptance rate: 1/8
Time to consider ms: 1-3 mos
Charts, pictures, tables
Foreign languages accepted: no
• REVIEWS
Seeking reviewers: no
Unsolicited reviews accepted: no
Materials reviewed: books, confer-
    ences
Review length: 500-600 wds
How to apply: letter

Include in application: professional degrees, institutional affiliation, areas of expertise, published works, foreign languages, current research, experience as a reviewer

Journal of Family History

History of the family, kinship, and population
Ed: Tamara K. Hareven
　　Department of Individual and
　　　Family Studies
　　University of Delaware
　　218 Alison Hall
　　Newark, DE 19716
Bk Rev Ed: Andrejs Plakans
　　Department of History
　　Iowa State University
　　Ames, IA 50011
4/yr, 100 pp; subs $55
Readership: academics
Indexed/Abstracted: ABC, AHCI,
　　CCSB, HI, IMB, SSCI
• MANUSCRIPTS
Query: no; *Abstract:* yes
Style guide: own
Preferred length: 40 pp
Copies: 3 + $15 submission fee
Notes: endnotes
Blind referee: yes
Charts, tables, graphs
Foreign languages accepted: no
• REVIEWS
Unsolicited reviews accepted: no
Materials reviewed: books
How to apply: letter
Include in application: professional degrees, institutional affiliation, areas of expertise, published works, current research

Journal of Folklore Research

Current theory and research in folklore studies
Affiliation: Indiana University Folklore Institute
Eds: John H. McDowell and Sandra Dolby

Folklore Institute
Indiana University
504 N. Fess Street
Bloomington, IN 47408
Bk Rev Ed: same
subs $15
Readership: academics, folklorists
Indexed/Abstracted: ABC, AHCI,
　　CCAH, MLA, WAH
• MANUSCRIPTS
Query: no; *Abstract:* no
Style guide: Chicago
Preferred length: varies
Copies: 2
Notes: endnotes
Blind referee: yes
Foreign languages accepted: no
• REVIEWS
Unsolicited reviews accepted: yes
Materials reviewed: books
Review length: 500 wds max

Journal of Garden History

History of individual gardens and
　　garden designers; garden design
　　theory
Ed: John Dixon Hunt
　　3 Pembroke Studios
　　Pembroke Gardens
　　London W8 6HX
　　U.K.
Bk Rev Ed: Mark Laird
　　67 Sullivan Street
　　Toronto, ON M5T 1C2
　　CANADA
4/yr, 100 pp; subs $180 institutional
Circ: 800
Readership: academics
Indexed/Abstracted: ABC, AHCI,
　　BHI, CCAH, WAH
• MANUSCRIPTS
Query: yes; *Abstract:* no
Style guide: MLA
Preferred length: varies
Copies: 2
Notes: endnotes
Blind referee: no
Acceptance rate: 3/5

Time to consider ms: 3–6 mos
Charts, pictures, tables, graphs, maps
Foreign languages accepted: French,
  Italian
• REVIEWS
Seeking reviewers: yes
Unsolicited reviews accepted: no
Materials reviewed· books
Review length: 2,0ʋʋ wds
How to apply: letter
Include in application: professional
  degrees, institutional affiliation,
  areas of expertise, published
  works, foreign languages, current
  research

Journal of
Historical Geography

Historical geography
Ed: Alan R. H. Baker
  Department of Geography
  University of Cambridge
  Downing Place
  Cambridge CB2 3EN
  U.K.
American Ed: John P. Radford
  Department of Geography
  York University
  4700 Keele Street
  North York, ON M3J 1P3
  CANADA
Bk Rev Ed: Gerry Kearns
  Department of Geography
  University of Liverpool
  Liverpool L69 3BX
  U.K.
American Bk Rev Ed: David Wishart
  Department of Geography
  University of Nebraska-Lincoln
  311 Avery Hall
  Lincoln, NE 68588-0135
4/yr, 132 pp; subs £48
Readership: academics
Indexed/Abstracted: ABC, AHCI,
  BRI, CCSB, IMB, SSCI, SSI,
  WAH
• MANUSCRIPTS
Query: no; *Abstract:* yes

Style guide: own
Preferred length: varies
Copies: 3
Notes: endnotes
Charts, pictures, tables, graphs, maps
Foreign languages accepted: no
• REVIEWS
Materials reviewed: books
Review length: varies

The Journal of
Historical Review

Twentieth century American and
  European history
Affiliation: Institute for Historical
  Review
Ed: Mark E. Weber
  1822½ Newport Boulevard
  #191
  Costa Mesa, CA 92627
Bk Rev Ed: John Ries
4/yr, 128 pp; subs $40
Circ: 3,000
Readership: academics, general public
• MANUSCRIPTS
Query: no; *Abstract:* no
Style guide: Chicago
Preferred length: 4,000–8,000 wds
Copies: 1
Notes: endnotes
Blind referee: no
Acceptance rate: 1/4
Time to consider ms: 2–4 mos
Charts, pictures, tables, graphs, maps
Foreign languages accepted: French,
  German, Italian, Spanish
• REVIEWS
Seeking reviewers: yes
Unsolicited reviews accepted: yes
Materials reviewed: books, films
Review length: 1,200 wds
How to apply: letter
Include in application: professional
  degrees, institutional affiliation,
  areas of expertise, published works,
  foreign languages, current research
• ADDITIONAL NOTES
The editors particularly welcome

skeptical ("revisionist") analysis of twentieth century U.S. and European history, and especially aspects of World War II history.

Journal of Historical Sociology

Historical sociology
American Ed: Daniel Nugent
 Department of Anthropology
 University of Arizona
 Tucson, AZ 85721
European Ed: Gavin Williams
 St. Peter's College
 Oxford OX1 2DL
 ENGLAND
Bk Rev Ed: Philip Corrigan
 contact through Gavin Williams
4/yr, 128 pp; subs $60
Circ: 350
Readership: academics
Indexed/Abstracted: ABC, IMB, SSCI
• MANUSCRIPTS
Query: yes; *Abstract:* yes
Style guide: own
Preferred length: 35 pp
Copies: 6
Notes: endnotes
Blind referee: yes
Acceptance rate: varies
Time to consider ms: 6 mos
Charts, tables, graphs, maps
Foreign languages accepted: no
• REVIEWS
Seeking reviewers: yes
Unsolicited reviews accepted: no
Materials reviewed: books, films, historical events
Review length: 15 pp
How to apply: invitation

Journal of Imperial and Commonwealth History

Imperial and Commonwealth history
Eds: A. J. Stockwell and Peter
 Burroughs
 c/o Frank Cass and Co. Ltd.
 Gainsborough House

11 Gainsborough Road
 London E11 1RS
 U.K.
Bk Rev Ed: same
3/yr; subs £28
Readership: academics
Indexed/Abstracted: ABC, AHCI, BHI, CCAH
• MANUSCRIPTS
Query: no; *Abstract:* no
Style guide: own
Preferred length: varies
Copies: 2
Notes: endnotes
Tables, diagrams, other suitable illustrations
Foreign languages accepted: no
• REVIEWS
Materials reviewed: books

Journal of Interdisciplinary History

The relationship of historical research and work in applied fields, such as economics and demographics
Affiliation: Lafayette College
Eds: Robert I. Rotberg
 Lafayette College
 316 Markle Hall
 Easton, PA 18042
 or
 Theodore K. Rabb
 Department of History
 Princeton University
 Princeton, NJ 08544
Bk Rev Ed: Lynda Miller
 Lafayette College
 316 Markle Hall
 Easton, PA 18042
4/yr, 182 pp; subs $32
Circ: 1,700
Readership: academics
Indexed/Abstracted: ABC, AHCI, BRI, CCAH, CCSB, HI, SSCI, WAH
• MANUSCRIPTS
Query: no; *Abstract:* no
Preferred length: 30 pp max

Copies: 2
Notes: endnotes
Blind referee: yes
Acceptance rate: 1/10
Time to consider ms: 3–8 wks
Charts, pictures, tables, graphs, maps
Foreign languages accepted: no
* REVIEWS
Seeking reviewers: yes
Unsolicited reviews accepted: occasionally
Materials reviewed: books, computer software
Review length: 2–3 pp
How to apply: letter
Include in application: professional degrees, institutional affiliation, areas of expertise
* ADDITIONAL NOTES
Send the original copy of the article to Robert I. Rotberg and the second copy to Theodore K. Rabb.

The Journal of Japanese Studies

Interdisciplinary studies of Japan
Affiliation: Society for Japanese Studies
Ed: Susan B. Hanley
    Thomson Hall DR-05
    University of Washington
    Seattle, WA 98195
Bk Rev Ed: same
2/yr, 285 pp; subs $25
Circ: 1,800
Readership: academics, government agencies, business
Indexed/Abstracted: ABC, AHCI, CCAH, HI, MLA
* MANUSCRIPTS
Query: no; *Abstract:* no
Style guide: modified Chicago
Preferred length: 30–40 pp
Copies: 3 + $15 submission fee
Notes: endnotes
Blind referee: yes
Acceptance rate: 1/10–1/4
Time to consider ms: 3 mos

All illustrations accepted
Foreign languages accepted: no
* REVIEWS
Seeking reviewers: no
Unsolicited reviews accepted: no
Materials reviewed: books

Journal of Jewish Studies

Jewish studies exclusive of modern politics
Affiliation: Oxford Centre for Postgraduate Hebrew Studies
Ed: Geza Vermes
    West Wood Cottage
    Foxcombe Lane
    Boars Hill
    Oxford OX1 5DH
    U.K.
Bk Rev Ed: same
2/yr, 150 pp; subs £18
Circ: 1,000
Readership: academics
Indexed/Abstracted: ABC, AHCI, BHI, CCAH, IMB
* MANUSCRIPTS
Query: yes; *Abstract:* yes
Preferred length: 5,000–6,000 wds
Notes: footnotes
Acceptance rate: 1/3
Time to consider ms: 3 mos
Pictures
Foreign languages accepted: no
* REVIEWS
Seeking reviewers: no
Unsolicited reviews accepted: rarely
Materials reviewed: books
Review length: 500–1,000 wds
How to apply: letter
Include in application: professional degrees, institutional affiliation, areas of expertise, published works, foreign languages

Journal of Latin American Studies

Latin America
Affiliation: Institute of Latin American Studies, University of London

Eds: V. Bulmer-Thomas and L.
  Whitehead
  Institute of Latin American
    Studies
  31 Tavistock Square
  London WC1H 9HA
  U.K.
Bk Rev Ed: same
3/yr, 250 pp; subs $54 U.S.
Circ: 1,500
Readership: academics
Indexed/Abstracted: ABC, AHCI,
  BHI, CCAH, CCSB, PAIS, SSCI,
  SSI
• MANUSCRIPTS
Query: no; *Abstract:* no
Preferred length: 10,000 wds
Copies: 2
Notes: footnotes
Blind referee: yes
Acceptance rate: 1/5
Charts, pictures, tables, graphs, maps
Foreign languages accepted: 1st sub-
  mission accepted in Spanish or
  Portuguese
• REVIEWS
Seeking reviewers: no
Unsolicited reviews accepted: no
Materials reviewed: books
Review length: 600–800 wds

Journal of Legal History

Legal history
Ed: Andrew Lewis
  Faculty of Laws
  University College London
  Bentham House
  Endsleigh Gardens
  London WC1H 0EG
  U.K.
Bk Rev Ed: Thomas G. Watkin
  Cardiff Law School
  University of Wales
  P.O. Box 427
  Cardiff CF1 1XD
  U.K.
3/yr, 125 pp; subs £30
Circ: 600

Readership: academics
Indexed/Abstracted: ABC, BHI
• MANUSCRIPTS
Abstract: no
Preferred length: 5,000–6,000 wds
Copies: 3
Notes: endnotes
Blind referee: yes
Time to consider ms: varies
Charts, pictures, tables, graphs, maps
Foreign languages accepted: no
• REVIEWS
Seeking reviewers: yes
Unsolicited reviews accepted: yes
Materials reviewed: books
Review length: 1,500 wds
How to apply: letter
Include in application: professional
  degrees, institutional affiliation,
  areas of expertise, published works,
  foreign languages, current research

Journal of Military History

Military history
Affiliation: Society for Military
  History
Ed: Henry S. Bausum
  George C. Marshall Library
  Virginia Military Institute
  Lexington, VA 24450
Bk Rev Ed: Bruce C. Vandervort
4/yr, 140 pp; subs $25
Circ: 2,792
Readership: academics, general pub-
  lic, military, public historians
Indexed/Abstracted: ABC, AHCI,
  CCAH, HI, WAH
• MANUSCRIPTS
Query: no; *Abstract:* no
Style guide: Chicago
Preferred length: open
Copies: 3
Notes: endnotes
Blind referee: yes
Acceptance rate: 1/5
Time to consider ms: 3 mos
Charts, pictures, tables, graphs, maps
Foreign languages accepted: no

- REVIEWS
Seeking reviewers: yes
Unsolicited reviews accepted: no
Materials reviewed: books
Review length: 450–600 wds
How to apply: letter, form
Include in application: professional
  degrees, institutional affiliation,
  areas of expertise, published
  works, foreign languages, current
  research

Journal of Mississippi History

History of Mississippi and the South
Affiliation: Mississippi Historical
  Society; University of Southern
  Mississippi; Mississippi Department
  of Archives and History
Ed: Kenneth McCarty
  University of Southern Mississippi
  Southern Station Box 8315
  Hattiesburg, MS 39406
Bk Rev Ed: Robert Jenkins
  Department of History
  Mississippi State University
  Mississippi State, MS 39762
4/yr, 85 pp; subs $15
Circ: 1,600
Readership: academics, general public
Indexed/Abstracted: ABC, WAH
- MANUSCRIPTS
Query: no; *Abstract:* no
Style guide: Chicago
Preferred length: 30 pp
Copies: 2
Notes: endnotes
Blind referee: yes
Acceptance rate: 1/5
Time to consider ms: 2 mos
Charts, pictures, tables, graphs, maps
Foreign languages accepted: no
- REVIEWS
Seeking reviewers: yes
Unsolicited reviews accepted: no
Materials reviewed: books
Review length: 3–5 pp
How to apply: letter
Include in application: professional

degrees, institutional affiliation,
areas of expertise, published
works, current research

Journal of Modern Greek Studies

Modern Greece
Affiliation: Modern Greek Studies
  Association; Dartmouth College
Ed: Peter Bien
  Department of English
  6032 Sanborn House
  Dartmouth College
  Hanover, NH 03755-3533
Bk Rev Ed: Mary Layoun
  Department of Comparative Lit-
  erature
  938 Van Hese Hall
  University of Wisconsin
  Madison, WI 53706
2/yr, 144 pp; subs $19
Circ: 700
Readership: academics, association
  members
Indexed/Abstracted: ABC, AHCI,
  CCAH, MLA
- MANUSCRIPTS
Query: no; *Abstract:* yes
Style guide: modified Chicago
Preferred length: 6,000–8,000 wds
Copies: 4
Notes: endnotes, parenthetical
  documentation
Blind referee: yes
Acceptance rate: 3/10
Time to consider ms: 3 mos
Charts, pictures, tables, graphs, maps
Foreign languages accepted: Greek
- REVIEWS
Seeking reviewers: no
Unsolicited reviews accepted: no
Materials reviewed: books
Review length: 750 wds

Journal of Modern Hellenism

History and culture of the Greek people from the 13th century to the
present

Affiliation: Hellenic College and Queens College of the City University of New York
Eds: Nomikos Michael Vaporis and Harry J. Psomiades
  50 Goddard Avenue
  Brookline, MA 02146
1/yr, 200 pp; subs $15
Circ: 1,000
Readership: academics, general public
• MANUSCRIPTS
Query: yes
Style guide: Chicago
Preferred length: 25-30 pp
Copies: 2
Notes: footnotes
Blind referee: yes
Acceptance rate: 1/2
Time to consider ms: 1 mo
Charts, graphs, maps
Foreign languages accepted: Greek

Journal of Modern History

European history, including Russia and the Balkans, from 1500 to the present
Affiliation: University of Chicago Press
Eds: John W. Boyer, Julias Kirshner
  SS #122
  1126 East Fifty-Ninth Street
  Chicago, IL 60637
Bk Rev Ed: Julias Kirshner
4/yr, 220 pp; subs $30
Circ: 4,000
Readership: academics
Indexed/Abstracted: ABC, AHCI, BRI, CCAH, CCSB, HI, IMB, SSCI, WAH
• MANUSCRIPTS
Query: no; *Abstract:* no
Style guide: Chicago
Preferred length: open
Copies: 2
Notes: endnotes
Blind referee: yes
Acceptance rate: 1/10
Time to consider ms: 3-5 mos

Charts, pictures, tables, graphs, maps
Foreign languages accepted: translations of French, German, Italian, Russian
• REVIEWS
Seeking reviewers: yes
Unsolicited reviews accepted: no
Materials reviewed: books
Review length: varies
How to apply: letter
Include in application: professional degrees, institutional affiliation, areas of expertise, published works, foreign languages, current research, vita

The Journal of Mormon History

History of the LDS, RLDS, and related churches
Affiliation: Mormon History Association
Ed: Lavina Fielding Anderson
  1519 Roberta Street
  Salt Lake City, UT 84115
Bk Rev Ed: Richard Jensen
  3862 S. 6580 W.
  West Valley City, UT 84120
2/yr, 180 pp; subs $15
Circ: 1,000
Readership: academics, general public, Mormons
Indexed/Abstracted: ABC
• MANUSCRIPTS
Query: no; *Abstract:* no
Style guide: Chicago
Preferred length: 25 pp
Copies: 3
Notes: footnotes
Blind referee: yes
Acceptance rate: 1/4
Time to consider ms: 10 wks
Charts, pictures, tables, graphs, maps
Foreign languages accepted: no
• REVIEWS
Seeking reviewers: yes
Unsolicited reviews accepted: no
Materials reviewed: books

Review length: 1,000 wds
How to apply: letter
Include in application: professional
    degrees, institutional affiliation,
    areas of expertise, published
    works, current research

Journal of Negro History

African and African American his-
tory
Affiliation: Morehouse College
Ed: Alton Hornsby, Jr.
    Morehouse College
    P.O. Box 20
    Atlanta, GA 30314
Bk Rev Ed: Marcellus C. Barksdale
4/yr, 70 pp; subs $30
Circ: 3,400
Readership: academics
Indexed/Abstracted: ABC, HI, WAH
• MANUSCRIPTS
Query: no; *Abstract:* no
Style guide: Turabian
Preferred length: 25 pp
Copies: 3
Notes: endnotes
Acceptance rate: 1/4
Time to consider ms: 4 wks
Tables, graphs
Foreign languages accepted: no
• REVIEWS
Seeking reviewers: no
Unsolicited reviews accepted: yes
Materials reviewed: books
Review length: 3 pp
How to apply: letter
Include in application: professional
    degrees, institutional affiliation,
    areas of expertise, published
    works, current research

Journal of Newspaper and Periodical History

All aspects of the different forms of
    serial output produced from the
    17th to the 20th century
Affiliation: Greenwood Publishing
    Group, Inc.

Ed: Michael Harris
    Centre for Extramural Studies
    Birkbeck College
    26 Russell Square
    London WC1B 5DQ
    U.K.
Bk Rev Ed: Jeremy Black
    Department of History
    University of Durham
    43-46 North Bailey
    Durham DH1 3EX
    U.K.
2/yr, 72 pp; subs $75
Indexed/Abstracted: ABC, MLA
• MANUSCRIPTS
Style guide: MLA
Preferred length: 4,000–6,000 wds
Copies: 2
Time to consider ms: 3 mos
No illustrations accepted
Foreign languages accepted: no
• REVIEWS
Seeking reviewers: yes
Unsolicited reviews accepted: no
Materials reviewed: books
How to apply: letter
Include in application: professional
    degrees, institutional affiliation,
    areas of expertise, published
    works, current research

Journal of Northeast Asian Studies

Social, political, economic, and mili-
    tary developments in post–World
    War II Northeast Asia
Affiliation: The Gaston Sigur Center
    for East Asian Studies, The George
    Washington University
Eds: Young C. Kim, Gaston J. Sigur
    The Gaston Sigur Center for
        East Asian Studies
    The George Washington Univer-
        sity
    2130 H Street, N.W.
    Suite 621
    Washington, DC 20052
4/yr, 80 pp; subs $34

Readership: academics
Indexed/Abstracted: ABC, PAIS
• MANUSCRIPTS
Query: no; *Abstract:* yes
Style guide: Chicago
Preferred length: 20-30 pp
Copies: 2
Notes: endnotes
Blind referee: yes
Time to consider ms: 1 mo
Charts, tables, graphs, maps
Foreign languages accepted: no

Journal of Peasant Studies

Multidisciplinary peasant studies including economics, history, anthropology, political science and sociology
Eds: T. J. Byres, Henry Berustein, Tom Brass
   c/o T. J. Byres
   School of Oriental and African Studies
   University of London
   Thornhaugh Street
   Russell Square
   London WC1H 0XG
   U.K.
Bk Rev Ed: R. G. Tiedemann
   Department of History
   School of Oriental and African Studies
   Thornhaugh Street
   Russell Square
   London WC1H 0XG
   U.K.
4/yr, 160 pp; subs $65 U.S.
Circ: 800
Readership: academics, general public
Indexed/Abstracted: ABC, BHI, CCSB, SSCI
• MANUSCRIPTS
Abstract: yes
Copies: 3
Notes: endnotes
• REVIEWS
Materials reviewed: books

Journal of Policy History

Development of public policy in a broad, historical, and theoretical context
Affiliation: Saint Louis University
Ed: Donald T. Critchlow
   256 DuBourg Hall
   221 N. Grand Boulevard
   Saint Louis University
   St. Louis, MO 63103
Bk Rev Ed: same
4/yr, 120 pp; subs $20
Circ: 1,000
Readership: academics
Indexed/Abstracted: ABC, WAH
• MANUSCRIPTS
Query: no; *Abstract:* preferred
Style guide: Chicago
Preferred length: 35 pp
Copies: 4
Notes: endnotes
Blind referee: yes
Acceptance rate: 1/5
Time to consider ms: 3-4 mos
Charts, tables, graphs
Foreign languages accepted: no
• REVIEWS
Seeking reviewers: yes
Unsolicited reviews accepted: no
Materials reviewed: books
Review length: 2,000-2,500 wds
How to apply: letter
Include in application: professional degrees, institutional affiliation, areas of expertise

Journal of Popular Culture

All aspects of culture regardless of time and place
Affiliation: Popular Culture Association and Bowling Green State University
Ed: Ray B. Browne
   Bowling Green State University
   Bowling Green, OH 43403
Bk Rev Ed: same
4/yr, 196 pp; subs $35
Circ: 3,000

Readership: academics
Indexed/Abstracted: ABC, AHCI,
   BRI, CCAH, HI, MLA, WAH
• MANUSCRIPTS
Query: no; *Abstract:* no
Style guide: MLA or Chicago
Preferred length: 10–15 pp
Copies: 2
Notes: endnotes
Blind referee: yes
Acceptance rate: 1/10
Time to consider ms: 1 wk to 1 mo
Charts, pictures, tables, graphs, maps
Foreign languages accepted: no
• REVIEWS
Seeking reviewers: no
Unsolicited reviews accepted: yes
Materials reviewed: books
Review length: 200 wds
How to apply: letter
Include in application: areas of
   expertise

The Journal of Psychohistory

Psychological sources of historical
   events
Affiliation: The Institute for Psycho-
   history
Ed: Lloyd deMause
   140 Riverside Drive
   Suite 14H
   New York, NY 10024
Bk Rev Ed: Henry Lawton
4/yr, 140 pp; subs $48
Circ: 5,000
Readership: academics, general pub-
   lic, mental health professionals
Indexed/Abstracted: ABC, WAH
• MANUSCRIPTS
Query: no; *Abstract:* no
Style guide: Chicago
Preferred length: 50 pp max
Copies: 1
Notes: endnotes or footnotes
Blind referee: yes
Acceptance rate: 1/5
Time to consider ms: 2 wks
Charts, pictures, tables, graphs, maps
Foreign languages accepted: no

• REVIEWS
Seeking reviewers: no
Unsolicited reviews accepted: yes
Materials reviewed: books
How to apply: letter
Include in application: areas of
   expertise

The Journal of Regional and Local Studies

Regional and local studies
Affiliation: University of Humberside
Ed: P. Swan
   School of Social and Profes-
      sional Studies
   University of Humberside
   Inglemire Avenue
   Hull
   U.K.
Bk Rev Ed: D. Neave
   University of Hull
   Cottingham Road
   Hull HU6 7RX
   U.K.
2/yr, 80 pp; subs £6.25
Circ: 400
Readership: academics
• MANUSCRIPTS
Query: no; *Abstract:* no
Copies: 1
Notes: endnotes
Blind referee: yes
Acceptance rate: 2/3
Charts, pictures, tables, graphs, maps
Foreign languages accepted: no
• REVIEWS
Seeking reviewers: yes
Unsolicited reviews accepted: yes
Materials reviewed: books
How to apply: letter
Include in application: institutional
   affiliation, areas of expertise, cur-
   rent research

Journal of San Diego History

History of San Diego region,
   southern California, and Baja California

Affiliation: San Diego Historical
Society
Ed: Richard W. Crawford
P.O. Box 81825
San Diego, CA 92138
Bk Rev Ed: Richard Griswold del
Castillo
Department of Mexican American Studies
San Diego State University
San Diego, CA 92182
4/yr, 80 pp; subs $35
Circ: 3,800
Readership: academics, general public
Indexed/Abstracted: ABC, WAH
● MANUSCRIPTS
Query: preferred; *Abstract:* no
Style guide: Chicago
Preferred length: 20–25 pp
Copies: 3 and computer disk preferred
Notes: endnotes
Blind referee: yes
Acceptance rate: 1/4
Time to consider ms: 6–8 wks
Charts, pictures, tables, graphs, maps
Foreign languages accepted: no
● REVIEWS
Seeking reviewers: yes
Unsolicited reviews accepted: no
Materials reviewed: books
Review length: 500 wds
How to apply: letter
Include in application: professional
degrees, institutional affiliation,
areas of expertise, published
works, current research

Journal of Social History

All periods and areas of social history
Affiliation: Carnegie Mellon University
Ed: Peter N. Stearns
Carnegie Mellon University
Pittsburgh, PA 15213
Bk Rev Ed: same
4/yr, 220 pp
Circ: 1,800

Readership: academics
Indexed/Abstracted: ABC, AHCI,
BRI, CCAH, CCSB, HI, IMB,
SSCI, SSI, WAH
● MANUSCRIPTS
Query: no; *Abstract:* preferred
Style guide: Chicago
Preferred length: 25–40 pp
Copies: 1
Notes: endnotes
Blind referee: yes
Acceptance rate: 1/6–1/5
Time to consider ms: 2 mos
Charts, pictures, tables, graphs, maps
Foreign languages accepted: no
● REVIEWS
Seeking reviewers: yes
Unsolicited reviews accepted: yes
Materials reviewed: books
Review length: 1,000 wds
How to apply: letter
Include in application: professional
degrees, institutional affiliation,
areas of expertise, published
works, foreign languages, current
research

Journal of South Asian and Middle Eastern Studies

In-depth analysis of political,
economic and social developments
in the modern Islamic and non–Islamic societies in South Asia, the
Middle East and North Africa
Affiliation: Villanova University
Ed: Hafeez Malik
111 Tolentine Hall
Villanova University
Villanova, PA 19085
Bk Rev Ed: Susan Hausman
4/yr, 94 pp; subs $20
Circ: 7,500
Readership: academics, general public
Indexed/Abstracted: ABC, PAIS
● MANUSCRIPTS
Query: no; *Abstract:* no
Preferred length: 25–30 pp
Copies: 2

Notes: footnotes
Blind referee: yes
Time to consider ms: 3–6 mos
Charts, tables, graphs, maps
Foreign languages accepted: no
• REVIEWS
Seeking reviewers: no
Unsolicited reviews accepted: no
Include in application: a two paragraph biography

Journal of Southern African Studies

Southern African studies
Affiliation: Oxford University Press
Eds: Colin Stoneman and others
 Centre for Southern African
  Studies
 University of York
 Heslington
 York YO1 5DD
 U.K.
Bk Rev Ed: Rob Turrell
 Queen Elizabeth House
 21 St. Giles
 Oxford OX1 3LA
 U.K.
4/yr; subs £26
Readership: academics
Indexed/Abstracted: ABC, AHCI,
 BHI, CCSB, SSCI
• MANUSCRIPTS
Query: no; *Abstract:* no
Style guide: own
Preferred length: varies
Copies: 3
• REVIEWS
Materials reviewed: books

Journal of Southern History

History of American South, including
 black history and history of abolitionism
Affiliation: The Southern Historical
 Association and Rice University
Ed: John B. Boles
 Department of History
 Rice University

P.O. Box 1892
 Houston, TX 77251
Bk Rev Ed: same
4/yr, 208 pp; subs $20
Circ: 4,800
Readership: academics
Indexed/Abstracted: ABC, AHCI,
 BRI, CCAH, HI, WAH
• MANUSCRIPTS
Query: preferred; *Abstract:* no
Style guide: Chicago
Preferred length: 30 pp
Copies: 3
Notes: endnotes
Blind referee: yes
Acceptance rate: 1/10
Time to consider ms: 1–3 mos
Charts, pictures, tables, graphs,
 maps
Foreign languages accepted: no
• REVIEWS
Seeking reviewers: yes
Unsolicited reviews accepted: no
Materials reviewed: books
Review length: varies
How to apply: letter, form
Include in application: professional
 degrees, institutional affiliation,
 areas of expertise, published
 works, current research

Journal of Southwest Georgia History

South Georgia history (16th–20th
 centuries)
Affiliation: Thronateeska Heritage
 Foundation and Albany State College
Ed: Lee W. Formwalt
 Department of History and Political Science
 Albany State College
 Albany, GA 31705
Bk Rev Ed: same
1/yr, 100 pp; subs $20
Circ: 400
Readership: academics, general public
Indexed/Abstracted: ABC

- MANUSCRIPTS
Query: no; *Abstract:* no
Style guide: Chicago
Preferred length: 15-20 pp
Copies: 2
Notes: footnotes
Blind referee: yes
Acceptance rate: 1/4
Time to consider ms: 1 mo
Charts, pictures, tables, graphs, maps
Foreign languages accepted: no
- REVIEWS
Seeking reviewers: yes
Unsolicited reviews accepted: no
Materials reviewed: books
Review length: 500 wds
How to apply: letter
Include in application: professional
degrees, institutional affiliation,
areas of expertise, published
works, current research
- ADDITIONAL NOTES
Although the focus of the articles
and edited documents is primarily
South Georgia history, many of the
book reviews are about various
aspects of Southern history.

Journal of Soviet Military Studies

Soviet/Russian military affairs since
Czarist times
Ed: Colonel David M. Glantz
615 Grant Avenue
Fort Leavenworth, KS 66027
Bk Rev Ed: Michael Parrish
School of Public and Environ-
mental Affairs
Indiana University
Bloomington, IN 47405
4/yr, 185 pp; subs $45
Circ: 550
Readership: academics, military
Indexed/Abstracted: ABC
- MANUSCRIPTS
Query: yes; *Abstract:* no
Style guide: own
Preferred length: 7,000-10,000 wds

Copies: 2
Notes: endnotes
Blind referee: yes
Time to consider ms: 1 yr
Charts, tables, graphs, maps
Foreign languages accepted: no
- REVIEWS
Seeking reviewers: yes
Unsolicited reviews accepted: yes
Materials reviewed: books
Review length: 600 wds
How to apply: letter
Include in application: professional
degrees, institutional affiliation,
areas of expertise, published works,
foreign languages, current research

Journal of Spelean History

International study of cave history
Affiliation: National Speleological
Society
Ed: Jack H. Speece
711 E. Atlantic Avenue
Altoona, PA 16602
Bk Rev Ed: same
4/yr, 20 pp; subs $6
Circ: 200
Readership: cavers
- MANUSCRIPTS
Query: preferred; *Abstract:* preferred
Style guide: open
Preferred length: 2-10 pp
Copies: 1
Notes: none
Blind referee: no
Acceptance rate: 9/10
Time to consider ms: 3 mos
Charts, pictures, tables, graphs, maps
Foreign languages accepted: no
- REVIEWS
Seeking reviewers: no
Unsolicited reviews accepted: yes
Materials reviewed: books
Review length: short

Journal of Sport History

History of sport
Affiliation: North American Society
for Sport History

Ed: Joseph L. Arbena
  Department of History
  Clemson University
  Clemson, SC 29634-1507
Bk Rev Ed: same
3/yr, 133 pp; subs $30
Circ: 930
Readership: academics, general public
Indexed/Abstracted: ABC, AHCI,
  CCSB, SSCI, WAH
• MANUSCRIPTS
Query: no; *Abstract:* no
Style guide: Chicago
Preferred length: 20-30 pp
Copies: 4
Notes: endnotes or footnotes
Blind referee: yes
Acceptance rate: 3/10
Time to consider ms: 8-12 wks
Charts, pictures, tables, graphs, maps
Foreign languages accepted: no
• REVIEWS
Seeking reviewers: yes
Unsolicited reviews accepted: no
Materials reviewed: books, films,
  museums, archives, videos
Review length: 500-750 wds
How to apply: letter
Include in application: professional
  degrees, institutional affiliation,
  areas of expertise, published
  works, foreign languages, current
  research

Journal of Strategic Studies

Strategic matters from the mid-nine-
teenth century to the present
Eds: John Gooch
  Department of History
  University of Lancaster
  Bailrigg
  Lancaster LA1 4YG
  U.K.
        or
  Amos Perlmutter
  School of Government
  The American University
  Washington, DC 20016

Bk Rev Ed: Geoffrey Till
  Department of History and
    International Affairs
  Royal Naval College
  Greenwich
  London SE10 9NN
  U.K.
4/yr, 140 pp; subs £35
Circ: 900
Readership: academics, military
Indexed/Abstracted: ABC, BHI,
  CCSB, SSCI, WAH
• MANUSCRIPTS
Query: yes; *Abstract:* no
Style guide: own
Preferred length: 7,000-10,000 wds
Copies: 2
Notes: endnotes
Blind referee: yes
Time to consider ms: 1 yr
Charts, tables, graphs, maps
Foreign languages accepted: no
• REVIEWS
Seeking reviewers: yes
Unsolicited reviews accepted: yes
Materials reviewed: books, videos
Review length: 600-1,000 wds
How to apply: letter
Include in application: professional
  degrees, institutional affiliation,
  areas of expertise, published
  works, foreign languages, current
  research

Journal of Texas Catholic History and Culture

Roman Catholic history and culture
  with an emphasis on Texas and the
  American Southwest
Affiliation: Texas Catholic Historical
  Society
Ed: Patrick Foley
  1113 Idlewood Avenue
  Azle, TX 76020-3647
Bk Rev Ed: Thomas W. Jodziewicz
  2801 Linden Lea
  Irving, TX 75861
1/yr, 115 pp; subs $10

Circ: 500–1,000
Readership: academics, persons interested in Catholic history
• MANUSCRIPTS
Query: preferred; *Abstract:* preferred
Style guide: Chicago
Preferred length: 30–35 pp
Copies: 2
Notes: endnotes
Blind referee: yes
Acceptance rate: 3/10
Time to consider ms: 2 mos
Charts, pictures, tables, graphs, maps
Foreign languages accepted: no
• REVIEWS
Seeking reviewers: yes
Unsolicited reviews accepted: no
Materials reviewed: books
Review length: 500 wds
How to apply: letter
Include in application: professional degrees, institutional affiliation, areas of expertise, published works, current research
• ADDITIONAL NOTES
The term "culture" in the journal's title broadly refers to Catholic architecture, music, literature, and related areas. Articles devoted to philosophy, theology, or politics are not published. The editors seek balanced and very scholarly articles, accepting no essays from the more radical camps seeking a platform. The majority of the articles are on Roman Catholic history.

Journal of the American Historical Society of Germans from Russia

History and culture of Germans who emigrated to Czarist Russia and of their descendants
Affiliation: American Historical Society of Germans from Russia
Ed: David Bagby
    AHSGR

    631 D Street
    Lincoln, NE 68502-1199
Bk Rev Ed: same
4/yr, 56 pp; subs $30
Circ: 5,400
Readership: academics, general public, society members
Indexed/Abstracted: ABC, WAH
• MANUSCRIPTS
Query: preferred; *Abstract:* no
Style guide: Chicago
Preferred length: 25 pp max
Copies: 2
Notes: endnotes
Blind referee: yes
Acceptance rate: 1/3
Time to consider ms: 3–6 mos
Charts, pictures, tables, graphs, maps
Foreign languages accepted: can assist in translating German or Russian
• REVIEWS
Seeking reviewers: yes
Unsolicited reviews accepted: yes
Materials reviewed: books
Review length: 250–350 wds
How to apply: letter
Include in application: professional degrees, institutional affiliation, areas of expertise, published works, foreign languages, current research

Journal of the Canadian Aviation Historical Society

Canadian aviation history
Affiliation: Canadian Aviation Historical Society
Ed: Bill Wheeler
    4 Rougecrest Drive
    Maritham, ON L3P 3B6
    CANADA
Bk Rev Ed: same
4/yr, 32 pp; subs $30
Circ: 1,200
Readership: aviation enthusiasts
Indexed/Abstracted: ABC
• MANUSCRIPTS
Query: preferred; *Abstract:* no

Preferred length: 12 pp
Notes: endnotes
Blind referee: no
Charts, pictures, tables, graphs, maps
Foreign languages accepted: no
• REVIEWS
Seeking reviewers: no
Unsolicited reviews accepted: yes
Materials reviewed: books

Journal of the Canadian Church Historical Society

All aspects of Canadian church
history
Affiliation: Canadian Church Histori-
cal Society
Eds: I. C. Storey, E. H. Jones
Trent University
Peterborough, ON K9J 7B8
CANADA
Bk Rev Ed: Joyce Banks
Rare Books Librarian
National Library
Ottawa, ON K1A 0N3
CANADA
2/yr, 50 pp; subs $20
Circ: 400
Readership: academics, interested
amateurs
Indexed/Abstracted: ABC
• MANUSCRIPTS
Query: no; *Abstract:* preferred
Style guide: own
Preferred length: 6,000 wds
Copies: 2
Notes: endnotes
Blind referee: yes
Acceptance rate: 1/2
Time to consider ms: 3-4 mos
Charts, tables, graphs, maps
Foreign languages accepted: French
• REVIEWS
Seeking reviewers: yes
Unsolicited reviews accepted: no
Materials reviewed: books, films
Review length: 250-500 wds
How to apply: letter
Include in application: professional

degrees, institutional affiliation,
areas of expertise, current research

Journal of the Early Republic

American history from 1789 to 1850
Affiliation: Indiana University-
Purdue University at Indianapolis
Ed: Ralph D. Gray
Department of History
425 University Boulevard
Indianapolis, IN 43202-5140
Bk Rev Ed: James C. Bradford
Department of History
Texas A & M University
College Station, TX 77843
4/yr, 150 pp; subs $15-$30 (income
based)
Circ: 1,200
Readership: academics
Indexed/Abstracted: ABC, HI, WAH
• MANUSCRIPTS
Query: no; *Abstract:* no
Style guide: Chicago
Preferred length: 20-40 pp
Copies: 3
Notes: endnotes
Blind referee: yes
Acceptance rate: 1/5
Time to consider ms: 90 days
Charts, pictures, tables, graphs, maps
Foreign languages accepted: no
• REVIEWS
Seeking reviewers: yes
Unsolicited reviews accepted: no
Materials reviewed: books
Review length: 250-500 wds
How to apply: letter
Include in application: professional
degrees, institutional affiliation,
areas of expertise, published
works, foreign languages, current
research
• ADDITIONAL NOTES
The best way to understand the ac-
cepted style is to read previous
issues. Contributions in political,
social, economic, cultural, military,
intellectual, diplomatic, and other

fields are welcome. The editors look for a fresh perspective on the period from 1789 to 1850.

The Journal of the Fort Smith Historical Society

History and genealogy of Fort Smith area
Affiliation: Fort Smith Historical Society
Ed: Amelia Martin
2121 Wolfe Lane
Fort Smith, AR 72901-6243
Bk Rev Ed: same
2/yr, 48 pp; subs $15
Circ: 600
Readership: general public
• MANUSCRIPTS
Query: preferred; *Abstract:* no
Preferred length: varies
Copies: 1
Notes: endnotes or footnotes
Blind referee: no
Charts, pictures, tables, graphs, maps
Foreign languages accepted: no
• REVIEWS
Seeking reviewers: no
Unsolicited reviews accepted: no
Materials reviewed: books
• ADDITIONAL NOTES
All book reviews are done by the journal staff.

Journal of the History of Ideas

Intellectual history
Affiliation: Rutgers University and Temple University
Ed: Donald R. Kelley
88 College Avenue
Rutgers University
New Brunswick, NJ 08903-5059
Bk Rev Ed: same
4/yr, 176 pp; subs $20
Circ: 3,100
Readership: academics
Indexed/Abstracted: ABC, AHCI, BRI, CCAH, CCSB, HI, MLA, SSCI, WAH

• MANUSCRIPTS
Query: no; *Abstract:* no
Style guide: Chicago
Preferred length: 9,000 wds max
Copies: 3
Notes: endnotes
Blind referee: yes
Acceptance rate: 1/8
Time to consider ms: 3–4 mos
Charts, pictures, tables, graphs, maps
Foreign languages accepted: no
• REVIEWS
Seeking reviewers: no
Unsolicited reviews accepted: no
Materials reviewed: books

Journal of the History of Medicine and Allied Sciences

History of medicine and allied sciences
Affiliation: Yale University School of Medicine
Ed: Stanley W. Jackson
333 Cedar Street
New Haven, CT 06510
Bk Rev Ed: Thomas Gariepy
Stonehill College
History of Science
North Easton, MA 02357
4/yr, 90 pp; subs $45
Circ: 1,500
Readership: academics
Indexed/Abstracted: ABC, AHCI, SSCI, WAH
• MANUSCRIPTS
Query: no; *Abstract:* preferred
Style guide: own
Preferred length: 15,000 wds max
Copies: 3
Notes: footnotes
Blind referee: yes
Acceptance rate: 1/4–1/3
Time to consider ms: 2–4 mos
Charts, pictures, tables, graphs, maps
Foreign languages accepted: no
• REVIEWS
Seeking reviewers: no
Unsolicited reviews accepted: no
Materials reviewed: books

Journal of the History of Philosophy

History of western philosophy
Affiliation: Emory University
Ed: Rudolf A. Makkreel
    Department of Philosophy
    Emory University
    Atlanta, GA 30322
Bk Rev Ed: Gerald A. Press
    Department of Philosophy
    Hunter College
    695 Park Avenue
    New York, NY 10021
4/yr, 160 pp; subs $20
Circ: 1,600
Readership: academics
Indexed/Abstracted: ABC, AHCI,
    CCAH, HI
• MANUSCRIPTS
Query: no; *Abstract:* no
Style guide: Chicago
Preferred length: 30 pp
Copies: 3
Notes: endnotes
Blind referee: yes
Acceptance rate: 1/8
Time to consider ms: 3 mos
Tables
Foreign languages accepted: French,
    German
• REVIEWS
Seeking reviewers: no
Unsolicited reviews accepted: no
Materials reviewed: books
Review length: 3 pp
How to apply: letter
Include in application: professional
    degrees, institutional affiliation,
    areas of expertise, published
    works, foreign languages, current
    research

Journal of the History of Sexuality

History of sexuality
Affiliation: University of Chicago
    Press; Bard College
Ed: John C. Fout

Bard College
    Annandale-on-Hudson, NY 12504
Bk Rev Ed: Michele D. Dominy
4/yr; subs $32
Readership: academics
Indexed/Abstracted: CCSB, IMB
• MANUSCRIPTS
Query: no; *Abstract:* no
Style guide: Chicago
Preferred length: 30–45 pp
Copies: 2
Notes: endnotes
Blind referee: yes
Tables, pictures, charts, other suit-
    able illustrations
Foreign languages accepted: no
• REVIEWS
Materials reviewed: books

Journal of the History of the Behavioral Sciences

History of the behavioral sciences
Affiliation: University of Massachu-
    setts-Boston
Ed: Barbara C. Ross
    Psychology Department
    UMASS-Boston
    100 Morrissey Boulevard
    Harbor Campus
    Boston, MA 02125-3393
Bk Rev Ed: same
4/yr, 100 pp; subs $45
Circ: 800
Readership: academics
Indexed/Abstracted: ABC, AHCI,
    CCSB, SSCI, WAH
• MANUSCRIPTS
Query: no; *Abstract:* yes
Style guide: Chicago
Preferred length: 15 pp
Copies: 3
Notes: endnotes
Blind referee: yes
Acceptance rate: 1/7
Pictures, tables
Foreign languages accepted: no
• REVIEWS
Seeking reviewers: yes

Unsolicited reviews accepted: no
Materials reviewed: books
Review length: 8 pp
How to apply: letter
Include in application: institutional affiliation, areas of expertise, foreign languages, current research
• ADDITIONAL NOTES
The term "behavioral sciences" includes history, anthropology, sociology, psychology, psychoanalysis, medicine; i.e. broadly defined.

Journal of the Lancaster County Historical Society

History and biography of Lancaster County and southeastern Pennsylvania
Affiliation: Lancaster County Historical Society
Ed: John W. W. Loose
    230 N. President Avenue
    Lancaster, PA 17603-3125
Bk Rev Ed: Thomas Winpenny
4/yr, 40 pp; subs $30
Circ: 1,830
Readership: society members
Indexed/Abstracted: ABC
• MANUSCRIPTS
Query: no; *Abstract:* preferred
Style guide: MLA or Chicago
Preferred length: 36–40 pp
Copies: 1
Notes: endnotes
Blind referee: no
Acceptance rate: 1/2
Time to consider ms: 3 wks
Charts, pictures, tables, maps
Foreign languages accepted: no
• REVIEWS
Seeking reviewers: yes
Unsolicited reviews accepted: yes
Materials reviewed: books
Review length: 3 pp
How to apply: letter
Include in application: professional degrees, institutional affiliation, areas of expertise

Journal of the Royal Asiatic Society

Multi-disciplinary studies of Asia, North Africa, and Ethiopia
Affiliation: Cambridge University Press; The Royal Asiatic Society of Great Britain and Ireland
Ed: D. O. Morgan
    Royal Asiatic Society
    60 Queen's Gardens
    London W2 3AF
    U.K.
Bk Rev Ed: same
3/yr, 170 pp; subs £28
Circ: 1,450
Readership: academics
Indexed/Abstracted: ABC, AHCI, BHI, CCAH, MLA
• MANUSCRIPTS
Query: no; *Abstract:* no
Style guide: own
Preferred length: 5,000–10,000 wds
Copies: 1
Notes: endnotes
Blind referee: no
Acceptance rate: 2/5
Time to consider ms: 2–3 mos
Charts, pictures, tables, maps
Foreign languages accepted: French, German
• REVIEWS
Seeking reviewers: no
Unsolicited reviews accepted: no
Materials reviewed: books
Review length: 1,000 wds

Journal of the Society of Architectural Historians

Architectural history
Affiliation: Society of Architectural Historians
Ed: Nicholas Adams
    Box 291
    Department of Art
    Vassar College
    Poughkeepsie, NY 12601
Bk Rev Ed: Kenneth Breisch

Southern California Institute of
Architecture
5454 Beethoven Street
Los Angeles, CA 90066
4/yr, 120 pp; subs membership
Circ: 4,000
Readership: academics, architects,
preservationists
Indexed/Abstracted: ABC, AHCI,
CCAH, IMB, WAH
• MANUSCRIPTS
Query: no; *Abstract:* yes
Style guide: own
Preferred length: varies
Copies: 2
Notes: endnotes
Blind referee: yes
Acceptance rate: 1/3
Time to consider ms: varies
Charts, pictures, tables, graphs, maps
Foreign languages accepted: no
• REVIEWS
Seeking reviewers: yes
Unsolicited reviews accepted: no
Materials reviewed: books
Review length: 1,500 wds
How to apply: letter
Include in application: professional
degrees, institutional affiliation,
areas of expertise, published
works, foreign languages, current
research

Journal of the Society of Archivists

Archives, conservation, records
management, all matters relating to
the study of records
Affiliation: Society of Archivists
Ed: C. C. Webb
The Borthwick Institute of His-
torical Research
University of York
St. Anthony's Hall
Peasholme Green
York YO1 2PW
U.K.
Bk Rev Ed: P. S. Bassett

Birmingham Central Library
Archives Division
Chamberlain Square
Birmingham B3 3HQ
U.K.
2/yr, 90 pp
Circ: 1,900
Readership: academics, general pub-
lic, archivists
Indexed/Abstracted: ABC, AHCI,
BHI, CCAH, IMB
• MANUSCRIPTS
Query: preferred; *Abstract:* no
Preferred length: 6,000 wds max
Copies: 2
Notes: footnotes
Blind referee: yes
Time to consider ms: 3-6 mos
Charts, tables, graphs
Foreign languages accepted: no
• REVIEWS
Seeking reviewers: no
Unsolicited reviews accepted: no
Materials reviewed: books, software

Journal of the Southwest

Multidisciplinary studies of the
Southwestern U.S. and Northern
Mexico
Affiliation: University of Arizona
Ed: Joseph C. Wilder
1052 North Highland Avenue
University of Arizona
Tucson, AZ 85721
Bk Rev Ed: Katherine Sturdevant
3970 Cyclone Drive
Colorado Springs, CO 80920
4/yr, 150 pp; subs $18
Circ: 1,100
Readership: academics
Indexed/Abstracted: ABC, AHCI,
CCAH, MLA, WAH
• MANUSCRIPTS
Query: no; *Abstract:* no
Style guide: Chicago
Preferred length: open
Copies: 2
Notes: footnotes

Blind referee: yes
Acceptance rate: 1/2
Time to consider ms: 3 mos
Charts, pictures, tables, graphs, maps
Foreign languages accepted: Spanish,
French, others
● REVIEWS
Seeking reviewers: yes
Unsolicited reviews accepted: occasionally
Materials reviewed: books, films
Review length: open
How to apply: letter
Include in application: professional
degrees, institutional affiliation,
areas of expertise, published
works, foreign languages, current
research
● ADDITIONAL NOTES
This journal publishes academic
papers, historic documents, essays,
reviews, and photographic essays
on the Greater Southwest Region.
The editors welcome manuscripts
from Mexican scholars.

Journal of the West

History and culture of the area west
of the Mississippi to Micronesia
and from Panama to the North
Pole
Affiliation: Kansas State University
Ed: Robin Higham
Box 1009
1531 Yuma
Manhattan, KS 66502-4228
Bk Rev Ed: same
4/yr, 112 pp; subs $30
Circ: 4,500
Readership: academics, general public
Indexed/Abstracted: ABC, AHCI,
CCAH, HI, WAH
● MANUSCRIPTS
Query: yes; *Abstract:* no
Style guide: own
Preferred length: 15 pp
Copies: 2
Notes: endnotes

Blind referee: no
Time to consider ms: 2 mos
Charts, pictures, tables, graphs, maps
Foreign languages accepted: no
● REVIEWS
Seeking reviewers: no
Unsolicited reviews accepted: no
Materials reviewed: books
Review length: 350 wds
How to apply: letter
Include in application: professional
degrees, institutional affiliation,
areas of expertise, published
works, current research, vita

Journal of Third World Studies

Multidisciplinary look at Third
World problems and issues and
U.S. relations with the developing
world
Ed: Harold Isaacs
P.O. Box 1232
Americus, GA 31709
2/yr, 400 pp; subs $30
Circ: 600
Readership: academics, government
officials, foreign service personnel
Indexed/Abstracted: ABC, PAIS
● MANUSCRIPTS
Query: preferred; *Abstract:* no
Style guide: Chicago
Preferred length: 20–25 pp
Copies: 4
Notes: endnotes
Blind referee: yes
Acceptance rate: 1/5
Time to consider ms: 4–6 wks
Charts, tables
Foreign languages accepted: no
● REVIEWS
Seeking reviewers: yes
Unsolicited reviews accepted: yes
Materials reviewed: books, films
Review length: 600–750 wds
How to apply: letter
Include in application: professional
degrees, institutional affiliation,

areas of expertise, published works, current research

Journal of Transport History

Economic and social history of transport in all periods and countries
Affiliation: Manchester University Press
Ed: John Armstrong
Polytechnic of West London
St. Mary's Road
Ealing
London W5 5RF
U.K.
Bk Rev Ed: same
2/yr, 100 pp; subs £25
Circ: 650
Readership: academics, general public, enthusiasts
Indexed/Abstracted: ABC, BHI, IMB, WAH
• MANUSCRIPTS
Query: preferred; *Abstract:* no
Style guide: own
Preferred length: 8,000 wds
Copies: 2
Notes: endnotes
Blind referee: yes
Acceptance rate: 1/2
Time to consider ms: 1–4 mos
Charts, pictures, tables, graphs, maps
Foreign languages accepted: no
• REVIEWS
Seeking reviewers: no
Unsolicited reviews accepted: no
Materials reviewed: books
Review length: 250–2,000 wds
How to apply: letter
Include in application: institutional affiliation

Journal of Ukrainian Studies

Ukrainian and Ukrainian Canadian topics in the humanities and social sciences
Affiliation: Canadian Institute of Ukrainian Studies
Ed: Zenon Kohut

352 Athabasca Hall
University of Alberta
Edmonton, AB T6G 2E8
CANADA
Bk Rev Ed: Alan Rutkowski
4-03 A
Cameron Library
University of Alberta
Edmonton, AB T6G 2J8
CANADA
2/yr, 120 pp; subs $15
Circ: 600
Readership: academics, others interested in Ukrainian studies
Indexed/Abstracted: ABC, MLA
• MANUSCRIPTS
Query: preferred; *Abstract:* preferred
Style guide: Chicago
Preferred length: 25 pp max
Copies: 3
Notes: endnotes
Blind referee: yes
Acceptance rate: 1/2
Time to consider ms: 3–6 mos
Charts, pictures, tables, graphs, maps
Foreign languages accepted: Ukrainian
• REVIEWS
Seeking reviewers: yes
Unsolicited reviews accepted: yes
Materials reviewed: books
Review length: 1,000–1,500 wds
How to apply: letter
Include in application: professional degrees, institutional affiliation, areas of expertise, published works, foreign languages, current research

Journal of Unconventional History

Original, unconventional work
Eds: Ann Elwood and Aline Hornaday
P.O. Box 459
Cardiff-by-the-Sea, CA 92007
Bk Rev Ed: same
3/yr, 70–80 pp; subs $20

Circ: 400
Readership: academics, general public, history buffs
Indexed/Abstracted: ABC
• MANUSCRIPTS
Query: no; *Abstract:* preferred
Style guide: any
Preferred length: 30 pp max
Copies: 1
Notes: endnotes
Blind referee: no
Acceptance rate: 4/5
Time to consider ms: 1–2 mos
Pictures, graphs, maps
Foreign languages accepted: no
• REVIEWS
Seeking reviewers: no
Unsolicited reviews accepted: occasionally
Materials reviewed: any historical material
Review length: 5 pp
How to apply: proposal

Journal of Urban History

Urban history
Affiliation: University of North Carolina at Charlotte
Ed: David R. Goldfield
History Department
UNC-Charlotte
Charlotte, NC 28223
Bk Rev Ed: Raymond A. Mohl
History Department
Florida Atlantic University
Boca Raton, FL 33432
4/yr, 130 pp; subs $40
Circ: 1,000
Readership: academics
Indexed/Abstracted: ABC, AHCI, BRI, CCAH, CCSB, HI, SSCI
• MANUSCRIPTS
Query: no; *Abstract:* no
Style guide: Chicago
Preferred length: 30–35 pp
Copies: 3
Notes: endnotes
Blind referee: yes

Acceptance rate: 1/6
Time to consider ms: 2 mos max
Charts, pictures, tables, graphs, maps
Foreign languages accepted: no
• REVIEWS
Seeking reviewers: yes
Unsolicited reviews accepted: no
Materials reviewed: books
How to apply: letter
Include in application: professional degrees, institutional affiliation, areas of expertise, published works

Journal of Women's History

History of women around the world
Affiliation: Indiana University
Eds: Christie Farnham, Joan Hoff
Indiana University
3/yr, 192 pp; subs $25
Circ: 1,500
Readership: academics, general public
Indexed/Abstracted: ABC, AHCI, WAH
• MANUSCRIPTS
Query: no; *Abstract:* no
Style guide: MLA
Notes: endnotes
Blind referee: yes

Journal of World History

Historical analysis from a global perspective
Affiliation: World History Association and University of Hawaii Press
Ed: Jerry H. Bentley
Department of History
Sakamaki Hall A-401
2530 Dole Street
Honolulu, HI 96822
Bk Rev Ed: Herbert Ziegler
Department of History
Sakamaki Hall A-403
2530 Dole Street
Honolulu, HI 96822
2/yr, 150 pp; subs $25
Circ: 1,350
Readership: academics, general public
Indexed/Abstracted: ABC, WAH

• MANUSCRIPTS
Query: no; *Abstract:* yes
Style guide: Chicago
Preferred length: 2,500–7,500 wds
Copies: 2
Notes: footnotes
Blind referee: yes
Acceptance rate: 1/4
Charts, pictures, tables, graphs, maps
Foreign languages accepted: no
• REVIEWS
Seeking reviewers: yes
Unsolicited reviews accepted: no
Materials reviewed: books, films
Review length: 1,000 wds
How to apply: letter
Include in application: areas of expertise, published works, foreign languages, current research

Journal of the United Reformed Church History Society

History of the Reformed tradition with emphasis on Great Britain
Ed: J. C. G. Binfield
   The Department of History
   The University of Sheffield
   Sheffield S10 2TN
   U.K.
Bk Rev Ed: David Cornick
   Westminster College
   Madingley Road
   Cambridge
   U.K.
2/yr, 64 pp; subs £5
Circ: 600
Readership: academics, general public, ministers
Indexed/Abstracted: ABC
• MANUSCRIPTS
Query: no; *Abstract:* no
Preferred length: 3,500–10,000 wds
Copies: 1
Notes: endnotes or footnotes
Blind referee: yes
Acceptance rate: 3/4
Time to consider ms: 1–3 mos

Charts, pictures, tables, graphs, maps
Foreign languages accepted: no
• REVIEWS
Seeking reviewers: no
Unsolicited reviews accepted: no
Materials reviewed: books
Review length: 250–1,700 wds
How to apply: letter
Include in application: professional degrees, institutional affiliation, areas of expertise, published works, foreign languages, current research

Journalism History

History of mass media, not including film
Affiliation: University of Nevada, Las Vegas
Ed: Barbara Cloud
   Greenspun School of Communication
   University of Nevada, Las Vegas
   Las Vegas, NV 89154-5007
Bk Rev Eds: Patrick Washburn,
   Robert Stewart
   Scripps School of Journalism
   Ohio University
   Athens, OH 45701
4/yr, 52 pp; subs $12
Circ: 700
Readership: academics, general public
Indexed/Abstracted: ABC, HI, WAH
• MANUSCRIPTS
Query: no; *Abstract:* no
Style guide: Turabian
Preferred length: 16–20 pp
Copies: 4
Notes: endnotes
Blind referee: yes
Time to consider ms: 2 mos
Charts, pictures, tables, graphs, maps
Foreign languages accepted: no
• REVIEWS
Seeking reviewers: yes
Unsolicited reviews accepted: sometimes
Materials reviewed: books

Review length: 500 wds
How to apply: letter
Include in application: areas of expertise, current research, vita

Jusūr: The UCLA Journal of Middle Eastern Studies

All areas of Middle Eastern Studies
Affiliation: Von Grunebaum Center for Near Eastern Studies, University of California, Los Angeles
Ed: Patricia Kabra
10286 Bunche Hall
Von Grunebaum Center for Near Eastern Studies
University of California, Los Angeles
Los Angeles, CA 90024
Bk Rev Ed: same
1/yr, 150 pp; subs $8
Circ: 500
Readership: academics
Indexed/Abstracted: ABC
• MANUSCRIPTS
Query: no; *Abstract:* no
Style guide: Chicago
Preferred length: 30–40 pp
Copies: 2
Notes: endnotes
Blind referee: yes
Acceptance rate: 1/5
Time to consider ms: 2 mos
Charts, pictures, tables, graphs, maps
Foreign languages accepted: will translate
• REVIEWS
Seeking reviewers: yes
Unsolicited reviews accepted: yes
Materials reviewed: books, films, theater
Review length: 2–6 pp
How to apply: letter
Include in application: professional degrees, institutional affiliation, areas of expertise, published works, current research

Kaiserzeit

Military history and collectibles of the German States and Empire, 1618–1918
Affiliation: Imperial German Military Collector's Association
Ed: Eric Johansson
P.O. Box 12212
Kansas City, KS 66112
Bk Rev Ed: same
irregular, 32 pp; subs $15
Circ: 500
Readership: academics, general public, military collectors
• MANUSCRIPTS
Query: preferred; *Abstract:* no
Style guide: any
Preferred length: varies
Copies: 2
Notes: endnotes
Blind referee: no
Acceptance rate: 19/20
Time to consider ms: varies
Charts, pictures, tables, graphs, maps
Foreign languages accepted: no
• REVIEWS
Seeking reviewers: yes
Unsolicited reviews accepted: yes
Materials reviewed: books, films
Review length: 1 pp
How to apply: letter
Include in application: areas of expertise, published works, current research

Kansas History: A Journal of the Central Plains

History of Kansas and the Central Plains
Affiliation: Kansas State Historical Society
Ed: Virgil W. Dean
Kansas State Historical Society
120 West Tenth Street
Topeka, KS 66612-1291
Bk Rev Ed: same
4/yr, 80 pp; subs $25
Circ: 3,500

Readership: academics, general public
Indexed/Abstracted: ABC, WAH
• MANUSCRIPTS
Query: preferred; *Abstract:* no
Style guide: Chicago
Preferred length: 25 pp
Copies: 1
Notes: endnotes
Blind referee: yes
Acceptance rate: 1/2
Time to consider ms: 8 wks
Charts, pictures, tables, graphs, maps
Foreign languages accepted: no
• REVIEWS
Seeking reviewers: yes
Unsolicited reviews accepted: no
Materials reviewed: books
Review length: 600 wds
How to apply: letter
Include in application: professional
degrees, institutional affiliation,
areas of expertise, published
works, current research

Kansas Quarterly

Kansas
Affiliation: Kansas State University
History Ed: Marion Gray
History Department
Kansas State University
Manhattan, KS 66506
4/yr, 144 pp; subs $20
Circ: 1,300
Readership: academics, general public
Indexed/Abstracted: ABC, AHI,
MLA, WAH
• MANUSCRIPTS
Query: preferred; *Abstract:* no
Style guide: Chicago
Preferred length: 1,000–5,000 wds
Copies: 1
Notes: endnotes
Blind referee: yes
Time to consider ms: 6 mos
Charts, pictures, tables, graphs, maps
Foreign languages accepted: no
• REVIEWS
Seeking reviewers: no
Unsolicited reviews accepted: no

• ADDITIONAL NOTES
Kansas Quarterly publishes one special topic history issue every two years.

Kiva: The Journal of Southwestern Anthropology and History

The prehistoric and historic archaeology, ethnology, history, and ethnohistory of the southwestern U.S. and northwestern Mexico
Affiliation: Arizona Archaeological
and Historical Society
Ed: Gayle Harrison Hartmann
Arizona Archaeological and Historical Society
Arizona State Museum
University of Arizona
Tucson, AZ 85721
Bk Rev Ed: John Ravesloot
4/yr, 88 pp; subs $25
Circ: 1,100
Readership: academics, general public
Indexed/Abstracted: ABC
• MANUSCRIPTS
Query: no; *Abstract:* yes
Style guide: modified Chicago
Preferred length: 30 pp max
Copies: 3
Notes: in text
Blind referee: yes
Acceptance rate: 4/5
Time to consider ms: 1–2 mos
Charts, pictures, tables, graphs, maps
Foreign languages accepted: an
abstract is printed in Spanish
• REVIEWS
Seeking reviewers: no
Unsolicited reviews accepted: no
Materials reviewed: books
Review length: 2–4 pp
How to apply: letter or telephone
Include in application: professional
degrees, institutional affiliation,
areas of expertise, published
works, foreign languages, current
research

Korean Studies

Korea and the Korean community
  abroad, with reference to the social
  sciences and humanities
Affiliation: Center for Korean
  Studies, University of Hawaii
Ed: Edward J. Shultz
  History Department
  University of Hawaii – West Oahu
  96-043 Ala Ike Street
  Pearl City, HI 96782
Bk Rev Ed: Center for Korean
  Studies
  1881 East-West Road
  University of Hawaii
  Honolulu, HI 96822
1/yr, 150 pp; subs $14
Circ: 160
Readership: academics, general public
Indexed/Abstracted: ABC
• MANUSCRIPTS
Query: no; *Abstract:* no
Style guide: Chicago
Preferred length: 5,000 wds
Copies: 2
Notes: endnotes
Blind referee: yes
Acceptance rate: 1/2
Time to consider ms: 2 mos
Charts, tables, graphs, maps
Foreign languages accepted: no
• REVIEWS
Seeking reviewers: yes
Unsolicited reviews accepted: no
Materials reviewed: books
Review length: 500–1,000 wds
How to apply: letter
Include in application: professional
  degrees, institutional affiliation

Labor History

History of labor
Affiliation: New York University
Ed: Dan Leab
  Tamiment Library
  70 Washington Square South
  10th Floor
  New York City, NY 10012

Bk Rev Ed: same
4/yr, 160 pp; subs $29
Circ: 2,000
Readership: academics, general public
Indexed/Abstracted: ABC, AHCI,
  CCAH, CCSB, HI, SSCI, WAH
• MANUSCRIPTS
Query: no; *Abstract:* no
Style guide: Turabian
Preferred length: 20–25 pp
Copies: 2
Notes: footnotes
Blind referee: yes
Acceptance rate: 3/10
Time to consider ms: 3–6 mos
Charts, pictures, tables, graphs, maps
Foreign languages accepted: no
• REVIEWS
Seeking reviewers: no
Unsolicited reviews accepted: no
Materials reviewed: books, films
Review length: 800–1,000 pp
How to apply: letter
Include in application: professional
  degrees, institutional affiliation,
  areas of expertise, published
  works, foreign languages, current
  research

Labor Studies Journal

Working class life, organized labor,
  labor education, industrial relations
Affiliation: University and College
  Labor Education Association
Ed: Higdon C. Roberts, Jr.
  Center for Labor Education and
  Research
  1044 11th Street South
  Birmingham, AL 35294-4500
Bk Rev Ed: Roberta Till-Retz
  Labor Center
  Oakdale Hall
  Iowa City, IA 52242
4/yr, 100 pp; subs $30
Circ: 1,000
Readership: academics, industrial
  relations practitioners
Indexed/Abstracted: ABC, PAIS

- MANUSCRIPTS
Query: no; *Abstract:* yes
Style guide: Chicago
Preferred length: 25 pp
Copies: 4
Notes: footnotes
Blind referee: yes
Acceptance rate: 1/5
Time to consider ms: 3–5 mos
Charts, graphs
Foreign languages accepted: no
- REVIEWS
Seeking reviewers: no
Unsolicited reviews accepted: no
Materials reviewed: books, films
- ADDITIONAL NOTES
Although no book or film reviewers are needed, the editors are seeking reviewers for peer review of articles. To apply, send a letter of interest and include professional degrees and areas of expertise.

Labor's Heritage

History of workers and the workplace
Affiliation: The George Meany Memorial Archives
Ed: Stuart B. Kaufman
    10000 New Hampshire Avenue
    Silver Spring, MD 20903
4/yr, 80 pp; subs $17.95
Circ: 10,000
Readership: academics, general public
Indexed/Abstracted: ABC
- MANUSCRIPTS
Query: preferred; *Abstract:* no
Style guide: Chicago
Preferred length: 15–30 pp
Copies: 1
Notes: endnotes
Blind referee: no
Acceptance rate: 3/5
Time to consider ms: 1–3 mos
Pictures
Foreign languages accepted: no
- ADDITIONAL NOTES
Labor's Heritage is an illustrated journal and seeks manuscripts with

the potential for eye-catching photographs and strong images. In addition to scholarly-based articles by historians, the journal carries essays of varying length based on labor history exhibits.

Labour / Le Travail

Social, working-class, and labour history
Affiliation: Canadian Historical Association
Ed: Gregory S. Kealey
    History Department
    Memorial University of Newfoundland
    St. John's, NF A1C 5S7
    CANADA
Bk Rev Ed: Bryan D. Palmer
    History Department
    Queen's University
    Kingston, ON K7L 3N6
    CANADA
2/yr, 440 pp; subs $20
Circ: 1,200
Readership: academics, unions
Indexed/Abstracted: ABC, AHCI, CCAH, PAIS, WAH
- MANUSCRIPTS
Query: preferred; *Abstract:* yes
Style guide: modified Chicago
Preferred length: 30 pp
Copies: 2
Notes: endnotes
Blind referee: yes
Acceptance rate: 2/3
Time to consider ms: 3 mos
Charts, pictures, tables, graphs, maps
Foreign languages accepted: French
- REVIEWS
Seeking reviewers: no
Unsolicited reviews accepted: yes
Materials reviewed: books
Review length: 1,000 wds
How to apply: letter
Include in application: professional degrees, institutional affiliation, areas of expertise, published

works, foreign languages, current research

Labour History Review

International labour history, emphasis on British
Affiliation: Society for the Study of Labour History
Ed: D. E. Martin
　Department of History
　The University
　Sheffield S10 2TN
　U.K.
Bk Rev Ed: Laurence Marlow
　Department of Social Sciences
　South Bank University
　103 Borough Road
　London SE1 0AA
　U.K.
3/yr, 85 pp; subs £15
Circ: 900
Readership: academics
Indexed/Abstracted: ABC
• MANUSCRIPTS
Query: preferred; *Abstract:* preferred
Style guide: own
Preferred length: 7,000 wds max
Copies: 2
Notes: endnotes
Blind referee: no
Acceptance rate: 6 mos
Time to consider ms: 1/3
Tables, graphs
Foreign languages accepted: no
• REVIEWS
Seeking reviewers: yes
Unsolicited reviews accepted: no
Materials reviewed: books
Review length: 200–2,000 wds
How to apply: letter
Include in application: areas of expertise
• ADDITIONAL NOTES
The *Review* publishes few essays of the type found in other historical journals; the editors find space for only two or three per year. Much of the journal is devoted to book reviews and bibliography. Also accepted are various short items (1,000–3,000 words). Contributors are advised to refer to recent issues.

Lake Superior Magazine

Contemporary and historical articles on the Lake Superior Region
Ed: Paul L. Hayden
　P.O. Box 16417
　Duluth, MN 55816-0417
6/yr, 80 pp; subs $21
Circ: 20,000
Readership: general public
• MANUSCRIPTS
Query: preferred; *Abstract:* no
Preferred length: 1,600–2,200 wds
Copies: 1
Notes: none
Blind referee: no
Acceptance rate: 1/20
Time to consider ms: 3–6 mos
Charts, pictures, maps
Foreign languages accepted: no
• ADDITIONAL NOTES
High quality photography is this journal's hallmark. All features must have appropriate graphics. Manuscripts should be written with a contemporary, well-educated audience in mind; conversational and well documented.

Lamar Journal of the Humanities

General humanities including history
Affiliation: Lamar University
Ed: Ronald Fritze
　Lamar University
　P.O. Box 10048
　Beaumont, TX 77710
Bk Rev Ed: same
2/yr, 50–60 pp; subs $6
Circ: 400
Readership: academics, general public
Indexed/Abstracted: ABC, MLA, WAH

- MANUSCRIPTS
Query: no; *Abstract:* no
Style guide: Chicago
Preferred length: 2,500–3,500 wds
Copies: 2
Notes: endnotes
Blind referee: yes
Acceptance rate: 1/3
Time to consider ms: 90 days
No illustrations accepted
Foreign languages accepted: no
- REVIEWS
Seeking reviewers: no
Unsolicited reviews accepted: no

The Landmark

Connecticut history, material culture, antiques, arts, architecture
Affiliation: The Antiquarian and Landmarks Society
Ed: Mary E. Baker
    Antiquarian and Landmarks Society, Inc.
    394 Main Street
    Hartford, CT 06103
Bk Rev Ed: same
3/yr, 20 pp; subs $25
Circ: 1,500
Readership: society members
- MANUSCRIPTS
Query: no; *Abstract:* preferred
Style guide: Chicago
Preferred length: 3–10 pp
Copies: 3
Notes: endnotes
Blind referee: occasionally
Acceptance rate: 1/2
Time to consider ms: 3–8 mos
Charts, pictures, tables, graphs, maps
Foreign languages accepted: no
- REVIEWS
Seeking reviewers: yes
Unsolicited reviews accepted: yes
Materials reviewed: anything on Connecticut history
Review length: ½ pp
How to apply: not necessary

Landscape

Cultural geography, historical geography, history of architecture and landscape architecture
Ed: Blair Boyd
    P.O. Box 7107
    Berkeley, CA 94707
Bk Rev Ed: Rebecca McKee
3/yr, 48 pp; subs $22
Circ: 3,000
Readership: academics, general public
Indexed/Abstracted: ABC, AHCI, CCAH, WAH
- MANUSCRIPTS
Query: no; *Abstract:* no
Preferred length: 2,000–5,000 wds
Copies: 1
Notes: none
Blind referee: yes
Acceptance rate: 1/5–1/4
Time to consider ms: 8–10 wks
Pictures, maps
Foreign languages accepted: no
- REVIEWS
Seeking reviewers: no
Unsolicited reviews accepted: seldom
Materials reviewed: books
How to apply: letter
Include in application: professional degrees, institutional affiliation, areas of expertise, published works, foreign languages, current research

Latah Legacy

History of Latah County, Idaho
Affiliation: Latah County Historical Society
Ed: Bert C. Cross
    Latah County Historical Society
    327 East Second Street
    Moscow, ID
Bk Rev Ed: same
2/yr, 38 pp; subs membership
Circ: 850
Readership: society members
- MANUSCRIPTS
Query: preferred; *Abstract:* no

Preferred length: varies
Copies: 1
Notes: endnotes
Blind referee: no
Time to consider ms: 6–8 wks
Charts, pictures, tables, maps
Foreign languages accepted: no
• REVIEWS
Seeking reviewers: no
Unsolicited reviews accepted: yes
Materials reviewed: books
Review length: 300–500 wds

Latin American Antiquity

Archaeology, prehistory, and ethno-
history of Latin America
Affiliation: Society for American
Archaeology
Ed: Dr. David M. Pendergast
Department of New World
Archaeology
Royal Ontario Museum
100 Queen's Park
Toronto, ON M5S 2C6
CANADA
Bk Rev Ed: Dr. Charles Stanish
Anthropology
Field Museum of Natural History
Roosevelt Road at Lake Shore
Drive
Chicago, IL 60605-2496
4/yr, 96 pp; subs $40
Circ: 917
Readership: academics, general pub-
lic, avocational archaeologists, cul-
tural-resource managers
• MANUSCRIPTS
Query: no; *Abstract:* yes
Style guide: own
Preferred length: 40–50 pp
Copies: 4
Notes: endnotes
Blind referee: yes
Acceptance rate: 3/10
Time to consider ms: 2–4 mos
Charts, pictures, tables, graphs, maps
Foreign languages accepted: Spanish
abstracts

• REVIEWS
Seeking reviewers: yes
Unsolicited reviews accepted: no
Materials reviewed: books, ms
Review length: open
How to apply: letter
Include in application: professional
degrees, institutional affiliation,
areas of expertise, foreign lan-
guages, current research, telephone
and fax numbers

Latin American Research Review

Latin American topics of research in
the social sciences, literature,
culture, and communications
Affiliation: University of New Mexico
Ed: Gilbert W. Merkx
Latin American Institute
801 Yale, N.E.
University of New Mexico
Albuquerque, NM 87131
Bk Rev Ed: Karen L. Remmer
3/yr, 288 pp; subs $25
Circ: 4,500
Readership: academics, general pub-
lic, U.S. military, government
Indexed/Abstracted: ABC, AHCI,
CCSB, PAIS, SSCI, SSI, WAH
• MANUSCRIPTS
Query: no; *Abstract:* no
Style guide: Chicago
Preferred length: 15–50 pp
Copies: 3
Notes: footnotes
Blind referee: yes
Acceptance rate: 1/5
Time to consider ms: 6 wks to 6 mos
Pictures, tables, maps
Foreign languages accepted: Spanish
• REVIEWS
Seeking reviewers: yes
Unsolicited reviews accepted: occa-
sionally
Materials reviewed: books
Review length: 15–20 pp
How to apply: letter

Include in application: professional degrees, institutional affiliation, areas of expertise, published works, foreign languages, current research, vita, proposal
• ADDITIONAL NOTES
LARR does not publish reviews of individual books. All reviews are essays treating at least three works.

Law and History Review

Legal history
Affiliation: American Society for Legal History
Ed: Bruce H. Mann
　　University of Pennsylvania Law School
　　3400 Chestnut Street
　　Philadelphia, PA 19004
Bk Rev Ed: same
2/yr, 224 pp; subs $35
Circ: 1,200
Readership: academics, lawyers, judges
Indexed/Abstracted: ABC, WAH
• MANUSCRIPTS
Query: no; *Abstract:* no
Style guide: Chicago
Preferred length: 40–60 pp
Copies: 1
Notes: endnotes
Blind referee: yes
Acceptance rate: 1/10
Time to consider ms: 6–8 wks
Charts, pictures, tables, graphs, maps
Foreign languages accepted: no
• REVIEWS
Seeking reviewers: yes
Unsolicited reviews accepted: yes
Materials reviewed: books
Review length: 1,500 wds
How to apply: letter
Include in application: professional degrees, institutional affiliation, areas of expertise, published work, current research

Legacies: A History Journal for Dallas and North Central Texas

History of Dallas and North Central Texas
Affiliation: Dallas Historical Society and Dallas County Heritage Society
Ed: Michael V. Hazel
　　Dallas Historical Society
　　P.O. Box 150038
　　Dallas, TX 75315
Bk Rev Ed: same
2/yr, 44 pp; subs $12.50
Circ: 2,500
Readership: general public
• MANUSCRIPTS
Query: preferred; *Abstract:* no
Preferred length: 15–20 pp
Copies: 1
Notes: endnotes
Blind referee: yes
Acceptance rate: 1/4
Time to consider ms: 2–3 mos
Pictures, graphs, maps
Foreign languages accepted: no
• REVIEWS
Seeking reviewers: yes
Unsolicited reviews accepted: no
Materials reviewed: books
Review length: 2 pp
How to apply: letter
Include in application: professional degrees, institutional affiliation, areas of expertise, current research
• ADDITIONAL NOTES
Contributors are paid $200–$400 per article.

Liberian Studies Journal

Social sciences and humanities of Liberia
Affiliation: The Liberian Studies Association
Ed: D. Elwood Dunn
　　Political Science Department
　　The University of the South
　　Sewanee, TN 37375
Bk Rev Ed: Alfred B. Konuwa

Business and Social Sciences
Butte College
3536 Butte Campus Drive
Oroville, CA 95965-8399
2/yr, 150 pp; subs $30
Readership: academics, general public, government officials, international organizations
Indexed/Abstracted: ABC, MLA
• MANUSCRIPTS
Query: no; *Abstract:* no
Preferred length: 25 pp
Copies: 3
Notes: endnotes
Blind referee: yes
Charts, pictures, tables, graphs, maps
Foreign languages accepted: no
• REVIEWS
Seeking reviewers: yes
Unsolicited reviews accepted: yes
Materials reviewed: books
Review length: 2 pp max
How to apply: letter
Include in application: professional degrees, institutional affiliation, areas of expertise, published works, current research

Libraries and Culture

History of books, libraries, and collections in the context of cultural and social history; international topics, ancient to modern periods
Affiliation: University of Texas at Austin
Ed: Donald G. Davis, Jr.
   Graduate School of Library and Information Science
   University of Texas at Austin
   Austin, TX 78712-1276
Bk Rev Ed: same
4/yr, 125 pp; subs $24
Circ: 800
Readership: academics, librarians, graduate students
Indexed/Abstracted: ABC, AHCI, BRI, CCSB, IMB, MLA, SSCI, WAH

• MANUSCRIPTS
Query: no; *Abstract:* yes
Style guide: Chicago
Preferred length: varies
Copies: 3
Notes: endnotes
Blind referee: yes
Acceptance rate: 3/10
Time to consider ms: 3–6 mos
Charts, pictures, tables, graphs, maps
Foreign languages accepted: no
• REVIEWS
Seeking reviewers: yes
Unsolicited reviews accepted: no
Materials reviewed: books
Review length: 500–700 wds
How to apply: letter
Include in application: professional degrees, institutional affiliation, areas of expertise, published works, foreign languages, current research

The Library

Bibliography — historical, textual, analytical
Affiliation: The Bibliographical Society
Ed: Martin Davies
   Incunabula
   The British Library
   Great Russell Street
   London WC1B 3DG
   U.K.
Bk Rev Ed: Christine Ferdinand
   Maedalen College
   Oxford OX1 4AU
   U.K.
4/yr, 95 pp; subs $80 overseas
Circ: 1,800
Readership: academics, bibliophiles, those in the book trade
Indexed/Abstracted: ABC, AHCI, BRI, CCAH, IMB, MLA
• MANUSCRIPTS
Abstract: no
Style guide: MLA
Preferred length: 20,000 wds max

Copies: 2
Notes: endnotes
Blind referee: no
Acceptance rate: 3/5
Time to consider ms: 6 mos
Charts, pictures, tables, graphs
Foreign languages accepted: no
• REVIEWS
Seeking reviewers: no
Unsolicited reviews accepted: no
Materials reviewed: books
Review length: 600–2,000 wds
• ADDITIONAL NOTES
The Library does not deal with
  modern library practice. It concen-
  trates on the printed word, but also
  accepts articles on medieval and
  later manuscript studies.

Library History

History of libraries, mainly British
Affiliation: The Library Association
Ed: K. A. Manley
  Institute of Historical Research
  University of London
  Senate House
  Malet Street
  London WC1E 7HU
  U.K.
Bk Rev Ed: same
1/yr, 80 pp; subs £11
Circ: 1,300
Readership: academics, librarians
Indexed/Abstracted: ABC, BHI,
  IMB
• MANUSCRIPTS
Query: preferred; *Abstract:* no
Style guide: own
Preferred length: 5,000–8,000 wds
Copies: 1
Notes: endnotes
Blind referee: yes
Acceptance rate: 3/4
Time to consider ms: 1–2 mos
Pictures, tables
Foreign languages accepted: no
• REVIEWS
Seeking reviewers: no

Unsolicited reviews accepted: no
Materials reviewed: books
Review length: 750 wds

Lincoln Herald

Abraham Lincoln
Affiliation: Lincoln Memorial Univer-
  sity Press
Ed: Thomas Turner
  Lincoln Memorial University
  Press
  Abraham Lincoln Museum
  Harrogate, TN 37752
Bk Rev Ed: same
4/yr, 40 pp; subs $20
Readership: academics, general public
Indexed/Abstracted: ABC, WAH
• MANUSCRIPTS
Query: no; *Abstract:* no
Style guide: own
Preferred length: varies
Copies: 1
Pictures, other suitable illustrations
Foreign languages accepted: no
• REVIEWS
Unsolicited reviews accepted: yes
Materials reviewed: books, other
  media related to Abraham Lincoln

Lituanus

The Baltic States, particularly Lith-
  uania
Affiliation: Lituanus Foundation, Inc.
Eds: Violeta Kelertas, Antanas
  Klimas, Robert A. Vitas
  6621 South Troy Street
  Chicago, IL 60629
Bk Rev Ed: Danute S. Harmon
4/yr, 96 pp; subs $10
Circ: 4,000
Readership: academics, general public
Indexed/Abstracted: ABC, MLA,
  PAIS
• MANUSCRIPTS
Query: no; *Abstract:* no
Style guide: Chicago
Preferred length: 10–25 pp
Copies: 1

Notes: endnotes
Blind referee: no
Acceptance rate: 1/2
Time to consider ms: varies
Charts, pictures, tables, graphs, maps
Foreign languages accepted: no
• REVIEWS
Seeking reviewers: yes
Unsolicited reviews accepted: yes
Materials reviewed: books
Review length: 3–10 pp
How to apply: letter
Include in application: professional
  degrees, institutional affiliation,
  areas of expertise, published
  works, current research

Living Historian

Historical reenactment and interpre-
tation
Affiliation: Living History Associa-
tion, Inc.
Ed: Stephen J. DelSignore
  P.O. Box 578
  Wilmington, VT 05363
Bk Rev Ed: Barry Wells
4/yr, 18 pp; subs $15
Circ: 5,000
Readership: academics, general pub-
lic, historic sites, museums
• MANUSCRIPTS
Query: no; *Abstract:* no
Preferred length: open
Copies: 1
Notes: endnotes, footnotes, or bib-
liography
Blind referee: yes
Acceptance rate: 1/2
Time to consider ms: 2 mos
Charts, pictures, tables, graphs, maps
Foreign languages accepted: no
• REVIEWS
Seeking reviewers: no
Unsolicited reviews accepted: yes
Materials reviewed: books, films, any
  medium related to historical inter-
  pretation or research
Review length: 2 pp

How to apply: letter
Include in application: institutional
  affiliation, areas of expertise

The Local Historian

British local history
Affiliation: British Association for
  Local History
Ed: Margaret Bonney
  7 Carisbrooke Park
  Knighton
  Leicester LE2 3PQ
  U.K.
Bk Rev Ed: Peter Christie
  30 Lime Grove
  Bideford
  Devon
  U.K.
4/yr, 56 pp; subs £15
Circ: 2,000
Readership: academics, general pub-
lic, archivists, librarians, history
teachers, local historians
Indexed/Abstracted: ABC, BHI,
  IMB
• MANUSCRIPTS
Query: preferred; *Abstract:* no
Style guide: own
Preferred length: 6,000 wds max
Copies: 2
Notes: endnotes
Blind referee: yes
Acceptance rate: 1/2–3/5
Time to consider ms: 1–2 mos
Charts, pictures, tables, graphs, maps,
  reproductions of original documents
Foreign languages accepted: no
• REVIEWS
Seeking reviewers: yes
Unsolicited reviews accepted: not
  usually
Materials reviewed: books
Review length: varies
How to apply: letter
Include in application: professional
  degrees, institutional affiliation,
  areas of expertise, published
  works, current research

Local History

History of Saratoga County, New
  York
Affiliation: Brookside Saratoga
  County History Center
Ed: Executive Director
    6 Charlton Street
    Bailston Spa, NY 12020
4/yr, 8 pp; subs $15
Circ: 750
Readership: general public
• MANUSCRIPTS
Query: preferred; *Abstract:* preferred
Preferred length: 8,500 wds
Copies: 1
Notes: footnotes
Blind referee: no
Time to consider ms: 3 wks
Charts, pictures, tables, graphs, maps
Foreign languages accepted: no

Locus: An Historical Journal of Regional Perspectives on National Topics

Topics that are locality specific but
  provide perspectives on broader na-
  tional issues
Affiliation: University of North Texas
Eds: Randolph B. Campbell and
  Donald E. Chipman
    Department of History
    Box 13735 NT Station
    University of North Texas
    Denton, TX 76203
Bk Rev Ed: William H. Wilson
2/yr, 120 pp; subs $8
Circ: 250
Readership: academics, general public
Indexed/Abstracted: ABC
• MANUSCRIPTS
Query: no; *Abstract:* no
Style guide: Chicago
Preferred length: 25–30 pp
Copies: 2
Notes: footnotes
Blind referee: yes
Acceptance rate: 1/3
Time to consider ms: 6 wks

Charts, pictures, tables, graphs, maps
Foreign languages accepted: no
• REVIEWS
Seeking reviewers: yes
Unsolicited reviews accepted: no
Materials reviewed: books
Review length: 400 wds
How to apply: letter
Include in application: professional
  degrees, institutional affiliation,
  areas of expertise, published
  works, current research
• ADDITIONAL NOTES
Locus welcomes article manuscripts
  on localities in the United States,
  Western Europe, Canada, and
  Latin America. The intent is to
  provide subscribers with articles
  and book reviews that illustrate
  how local history supplies answers
  to major historical questions.

Long Island Forum

Long Island studies—history, politics,
  society, natural history
Ed: Richard F. Welch
    P.O. Box 277
    Woodbury, NY 11797
Bk Rev Ed: same
4/yr, 44 pp; subs $20 (2 yr)
Circ: 1,800
Readership: academics, general public
• MANUSCRIPTS
Query: no; *Abstract:* no
Preferred length: 500–1,500 wds
Copies: 2
Notes: endnotes
Blind referee: no
Acceptance rate: 3/5
Time to consider ms: 1 mo
Charts, pictures, tables, graphs, maps
Foreign languages accepted: no
• REVIEWS
Seeking reviewers: yes
Unsolicited reviews accepted: yes
Materials reviewed: books, exhibi-
  tions
Review length: 100–200 wds

How to apply: letter
Include in application: professional
   degrees, institutional affiliation,
   areas of expertise, published
   works, current research

Long Island Historical Journal

All aspects of Long Island history
Affiliation: SUNY at Stony Brook
Ed: Roger Wunderlich
   Department of History
   SUNY at Stony Brook
   Stony Brook, NY 11794-4348
Bk Rev Ed: Thomas Beal
2/yr, 150 pp; subs $15
Circ: 1,000
Readership: academics, general public
Indexed/Abstracted: ABC, WAH
• MANUSCRIPTS
Query: no; *Abstract:* no
Style guide: Chicago
Preferred length: 20–30 pp
Copies: 2 and on computer disk
Notes: endnotes
Blind referee: yes
Acceptance rate: 1/2
Time to consider ms: 3 mos
Pictures, tables
Foreign languages accepted: no
• REVIEWS
Seeking reviewers: no
Unsolicited reviews accepted: yes
Materials reviewed: books, films
Review length: 1,000 wds
How to apply: letter
Include in application: areas of
   expertise

Louisiana History

Louisiana (colonial and state) history
Affiliation: The Louisiana Historical
   Association; University of South-
   western Louisiana
Ed: Glenn R. Conrad
   P.O. Box 40831
   University of Southwestern
   Louisiana
   Lafayette, LA 70504-0831

Bk Rev Ed: same
4/yr, 112 pp; subs $15
Circ: 1,200
Readership: academics, general public
Indexed/Abstracted: ABC, WAH
• MANUSCRIPTS
Query: no; *Abstract:* no
Style guide: Chicago
Preferred length: 30–35 pp max
Copies: 2
Notes: endnotes
Blind referee: yes
Acceptance rate: 17/20
Time to consider ms: varies
Charts, pictures, tables, graphs, maps
Foreign languages accepted: no
• REVIEWS
Seeking reviewers: yes
Unsolicited reviews accepted: no
Materials reviewed: books
Review length: 750–1,000 wds
How to apply: letter
Include in application: professional
   degrees, institutional affiliation,
   areas of expertise, published works

The Loyalist Gazette

United Empire Loyalists' history and
   genealogy
Affiliation: The United Empire Loyal-
   ists' Association
Ed: David Dorward
   c/o The United Empire Loyalists'
      Association
   50 Baldwin Street
   Toronto, ON M5T 1L4
   CANADA
Bk Rev Ed: same
2/yr, 36 pp; subs $12.50
Circ: 2,500
Readership: academics, general pub-
   lic, genealogists
• MANUSCRIPTS
Query: yes
Preferred length: varies
Copies: 2
Notes: none
Blind referee: no

Charts, pictures
Foreign languages accepted: no
• REVIEWS
Seeking reviewers: no
Unsolicited reviews accepted: no
Materials reviewed: books
Include in application: areas of expertise

Luso-Brazilian Review

Portuguese, Brazilian and Lusophone
    African culture with a special emphasis on the social sciences, history and literature
Affiliation: University of Wisconsin
    Press
Ed: Robert M. Levine
    Department of History
    Box 248107
    University of Miami
    Coral Gables, FL 33124
Bk Rev Ed: same
2/yr, 140 pp; subs $27
Circ: 600
Readership: academics
Indexed/Abstracted: ABC, MLA
• MANUSCRIPTS
Query: no; *Abstract:* no
Style guide: Chicago
Preferred length: 15–30 pp
Notes: endnotes
Blind referee: no
Acceptance rate: 1/2
Time to consider ms: 3–4 mos
Charts, pictures, tables, graphs,
    maps
Foreign languages accepted: Portuguese, Spanish
• REVIEWS
Seeking reviewers: yes
Unsolicited reviews accepted: yes
Materials reviewed: books, videos
Review length: 500–750 wds
How to apply: letter
Include in application: professional
    degrees, institutional affiliation,
    areas of expertise, foreign languages

MHQ: The Quarterly Journal of Military History

Military history
Ed: Robert Cowley
    29 W. 38th Street
    New York, NY 10018
Bk Rev Ed: same
4/yr, 112 pp; subs $60
Circ: 25,000
Readership: academics, general public
Indexed/Abstracted: ABC, WAH
• MANUSCRIPTS
Query: yes; *Abstract:* no
Preferred length: 4,000 wds
Copies: 1
Notes: endnotes
Blind referee: no
Acceptance rate: very few
Pictures, maps
Foreign languages accepted: no
• REVIEWS
Seeking reviewers: no
Unsolicited reviews accepted: no
Materials reviewed: books

Magazine of Albermarle County History

Events and individuals in or related
    to Albemarle County
Affiliation: Albemarle County Historical Society
Ed: Dorothy Twohig
    c/o Albemarle County Historical
        Society
    220 Court Square
    Charlottesville, VA 22902
1/yr, 100 pp; subs $25
Circ: 850
Readership: academics, general public
Indexed/Abstracted: ABC
• MANUSCRIPTS
Query: no; *Abstract:* no
Preferred length: open
Copies: 8
Notes: endnotes
Blind referee: no
Acceptance rate: 3/4
Time to consider ms: 2 mos

Charts, pictures, tables, graphs, maps
Foreign languages accepted: no

The Maghreb Review

All aspects of North African and
Islamic studies from 600 A.D. to
the present
Ed: Mohamed Ben Madani
45 Burton Street
London WC1H 9AL
U.K.
Bk Rev Ed: same
4/yr, 144 pp; subs £130
Circ: 9,000
Readership: academics, North
African and Islamic specialists
Indexed/Abstracted: ABC
• MANUSCRIPTS
Query: yes; *Abstract:* yes
Style guide: own
Preferred length: 25–40 pp
Copies: 2
Notes: endnotes
Blind referee: yes
Time to consider ms: 30–40 days
Charts, pictures, tables, graphs, maps
Foreign languages accepted: French
• REVIEWS
Seeking reviewers: no
Unsolicited reviews accepted: yes
Materials reviewed: books
Review length: 4–25 pp
How to apply: letter
Include in application: professional
degrees, institutional affiliation,
published works, foreign lan-
guages, current research

Maine Historical Society Quarterly

Maine history and prehistory
Ed: Richard W. Judd
170 Stevens Hall
University of Maine
Orono, ME 04474
Bk Rev Ed: Stanley R. Howe
Bethel Historical Society
Bethel, ME 04217

4/yr, 60 pp
Circ: 2,000
Readership: academics, general public
Indexed/Abstracted: ABC, WAH
• MANUSCRIPTS
Query: no; *Abstract:* no
Style guide: Chicago
Preferred length: 25–30 pp
Copies: 1
Notes: endnotes
Blind referee: yes
Acceptance rate: 1/4
Time to consider ms: 6 wks
Charts, pictures, tables, graphs, maps
Foreign languages accepted: no
• REVIEWS
Seeking reviewers: yes
Unsolicited reviews accepted: yes
Materials reviewed: books
Review length: 600–800 wds
How to apply: letter
Include in application: professional
degrees, institutional affiliation,
areas of expertise

Manuscripta

Textual studies and analyses based on
original manuscript research;
preferred periods range generally
from classical antiquity to the early
modern period
Affiliation: St. Louis University
Ed: Charles J. Ermatinger
3650 Lindell Boulevard
St. Louis University
St. Louis, MO 63108
Bk Rev Ed: same
3/yr, 85 pp; subs $18
Circ: 900
Readership: academics
Indexed/Abstracted: ABC, AHCI,
AHI, CCAH, IMB, MLA
• MANUSCRIPTS
Query: no; *Abstract:* no
Style guide: Chicago or MLA
Preferred length: 20 pp
Copies: 1
Notes: endnotes

Blind referee: no
Acceptance rate: 9/10
Time to consider ms: 6 mos
Charts, pictures, tables
Foreign languages accepted: Latin,
French, German, Italian, Spanish,
Portuguese, Old English
• REVIEWS
Seeking reviewers: yes
Unsolicited reviews accepted: yes
Materials reviewed: books
Review length: 1,000 wds
How to apply: letter
Include in application: professional
degrees, institutional affiliation

The Mariner's Mirror: The Journal of the Society for Nautical Research

All aspects of maritime research
Affiliation: Society for Nautical Re-
search; The National Maritime
Museum
Ed: Michael Duffy
Department of History
University of Exeter
Queen's Building
The Queen's Drive
Exeter EX4 4QH
U.K.
Bk Rev Ed: David J. Starkey
Centre for Maritime Historical
Studies
University of Exeter
Amory Building
Rennes Drive
Exeter EX4 4PJ
U.K.
4/yr, 126 pp; subs £20
Circ: 2,200
Readership: academics, society mem-
bers, others interested in maritime
history
Indexed/Abstracted: ABC, AHCI,
BHI, CCAH, IMB, WAH
• MANUSCRIPTS
Query: no; *Abstract:* no
Style guide: own

Preferred length: 8,000 wds max
Copies: 1
Notes: endnotes
Blind referee: yes
Acceptance rate: 3/5
Time to consider ms: 3-6 mos
Charts, pictures, tables, graphs, maps
Foreign languages accepted: no
• REVIEWS
Seeking reviewers: yes
Unsolicited reviews accepted: no
Materials reviewed: books
Review length: 500 wds
How to apply: letter
Include in application: professional
degrees, institutional affiliation,
areas of expertise, published works,
foreign languages, current research

The Maryland Historian

History (contributions by graduate
students and faculty from all insti-
tutions)
Affiliation: University of Maryland
Ed: John Martin
Department of History
Francis Scott Hall
University of Maryland
College Park, MD 20742
Bk Rev Ed: varies; address to Bk Rev
Ed
2/yr, 80 pp; subs $10
Circ: 350-500
Readership: academics, general public
Indexed/Abstracted: ABC, WAH
• MANUSCRIPTS
Query: preferred; *Abstract:* no
Style guide: Chicago
Preferred length: 25-35 pp
Copies: 4
Notes: endnotes
Blind referee: yes
Acceptance rate: 1/5
Time to consider ms: 4-6 mos
Charts, pictures, tables, graphs, maps
Foreign languages accepted: no
• REVIEWS
Seeking reviewers: yes

Unsolicited reviews accepted: no
Materials reviewed: books
Review length: 750–1,000 wds
How to apply: letter
Include in application: professional
  degrees, institutional affiliation,
  areas of expertise, current research

Maryland Historical Magazine

Maryland/Chesapeake history and
  culture
Affiliation: Maryland Historical So-
  ciety
Ed: Robert J. Brugger
  201 W. Monument Street
  Baltimore, MD 21201
Bk Rev Ed: same
4/yr, 128 pp; subs $35
Circ: 4,500
Readership: academics, general public
Indexed/Abstracted: ABC, WAH
• MANUSCRIPTS
Query: preferred; *Abstract:* preferred
Style guide: Chicago
Preferred length: 25–30 pp
Copies: 2
Notes: endnotes
Blind referee: yes
Acceptance rate: 1/4
Time to consider ms: 6–8 wks
Charts, pictures, tables, graphs, maps
Foreign languages accepted: no
• REVIEWS
Seeking reviewers: yes
Unsolicited reviews accepted: no
Materials reviewed: books, CDs
Review length: 500–600 wds
How to apply: letter
Include in application: professional
  degrees, institutional affiliation,
  areas of expertise, published
  works, current research

Material Culture

Documentation and explanation of
  the material culture landscape
Affiliation: Pioneer America Society
Ed: William D. Walters, Jr.

Department of Geography
Illinois State University
Normal, IL 61701
Bk Rev Ed: Megan Ferrell
  University of Southwestern Loui-
  siana
  R.R. 4, Box 500
  Breaux Bridge, LA 70517
3/yr, 70 pp; subs $20
Circ: 450
Readership: academics, general public
Indexed/Abstracted: ABC, MLA
• MANUSCRIPTS
Query: no; *Abstract:* no
Style guide: own
Preferred length: open
Copies: 3
Notes: endnotes
Blind referee: yes
Time to consider ms: 1–2 mos
Charts, pictures, tables, graphs, maps
Foreign languages accepted: no
• REVIEWS
Seeking reviewers: no
Unsolicited reviews accepted: no
Materials reviewed: books
• ADDITIONAL NOTES
Material Culture deals with the
  material remains of the North
  American past. Authors come from
  a wide range of disciplines includ-
  ing anthropology, architecture,
  geography, history and historic
  preservation. Many articles relate
  to the common structures and artifacts of North American history,
  but the journal also welcomes theoretical articles on material culture
  and articles on related topics.

Material History Review

Material history, material culture
  studies
Affiliation: National Museum of
  Science and Technology
Ed: Geoffrey Rider
  National Museum of Science and
  Technology

P.O. Box 9724, Ottawa Terminal
Ottawa, ON K1G 5A3
CANADA
Bk Rev Ed: Garth Wilson
2/yr, 91 pp; subs $15
Readership: academics, general public, museum curators
Indexed/Abstracted: ABC
• MANUSCRIPTS
Query: preferred; *Abstract:* yes
Style guide: Chicago
Preferred length: 10–30 pp
Copies: 1
Notes: endnotes
Blind referee: yes
Time to consider ms: 4 wks
Charts, pictures, tables, graphs, maps
Foreign languages accepted: French
• REVIEWS
Seeking reviewers: yes
Unsolicited reviews accepted: yes
Materials reviewed: books, films, conferences, educational programs, exhibits
Review length: 5 pp
How to apply: letter
Include in application: professional degrees, institutional affiliation, areas of expertise
• ADDITIONAL NOTES
MHR's primary focus is Canada, but frequently presents material reflecting the latest scholarship in the field from the U.S. and Europe.

Media History Digest

Media history
Affiliation: Editor and Publisher Magazine
Ed: Hiley H. Ward
c/o Editor and Publisher
11 W. 19th Street
New York, NY 10011
Bk Rev Ed: same
2/yr, 64 pp; subs $7.50
Circ: 2,000
Readership: academics, general public, media professionals

• MANUSCRIPTS
Query: preferred; *Abstract:* no
Preferred length: 2,500 wds
Copies: 1
Notes: endnotes or footnotes
Blind referee: no
Time to consider ms: 3 mos
Charts, pictures, maps
Foreign languages accepted: no
• REVIEWS
Seeking reviewers: no
Unsolicited reviews accepted: yes

Mediaeval Studies

All areas of medieval studies, especially philosophy, theology, history, literature and language, and paleography
Affiliation: Pontifical Institute of Mediaeval Studies
Ed: Jonathon Black
Pontifical Institute of Mediaeval Studies
59 Queen's Park Crescent East
Toronto, ON M5S 2C4
CANADA
1/yr, 350 pp; subs $55
Circ: 1,250
Readership: academics
Indexed/Abstracted: AHCI, CCAH, MLA
• MANUSCRIPTS
Query: no; *Abstract:* no
Style guide: Chicago
Preferred length: 15–75 pp
Copies: 3
Notes: endnotes
Blind referee: yes
Acceptance rate: 1/5
Time to consider ms: 5 mos
Charts, pictures, tables, graphs
Foreign languages accepted: French, others may be considered

Medical History

All aspects of the history of medicine
Affiliation: Wellcome Institute for the History of Medicine

Eds: W. F. Bynum and Vivian Nutton
   Wellcome Institute for the History of Medicine
   183 Euston Road
   London NW1 2BN
   U.K.
Bk Rev Ed: same
4/yr, 120 pp; subs £14
Circ: 1,000
Readership: academics, physicians
Indexed/Abstracted: ABC, AHCI, SSCI
● MANUSCRIPTS
Query: no; *Abstract:* no
Preferred length: 10,000 wds
Copies: 2
Notes: endnotes
Blind referee: no
Acceptance rate: 9/20
Time to consider ms: 1–3 mos
Charts, pictures, tables, graphs, maps
Foreign languages accepted: no
● REVIEWS
Seeking reviewers: yes
Unsolicited reviews accepted: no
Materials reviewed: books
Review length: 500 wds
How to apply: letter
Include in application: professional degrees, institutional affiliation, areas of expertise, published works, foreign languages, current research

Medieval Prosopography

Collective biography
Affiliation: Western Michigan University
Ed: Candace Porath
   Medieval Institute Publications
   Western Michigan University
   Kalamazoo, MI 49008-3851
2/yr, 130 pp; subs $20
Circ: 350
Readership: academics
Indexed/Abstracted: IMB
● MANUSCRIPTS
Query: preferred; *Abstract:* no

Style guide: modified Chicago
Preferred length: 25–30 pp
Copies: 2
Notes: endnotes
Blind referee: no

Medievalia et Humanistica: Studies in Medieval and Renaissance Culture

Medieval and Renaissance studies
Affiliation: University of North Texas
Ed: Paul M. Clogan
   P.O. Box 13348
   University of North Texas
   Denton, TX 76203
Bk Rev Ed: same
1/yr, 300 pp; subs $37.50
Circ: 2,000
Readership: academics
Indexed/Abstracted: IMB, MLA
● MANUSCRIPTS
Query: no; *Abstract:* no
Style guide: Chicago
Preferred length: 2,500–9,000 wds
Copies: 3
Notes: endnotes
Blind referee: yes
Time to consider ms: 2–3 mos
Charts, pictures, tables, graphs, maps
Foreign languages accepted: no
● REVIEWS
Seeking reviewers: no
Unsolicited reviews accepted: no
Materials reviewed: books
How to apply: letter
Include in application: professional degrees, institutional affiliation, areas of expertise, published works, foreign languages, current research
● ADDITIONAL NOTES
Articles should: (1) make a marked contribution to knowledge or understanding; or (2) employ an interdisciplinary approach of importance to the understanding of the subject; or (3) treat a broad theme or topic; or (4) discuss new direc-

tions in humanistic scholarship; or (5) review major areas of current concern within particular fields.

Mennonite Historical Bulletin

Anabaptist and Mennonite history
Affiliation: Historical Committee of the Mennonite Church
Ed: Levi Miller
    1700 South Main Street
    Goshen, IN 46526
Bk Rev Ed: Steven Reschly
4/yr, 16 pp; subs $20
Circ: 500
Readership: academics, general public
● MANUSCRIPTS
Query: yes; *Abstract:* no
Style guide: Chicago
Preferred length: 3,000 wds
Copies: 1
Notes: endnotes
Blind referee: no
Acceptance rate: 1/4
Time to consider ms: 1 mo
All illustrations accepted
Foreign languages accepted: no
● REVIEWS
Seeking reviewers: no
Unsolicited reviews accepted: seldom
Materials reviewed: books, films

Mennonite Quarterly Review

Anabaptist, Radical Reformation, Mennonite, Amish, Hutterite history, sociology, religious thought, life affairs
Affiliation: Goshen College and Associated Mennonite Biblical Seminaries
Ed: John D. Roth
    Goshen College
    Goshen, IN 46526
Bk Rev Ed: Marlin Jeschke
4/yr, 120 pp; subs $20
Circ: 1,000
Readership: academics, general public
Indexed/Abstracted: ABC, WAH

● MANUSCRIPTS
Query: no; *Abstract:* no
Style guide: Chicago
Preferred length: 25–30 pp
Copies: 2
Notes: endnotes
Blind referee: yes
Acceptance rate: 1/2–3/5
Time to consider ms: 2–3 mos
Foreign languages accepted: (must be translated) German, Dutch, Latin, French
● REVIEWS
Seeking reviewers: yes
Unsolicited reviews accepted: no
Materials reviewed: books
Review length: 600–1,000 wds
How to apply: letter
Include in application: professional degrees, institutional affiliation, areas of expertise, published works, foreign languages

Methodist History

History of the United Methodist Church, its antecedents, and other Methodist bodies
Affiliation: United Methodist Church
Ed: Charles Yrigoyen, Jr.
    P.O. Box 127
    Madison, NJ 07940
Bk Rev Ed: same
4/yr, 64 pp; subs $12
Circ: 1,200
Readership: academics, general public
Indexed/Abstracted: ABC, WAH
● MANUSCRIPTS
Query: no; *Abstract:* no
Style guide: Turabian
Preferred length: 15–20 pp
Copies: 1
Notes: footnotes
Blind referee: yes
Acceptance rate: 3/4
Time to consider ms: 3–4 mos
Charts, pictures, tables, graphs, maps
Foreign languages accepted: no

- REVIEWS
Seeking reviewers: no
Unsolicited reviews accepted: no
Materials reviewed: books
Review length: 500 wds
How to apply: letter
Include in application: professional
degrees, institutional affiliation,
areas of expertise

Mexican Studies/
Estudios Mexicanos

Study of Mexico and its relation to
the United States
Affiliation: University of California,
Irvine
Ed: Jaime E. Rodriguez
University of California, Irvine
340 Humanities Office Building
Irvine, CA 92717
Bk Rev Ed: same
2/yr, 214 pp; subs $19
Circ: 1,225
Readership: academics
Indexed/Abstracted: ABC
- MANUSCRIPTS
Query: no; *Abstract:* yes
Style guide: Chicago
Preferred length: open
Copies: 2
Notes: endnotes or footnotes
Blind referee: yes
Acceptance rate: 1/5
Time to consider ms: 2–3 mos
Charts, pictures, tables, graphs, maps
Foreign languages accepted: Spanish
- REVIEWS
Seeking reviewers: yes
Unsolicited reviews accepted: yes
Materials reviewed: books
Review length: 15–20 pp
How to apply: letter
Include in application: professional
degrees, institutional affiliation,
areas of expertise, current research

Michigan Historical Review

Michigan and Great Lakes regional
history

Affiliation: Clarke Historical Library,
Central Michigan University, and
Historical Society of Michigan
Ed: William T. Bulger
Clarke Historical Library
Central Michigan University
Mount Pleasant, MI 48859
Bk Rev Ed: Dennis Thavenet
2/yr, 100 pp; subs $12.50
Circ: 5,000
Readership: academics, general public
Indexed/Abstracted: ABC, AHCI,
CCAH, WAH
- MANUSCRIPTS
Query: yes; *Abstract:* yes
Style guide: Chicago
Preferred length: 6,000 wds max
Copies: 3
Notes: endnotes
Blind referee: yes
Acceptance rate: 1/4
Time to consider ms: 3 mos
Charts, pictures, tables, graphs, maps
Foreign languages accepted: no
- REVIEWS
Seeking reviewers: yes
Unsolicited reviews accepted: yes
Materials reviewed: books
Review length: 500 wds
How to apply: letter
Include in application: professional
degrees, institutional affiliation,
areas of expertise, current research

Mid-America

United States, including the colonial
period
Affiliation: Loyola University,
Chicago
Ed: William J. Galush
6525 N. Sheridan Road
Chicago, IL 60626
Bk Rev Ed: same
3/yr, 90 pp; subs $9
Circ: 600
Readership: academics, general public
Indexed/Abstracted: ABC, AHCI,
BRI, CCAH, WAH

● MANUSCRIPTS
Query: no; *Abstract:* no
Style guide: Chicago
Preferred length: 40 pp max
Copies: 1
Notes: endnotes
Blind referee: yes
Acceptance rate: 1/3
Time to consider ms: 90 days
Charts, tables, graphs, maps
Foreign languages accepted: no
● REVIEWS
Seeking reviewers: yes
Unsolicited reviews accepted: yes
Materials reviewed: books
Review length: 10–20 pp
How to apply: letter
Include in application: vita
● ADDITIONAL NOTES
The reviews should discuss the state
of the topic in the form of an his-
toriographical and bibliographical
essay. Several works should be dis-
cussed and suggestions for further
research or perspectives might be
made.

Middle East Studies Association Bulletin

All fields of Middle East studies from
7th century C.E. to the present
Affiliation: Middle East Studies
Association
Ed: Jon W. Anderson
200 Life Cycle Institute
Catholic University of America
Washington, DC 20064
Bk Rev Ed: same
2/yr, 160 pp; subs membership
Circ: 4,000
Readership: academics, government,
researchers
Indexed/Abstracted: ABC
● MANUSCRIPTS
Query: preferred; *Abstract:* no
Style guide: MLA or Chicago
Preferred length: 10 pp
Copies: 2

Notes: footnotes
Blind referee: yes
Time to consider ms: 3 mos
Charts, pictures, tables, graphs, maps
Foreign languages accepted: no
● REVIEWS
Seeking reviewers: yes
Unsolicited reviews accepted: no
Materials reviewed: books, films, ex-
hibitions, recordings
Review length: 500 wds
How to apply: letter
Include in application: professional
degrees, areas of expertise, pub-
lished works, foreign languages,
current research

Middle Eastern Studies

Middle East Studies
Ed: Elie Kedourie
London School of Economics
Houghton Street
Aldwych
London WC2 2AE
U.K.
Bk Rev Ed: same
4/yr; subs £38
Readership: academics
Indexed/Abstracted: ABC, AHCI,
BHI, CCSB, SSCI, SSI
● MANUSCRIPTS
Query: no; *Abstract:* no
Style guide: own
Preferred length: varies
Copies: 1
Notes: endnotes
Tables, graphs, other suitable illustra-
tions
● REVIEWS
Materials reviewed: books

Midwest Quarterly

Contemporary issues or cutting-edge
scholarship addressed to a non-specialist audience across a campus-
wide spectrum of disciplines
Affiliation: Pittsburg State University
Ed: James B. M. Schick

c/o Midwest Quarterly
Pittsburg State University
Pittsburg, KS 66762
Bk Rev Ed: Dudley T. Cornish
Department of History
Pittsburg State University
Pittsburg, KS 66762
4/yr, 100 pp; subs $10
Circ: 800
Readership: academics
Indexed/Abstracted: ABC, AHCI,
CCAH, HI, MLA, WAH
• MANUSCRIPTS
Query: no; *Abstract:* no
Style guide: any
Preferred length: 17 pp max
Copies: 2
Notes: sources for quotes
Blind referee: yes
Acceptance rate: 3/5
Time to consider ms: 4–6 mos
Charts, tables
Foreign languages accepted: no
• REVIEWS
Seeking reviewers: yes
Unsolicited reviews accepted: yes
Materials reviewed: books
Review length: 2 pp
How to apply: letter
Include in application: professional
degrees, institutional affiliation,
areas of expertise, published
works, current research

The Midwest Review

History and culture of Midwest/
Great Plains
Affiliation: Wayne State College
Ed: Kent Blaser
History Department
Wayne State College
Wayne, NE 68787
Bk Rev Ed: same
1/yr, 80 pp
Circ: 800–900
Readership: academics
Indexed/Abstracted: ABC, WAH
• MANUSCRIPTS
Query: no; *Abstract:* no

Preferred length: 15–30 pp
Copies: 3
Notes: endnotes
Blind referee: yes
Acceptance rate: 1/2–3/4
Time to consider ms: 4–8 wks
Charts, pictures, tables, graphs, maps
Foreign languages accepted: no
• REVIEWS
Seeking reviewers: no
Unsolicited reviews accepted: no
Review length: 1,500–2,000 wds
How to apply: letter
Include in application: professional
degrees, institutional affiliation,
areas of expertise, published
works, current research

Military Historical Society Bulletin

All periods of British and Common-
wealth military history
Affiliation: Military Historical Society
Ed: Lt. Col. R. J. Wyatt
33 Sturges Road
Wokingham
Berks RG11 2HG
U.K.
Bk Rev Ed: same
4/yr, 56 pp; subs £10
Circ: 1,400
Readership: academics, society
members, military history enthu-
siasts
• MANUSCRIPTS
Query: yes; *Abstract:* no
Preferred length: 500–5,000 wds
Copies: 2
Notes: endnotes or footnotes
Blind referee: no
Acceptance rate: 9/10
Time to consider ms: 1 wk
Charts, pictures, tables, graphs,
maps, any others
Foreign languages accepted: no
• REVIEWS
Seeking reviewers: no
Unsolicited reviews accepted: yes

Materials reviewed: books, videos, journals
Review length: 200–500 wds
How to apply: letter
Include in application: areas of expertise

Military History

All aspects of military history
Affiliation: Empire Press
Ed: C. Brian Kelly
602 King Street
Suite 300
Leesburg, VA 22075
Bk Rev Ed: varies
6/yr, 88 pp; subs $19.95
Circ: 193,000
Readership: academics, general public
Indexed/Abstracted: ABC
• MANUSCRIPTS
Query: yes; *Abstract:* no
Style guide: own
Copies: 1
Notes: endnotes
Blind referee: no
Acceptance rate: 1/4
Time to consider ms: 4–6 mos
Charts, pictures, tables, graphs, maps
Foreign languages accepted: no
• REVIEWS
Seeking reviewers: no
Unsolicited reviews accepted: no
Materials reviewed: books, films
How to apply: letter
Include in application: institutional affiliation, areas of expertise

Military History of the West

Military history of the United States west of the Mississippi River; all topics from exploration to present
Affiliation: University of North Texas
Ed: Richard Lowe
Department of History
University of North Texas
Denton, TX 76203
Bk Rev Ed: G. L. Seligmann
2/yr, 128 pp; subs $8

Circ: 500–600
Readership: academics, general public
Indexed/Abstracted: ABC, WAH
• MANUSCRIPTS
Query: no; *Abstract:* no
Style guide: modified Chicago
Preferred length: 30–40 pp
Copies: 3
Notes: endnotes
Blind referee: yes
Acceptance rate: 1/3
Time to consider ms: 2 mos max
Charts, pictures, tables, graphs, maps
Foreign languages accepted: no
• REVIEWS
Seeking reviewers: yes
Unsolicited reviews accepted: no
Materials reviewed: books
Review length: 400–500 wds
How to apply: letter
Include in application: professional degrees, institutional affiliation, areas of expertise, published works

Military Images

U.S. military photography, 1839–1900
Ed: Harry Roach
RD 1, Box 99A
Lesoine Drive
Henryville, PA 18332
Bk Rev Ed: same
6/yr, 36 pp; subs $20
Circ: 2,300
Readership: academics, general public, collectors
Indexed/Abstracted: ABC
• MANUSCRIPTS
Query: yes; *Abstract:* no
Copies: 1
Notes: none
Blind referee: no
Photos
Foreign languages accepted: no
• REVIEWS
Seeking reviewers: no
Unsolicited reviews accepted: occasionally
Materials reviewed: books, films

Milwaukee History

Milwaukee County history
Affiliation: Milwaukee County Historical Society
Ed: Ralph M. Aderman
    Milwaukee County Historical Society
    910 N. Old World 3rd Street
    Milwaukee, WI 53203
4/yr, 36 pp; subs $12
Circ: 1,300
Readership: academics, general public
Indexed/Abstracted: ABC, WAH
• MANUSCRIPTS
Query: no; *Abstract:* no
Preferred length: 20–30 pp
Copies: 2
Notes: endnotes or footnotes
Blind referee: no
Acceptance rate: majority
Time to consider ms: 3 mos
Charts, pictures, tables, graphs, maps
Foreign languages accepted: no

Minnesota History

Minnesota state, territorial, and regional history
Affiliation: Minnesota Historical Society
Ed: Anne R. Kaplan
    Minnesota Historical Society
    160 John Ireland Boulevard
    St. Paul, MN 55102
Bk Rev Ed: same
4/yr, 40 pp; subs $20
Circ: 8,000
Readership: academics, general public
Indexed/Abstracted: ABC, WAH
• MANUSCRIPTS
Query: preferred; *Abstract:* no
Style guide: Chicago
Preferred length: 25 pp
Copies: 2
Notes: endnotes
Blind referee: yes
Acceptance rate: 2/5
Time to consider ms: 2–3 mos

Charts, pictures, tables, graphs, maps
Foreign languages accepted: no
• REVIEWS
Seeking reviewers: yes
Unsolicited reviews accepted: no
Materials reviewed: books
Review length: 500–700 wds
How to apply: letter
Include in application: professional degrees, institutional affiliation, areas of expertise, published works, current research

Mississippi Quarterly: The Journal of Southern Culture

Humanities and social sciences dealing with the South and Southerners, past and present
Affiliation: Mississippi State University
Ed: Robert L. Phillips, Jr.
    P.O. Box 5272
    Mississippi State, MS 39762
Bk Rev Ed: same
4/yr, 115 pp; subs $12
Circ: 850
Readership: academics
Indexed/Abstracted: ABC, AHCI, CCAH, HI, MLA, WAH
• MANUSCRIPTS
Query: no; *Abstract:* no
Style guide: MLA
Preferred length: 4,000
Copies: 1
Notes: endnotes
Blind referee: yes
Acceptance rate: 1/7
Time to consider ms: 2–4 mos
Illustrations rarely accepted
Foreign languages accepted: no
• REVIEWS
Seeking reviewers: no
Unsolicited reviews accepted: no
Materials reviewed: books
Review length: 800–3,000 wds
How to apply: letter
Include in application: areas of expertise

Missouri Historical Review

History of Missouri and other fields
of American history relevant to the
history of Missouri or the West
Affiliation: State Historical Society of
Missouri
Ed: James W. Goodrich
State Historical Society of Missouri
1020 Lowry
Columbia, MO 65201
Bk Rev Ed: same
4/yr, 128 pp; subs $10
Circ: 9,000
Readership: academics, general public
Indexed/Abstracted: ABC, WAH
• MANUSCRIPTS
Query: no; *Abstract:* no
Style guide: Chicago
Preferred length: 7,500 wds max
Copies: 2
Notes: endnotes
Blind referee: no
Acceptance rate: 1/3
Time to consider ms: 1–3 mos
Pictures, maps
Foreign languages accepted: no
• REVIEWS
Seeking reviewers: yes
Unsolicited reviews accepted: no
Materials reviewed: books
Review length: 500 wds
How to apply: letter
Include in application: professional
degrees, institutional affiliation,
areas of expertise, published
works, current research

Modern and Contemporary France

French area studies
Affiliation: Portsmouth Polytechnic
Eds: B. Jenkins and T. Chafer
School of Languages and Area
Studies
Portsmouth Polytechnic
Portsmouth PO1 2BU
U.K.

Bk Rev Ed: same
4/yr, 100 pp; subs $40 U.S.
Circ: 400
Readership: academics, secondary
school and further education
teachers
Indexed/Abstracted: ABC
• MANUSCRIPTS
Query: preferred; *Abstract:* no
Style guide: yes
Preferred length: 5,000 wds
Copies: 2
Notes: endnotes
Blind referee: yes
• REVIEWS
Materials reviewed: books

Modern Asian Studies

History, geography, and social
sciences related to modern Asia
Affiliation: Cambridge University
Press
Ed: Gordon Johnson
Selwyn College
Cambridge CB3 9DQ
U.K.
Bk Rev Ed: same
4/yr, 224 pp
Circ: 1,500
Readership: academics
Indexed/Abstracted: ABC, AHCI,
CCSB, SSCI, SSI
• MANUSCRIPTS
Query: no; *Abstract:* no
Style guide: any
Preferred length: 8,000 wds
Copies: 2
Notes: endnotes or footnotes
Blind referee: yes
Time to consider ms: 3–6 mos
Charts, tables, graphs, maps
Foreign languages accepted: no
• REVIEWS
Seeking reviewers: no
Unsolicited reviews accepted: no
Materials reviewed: books
Review length: 800–4,000 wds
How to apply: letter

Include in application: professional degrees, institutional affiliation, published works

Modern China

Modern China history and social science
Ed: Philip C. C. Huang
  Department of History
  University of California
  Los Angeles, CA 90024
Bk Rev Ed: same
4/yr; subs $45
Readership: academics
Indexed/Abstracted: ABC, AHCI, CCSB, PAIS, SSCI, SSI
● MANUSCRIPTS
Query: no; *Abstract:* no
Style guide: own
Preferred length: varies
Copies: 3
Notes: endnotes
Blind referee: yes
Time to consider ms: 2 mos
Charts, tables
● REVIEWS
Unsolicited reviews accepted: yes
Materials reviewed: books
Review length: varies

Modern History Review

Modern British and European history from 1815 onwards
Affiliation: Institute of Contemporary British History
Ed: Peter Catterall
  Institute of Contemporary British History
  34 Tavistock Square
  London WC1H 9E2
  U.K.
Bk Rev Ed: Richard Cockett
  91d Clarendon Road
  London W11
  U.K.
4/yr, 33 pp; subs £7.50
Circ: 13,000

Readership: general public, students
Indexed/Abstracted: ABC
● MANUSCRIPTS
Query: no; *Abstract:* no
Style guide: own
Preferred length: 3,000 wds max
Copies: 2
Notes: endnotes
Blind referee: no
● REVIEWS
Materials reviewed: books
● ADDITIONAL NOTES
Articles should be written at a level which able sixth-formers and first year undergraduates should find easy to absorb. Articles therefore need to be informative, interesting, clear and succinct. Authors are reminded not to assume prior knowledge on the part of their readers.

Montana the Magazine of Western History

Western American history, Montana history
Affiliation: Montana Historical Society
Ed: Charles E. Rankin
  Montana Historical Society
  225 N. Roberts Street
  Helena, MT 59620
Bk Rev Ed: same
4/yr, 96 pp; subs $20
Circ: 10,000
Readership: academics, general public, history buffs
Indexed/Abstracted: ABC, AHCI, CCAH, WAH
● MANUSCRIPTS
Query: no; *Abstract:* no
Style guide: modified Chicago
Preferred length: 25 pp
Copies: 2
Notes: endnotes
Blind referee: yes
Acceptance rate: 1/4
Time to consider ms: 6–8 wks
Charts, pictures, tables, maps
Foreign languages accepted: no

• REVIEWS
Seeking reviewers: no
Unsolicited reviews accepted: no
Materials reviewed: books, films, museum exhibits
Review length: 500 wds
How to apply: letter
Include in application: professional degrees, institutional affiliation, areas of expertise, published works, current research

Museum of the Fur Trade Quarterly

Materials and methods of the North American frontier
Affiliation: Museum Association of the American Frontier
Ed: Charles E. Hanson, Jr.
    Museum of the Fur Trade
    HC 74 Box 18
    Chadron, NE 69337
Bk Rev Ed: same
4/yr, 16 pp; subs $6
Circ: 2,400
Readership: academics, general public, living history workers
Indexed/Abstracted: ABC
• MANUSCRIPTS
Query: yes; *Abstract:* no
Preferred length: 2,800–3,500 wds
Copies: 2
Notes: endnotes
Blind referee: no
Pictures, tables, maps
Foreign languages accepted: no
• REVIEWS
Seeking reviewers: no
Unsolicited reviews accepted: no
Materials reviewed: books, films
Review length: 3–4 paragraphs

The Musk-Ox

Arctic and Subarctic
Affiliation: University of Saskatchewan
Ed: W. O. Kupsch
    Department of Geological
    Sciences

University of Saskatchewan
Saskatoon, SK S7N 0W0
CANADA
Bk Rev Ed: W. A. Waiser
    Department of History
    University of Saskatchewan
    Saskatoon, SK S7N 0W0
    CANADA
1/yr, 100 pp; subs $30
Circ: 900
Readership: academics, general public
• MANUSCRIPTS
Query: no; *Abstract:* yes
Style guide: own
Preferred length: open
Copies: 2
Notes: endnotes
Blind referee: yes
Acceptance rate: 1/2
Time to consider ms: 6 mos
Charts, pictures, tables, graphs, maps
Foreign languages accepted: French
• REVIEWS
Seeking reviewers: no
Unsolicited reviews accepted: yes
Materials reviewed: books
Review length: open
How to apply: letter
Include in application: professional degrees, institutional affiliation, areas of expertise

National Railway Bulletin

History and operations of North American railroads
Affiliation: National Railway Historical Society
Ed: Frank G. Tatnall
    P.O. Box 58153
    Philadelphia, PA 19102-8153
Bk Rev Ed: James N. J. Henwood
6/yr, 48 pp; subs membership
Circ: 17,500
Readership: society members
• MANUSCRIPTS
Query: no; *Abstract:* no
Preferred length: 5,000 wds max
Copies: 1

Notes: not required
Blind referee: no
Acceptance rate: 1/2
Time to consider ms: varies
Charts, pictures, graphs, maps
Foreign languages accepted: no
• REVIEWS
Seeking reviewers: no
Unsolicited reviews accepted: no
Materials reviewed: books, videos
Review length: 100–300 wds
• ADDITIONAL NOTES
This magazine is published by and
for members of the National Rail-
way Historical Society. Outside
contributions are discouraged.

Natural History Magazine

Evolution, ecology, biological
sciences, anthropology, earth
sciences, astronomy, archaeol-
ogy
Affiliation: American Museum of
Natural History
Ed: Alan Ternes
79th and Central Park West
New York, NY 10024
Bk Rev Ed: Jenny Lawrence
12/yr, 92 pp; subs $25
Circ: 500,000
Readership: general public
Indexed/Abstracted: AHCI, BRD,
BRI, RG, SSCI
• MANUSCRIPTS
Query: yes; *Abstract:* no
Preferred length: 1,500–3,000 wds
Copies: 1
Notes: none
Blind referee: no
Time to consider ms: 3 mos
No illustrations accepted
Foreign languages accepted: no
• REVIEWS
Seeking reviewers: no
Unsolicited reviews accepted: no
Materials reviewed: books
Review length: 1,500 wds

Nature, Society, and Thought

Interdisciplinary; dialectical and
historical materialism
Ed: Erwin Marquit
University of Minnesota
116 Church Street, S.E.
Minneapolis, MN 55455-0112
Bk Rev Ed: Doris Grieser
4/yr, 128 pp; subs $15
Circ: 700
Readership: academics, general public
• MANUSCRIPTS
Query: no; *Abstract:* no
Style guide: own
Preferred length: 3,000–10,000 wds
Copies: 3
Notes: endnotes
Blind referee: no

Nautical Research Journal

The study of maritime history and
nautical research as applied to
documentary ship model building
Affiliation: The Nautical Research
Guild
Ed: Rob Napier
62 Marlboro Street
Newburyport, MA 01950-3134
Bk Rev Ed: same
4/yr, 64 pp; subs $25
Circ: 1,500
Readership: academics, general public
Indexed/Abstracted: ABC, WAH
• MANUSCRIPTS
Query: preferred; *Abstract:* no
Preferred length: 10,000 wds max
Copies: 1
Notes: endnotes or footnotes
Blind referee: no
Acceptance rate: high
Time to consider ms: 3 mos
Charts, pictures, tables, graphs,
maps, ship plans
Foreign languages accepted: no
• REVIEWS
Seeking reviewers: no
Unsolicited reviews accepted: no

Materials reviewed: books, published ship plans, ship modelers tools
Review length: 600 wds
How to apply: letter

Naval History

Naval and maritime history, specifically the U.S. Navy, Marine Corps, and Coast Guard
Affiliation: U.S. Naval Institute
Ed: Paul Stillwell
    118 Maryland Avenue
    Annapolis, MD 21402-5035
Bk Rev Ed: Linda O'Doughda
4/yr, 80 pp; subs $20
Circ: 29,000
Readership: general public, Naval Institute members
Indexed/Abstracted: ABC
• MANUSCRIPTS
Query: preferred; *Abstract:* preferred
Preferred length: 3,500 wds max
Copies: 1
Notes: endnotes
Blind referee: no
Acceptance rate: 1/6–1/5
Time to consider ms: 2–3 mos
Charts, pictures, tables, graphs, maps
Foreign languages accepted: no
• REVIEWS
Seeking reviewers: no
Unsolicited reviews accepted: occasionally
Materials reviewed: books
Review length: 600 wds max
How to apply: letter
Include in application: areas of expertise, published works

Naval War College Review

Military history, naval history, strategy
Affiliation: Naval War College
Ed: Frank Uhlig, Jr.
    Code 32
    Newport, RI 02841-5010
Bk Rev Ed: Phyllis P. Winkler

4/yr, 148 pp; subs free to qualified subscribers
Readership: academics, military professionals
Indexed/Abstracted: ABC
• MANUSCRIPTS
Query: preferred; *Abstract:* no
Preferred length: varies
Copies: 2
Notes: endnotes
Blind referee: no
Time to consider ms: 2–3 mos
Charts, pictures, tables, graphs, maps
Foreign languages accepted: (translation preferred) Russian, German
• REVIEWS
Unsolicited reviews accepted: occasionally
Materials reviewed: books
Review length: 500–700 wds
How to apply: letter
Include in application: professional degrees, institutional affiliation, areas of expertise, published works

Nebraska History

History of Nebraska and the Great Plains
Affiliation: Nebraska State Historical Society
Ed: James E. Potter
    Nebraska State Historical Society
    Box 82554
    Lincoln, NE 68501
Bk Rev Ed: same
4/yr, 50 pp; subs $15
Circ: 4,000
Readership: academics, general public
Indexed/Abstracted: ABC, WAH
• MANUSCRIPTS
Query: no; *Abstract:* no
Style guide: Chicago
Preferred length: 3,000–7,500 wds
Copies: 1
Notes: endnotes
Blind referee: yes
Acceptance rate: 1/2
Time to consider ms: 60 days

Charts, pictures, tables, graphs, maps
Foreign languages accepted: no
• REVIEWS
Seeking reviewers: no
Unsolicited reviews accepted: no
Materials reviewed: books
Review length: 500–1,000 wds
How to apply: letter
Include in application: professional
degrees, institutional affiliation,
areas of expertise, published
works, current research

Nevada Historical Society Quarterly

History of Nevada and the West
Affiliation: Nevada Historical Society
Ed: William D. Rowley
1650 N. Virginia Street
Reno, NV 89503
Bk Rev Ed: Jerome E. Edwards
4/yr, 100 pp; subs $25
Circ: 1,200–1,500
Readership: academics, general public
Indexed/Abstracted: ABC, WAH
• MANUSCRIPTS
Query: no; *Abstract:* no
Style guide: own
Preferred length: 25 pp
Copies: 1
Notes: endnotes
Blind referee: yes
Charts, pictures, tables, graphs, maps
Foreign languages accepted: no
• REVIEWS
Seeking reviewers: yes
Unsolicited reviews accepted: no
Materials reviewed: books
Review length: 400–500 wds
How to apply: letter
Include in application: professional
degrees, institutional affiliation,
areas of expertise, published
works, current research

New England Journal of History

History of New England, United
States and Europe in all fields

Affiliation: New England History
Teachers Association
Ed: James Weland
Department of History
Bentley College
Waltham, MA 02154
Bk Rev Ed: Vera Laska
Regis College
Weston, MA 02193
3/yr, 90 pp; subs $15
Circ: 400
Readership: academics, general public, history teachers
Indexed/Abstracted: ABC
• MANUSCRIPTS
Query: no; *Abstract:* no
Style guide: Chicago
Preferred length: 2,000–10,000 wds
Copies: 2
Notes: endnotes
Blind referee: no
Acceptance rate: 1/4
Time to consider ms: 2–3 mos
Charts, pictures, tables, graphs, maps
Foreign languages accepted: no
• REVIEWS
Seeking reviewers: no
Unsolicited reviews accepted: no
Include in application: professional
degrees, institutional affiliation,
areas of expertise
• ADDITIONAL NOTES
Secondary school teachers of history
make up a large part of the readership. Articles that pertain directly
to the classroom are especially
welcome, both substantive historical matters and pedagogy in the
history classroom. The editors encourage history teachers to share
their classroom experiences and
techniques where they may be
useful to other history teachers.

The New England Quarterly

New England history and literature;
all periods
Ed: William M. Fowler, Jr.

227 Meserve Hall
Northeastern University
Boston, MA 02115
Bk Rev Eds: William Fowler and
Linda Rhodes
4/yr, 176 pp
Circ: 2,400
Readership: academics, general public
Indexed/Abstracted: ABC, AHCI,
BRD, BRI, CCAH, HI, MLA,
WAH
● MANUSCRIPTS
Query: no; *Abstract:* no
Style guide: Chicago
Preferred length: 25–30 pp
Copies: 2
Notes: endnotes
Blind referee: yes
Acceptance rate: 1/10
Time to consider ms: 6–8 wks
Charts, pictures, tables, graphs,
maps
Foreign languages accepted: no
● REVIEWS
Seeking reviewers: yes
Unsolicited reviews accepted: no
Materials reviewed: books
How to apply: letter
Include in application: published
works, current research, book to
be reviewed

New Jersey History

History of New Jersey
Affiliation: New Jersey Historical
Society
Ed: Mark Edward Lender
T-132, Grants Office
Kean College of New Jersey
Morris Avenue
Union, NJ 07083
Bk Rev Ed: Eugene Sheridan
Papers of Thomas Jefferson
Firestone Library
Princeton University
Princeton, NJ 08540
4/yr, 96 pp; subs $30
Circ: 3,500

Readership: academics, general public
Indexed/Abstracted: ABC, WAH
● MANUSCRIPTS
Query: no; *Abstract:* no
Style guide: Chicago
Preferred length: open
Copies: 2
Notes: endnotes
Blind referee: yes
Acceptance rate: 1/3
Time to consider ms: 2–3 mos
Charts, pictures, tables, graphs,
maps
Foreign languages accepted: no
● REVIEWS
Seeking reviewers: yes
Unsolicited reviews accepted: yes
Materials reviewed: books, films
Review length: 1,000 wds
How to apply: letter
Include in application: professional
degrees, institutional affiliation,
areas of expertise, current research

New Literary History

Literary history
Affiliation: Johns Hopkins University
Press; University of Virginia
Ed: Ralph Cohen
Department of English
234 Wilson Hall
University of Virginia
Charlottesville, VA 22903
4/yr, 250 pp; subs $22
Circ: 2,000
Readership: academics
Indexed/Abstracted: ABC, AHCI,
CCAH, HI, IMB, MLA
● MANUSCRIPTS
Query: no; *Abstract:* no
Style guide: Chicago
Preferred length: 25 pp
Copies: 1
Notes: footnotes
Blind referee: yes
Acceptance rate: 1/5
Time to consider ms: 4 mos
Charts, pictures, tables, graphs, maps

Foreign languages accepted: yes, but
will be published in English

New Mexico Historical Review

History and culture of New Mexico
and the greater Southwest
Affiliation: University of New Mexico
Ed: Robert Himmerich y Valencia
The University of New Mexico
Mesa Vista Hall, Room 1013
Albuquerque, NM 87131-1186
Bk Rev Ed: same
4/yr, 100 pp; subs $24
Circ: 1,300
Readership: academics, general pub-
lic, historical society members
Indexed/Abstracted: ABC, AHCI,
CCAH, WAH
• MANUSCRIPTS
Query: no; *Abstract:* no
Style guide: Chicago
Preferred length: 20–30 pp
Copies: 2
Notes: endnotes
Blind referee: yes
Time to consider ms: 2 mos
Charts, pictures, tables, graphs, maps
Foreign languages accepted: Spanish
• REVIEWS
Seeking reviewers: yes
Unsolicited reviews accepted: no
Materials reviewed: books
Review length: 250–400 wds
How to apply: letter
Include in application: professional
degrees, institutional affiliation,
areas of expertise, published
works, foreign languages, current
research, vita

New York History

History of New York state
Affiliation: New York State Historical
Association
Ed: Wendell Tripp
New York State Historical Asso-
ciation
P.O. Box 800
Cooperstown, NY 13326

Bk Rev Ed: same
4/yr, 128 pp; subs $20
Circ: 2,900
Readership: academics, general public
Indexed/Abstracted: ABC, AHCI,
CCAH, WAH
• MANUSCRIPTS
Query: no; *Abstract:* no
Style guide: modified Chicago
Preferred length: 4,000–6,000 wds
Copies: 2
Notes: endnotes
Blind referee: yes
Acceptance rate: 1/5
Time to consider ms: 3 mos
Charts, pictures, tables, graphs,
maps, cartoons
Foreign languages accepted: no
• REVIEWS
Seeking reviewers: yes
Unsolicited reviews accepted: no
Materials reviewed: books
Review length: 500 wds
How to apply: letter
Include in application: professional
degrees, institutional affiliation,
areas of expertise, published
works, current research

Newfoundland Studies

Interdisciplinary; society and culture
of Newfoundland
Affiliation: Memorial University of
Newfoundland
Ed: Patrick O'Flaherty
English Department
Memorial University of New-
foundland
St. John's, NF A1C 5S7
CANADA
Bk Rev Ed: same
2/yr, 125 pp; subs $15
Circ: 500
Readership: academics, general pub-
lic, bureaucrats
Indexed/Abstracted: ABC
• MANUSCRIPTS
Query: no; *Abstract:* no

Preferred length: open
Copies: 2
Notes: endnotes
Blind referee: yes
Acceptance rate: 2/5
Time to consider ms: 6–12 mos
Charts, pictures, tables, graphs, maps
Foreign languages accepted: French
• REVIEWS
Seeking reviewers: no
Unsolicited reviews accepted: no
Materials reviewed: books
Review length: open
How to apply: letter
Include in application: professional
    degrees, institutional affiliation,
    areas of expertise, published
    works, foreign languages, current
    research

Newport History

History of Newport County, Rhode
    Island
Affiliation: Newport Historical Society
Ed: Publications Committee
    Newport Historical Society
    82 Touro Street
    Newport, RI 02889
4/yr, 40 pp; subs membership
Circ: 2,000
Readership: general public, society
    members
Indexed/Abstracted: ABC
• MANUSCRIPTS
Query: no; *Abstract:* no
Preferred length: open
Copies: 2
Notes: footnotes
Blind referee: no
Acceptance rate: 4/5
Time to consider ms: 4–6 mos
Charts, pictures, maps
Foreign languages accepted: no

News and Journal

History and genealogy of Tippah
    County, Mississippi
Affiliation: Ripley Public Library

Ed: Tommy Covington
    308 North Commerce
    Ripley, MS 38663
4/yr, 25 pp; subs $12
Circ: 250
Readership: general public
• MANUSCRIPTS
Query: no; *Abstract:* no
Style guide: none
Preferred length: 1–4 pp
Copies: 1
Notes: none
Blind referee: no
Acceptance rate: 3/4
Pictures
Foreign languages accepted: no

Nine: A Journal of Baseball History and Social Policy Perspectives

Scholarly study of all aspects of base-
    ball history and social trends
Ed: Bill Kirwin
    Faculty of Social Work
    #300, 8625–112 Street
    Edmonton, AB T6G 1K8
    CANADA
Bk Rev Ed: same
2/yr, 120 pp; subs $20
Circ: 300
Readership: academics, baseball his-
    torians
• MANUSCRIPTS
Query: no; *Abstract:* no
Style guide: any
Preferred length: 2,000–5,000 wds
Copies: 3
Notes: endnotes
Blind referee: yes
Acceptance rate: 1/4
Time to consider ms: 3 mos
Charts, pictures, tables
Foreign languages accepted: French
• REVIEWS
Seeking reviewers: yes
Unsolicited reviews accepted: no
Materials reviewed: books, films
Review length: 750 wds

How to apply: letter
Include in application: institutional affiliation, current research
• ADDITIONAL NOTES
Nine regularly features an oral history of about 1,500–2,000 words. Another regular feature, also 1,500–2,000 words is Elysian Fields which focuses on ballparks themselves. Also included are 1–2 small fiction pieces.

Nineteenth Century Studies

Scholarly studies of nineteenth century culture, literature, science, religion, politics, art, music, etc. with an emphasis on cross-disciplinary research
Affiliation: The Citadel and Southeastern Nineteenth Century Studies Association
Ed: Suzanne O. Edwards
    Department of English
    The Citadel
    Charleston, SC 29409
Bk Rev Ed: same
1/yr, 110 pp; subs $15
Circ: 250
Readership: academics
Indexed/Abstracted: ABC, MLA
• MANUSCRIPTS
Query: no; *Abstract:* no
Style guide: MLA
Preferred length: 15–30 pp
Copies: 2
Notes: endnotes
Blind referee: yes
Acceptance rate: 1/20–1/10
Time to consider ms: 3 mos
Charts, pictures, tables, graphs, maps
• REVIEWS
Seeking reviewers: yes
Unsolicited reviews accepted: no
Materials reviewed: books
Review length: 5–8 pp
How to apply: letter
Include in application: professional degrees, areas of expertise, published works, current research

Nineteenth Century Theatre

Nineteenth century theatre studies
Affiliation: University of Massachusetts at Amherst
Ed: Joseph Donohue
    Department of English
    Bartlett Hall
    University of Massachusetts
    Amherst, MA 01003
Bk Rev Ed: Thomas Postlewait
    contact the editor directly
2/yr, 80 pp; subs $12
Readership: academics, theatre professionals
Indexed/Abstracted: ABC, MLA
• MANUSCRIPTS
Query: no; *Abstract:* no
Style guide: MLA
Preferred length: varies
Copies: 3
Notes: endnotes
Foreign languages accepted: no
• REVIEWS
Materials reviewed: books
Review length: varies

North Carolina Historical Review

North Carolina and Southern history
Affiliation: North Carolina Division of Archives and History
Ed-in-Chief: Jeffrey J. Crowe
Ed: Katthleen B. Wyche
    109 E. Jones Street
    Raleigh, NC 27601-2807
4/yr, 128 pp; subs $25
Circ: 1,500
Readership: academics, general public
Indexed/Abstracted: ABC, MLA, WAH
• MANUSCRIPTS
Query: no; *Abstract:* no
Style guide: Chicago
Preferred length: 25 pp
Copies: 2
Notes: footnotes
Blind referee: yes
Acceptance rate: 1/4

Time to consider ms: 6–8 wks
Charts, pictures, tables, graphs, maps
Foreign languages accepted: no
• REVIEWS
Seeking reviewers: yes
Unsolicited reviews accepted: no
Materials reviewed: books
Review length: 350 wds
How to apply: letter
Include in application: professional
  degrees, institutional affiliation,
  areas of expertise, published
  works, current research

North Dakota History: Journal of the Northern Plains

History and culture of North Dakota
  and the northern Great Plains
Affiliation: State Historical Society of
  North Dakota
Ed: Virginia L. Heidenreich
  State Historical Society of North
    Dakota
  North Dakota Heritage Center
  612 East Boulevard
  Bismark, ND 58501
Bk Rev Ed: same
4/yr, 40 pp; subs $15
Circ: 1,750
Readership: academics, general public
Indexed/Abstracted: ABC, WAH
• MANUSCRIPTS
Query: preferred; *Abstract:* no
Style guide: Chicago
Preferred length: 20–30 pp
Copies: 2
Notes: endnotes
Blind referee: yes
Acceptance rate: 1/2
Time to consider ms: 60–90 days
Charts, pictures, tables, graphs, maps
Foreign languages accepted: no
• REVIEWS
Seeking reviewers: occasionally
Unsolicited reviews accepted: no
Materials reviewed: books
Review length: 600 wds
How to apply: letter

Include in application: professional
  degrees, institutional affiliation,
  areas of expertise, published
  works, current research, vita

North Dakota Horizons

North Dakota's history; places and
  people in North Dakota
Affiliation: North Dakota State Tour-
  ism Department
Ed: Sheldon Green
  P.O. Box 2467
  Fargo, ND 58108
Bk Rev Ed: same
4/yr, 36 pp; subs $15
Circ: 18,000
Readership: general public
• MANUSCRIPTS
Query: preferred; *Abstract:* no
Preferred length: 6–8 pp
Copies: 1
Notes: footnotes
Blind referee: no
Charts, pictures, tables, graphs, maps
Foreign languages accepted: no
• REVIEWS
Seeking reviewers: no
Unsolicited reviews accepted: no
Materials reviewed: books

North Dakota Quarterly

Humanities and social sciences;
  northern plains, American Indian
Affiliation: University of North
  Dakota
Ed: Robert W. Lewis
  Box 8237
  University of North Dakota
  Grand Forks, ND 58202
Bk Rev Ed: same
4/yr, 250 pp; subs $15
Circ: 800
Readership: academics, general public
Indexed/Abstracted: ABC, AHI,
  MLA, WAH
• MANUSCRIPTS
Query: no; *Abstract:* no
Style guide: MLA

Preferred length: 15–25 pp
Copies: 1
Notes: endnotes
Blind referee: no
Acceptance rate: 1/10
Time to consider ms: 4–8 wks
Charts, pictures, tables, graphs, maps
Foreign languages accepted: no
• REVIEWS
Seeking reviewers: yes
Unsolicited reviews accepted: no
Materials reviewed: books
Review length: 500–1,000 wds
How to apply: letter
Include in application: professional
 degrees, institutional affiliation,
 areas of expertise, published works

North Louisiana Historical Association Journal

North Louisiana history
Affiliation: North Louisiana Histori-
 cal Association; Louisiana State
 University in Shreveport
Ed: Alan Thompson
 Department of History and
  Social Sciences
 Louisiana State University in
  Shreveport
 Shreveport, LA 71115
Bk Rev Ed: same
3/yr, 48 pp; subs $10
Circ: 450
Readership: academics, general public
Indexed/Abstracted: ABC
• MANUSCRIPTS
Query: preferred; *Abstract:* no
Style guide: Chicago
Preferred length: 15–25 pp
Copies: 1
Notes: endnotes
Blind referee: no
Acceptance rate: 3/4
Time to consider ms: 1 mo
Charts, pictures, tables, graphs, maps
Foreign languages accepted: no
• REVIEWS
Seeking reviewers: yes

Unsolicited reviews accepted: no
Materials reviewed: books
Review length: 350 wds
How to apply: letter
Include in application: professional
 degrees, institutional affiliation,
 areas of expertise, published
 works, current research

Northeastern Nevada Historical Society Quarterly

History of Northeastern Nevada
Affiliation: Northeastern Nevada His-
 torical Society
Ed: Howard Hickson
 1515 Idaho Street
 Elko, NV 89801
Bk Rev Ed: same
4/yr, 40 pp; subs $10
Circ: 1,500
Readership: general public
Indexed/Abstracted: ABC, WAH
• MANUSCRIPTS
Query: no; *Abstract:* no
*Style guide: The Associated Press
 Style Book and Libel Manuel*
Preferred length: 10–20 pp
Copies: 1
Notes: endnotes
Blind referee: no
Acceptance rate: 3/4
Time to consider ms: 6 wks
Charts, pictures, tables, graphs, maps
Foreign languages accepted: no
• REVIEWS
Seeking reviewers: no
Unsolicited reviews accepted: no

Northwest Ohio Quarterly

History of Northwest Ohio and the
 Middle West in general
Affiliation: Maumee Valley Historical
 Society
Ed: David Curtis Skaggs
 Department of History
 Bowling Green State University
 Bowling Green, OH 43403-0220
Bk Rev Ed: Sturt R. Givens

4/yr, 38 pp; subs $15
Circ: 500
Readership: academics
Indexed/Abstracted: ABC, MLA, WAH
• MANUSCRIPTS
Query: preferred; *Abstract:* no
Style guide: Turabian
Preferred length: 15–25 pp
Copies: 3
Notes: endnotes
Blind referee: yes
Acceptance rate: 3/4
Time to consider ms: 2 mos
Charts, pictures, tables, graphs, maps
Foreign languages accepted: no
• REVIEWS
Seeking reviewers: yes
Unsolicited reviews accepted: no
Materials reviewed: books
Review length: 1,000–2,000 wds
How to apply: letter
Include in application: professional degrees, institutional affiliation, areas of expertise, published works, current research
• ADDITIONAL NOTES
This journal has multidisciplinary interests related to the region and accepts articles in science, political science, sociology, education, literature, economics, etc. that relate to regional development. Book review essays almost totally relate to Ohio and the Middle West.

Notes and Queries

English language and literature, lexicography, history, and scholarly antiquarianism; emphasis on factual rather than speculative
Affiliation: Oxford University Press
Eds: E. G. Stanley, Douglas Hewitt, L. G. Black
      Pembroke College
      Oxford OX1 1DW
      U.K.
Bk Rev Ed: same

4/yr, 144 pp; subs £47
Circ: 3,000
Readership: academics
Indexed/Abstracted: ABC, AHCI, BHI, CCAH, HI, IMB, MLA
• MANUSCRIPTS
Query: no; *Abstract:* no
Style guide: Hart's Rules for Compositors and Readers at the University Press, Oxford
Preferred length: short
Copies: 1
Notes: endnotes
Blind referee: no
Acceptance rate: 1/2
Time to consider ms: 3 mos
Charts, pictures, tables, graphs
Foreign languages accepted: no
• REVIEWS
Seeking reviewers: occasionally
Unsolicited reviews accepted: no
Materials reviewed: books
Review length: 600 wds
How to apply: letter
Include in application: professional degrees, institutional affiliation, areas of expertise, published works, current research

Notes and Queries for Somerset and Dorset

Local history and related studies of Somerset and Dorset
Somerset Ed: D. M. M. Shorrocks
      222 Staplegrove Roads
      Taunton
      Somerset TA2 6AL
      U.K.
Dorset and Bk Rev Ed: G. J. Davies
      16, Melcombe Avenue
      Weymouth
      Dorset DT4 7TH
      U.K.
2/yr, 44 pp; subs £5
Circ: 600
Readership: academics, general public
• MANUSCRIPTS
Query: preferred; *Abstract:* no

Preferred length: short
Copies: 2
Notes: endnotes
Blind referee: no
Acceptance rate: 3/4
Time to consider ms: 1–2 mos
Pictures, tables, maps
Foreign languages accepted: no
• REVIEWS
Seeking reviewers: no
Unsolicited reviews accepted: no
Materials reviewed: books

Nova Scotia Historical Review

Scholarly history of Nova Scotia and
    New Brunswick
Affiliation: Public Archives of Nova
    Scotia
Ed: Barry Cahill
    Public Archives of Nova Scotia
    6016 University Avenue
    Halifax, NS B3H 1W4
    CANADA
Bk Rev Ed: Allen B. Robertson
2/yr, 150 pp; subs $20
Circ: 800
Readership: academics, general public
Indexed/Abstracted: ABC
• MANUSCRIPTS
Query: preferred; *Abstract:* no
Style guide: Chicago
Preferred length: 10,000 wds max
Copies: 1
Notes: footnotes
Blind referee: no
Acceptance rate: 9/10
Time to consider ms: 4–6 wks
Pictures, tables, graphs, maps
Foreign languages accepted: French
• REVIEWS
Seeking reviewers: no
Unsolicited reviews accepted: no
Materials reviewed: books

Now and Then Magazine

Appalachian issues and literature
Affiliation: East Tennessee State
    University

Ed: Pat Arnow
    Box 70665
    East Tennessee State University
    Johnson City, TN 37614-0556
Bk Rev Ed: same
3/yr, 40 pp; subs $10
Circ: 1,200
Readership: academics, general public
Indexed/Abstracted: MLA
• MANUSCRIPTS
Query: preferred; *Abstract:* no
*Style guide: The Associated Press
    Style Book and Libel Manual*
Preferred length: 2,500 wds max
Copies: 1
Notes: none
Blind referee: no
Acceptance rate: 1/5
Time to consider ms: 4 mos max
Charts, pictures, tables, graphs, maps
Foreign languages accepted: no
• REVIEWS
Seeking reviewers: yes
Unsolicited reviews accepted: yes
Materials reviewed: books, films,
    music
Review length: 750 wds
How to apply: letter
Include in application: professional
    degrees, institutional affiliation,
    areas of expertise, published
    works, current research
• ADDITIONAL NOTES
Each issue has a special focus. Every-
    thing published has to pertain to
    this region and to the focus issue in
    some way. The style is more jour-
    nalistic than scholarly, though
    many of the contributors are aca-
    demics. The editors try to appeal
    to a broad range of people in-
    terested in Appalachia.

OAH Magazine of History

American history
Affiliation: Organization of American
    Historians
Ed: Michael Regoli

Organization of American Historians
112 North Bryan Street
Bloomington, IN 47408-4199
Bk Rev Ed: same
4/yr, 64 pp; subs $20
Circ: 6,000
Readership: academics, secondary school teachers
• MANUSCRIPTS
Query: yes; *Abstract:* no
Style guide: Chicago
Preferred length: 3,000 wds max
Copies: 2
Notes: endnotes
Blind referee: yes
Acceptance rate: 9/10
Time to consider ms: 6 wks
Charts, pictures, tables, graphs, maps
Foreign languages accepted: no
• REVIEWS
Seeking reviewers: yes
Unsolicited reviews accepted: yes
Materials reviewed: books, films
Review length: 500 wds
How to apply: letter
Include in application: professional degrees, institutional affiliation, areas of expertise, published works, current research, vita
• ADDITIONAL NOTES
The OAH Magazine of History is designed to supplement materials in the history classroom. The audience is primarily junior and senior high school, with some college and university level subscribers. The editors welcome any and all manuscripts dealing with the particular theme in American history that each issue covers. Please query the editor before submitting materials.

Ohio History

History of Ohio and the Middle West
Affiliation: Ohio Historical Society
Ed: Robert L. Daugherty

Ohio Historical Society
1982 Velma Avenue
Columbus, OH 43211
Bk Rev Ed: Laura Russell
2/yr, 96 pp; subs $10
Circ: 3,500
Readership: academics, general public, society members
Indexed/Abstracted: ABC, WAH
• MANUSCRIPTS
Query: no; *Abstract:* no
Style guide: Turabian or Chicago
Preferred length: 10–40 pp
Copies: 2
Notes: endnotes
Blind referee: yes
Acceptance rate: 1/10
Time to consider ms: 1–2 mos
Charts, pictures, tables, graphs, maps
Foreign languages accepted: no
• REVIEWS
Seeking reviewers: yes
Unsolicited reviews accepted: no
Materials reviewed: books
Review length: 600 wds
How to apply: letter, form
Include in application: professional degrees, institutional affiliation, areas of expertise, published works, current research
• ADDITIONAL NOTES
The primary purpose of the journal is to publish articles, documents, notes, and reviews concerning the political, social, economic, and cultural history of Ohio and the Middle West. The editors welcome studies in general fields of American history if they possess obvious relevance to Ohio and the Middle West.

Old Mill News

Water, steam, animal or wind powered mills
Affiliation: Society for the Preservation of Old Mills
Ed: Michael La Forest

604 Ensley, Rt. 29
Knoxville, TN 37920
Bk Rev Ed: same
4/yr, 24 pp; subs $10
Circ: 2,000
Readership: academics, general public
• MANUSCRIPTS
Query: no; *Abstract:* no
Preferred length: 1,000–1,500 wds
Copies: 1
Notes: endnotes
Blind referee: no
Charts, pictures, tables, maps,
cartoons
Foreign languages accepted: no
• REVIEWS
Materials reviewed: books
Review length: 500–600 wds

The Old Northwest: A Journal of Regional Life and Letters

The greater Midwest
Affiliation: Miami University
Eds: Robert Kettler, Andrew Carlon,
Jerome Rosenberg
302 Bachelor Hall
Miami University
Oxford, OH 45056
Bk Rev Ed: Robert Kettler
4/yr, 100 pp; subs $10
Circ: 700
Readership: academics
Indexed/Abstracted: ABC, MLA
• MANUSCRIPTS
Query: no; *Abstract:* no
Style guide: MLA
Preferred length: 50 pp max
Copies: 1
Notes: endnotes
Blind referee: yes
Acceptance rate: 2/5
Charts, pictures, tables, graphs, maps
Foreign languages accepted: no
• REVIEWS
Seeking reviewers: yes
Unsolicited reviews accepted: no
Materials reviewed: books, films
Review length: 600–1,000 wds

How to apply: letter
Include in application: areas of expertise, current research

Old West

History of the trans–Mississippi West
from prehistory to about 1930
Ed: John Joerschke
P.O. Box 2107
Stillwater, OK 74076
Bk Rev Ed: same
4/yr, 68 pp; subs $10.95
Circ: 30,000
Readership: general public
• MANUSCRIPTS
Query: preferred; *Abstract:* no
Style guide: any
Preferred length: 3,000–4,000 wds
Copies: 1
Notes: footnotes or endnotes are
preferred
Blind referee: no
Acceptance rate: 1/6
Time to consider ms: 6–8 wks
Pictures, maps, documents
Foreign languages accepted: no
• REVIEWS
Seeking reviewers: yes
Unsolicited reviews accepted: occasionally
Materials reviewed: books, films
Review length: 300 wds
How to apply: letter
Include in application: professional
degrees, areas of expertise, published works, current research
• ADDITIONAL NOTES
The editors are very interested in
manuscripts written by professional
historians for a general readership.

Ontario History

Various aspects of the history of
Ontario
Affiliation: The Ontario Historical
Society
Ed: Jean Burnet
5151 Yonge Street

Willowdale, ON M2N 5P5
CANADA
Bk Rev Ed: James Clemens
4/yr, 92 pp; subs $45
Circ: 1,300
Readership: academics, general public
Indexed/Abstracted: ABC
• MANUSCRIPTS
Query: preferred; *Abstract:* no
Style guide: own
Preferred length: open
Copies: 3
Notes: endnotes or footnotes
Blind referee: yes
Acceptance rate: 3/5
Time to consider ms: 2 mos
Charts, pictures, tables, graphs, maps
Foreign languages accepted: no
• REVIEWS
Seeking reviewers: yes
Unsolicited reviews accepted: no
Materials reviewed: books, ms
Review length: open
How to apply: letter
Include in application: professional
degrees, institutional affiliation,
areas of expertise

Oral History

Oral history
Affiliation: University of Essex;
British Library National Sound
Archive
Ed: Rob Perks and others
British Library National Sound
Archive
29 Exhibition Road
London SW7 2AS
U.K.
Bk Rev Ed: Brenda Corti
Sociology Department
Essex University
Wivenhoe Park
Colchester
Essex CO4 3SQ
U.K.
2/yr, 88 pp; subs £12
Circ: 1,000

Readership: academics, general pub-
lic, care professionals, museum
curators, archivists
Indexed/Abstracted: BHI, MLA
• MANUSCRIPTS
Query: preferred; *Abstract:* preferred
Style guide: own
Preferred length: 5,000 wds max
Copies: 2
Notes: endnotes
Blind referee: no
Acceptance rate: 3/4
Time to consider ms: 3 mos
Charts, pictures, tables, graphs, maps
Foreign languages accepted: no
• REVIEWS
Seeking reviewers: yes
Unsolicited reviews accepted: yes
Materials reviewed: books, films,
audio-visual publications, television
programs
Review length: varies
How to apply: letter
Include in application: professional
degrees, institutional affiliation,
areas of expertise, published
works, current research

Oral History Review

Oral history
Affiliation: Oral History Association
Ed: Michael Frisch
565 Park Hall
SUNY-Buffalo
Buffalo, NY 14260
Bk Rev Ed: Linda Shopes
Division of History
Pennsylvania Historical and
Museum Commission
William Penn Building
Harrisburg, PA 17108-1026
2/yr, 200 pp; subs $50
Circ: 1,300
Readership: academics, general public
Indexed/Abstracted: ABC, HI
• MANUSCRIPTS
Query: no; *Abstract:* no
Style guide: Chicago

Preferred length: 7,500 wds
Copies: 3
Notes: endnotes or footnotes
Blind referee: yes
Acceptance rate: 1/8
Time to consider ms: 2 mos
Charts, pictures, tables, graphs, maps
Foreign languages accepted: translation can be provided
• REVIEWS
Seeking reviewers: yes
Unsolicited reviews accepted: no
Materials reviewed: books, films, exhibits, other kinds of media and public history presentations
Review length: 750 wds
How to apply: letter
Include in application: professional degrees, institutional affiliation, areas of expertise, published works, foreign languages, current research

Oregon Historical Quarterly

History and culture of the Pacific Northwest
Affiliation: Oregon Historical Society
Ed: Rick Harmon
　1230 S.W. Park Avenue
　Portland, OR 97205
Bk Rev Ed: same
4/yr, 112 pp; subs $25
Circ: 8,000
Readership: academics, general public
Indexed/Abstracted: ABC, AHCI, CCAH, WAH
• MANUSCRIPTS
Query: no; *Abstract:* no
Style guide: Chicago
Preferred length: open
Copies: 2
Notes: endnotes
Blind referee: yes
Acceptance rate: 1/5
Time to consider ms: 6–12 mos
Pictures, maps
Foreign languages accepted: no
• REVIEWS
Seeking reviewers: yes

Unsolicited reviews accepted: yes
Materials reviewed: books, films, videos, exhibits, maps
Review length: 400–600 wds
How to apply: letter
Include in application: professional degrees, institutional affiliation, areas of expertise, published works, current research

Overland Journal

All aspects of the western emigrant trails — Oregon Trail and its many cutoffs, California Trail, Mormon Trail, etc.
Affiliation: Oregon-California Trails Association
Ed: Lois Daniel
　3533 Wyandotte
　Kansas City, MO 64111
Bk Rev Ed: Harold Smith
　206 Summer
　Parkville, MO 64152
4/yr, 36 pp; subs membership
Circ: 2,200
Readership: academics, general public, association members
Indexed/Abstracted: ABC
• MANUSCRIPTS
Query: preferred; *Abstract:* no
Style guide: Chicago
Preferred length: 35 pp
Copies: 1
Notes: endnotes
Blind referee: no
Time to consider ms: 1 mo
Charts, pictures, tables, graphs, maps
Foreign languages accepted: no
• REVIEWS
Seeking reviewers: no
Unsolicited reviews accepted: yes
Materials reviewed: books
Review length: 1–3 pp
How to apply: letter
• ADDITIONAL NOTES
Although not totally a scholarly magazine, the editors look for articles with an original point of view

about some aspect of the migration: the effect of weather, use of weapons, specific trail sites examined, etc, not just compilations of previously published material. They do publish and actively seek entire trail diaries that have not previously been published. Research based on unpublished or difficult to access material is a high priority.

Pacific Affairs

Asia and the Pacific
Affiliation: University of British Columbia
Ed: Ian D. Slater
University of British Columbia
2029 West Mall
Vancouver, BC V6T 1Z2
Bk Rev Ed: same
4/yr, 160 pp; subs $35
Circ: 4,000
Readership: academics
Indexed/Abstracted: ABC, AHCI, BRI, CCSB, HI, PAIS, SSCI, SSI
• MANUSCRIPTS
Query: no; *Abstract:* yes
Style guide: Chicago
Preferred length: 25 pp max
Copies: 4
Notes: footnotes
Blind referee: yes
Acceptance rate: 1/5
Time to consider ms: 3 mos max
Charts, tables, graphs, maps
Foreign languages accepted: no
• REVIEWS
Seeking reviewers: yes
Unsolicited reviews accepted: no
Materials reviewed: books
Review length: varies
How to apply: letter
Include in application: professional degrees, institutional affiliation, areas of expertise, published works, foreign languages

Pacific Historical Review

History of American expansion to the Pacific and beyond; post-frontier developments of the 20th century American West
Affiliation: University of California, Los Angeles
Ed: Norris Hundley, Jr.
University of California, Los Angeles
Ralphe Bunche Hall
Los Angeles, CA 90024-1473
Bk Rev Ed: same
4/yr, 150 pp; subs $19
Circ: 2,000
Readership: academics
Indexed/Abstracted: ABC, AHCI, BRI, CCAH, HI, WAH
• MANUSCRIPTS
Query: no; *Abstract:* no
Style guide: own
Preferred length: 25-35 pp
Copies: 3
Notes: footnotes
Blind referee: yes
Time to consider ms: 4-12 wks
Charts, pictures, tables, graphs, maps
Foreign languages accepted: no
• REVIEWS
Seeking reviewers: yes
Unsolicited reviews accepted: no
Materials reviewed: books
Review length: 400-500 wds
How to apply: letter
Include in application: professional degrees, institutional affiliation, areas of expertise, published works, foreign languages, current research

Pacific Northwest Forum

Pacific Northwest history
Affiliation: Eastern Washington University
Ed: J. William T. Youngs
Department of History
MS 27
Eastern Washington University
Cheney, WA 99004

Bk Rev Ed: same
2/yr, 120 pp; subs $8
Circ: 500
Readership: academics, general public
• MANUSCRIPTS
Query: no; *Abstract:* no
Preferred length: 8–30 pp
Copies: 2
Notes: endnotes
Blind referee: no
Acceptance rate: 1/2
Time to consider ms: 2 mos
Pictures, maps
Foreign languages accepted: no
• REVIEWS
Seeking reviewers: no
Unsolicited reviews accepted: no
Materials reviewed: books
• ADDITIONAL NOTES
Each year, one theme issue is published. Articles on the year's theme are particularly useful. Please write for information on forthcoming themes. The editors also like to publish edited documents, especially diaries and letters.

Pacific Northwest Quarterly

History of Pacific Northwest, including Alaska, western Montana, British Columbia, Washington, Oregon, and Idaho
Affiliation: University of Washington
Ed: Lewis O. Saum
4045 Brooklyn Avenue, N.E.
University of Washington
Seattle, WA 98105
Bk Rev Ed: same
4/yr, 40 pp; subs $15
Circ: 1,400
Readership: academics, general public
Indexed/Abstracted: ABC, AHCI, CCAH, WAH
• MANUSCRIPTS
Query: no; *Abstract:* no
Preferred length: 3–25 pp
Copies: 2
Notes: endnotes

Blind referee: yes
Acceptance rate: 1/2
Time to consider ms: 3–6 mos
Charts, pictures, tables, graphs, maps
Foreign languages accepted: no
• REVIEWS
Seeking reviewers: no
Unsolicited reviews accepted: no
Materials reviewed: books, films
How to apply: letter
Include in application: professional degrees (if any), institutional affiliation, areas of expertise, current research
• ADDITIONAL NOTES
The editors accept photo essays, e.g., the work of a Pacific Northwest photographer, views of a place or event or activity significant in or representative of the region. Text should give context of visual materials.

Pacific Studies

The people of the Pacific Islands
Affiliation: Brigham Young University-Hawaii Campus
Ed: Dale B. Robertson
Box 1829, BYU-HC
Laie, HI 96762
Bk Rev Ed: same
4/yr, 200 pp; subs $30
Circ: 500
Readership: academics
Indexed/Abstracted: ABC, BRI, PAIS, WAH
• MANUSCRIPTS
Query: no; *Abstract:* no
Style guide: MLA
Preferred length: 20 pp
Copies: 1
Notes: endnotes
Blind referee: yes
Acceptance rate: 1/2
Time to consider ms: 3 mos
Charts, pictures, tables, graphs, maps
Foreign languages accepted: no

- REVIEWS
Seeking reviewers: yes
Unsolicited reviews accepted: no
Materials reviewed: books, films
How to apply: form
Include in application: professional degrees, institutional affiliation, areas of expertise, published works, current research

Palimpsest

Iowa history
Affiliation: State Historical Society of Iowa
Ed: Ginale Swaim
402 Iowa Avenue
Iowa City, IA 52240
4/yr, 48 pp; subs $15
Circ: 4,000
Readership: academics, general public
Indexed/Abstracted: ABC, MLA, WAH
- MANUSCRIPTS
Query: preferred; *Abstract:* no
Style guide: Chicago
Preferred length: 20 pp
Copies: 2
Notes: endnotes or footnotes
Blind referee: occasionally
Acceptance rate: 1/2
Time to consider ms: 2 mos
Pictures
Foreign languages accepted: no

Panhandle-Plains Historical Review

Great Plains south of the Arkansas River
Affiliation: Panhandle-Plains Historical Society
Ed: Frederick W. Rathjen
Box 967 W. T. Station
Canyon, TX 79016
Bk Rev Ed: same
1/yr, 110 pp; subs $20
Circ: 800
Readership: academics, general public
Indexed/Abstracted: ABC

- MANUSCRIPTS
Query: preferred; *Abstract:* no
Style guide: Chicago
Preferred length: 20–30 pp
Copies: 2
Notes: endnotes
Blind referee: yes
Acceptance rate: 3/5
Time to consider ms: 1 yr
Any appropriate illustrations accepted
Foreign languages accepted: no
- REVIEWS
Seeking reviewers: no
Unsolicited reviews accepted: no
Materials reviewed: books
Review length: 300 wds
How to apply: letter
Include in application: professional degrees, institutional affiliation, areas of expertise, published works
- ADDITIONAL NOTES
The bulk of the readership comprises the membership of the Panhandle-Plains Historical Society. The editors, therefore, aim at a reasonably well informed "lay" readership as well as to the academic community. The Review maintains the highest possible standards of research, documentation, and writing and will consider any manuscript which meets those standards and falls within the editorial purview. Book reviewers are chosen on the basis of established scholarship, expertise, and professional integrity.

Papers of the Bibliographical Society of America

Descriptive, analytical, and historical bibliography; textual scholarship
Affiliation: Bibliographical Society of America
Ed: William S. Peterson
Department of English
University of Maryland
College Park, MD 20742
Bk Rev Ed: same

4/yr, 120 pp; subs $30
Circ: 1,250
Readership: academics, librarians,
  collectors, booksellers
Indexed/Abstracted: ABC, AHCI,
  BRI, CCAH, HI, IMB, MLA,
  WAH
● MANUSCRIPTS
Query: no; *Abstract:* no
Style guide: Chicago
Preferred length: 30 pp
Copies: 1
Notes: endnotes
Blind referee: sometimes
Acceptance rate: 3/10
Time to consider ms: 2–6 mos
Pictures, tables
Foreign languages accepted: no
● REVIEWS
Seeking reviewers: no
Unsolicited reviews accepted: no
Materials reviewed: books
Review length: 1,000 wds
● ADDITIONAL NOTES
In general, the *Papers* do not deal
with enumerative bibliography.

Parliamentary History

British parliamentary history from
  the Middle Ages to the 20th cen-
  tury including Scottish and Irish
  parliaments and British colonial
  legislatures
Ed: Clyve Jones
  Institute of Historical Research
  University of London
  Senate House
  Malet Street
  London WC1E 7HU
  U.K.
Bk Rev Ed: Stephen Taylor
  Department of History
  University of Reading
  Reading RG6 2AA
  U.K.
3/yr, 120 pp; subs £25
Circ: 450
Readership: academics
Indexed/Abstracted: ABC, BHI

● MANUSCRIPTS
Query: no; *Abstract:* no
Style guide: own
Preferred length: 8,000–10,000 wds
Copies: 2
Notes: endnotes
Blind referee: yes
Acceptance rate: 1/2
Time to consider ms: 3 mos
Charts, pictures, tables, graphs, maps
Foreign languages accepted: no
● REVIEWS
Seeking reviewers: no
Unsolicited reviews accepted: no
Materials reviewed: books
Review length: varies
How to apply: letter
Include in application: professional
  degrees, institutional affiliation,
  areas of expertise, published
  works, current research

Parliaments, Estates & Repre-
sentation/Parlements, Etats
& Representation

History of representative and
  parliamentary institutions
Affiliation: International Commission
  for the History of Representative
  and Parliamentary Institutions
Ed: I. A. A. Thompson
  Department of History
  University of Keele
  Keele
  Staffs ST5 5BG
  U.K.
Bk Rev Ed: same
2/yr, 96 pp; subs £55
Circ: 450
Readership: academics
Indexed/Abstracted: ABC, IMB
● MANUSCRIPTS
Query: no; *Abstract:* yes
Style guide: MLA or ModHum
Preferred length: 8,000 wds
Copies: 2
Notes: endnotes
Blind referee: no

Acceptance rate: 1/2
Time to consider ms: 1–2 mos
Charts, tables, graphs, maps
Foreign languages accepted: French,
    German
• REVIEWS
Seeking reviewers: no
Unsolicited reviews accepted: yes
Materials reviewed: books, con-
    ferences, major articles
Review length: 600–1,200 wds
How to apply: letter
Include in application: institutional
    affiliation, areas of expertise, pub-
    lished works, foreign languages,
    current research

Past and Present: A Journal of Historical Studies

Social, economic, and cultural history
    of all periods and all parts of the
    world
Affiliation: The Past and Present
    Society
Eds: Paul Slack and Joanna Innes
    175 Banbury Road
    Oxford OX2 7AW
    U.K.
Bk Rev Ed: same
4/yr, 200 pp; subs £20.50
Circ: 3,400
Readership: academics
Indexed/Abstracted: ABC, AHCI,
    BHI, CCAH, CCSB, HI, IMB,
    SSCI, WAH
• MANUSCRIPTS
Query: no; *Abstract:* preferred
Style guide: own
Preferred length: 6,000–8,000 wds
Copies: 2–3
Notes: endnotes or footnotes
Blind referee: no
Time to consider ms: 2–3 mos
Charts, pictures, tables, graphs, maps
Foreign languages accepted: no
• REVIEWS
Seeking reviewers: no
Unsolicited reviews accepted: yes

Materials reviewed: books
Review length: 3,000–8,000 wds

Pennsylvania Folklife

Folklife, folklore, history and geog-
    raphy of Pennsylvania from co-
    lonial times to present
Affiliation: Pennsylvania Folklife
    Society and Ursinus College
Ed: Nancy K. Gaugler
    P.O. Box 92
    Collegeville, PA 19426
Bk Rev Ed: same
3/yr, 48 pp; subs $10
Readership: academics, general public
Indexed/Abstracted: ABC, MLA
• MANUSCRIPTS
Query: no; *Abstract:* no
Style guide: MLA
Preferred length: 4–100 pp
Copies: 1
Notes: endnotes
Blind referee: no
Acceptance rate: 3/4
Time to consider ms: 60 days
Charts, pictures, tables, graphs, maps
Foreign languages accepted: no
• REVIEWS
Seeking reviewers: no
Unsolicited reviews accepted: no

Pennsylvania History

History of Pennsylvania
Affiliation: Gettysburg College
Ed: Michael J. Birkner
    Department of History
    Gettysburg College
    Gettysburg, PA 17325
Bk Rev Ed: Jack Bauman
    Department of History
    California University of Penn-
    sylvania
    California, PA 15419
4/yr, 100 pp; subs $20
Circ: 800
Readership: academics, general public
Indexed/Abstracted: ABC, WAH
• MANUSCRIPTS
Query: no; *Abstract:* no

Style guide: Turabian or Chicago
Preferred length: 20–25 pp
Copies: 2
Notes: endnotes
Blind referee: yes
Acceptance rate: 1/3
Time to consider ms: 3 mos
Charts, pictures, tables, graphs, maps
Foreign languages accepted: no
• REVIEWS
Seeking reviewers: yes
Unsolicited reviews accepted: no
Materials reviewed: books, films, exhibits
Review length: 500 wds
How to apply: letter
Include in application: professional degrees, institutional affiliation, areas of expertise, published works, current research

Pennsylvania Magazine of History and Biography

History of Pennsylvania and the Mid-Atlantic region
Affiliation: Historical Society of Pennsylvania
Ed: Ian M. G. Quimby
Historical Society of Pennsylvania
1300 Locust Street
Philadelphia, PA 19107
Bk Rev Ed: same
4/yr, 160 pp; subs $30
Circ: 3,300
Readership: academics, general public, society members
Indexed/Abstracted: ABC, AHCI, CCAH, MLA, WAH
• MANUSCRIPTS
Query: preferred; *Abstract:* no
Style guide: Chicago
Preferred length: 25–30 pp
Copies: 2
Notes: endnotes
Blind referee: yes
Acceptance rate: 1/5
Time to consider ms: 2–3 mos

Charts, pictures, tables, graphs, maps
Foreign languages accepted: no
• REVIEWS
Seeking reviewers: yes
Unsolicited reviews accepted: no
Materials reviewed: books
Review length: 600 wds
How to apply: letter
Include in application: professional degrees, institutional affiliation, areas of expertise, published works, current research

Pennsylvania Mennonite Heritage

History of Amish and Mennonites in Pennsylvania, their origins in Europe and daughter settlements in North America
Affiliation: Lancaster Mennonite Historical Society
Ed: David J. Rempel Smucker
2215 Millstream Road
Lancaster, PA 17602
Bk Rev Ed: same
4/yr, 42 pp; subs $25
Circ: 3,000
Readership: academics, general public
Indexed/Abstracted: ABC, WAH
• MANUSCRIPTS
Query: no; *Abstract:* preferred
Style guide: Chicago
Preferred length: 15–35 pp
Copies: 1
Notes: footnotes
Blind referee: no
Acceptance rate: 4/5
Time to consider ms: 4 mos
Charts, pictures, tables, graphs, maps
Foreign languages accepted: translated; German and French
• REVIEWS
Seeking reviewers: yes
Unsolicited reviews accepted: no
Materials reviewed: books, films, museum exhibits
How to apply: letter
Include in application: professional

degrees, institutional affiliation,
areas of expertise, current research

Pensacola History Illustrated

Local history of Northwest Florida
and South Alabama
Affiliation: Pensacola Historical So-
ciety
Ed: Virginia Parks
Pensacola Historical Museum
405 S. Adams Street
Pensacola, FL 32501
Bk Rev Ed: Mary Dawkins
2/yr, 34 pp; subs membership
Circ: 800
Readership: academics, general public
Indexed/Abstracted: ABC
• MANUSCRIPTS
Query: preferred; *Abstract:* preferred
Style guide: Turabian
Preferred length: 10–20 pp
Copies: 2
Notes: endnotes
Blind referee: no
Acceptance rate: 7/10
Time to consider ms: varies
Charts, pictures, tables, graphs, maps
Foreign languages accepted: no
• REVIEWS
Seeking reviewers: no
Unsolicited reviews accepted: yes
Materials reviewed: books
Review length: 2–4 pp
How to apply: letter
Include in application: professional
degrees, institutional affiliation,
areas of expertise, published
works, current research

Pharmacy in History

History of pharmaceutical practice,
including history of drugs and ther-
apeutics and related facets of the
medical sciences
Affiliation: American Institute of the
History of Pharmacy
Ed: Gregory J. Higby
American Institute of the History
of Pharmacy

Bk Rev Ed: Elaine C. Stroud
4/yr, 60 pp; subs $25
Circ: 1,200
Readership: academics, pharmacy
professionals
Indexed/Abstracted: ABC, WAH
• MANUSCRIPTS
Query: no; *Abstract:* no
Style guide: own
Preferred length: 10,000 wds max
Copies: 2
Notes: endnotes
Blind referee: yes
Acceptance rate: 1/2
Time to consider ms: 3–6 wks
Charts, pictures, tables
Foreign languages accepted: no
• REVIEWS
Seeking reviewers: yes
Unsolicited reviews accepted: no
Materials reviewed: books
How to apply: letter
Include in application: professional
degrees, institutional affiliation,
areas of expertise, published
works, foreign languages, current
research

Photographic Canadiana

Photographic history, collection of
artifacts
Affiliation: Photographic Historical
Society of Canada
Ed: Everett Roseborough
4174 Dundas Street, W., -203
Etobicoke, ON M8X 1X3
CANADA
Bk Rev Eds: Robert Wilson, Stanley
J. White
5/yr, 22 pp; subs membership
Circ: 450
Readership: academics, general pub-
lic, society members
• MANUSCRIPTS
Query: preferred; *Abstract:* preferred
Preferred length: 1,000–3,000 wds
Copies: 1
Blind referee: no

Acceptance rate: 3/5
Time to consider ms: 2 wks
Charts, pictures, tables, graphs, maps
Foreign languages accepted: no
• REVIEWS
Seeking reviewers: no
Materials reviewed: books
Review length: 1,000 wds

The Pickaway Quarterly

History of Pickaway County, Ohio
Affiliation: Pickaway County Histori-
cal Society
Ed: Steve Jones
    10979 Heffner Road
    Circleville, OH 43113
4/yr, 24 pp; subs $12
Circ: 800
Readership: academics, general public
• MANUSCRIPTS
Query: yes
Notes: footnotes
Blind referee: no
Charts, pictures, tables, graphs, maps
Foreign languages accepted: no

Pilipinas: A Journal of Philippine Studies

Research concerning the Philippines,
in all scholarly disciplines
Affiliation: Arizona State University
Ed: James F. Eder
    Program for Southeast Asian
    Studies
    Arizona State University
    Tempe, AZ 85287-3101
Bk Rev Ed: Roger Bresnahan
    Department of American
    Thought and Languages
    Michigan State University
    East Lansing, MI 48823
2/yr, 125 pp; subs $16
Circ: 200
Readership: academics, general public
• MANUSCRIPTS
Query: no; *Abstract:* yes
Style guide: own
Preferred length: 20-40 pp

Copies: 1
Notes: endnotes
Blind referee: yes
Acceptance rate: 1/2
Time to consider ms: 3 mos
Tables
Foreign languages accepted: no
• REVIEWS
Seeking reviewers: yes
Unsolicited reviews accepted: no
Materials reviewed: books, films
Review length: 2-4 pp
How to apply: letter
Include in application: professional
    degrees, institutional affiliation,
    areas of expertise, published
    works, current research

Pittsburgh History: A Magazine of the City and Its Region

History of western Pennsylvania
    region, including northern West
    Virginia and eastern Ohio; espec-
    ially general social history of Pitts-
    burgh
Affiliation: Historical Society of West
    Pennsylvania
Ed: Paul Roberts
    4338 Bigelow Boulevard
    Pittsburgh, PA 15213
Bk Rev Ed: same
4/yr, 50 pp; subs $30
Circ: 3,000
Readership: society members
Indexed/Abstracted: ABC, WAH
• MANUSCRIPTS
Query: preferred; *Abstract:* preferred
Preferred length: open
Copies: 3
Notes: endnotes
Blind referee: yes
Acceptance rate: 7/10
Time to consider ms: 2-6 mos
Charts, pictures, tables, graphs, maps
Foreign languages accepted: no
• REVIEWS
Seeking reviewers: yes

Unsolicited reviews accepted: yes
Materials reviewed: books, films
How to apply: letter
Include in application: professional
   degrees, institutional affiliation,
   areas of expertise, current research

Plateau

Colorado Plateau
Affiliation: Museum of Northern Arizona
Ed: Diana Clark Lubick
   Rt. 4, Box 720
   Flagstaff, AZ 86001
4/yr, 32 pp; subs $20
Circ: 6,000
Readership: academics, general public
Indexed/Abstracted: ABC
• MANUSCRIPTS
Query: yes; *Abstract:* no
Preferred length: 28–35 pp
Copies: 1
Notes: none
Blind referee: no
Charts, pictures, tables, graphs, maps
Foreign languages accepted: no

The Polish Review

Poland and Polish subjects in various
   fields of study
Affiliation: Polish Institute of Arts
   and Sciences in America
Ed: Joseph W. Wieczerzak
   208 East 30th Street
   New York, NY 10016
Bk Rev Ed: Krystyna S. Olszer
4/yr, 128 pp
Circ: 1,200
Readership: academics
Indexed/Abstracted: ABC, MLA,
   WAH
• MANUSCRIPTS
Query: preferred; *Abstract:* no
Style guide: own
Preferred length: 25 pp
Copies: 3
Notes: footnotes
Blind referee: yes

Acceptance rate: 4/5
Time to consider ms: 1 mo
Charts, pictures, tables, graphs, maps
Foreign languages accepted: no
• REVIEWS
Seeking reviewers: yes
Unsolicited reviews accepted: yes
Materials reviewed: books, films,
   other media
Review length: 5 pp
How to apply: letter
Include in application: professional
   degrees, institutional affiliation,
   published works, current research

Polyphony: Bulletin of the Multicultural History Society of Ontario

All cultures in Ontario and Canada
Ed: Gabriele Scardellato
   43 Queen's Park Crescent East
   Toronto, ON M4S 2C3
   CANADA
Bk Rev Ed: same
2/yr, 200 pp; subs $20
Circ: 300
Readership: academics, general public, cultural centers
Indexed/Abstracted: ABC
• MANUSCRIPTS
Query: preferred; *Abstract:* yes
Preferred length: 3–5 pp
Copies: 1
Notes: endnotes
Blind referee: no
Acceptance rate: 1/10
Time to consider ms: 2 mos
Charts, pictures, tables, graphs,
   maps
Foreign languages accepted: no
• REVIEWS
Seeking reviewers: no
Unsolicited reviews accepted: no
Materials reviewed: books
Review length: 2–3 pp
How to apply: letter
Include in application: institutional
   affiliation, areas of expertise,

published works, current research, personal cultural interest

Prairie Forum

Canadian plains and the Great Plains
Affiliation: University of Regina
Ed: Alvin Finkel
    c/o Canadian Plains Research
      Center
    University of Regina
    Regina, SK S4S 0A2
    CANADA
Bk Rev Ed: Phil Hansen
2/yr, 150 pp; subs $20
Circ: 350
Readership: academics
Indexed/Abstracted: ABC
• MANUSCRIPTS
Query: preferred; *Abstract:* yes
Style guide: Chicago
Preferred length: 3,500–5,000 wds
Copies: 3
Notes: endnotes
Blind referee: yes
Acceptance rate: 3/10
Time to consider ms: 18–24 mos
Charts, pictures, tables, graphs, maps
Foreign languages accepted: French
• REVIEWS
Seeking reviewers: no
Unsolicited reviews accepted: no

Presidential Studies Quarterly

American presidency; relations with
    Congress and the courts; foreign
    and domestic policies
Affiliation: Center for the Study of
    the Presidency
Ed: R. Gordon Hoxie
    208 East 75th Street
    New York, NY 10021
Bk Rev Ed: Philip R. Rulon
    Professor of History
    Northern Arizona University
    Box 5725
    Flagstaff, AZ 86001
4/yr, 212 pp; subs $25
Circ: 14,500

Readership: academics, general public
Indexed/Abstracted: ABC, BRI,
    PAIS, SSI, WAH
• MANUSCRIPTS
Query: preferred; *Abstract:* yes
Style guide: Chicago
Preferred length: 4,000 wds
Copies: 3
Notes: endnotes
Blind referee: yes
Acceptance rate: 1/4
Time to consider ms: 6–12 mos
Charts, tables, graphs
Foreign languages accepted: no
• REVIEWS
Seeking reviewers: yes
Unsolicited reviews accepted: yes
Materials reviewed: books
Review length: 500–800 wds
How to apply: letter
Include in application: professional
    degrees, institutional affiliation,
    areas of expertise, published
    works, current research

Princeton History

History of Princeton, New Jersey
Affiliation: Historical Society of
    Princeton
Ed: Gloria B. Halpern
    Historical Society of Princeton
    158 Nassau Street
    Princeton, NJ 08542
Bk Rev Ed: same
1/yr, 60 pp; subs membership
Circ: 1,200
Readership: academics, general public
Indexed/Abstracted: ABC
• MANUSCRIPTS
Query: preferred; *Abstract:* no
Style guide: Chicago
Preferred length: 20–25 pp
Copies: 1
Notes: endnotes or footnotes
Blind referee: no
Acceptance rate: 2/3
Time to consider ms: 3 wks
Charts, pictures, tables, maps
Foreign languages accepted: no

- REVIEWS
Seeking reviewers: yes
Unsolicited reviews accepted: yes
Materials reviewed: books
Review length: open
How to apply: letter
Include in application: professional
  degrees, institutional affiliation,
  areas of expertise, published
  works, current research

Princeton University Library Chronicle

Humanities, social and natural
  sciences, and books and book col-
  lecting; based on research con-
  ducted in the Library's Department
  of Rare Books and Special Collec-
  tions
Affiliation: Princeton University
Ed: Patricia H. Marks
    Rare Books and Special Collec-
    tions
    Princeton University Libraries
    One Washington Road
    Princeton, NJ 08544
3/yr, 125 pp; subs $50
Circ: 1,250–1,750
Readership: academics, general public
Indexed/Abstracted: ABC, IMB,
  MLA, WAH
- MANUSCRIPTS
Query: no; *Abstract:* no
Style guide: Chicago
Preferred length: 25–40 pp
Copies: 1
Notes: footnotes
Blind referee: no
Acceptance rate: 4/5
Time to consider ms: 2–3 mos
Charts, pictures, tables, graphs,
  maps
Foreign languages accepted: no
- ADDITIONAL NOTES
The editors seek articles of scholarly
  importance written for the edu-
  cated non-specialist.

Print Quarterly

History of printmaking
Ed: David Landau
    80 Carlton Hill
    London NW8 0ER
    U.K.
Bk Rev Ed: same
4/yr, 124 pp; subs $56 U.S.
Circ: 1,500
Readership: academics, collectors,
  dealers
Indexed/Abstracted: ABC, AHCI,
  CCAH
- MANUSCRIPTS
Query: yes; *Abstract:* no
Style guide: own
Preferred length: 6,000 wds
Copies: 1
Notes: endnotes
Blind referee: yes
Acceptance rate: 3/10
Time to consider ms: 3 mos
All illustrations accepted
Foreign languages accepted: no
- REVIEWS
Seeking reviewers: no
Unsolicited reviews accepted: no
Materials reviewed: books
Review length: 1,500 wds

Printing History

Printing history, type design, book-
  making
Affiliation: American Printing His-
  tory Association
Ed: David Pankow
    Cary Collection
    Rochester Institute of Technology
    One Lomb Memorial Drive
    Rochester, NY 14623
Bk Rev Ed: same
2/yr, 48 pp; subs $30
Circ: 1,300
Readership: academics, general pub-
  lic, association members
Indexed/Abstracted: IMB, MLA,
  WAH

- MANUSCRIPTS
Query: preferred; *Abstract:* preferred
Style guide: Chicago
Preferred length: varies
Copies: 1
Notes: endnotes
Blind referee: yes
Acceptance rate: 3/4
Time to consider ms: 2 mos
Any suitable illustrations accepted
Foreign languages accepted: no
- REVIEWS
Seeking reviewers: yes
Unsolicited reviews accepted: yes
Materials reviewed: books
Review length: 750 wds
How to apply: letter
Include in application: professional
degrees, institutional affiliation,
areas of expertise

Proceedings of the American Antiquarian Society: A Journal of American History and Culture Through 1876

American history and culture through
1876
Affiliation: American Antiquarian
Society
Ed: John B. Hench
American Antiquarian Society
185 Salisbury Street
Worcester, MA 01609
2/yr; subs $45
Circ: 1,000
Readership: academics, general pub-
lic, society members
Indexed/Abstracted: ABC, AHCI,
CCAH, MLA, WAH
- MANUSCRIPTS
Query: preferred; *Abstract:* no
Style guide: modified Chicago
Copies: 2
Notes: endnotes
Blind referee: yes
Acceptance rate: 1/4
Time to consider ms: 2–6 mos

Charts, pictures, tables, graphs, maps
Foreign languages accepted: no
- ADDITIONAL NOTES
The *Proceedings of the American
Antiquarian Society,* one of the
country's oldest learned journals,
publishes articles within the general
field of American history and culture through 1876. The *Proceedings*
has become a principal medium for
the publication of scholarship in
the new interdisciplinary field of
the history of the book in American culture. The *Proceedings* also
emphasizes the publication of mid-
length works and the publication
of tools for scholarship, such as
bibliographies and primary documents.

Proceedings of the American Philosophical Society

History, sciences, social sciences
Affiliation: American Philosophical
Society
Ed: Herman H. Goldstine
104 South Fifth Street
Philadelphia, PA 19106
4/yr, 120 pp; subs $27
Circ: 1,800
Readership: academics
Indexed/Abstracted: ABC, AHCI,
CCAH, MLA, WAH
- MANUSCRIPTS
Query: no; *Abstract:* no
Style guide: Chicago
Preferred length: 100 pp max
Copies: 2
Blind referee: yes
Acceptance rate: 1/2
Time to consider ms: 6 mos
Charts, pictures, tables, graphs, maps
Foreign languages accepted: all

Proceedings of the Wesley Historical Society

Methodist history, chiefly British
Affiliation: Wesley Historical Society

Ed: E. A. Rose
 26 Roe Cross Green
 Mottram
 Hyde
 Cheshire SK14 6LP
 U.K.
Bk Rev Ed: same
3/yr, 32 pp; subs £6
Circ: 900
Readership: academics, general public
Indexed/Abstracted: ABC
• MANUSCRIPTS
Query: preferred; *Abstract:* no
Preferred length: 5,000–6,000 wds
Copies: 1
Notes: footnotes
Blind referee: no
Acceptance rate: 3/5
Time to consider ms: 3 mos
Charts, pictures, tables, graphs, maps
Foreign languages accepted: no
• REVIEWS
Seeking reviewers: no
Unsolicited reviews accepted: no
Materials reviewed: books
Review length: 500 wds
How to apply: letter
Include in application: areas of
 expertise

Prologue: Quarterly of the National Archives

History of the United States, 1774–
present; based in whole or in part
on the holdings and programs of
the National Archives, its regional
archives, and the presidential li-
braries
Affiliation: National Archives and
 Records Administration
Ed: Henry J. Gwiazda II
 National Archives
 NEPP
 Washington, DC 20408
4/yr, 112 pp; subs $12
Circ: 4,500
Readership: academics, general pub-
lic, genealogists

Indexed/Abstracted: ABC, AHCI,
 CCAH, WAH
• MANUSCRIPTS
Query: preferred; *Abstract:* no
Style guide: Chicago
Preferred length: varies
Copies: 1
Notes: endnotes
Blind referee: sometimes
Acceptance rate: relatively high
Time to consider ms: 6–12 mos
Charts, pictures, tables, graphs, maps
Foreign languages accepted: no
• ADDITIONAL NOTES
Inquiries prior to submission of a
manuscript are highly desirable.
Telephone inquiries are welcome
(202-724-0086). Besides the use of
National Archives records, other
factors that are considered include
general interest, breadth of topic,
and quality of expression. Manu-
scripts that are politically partisan
or deal with contemporary political
issues will not be accepted.

Psychohistory Review

Application of psychology to history
Affiliation: Sangamon State Univer-
 sity
Ed: Larry Shiner
 Brookens 385
 Sangamon State University
 Springfield, IL 62794
Bk Rev Ed: Mark Johnson
3/yr, 120 pp; subs $22
Circ: 400
Readership: academics, psychiatrists
Indexed/Abstracted: ABC
• MANUSCRIPTS
Query: no; *Abstract:* no
Style guide: Chicago
Preferred length: 20 pp
Copies: 2
Notes: footnotes
Blind referee: no
Acceptance rate: 1/3
Time to consider ms: 2–3 mos

Charts, pictures, tables, graphs, maps
Foreign languages accepted: no
• REVIEWS
Seeking reviewers: yes
Unsolicited reviews accepted: yes
Materials reviewed: books
Review length: 3–5 pp
How to apply: letter
Include in application: professional
degrees, institutional affiliation,
areas of expertise, published
works, foreign languages, current
research

Public Historian

Public history
Affiliation: University of California,
Santa Barbara
Ed: Otis L. Graham, Jr.
Ellison Hall
University of California, Santa
Barbara
Santa Barbara, CA 93106
Bk Rev Ed: Michael Osborne
4/yr, 128 pp; subs $37
Circ: 1,300
Readership: academics, general pub-
lic, public historians
Indexed/Abstracted: ABC, AHCI,
CCAH, WAH
• MANUSCRIPTS
Query: no; *Abstract:* yes
Style guide: Chicago
Preferred length: 20–30 pp
Copies: 4
Notes: endnotes
Blind referee: yes
Acceptance rate: 1/4
Time to consider ms: 2 mos
Charts, pictures, tables, graphs, maps
Foreign languages accepted: no
• REVIEWS
Seeking reviewers: yes
Unsolicited reviews accepted: no
Materials reviewed: books, films, ex-
hibits, software, archives
Review length: 2–3 pp
How to apply: letter

Include in application: professional
degrees, institutional or public
history affiliation, areas of expertise, published works, current
research

Publishing History

Social, economic, and literary history
of book, newspaper, and magazine
publishing
Eds: Michael L. Turner and Simon
Eliot
The Bodleian Library
Oxford OX1 3BG
U.K.
Bk Rev Ed: Michael L. Turner
2/yr, 90 pp; subs $48 U.S.
Circ: 400
Readership: academics
Indexed/Abstracted: ABC, AHCI,
BHI, CCAH, IMB, MLA
• MANUSCRIPTS
Query: no; *Abstract:* no
Preferred length: open
Copies: 2
Notes: endnotes
Blind referee: no
Charts, tables, graphs
Foreign languages accepted: no
• REVIEWS
Unsolicited reviews accepted: no
Materials reviewed: books
Review length: 1,500–2,000 wds
How to apply: letter

Quaker History

The history of the Religious Society
of Friends
Affiliation: Haverford College,
Swarthmore College, and Villanova
University
Ed: Charles L. Cherry
Office of Academics Affairs
Villanova University
Villanova, PA 19085
Bk Rev Ed: Thomas D. Hamm
Lilly Library
Earlham College
Richmond, IN 47374

2/yr, 64 pp; subs $15
Circ: 850
Readership: academics, general public, genealogists
Indexed/Abstracted: ABC, WAH
• MANUSCRIPTS
Query: no; *Abstract:* no
Style guide: MLA
Preferred length: 10–20 pp
Copies: 1
Notes: endnotes
Blind referee: no
Acceptance rate: 1/5–1/4
Time to consider ms: 4–8 wks
Charts, pictures, tables, graphs, maps
Foreign languages accepted: no
• REVIEWS
Seeking reviewers: no
Unsolicited reviews accepted: no
Materials reviewed: books
Review length: 1–2 pp
How to apply: letter
Include in application: professional degrees, institutional affiliation, areas of expertise, published works, current research

Quebec Studies

All aspects of Quebec society and French-Canadian culture
Affiliation: American Council for Quebec Studies
Ed: Karen Gould
   Department of Romance Languages
   Bowling Green State University
   Bowling Green, OH 43403
Bk Rev Ed: Emilie Talbot
contact the editor directly
2/yr, 120 pp; subs $30
Readership: academics
• MANUSCRIPTS
Query: no; *Abstract:* yes
Style guide: MLA
Preferred length: 15–20 pp
Copies: 3
Notes: endnotes
Blind referee: yes
Foreign languages accepted: French

• REVIEWS
Unsolicited reviews accepted: yes
Materials reviewed: books
Review length: varies

Queen's Quarterly

A wide variety of subjects, including science, humanities, arts and letters, politics and history for the educated reader
Affiliation: Queen's University
Ed: Boris Castel
   Queen's University
   Kingston, ON K7L 3N6
   CANADA
Bk Rev Ed: same
4/yr, 224 pp; subs $20
Circ: 3,000
Readership: academics
Indexed/Abstracted: ABC, AHCI, BRI, CCAH, MLA
• MANUSCRIPTS
Query: no; *Abstract:* no
Preferred length: 2,000–3,500 wds
Copies: 3
Notes: endnotes
Blind referee: yes
Time to consider ms: 6 wks
• REVIEWS
Seeking reviewers: no
Unsolicited reviews accepted: occasionally
Materials reviewed: books

Radical America

Socialist/feminist journal of politics and culture
Ed: 12 member board
   1 Summer Street
   Somerville, MA 02143
Bk Rev Ed: same
4/yr, 88 pp; subs $20
Circ: 5,000
Readership: academics, general public
Indexed/Abstracted: ABC
• MANUSCRIPTS
Query: no; *Abstract:* no
Preferred length: varies

Copies: 1
Notes: endnotes
Blind referee: no
Time to consider ms: varies
Charts, pictures, tables, graphs, maps
Foreign languages accepted: French,
  Spanish
• REVIEWS
Seeking reviewers: yes
Unsolicited reviews accepted: yes
Materials reviewed: books
Review length: 1-2 pp
How to apply: letter
Include in application: professional
  degrees, areas of expertise, pub-
  lished works, current research

Radical History Review

Examines important new scholarship
  and analyzes the uses and abuse of
  history in the popular media, his-
  tory museums, and other public
  forms
Ed: Molly McGarry
  Tamiment Library
  70 Washington Square South
  New York, NY 10012
Bk Rev Ed: Jon Wiener
3/yr, 200 pp; subs $24
Circ: 2,000
Readership: academics, general public
Indexed/Abstracted: ABC, AHCI,
  CCAH, WAH
• MANUSCRIPTS
Query: no; *Abstract:* no
Style guide: Chicago
Copies: 4
Notes: endnotes
Blind referee: yes
Charts, pictures, maps
Foreign languages accepted: no
• REVIEWS
Seeking reviewers: no
Unsolicited reviews accepted: no
Materials reviewed: books, films,
  museum exhibits
How to apply: letter
Include in application: professional

degrees, institutional affiliation,
  areas of expertise, published
  works, foreign languages, current
  research, abstract

Railroad History

Railroad history
Affiliation: The University of Akron;
  The Smithsonian Institution
Ed: H. Roger Grant
  Department of History
  The University of Akron
  Akron, OH 44325-1902
Bk Rev Ed: James N. J. Henwood
  Department of History
  East Stroudsburg University
  East Stroudsburg, PA 18301
2/yr, 148 pp; subs $18
Circ: 3,500
Readership: academics, general pub-
  lic, railfans
Indexed/Abstracted: ABC
• MANUSCRIPTS
Query: no; *Abstract:* no
Style guide: Chicago
Preferred length: 50 pp max
Copies: 2
Notes: endnotes
Blind referee: yes
Time to consider ms: 4-6 wks
Charts, pictures, tables, graphs, maps
Foreign languages accepted: no
• REVIEWS
Seeking reviewers: yes
Unsolicited reviews accepted: no
Materials reviewed: books
Review length: 500-750 wds
How to apply: letter
Include in application: areas of
  expertise

Recusant History

History of the Roman Catholic
  church since Reformation, espec-
  ially Great Britain and Ireland
Affiliation: Catholic Record Society
Ed: V. A. M. Clelland
  School of Education

The University of Hull
Hull HU6 7RX
U.K.
2/yr, 150 pp; subs $15
Readership: academics, general public
Indexed/Abstracted: ABC, BHI
• MANUSCRIPTS
Query: preferred; *Abstract:* preferred
Style guide: own
Preferred length: 8,000–9,000 wds
Copies: 2
Notes: endnotes
Blind referee: yes
Acceptance rate: 1/2
Time to consider ms: 1 mo
Charts, pictures, tables, graphs,
    maps, manuscript reproductions
Foreign languages accepted: no

The Register of the Kentucky Historical Society

Kentucky history
Affiliation: Kentucky Historical So-
    ciety
Ed: Thomas H. Appleton, Jr.
    P.O. Box H
    Old Capitol Annex
    Frankfort, KY 40602-2108
Bk Rev Ed: same
4/yr, 120 pp; subs $25
Circ: 6,000
Readership: academics, general public
Indexed/Abstracted: ABC, WAH
• MANUSCRIPTS
Query: no; *Abstract:* no
Style guide: Chicago
Preferred length: 25–35 pp
Copies: 3
Notes: footnotes
Blind referee: yes
Acceptance rate: 1/3
Time to consider ms: 3 mos
Pictures, tables, maps
Foreign languages accepted: no
• REVIEWS
Seeking reviewers: yes
Unsolicited reviews accepted: no
Materials reviewed: books

Review length: 300–350 wds
How to apply: letter
Include in application: professional
    degrees, institutional affiliation,
    areas of expertise, published
    works, current research
• ADDITIONAL NOTES
Manuscripts may be from professional or academic historians.
Authors whose papers are accepted
are encouraged to submit their own
illustrations or ideas on where to
obtain them. In addition to the
regular single-work book reviews,
review essays are occasionally published.

Religion

Religious studies
European Ed: Adrian Cunningham
    Department of Religious Studies
    Lancaster University
    Lancaster LA1 4YG
    U.K.
U.S. Ed: Ivan Strenski
    3463 Meier Street
    Mar Vista
    Los Angeles, CA 90066-1701
European Bk Rev Ed: J. F. A. Sawyer
    Department of Religious Studies
    The University of Newcastle
        upon Tyne
    Newcastle upon Tyne NE1 7RU
    U.K.
U.S. Bk Rev Ed: Ivan Strenski
4/yr, 100 pp; subs £25
Readership: academics
Indexed/Abstracted: AHCI, CCAH,
    HI, IMB
• MANUSCRIPTS
Query: no; *Abstract:* yes
Style guide: own
Preferred length: 5,000 wds max
Copies: 2
Notes: endnotes
Time to consider ms: 12 wks
Pictures
Foreign languages accepted: no

• REVIEWS
Materials reviewed: books
Review length: varies

Renaissance and Reformation/ Renaissance et Reforme

Multidisciplinary studies on the Renaissance
Affiliation: University of Guelph
Ed: François Pare
  Department of French Studies
  University of Guelph
  Guelph, ON N1G 2W1
  CANADA
English Bk Rev Ed: Daniel Doerksen
  Department of English
  University of New Brunswick
  P.O. Box 4400
  Fredericton, NB E3B 5A3
  CANADA
French Bk Rev Ed: Pierre-Louis
  Vaillancourt
  Lettres françaises
  Université d'Ottawa
  Ottawa, ON K1N 6N5
  CANADA
4/yr, 100 pp; subs $20
Circ: 800
Readership: academics
Indexed/Abstracted: ABC, AHCI,
  BRI, CCAH, MLA
• MANUSCRIPTS
Query: no; *Abstract:* no
Style guide: MLA for English; any
  standard format for French
Preferred length: 50 pp max
Copies: 2
Notes: endnotes
Blind referee: yes
Acceptance rate: 1/4
Time to consider ms: 6–8 mos
Charts, pictures, tables, graphs, maps
Foreign languages accepted: French
• REVIEWS
Seeking reviewers: yes
Unsolicited reviews accepted: no
Materials reviewed: books
Review length: 500–800 wds

How to apply: letter
Include in application: professional
  degrees, institutional affiliation,
  areas of expertise, foreign languages

Renaissance Quarterly

Interdisciplinary Renaissance studies
Ed: Rona Goffen
  1161 Amsterdam Avenue
  New York, NY 10027
Bk Rev Ed: Bridget Gellert Lyons
4/yr, 200 pp; subs $50
Circ: 3,500
Readership: academics
Indexed/Abstracted: ABC, AHCI,
  CCAH, HI, IMB, MLA
• MANUSCRIPTS
Query: no; *Abstract:* no
Style guide: MLA
Preferred length: 30–40 pp
Copies: 2
Notes: endnotes
Blind referee: yes
Acceptance rate: 1/7
Time to consider ms: 3–4 mos
Charts, pictures, tables, graphs, maps
Foreign languages accepted: Italian,
  French, German, Spanish
• REVIEWS
Seeking reviewers: yes
Unsolicited reviews accepted: occa-
  sionally
Materials reviewed: books
Review length: 600 wds
How to apply: letter
Include in application: professional
  degrees, institutional affiliation,
  areas of expertise, published
  works, foreign languages, current
  research, vita

Renaissance Studies

Multidisciplinary studies of Renaissance Europe—history, art, architecture, religion, literature and
language
Affiliation: The Society for Renaissance Studies

Assoc Ed: John Law
Department of History
University College of Swansea
Singleton Park
Swansea SA2 8PP
U.K.
Bk Rev Ed: Stephen Bamforth
Department of French
University of Nottingham
Nottingham NG7 2RD
U.K.
Exhibition Rev Ed: Susan Foister
The National Gallery
Trafalgar Square
London WC2N 5DN
U.K.
4/yr, 125 pp; subs £54
Circ: 500
Readership: academics
Indexed/Abstracted: ABC, BHI,
MLA
• MANUSCRIPTS
Query: no; *Abstract:* no
Style guide: own
Preferred length: open
Copies: 3
Notes: endnotes
Acceptance rate: 1/4
Time to consider ms: 2 mos
Charts, pictures, tables, graphs, maps
Foreign languages accepted: no
• REVIEWS
Seeking reviewers: no
Unsolicited reviews accepted: yes
Materials reviewed: books, exhibitions
Review length: 2,500 wds
How to apply: letter
Include in application: professional
degrees, institutional affiliation,
areas of expertise, published
works, foreign languages, current
research

Resources for Feminist Research

Women's studies, feminist research
Affiliation: Ontario Institute for
Studies in Education

Ed: Philinda Masters
Ontario Institute for Studies in
Education
252 Bloor Street West
Toronto, ON M5S 1V6
CANADA
Bk Rev Ed: same
4/yr, 130 pp; subs $40
Circ: 2,000
Readership: academics
Indexed/Abstracted: ABC, AHI
• MANUSCRIPTS
Query: no; *Abstract:* no
Style guide: Chicago
Preferred length: 3,000 wds
Copies: 3
Notes: endnotes
Blind referee: yes
Acceptance rate: 2/5
Time to consider ms: 6 mos
Foreign languages accepted: French
• REVIEWS
Seeking reviewers: yes
Unsolicited reviews accepted: rarely
Materials reviewed: books
Review length: 500 wds
How to apply: letter or form
Include in application: institutional
affiliation, areas of expertise, cur-
rent research, knowledge of Cana-
dian feminist research

Restoration and 18th Century Theatre Research

Restoration and 18th century theatre
Affiliation: Loyola University of
Chicago
Ed: Douglas H. White
English Department
Loyola University of Chicago
6525 N. Sheridan Road
Chicago, IL 60626
Bk Rev Ed: same
2/yr, 63 pp; subs $8
Circ: 600
Readership: academics
Indexed/Abstracted: ABC, MLA

- MANUSCRIPTS
Query: no; *Abstract:* no
Style guide: Chicago
Preferred length: 8,000 wds
Copies: 2
Notes: endnotes
Blind referee: usually
Acceptance rate: 1/2
Time to consider ms: 3–6 mos
Charts, pictures, tables, graphs,
  maps
Foreign languages accepted: no
- REVIEWS
Seeking reviewers: yes
Unsolicited reviews accepted: yes
Materials reviewed: books
Review length: 1,000 wds
How to apply: letter
Include in application: professional
  degrees, areas of expertise, pub-
  lished works

Review of International Studies

International relations
Affiliation: British International Stu-
  dies Association
Ed: Richard Little
  Department of Politics and Inter-
    national Relations
  Lancaster University
  Lancaster LA1 4YL
  U.K.
4/yr, 97 pp; subs $42 U.S.
Circ: 1,200
Readership: academics
Indexed/Abstracted: ABC, BHI,
  PAIS
- MANUSCRIPTS
Query: no; *Abstract:* no
Style guide: own
Preferred length: 8,000 wds
Copies: 3
Notes: footnotes
Blind referee: yes
Acceptance rate: 1/4
Time to consider ms: 3 mos
Charts, tables, graphs, maps
Foreign languages accepted: no

Reviews in American History

Book reviews, historiography, retro-
  spectives
Ed: Stanley I. Kutler
4/yr, 175 pp; subs $12
Circ: 6,000
Readership: academics, general public
Indexed/Abstracted: ABC, AHCI,
  BRD, BRI, CCAH, HI
- REVIEWS
Seeking reviewers: yes
Unsolicited reviews accepted: no
Materials reviewed: books, films
Review length: 2,000–3,000 wds
How to apply: letter
Include in application: professional
  degrees, institutional affiliation,
  areas of expertise, published works,
  foreign languages, current research

Revolutionary Russia

History of Russia in the revolu-
  tionary periods of 1905 and 1917
Ed: John Slatter
  Department of Russian
  University of Durham
  Durham DH1 3HP
  U.K.
Bk Rev Ed: David Saunders
  Department of History
  University of Newcastle upon
    Tyne
  Newcastle upon Tyne NE1 7RU
  U.K.
2/yr, 150 pp; subs $38 U.S.
Circ: 120
Readership: academics, general public
Indexed/Abstracted: ABC
- MANUSCRIPTS
Notes: endnotes
- REVIEWS
Materials reviewed: books

La Revue d'Histoire de la So-
ciété Historique Nicolas-Denys

History of Northeastern New Brunswick

Affiliation: Société historique Nicolas-Denys
Ed: Eloi DeGrace
  Centre universitaire
  Shippagan, NB E0B 2P0
  CANADA
Bk Rev Ed: same
3/yr, 90 pp; subs $20
Circ: 1,000
Readership: general public
• MANUSCRIPTS
Query: yes; *Abstract:* no
Preferred length: 5–10 pp
Copies: 1
Notes: footnotes
Blind referee: yes
Acceptance rate: 4/5
Time to consider ms: 2–3 mos
Charts, pictures, tables, graphs, maps
Foreign languages accepted: French
• REVIEWS
Seeking reviewers: yes
Unsolicited reviews accepted: yes
Materials reviewed: books
Review length: 500–800 wds
How to apply: letter
Include in application: professional
  degrees, institutional affiliation

Revue d'Histoire de l'Amérique Française

History of the Francophone communities of Quebec, Canada, and the American continent
Affiliation: Institut d'Histoire de l'Amérique Française
Ed: Pierre Trepanier
  261, avenue Bloomfield
  Outremont, PQ H2V 3R6
  CANADA
Bk Rev Ed: Lucia Ferretti
4/yr, 175 pp; subs $41.54
Circ: 1,300
Readership: academics
Indexed/Abstracted: ABC, AHCI, CCAH, MLA
• MANUSCRIPTS
Query: no; *Abstract:* yes

Style guide: own
Preferred length: 10,000 wds max
Copies: 1
Notes: endnotes
Blind referee: yes
Acceptance rate: 2/5
Time to consider ms: 6 mos
Charts, pictures, tables, graphs, maps
Foreign languages accepted: French
• REVIEWS
Seeking reviewers: yes
Unsolicited reviews accepted: yes
Materials reviewed: books
Review length: 1,000 wds
How to apply: letter
Include in application: institutional
  affiliation, areas of expertise, a
  review to be published
• ADDITIONAL NOTES
This journal publishes only in French. Translations of English manuscripts are sometimes published. All reviewers must possess a reading knowledge of French.

Rhetorica: A Journal of the History of Rhetoric

History of rhetoric
Affiliation: International Society for the History of Rhetoric
Ed: Michael Leff
  Department of Communication Studies
  Northwestern University
  1815 Chicago Avenue
  Evanston, IL 60208-1340
Bk Rev Ed: Kees Meerhoff
  University of Amsterdam
  Instituut voor Romanistiek
  Office 320
  P.C. Hoofthuis
  Spuistraat 134
  1012 VB Amsterdam
  NETHERLANDS
4/yr, 100 pp; subs $30
Readership: academics
Indexed/Abstracted: ABC, AHCI, CCAH, IMB, MLA

• MANUSCRIPTS
Query: no; *Abstract:* yes
Style guide: own
Preferred length: varies
Copies: 3
Notes: endnotes
Blind referee: yes
• REVIEWS
Unsolicited reviews accepted: yes
Materials reviewed: books
Review length: varies

Rhode Island History

State and local history of Rhode
Island
Affiliation: Rhode Island Historical
Society
Ed: Albert T. Keyberg
110 Benevolent Street
Providence, RI 02906
4/yr, 32 pp; subs $20
Circ: 2,500
Readership: academics, general public
Indexed/Abstracted: ABC, WAH
• MANUSCRIPTS
Query: preferred; *Abstract:* no
Preferred length: 20 pp
Copies: 1
Notes: endnotes
Blind referee: no
Acceptance rate: 1/2
Time to consider ms: 2 wks
Charts, pictures, tables, maps
Foreign languages accepted: no

The Ricardian

English 15th century history with
special reference to the reign of
Richard III
Affiliation: Richard III Society
Ed: Anne F. Sutton
17 Enfield Cloisters
Fanshaw Street
London N1 6LD
U.K.
Bk Rev Ed: same
4/yr, 48 pp; subs £9
Circ: 4,500

Readership: academics, society mem-
bers
Indexed/Abstracted: IMB
• MANUSCRIPTS
Query: no; *Abstract:* no
Style guide: own
Preferred length: varies
Copies: 1
Notes: endnotes
Blind referee: yes
Acceptance rate: 4/5
Time to consider ms: 2-6 wks
Pictures, maps, others as appropriate
Foreign languages accepted: no
• REVIEWS
Seeking reviewers: no
Unsolicited reviews accepted: no
Materials reviewed: books
Review length: 500-1,000 wds
How to apply: letter

Ricardian Register

Richard III and related periods of
English history
Affiliation: Richard III Society, Inc.
Ed: Carole M. Rike
P.O. Box 13786
New Orleans, LA 70185-3786
Bk Rev Ed: Myrna Smith
4/yr, 24 pp; subs membership
Circ: 750
Readership: academics, general public
• MANUSCRIPTS
Query: no; *Abstract:* no
Preferred length: varies
Copies: 1
Notes: endnotes
Blind referee: no
Charts, pictures, tables, graphs, maps
Foreign languages accepted: no
• REVIEWS
Seeking reviewers: yes
Unsolicited reviews accepted: yes
Materials reviewed: books, films,
other media
How to apply: letter
Include in application: current re-
search

Richmond County Journal

History and genealogy of Augusta,
   Georgia
Affiliation: Richmond County His-
   torical Society
Ed: Helen H. Callahan
   2500 Walton Way
   Reese Library
   Augusta, GA 30910
Bk Rev Ed: same
2/yr, 50 pp; subs $6.50
Circ: 450
Readership: general public, society
   members
• MANUSCRIPTS
Query: preferred; *Abstract:* preferred
Preferred length: 10 pp
Copies: 2
Notes: footnotes
Blind referee: no
Charts, pictures, tables, graphs,
   maps
Foreign languages accepted: no
• REVIEWS
Seeking reviewers: no
Unsolicited reviews accepted: yes
Materials reviewed: books
How to apply: letter
Include in application: professional
   degrees, institutional affiliation,
   areas of expertise, published
   works, current research
• ADDITIONAL NOTES
Most of the articles contained within
   this journal are written by local
   college historians, genealogists,
   and/or interested society members.

The Richmond Literature and History Quarterly

History of Richmond and its en-
   virons; short stories and poetry by
   Richmond area authors
Ed: Julia C. Killian
   2405 Vollmer Road
   Richmond, VA 23229
Bk Rev Ed: same
4/yr, 48 pp; subs $16

Circ: 250
Readership: academics, general public
• MANUSCRIPTS
Query: no; *Abstract:* no
Style guide: any
Preferred length: 2,500 wds max
Copies: 1
Notes: endnotes or footnotes
Blind referee: no
Acceptance rate: 1/2
Time to consider ms: 3 mos
Charts, pictures, tables, graphs, maps
Foreign languages accepted: no
• REVIEWS
Seeking reviewers: no
Unsolicited reviews accepted: yes
Materials reviewed: books
Review length: 2,500 wds max
How to apply: letter
Include in application: professional
   degrees, institutional affiliation,
   areas of expertise, published
   works, current research

Rochester History

History of upstate New York between
   Buffalo and Syracuse with some re-
   lationship to Rochester area
Affiliation: Rochester Public Library
   and Office of the City Historian
Ed: Ruth Rosenberg Naparsteck
   Office of the City Historian
   Rochester Public Library
   115 South Avenue
   Rochester, NY 14604
4/yr, 28 pp; subs $6
Readership: academics, general pub-
   lic, municipal officials
Indexed/Abstracted: ABC, WAH
• MANUSCRIPTS
Query: preferred; *Abstract:* no
Style guide: own
Preferred length: 10,000–12,000 wds
Copies: 1
Notes: endnotes
Blind referee: no
Acceptance rate: 3/5
Time to consider ms: 4 wks

Charts, pictures, tables, graphs, maps
Foreign languages accepted: no

Roots

Minnesota history
Affiliation: Minnesota Historical Society
Ed: James P. Smith
  345 Kellogg Boulevard West
  St. Paul, MN 55102-1906
2/yr, 32 pp; subs $6
Circ: 4,700
Readership: general public, society members, school teachers, secondary school students
• MANUSCRIPTS
Query: yes; *Abstract:* no
Style guide: Chicago
Preferred length: 2,000 wds
Copies: 1
Notes: none, but full documentation needed for files
Blind referee: no
Time to consider ms: 3 mos
Charts, pictures, tables, graphs, maps
Foreign languages accepted: no

Rural History

Rural history
Affiliation: Cambridge University Press
Eds: Liz Bellamy and Tom Williamson
  Centre of East Anglian Studies
  University of East Anglia
  Norwich NR4 7TJ
  U.K.
    or
  Keith D. M. Snell
  Department of English Local History
  University of Leicester
  Leicester LE1 7RH
  U.K.
Bk Rev Ed: same
2/yr; subs £39
Readership: academics
Indexed/Abstracted: ABC, BHI

• MANUSCRIPTS
Query: no; *Abstract:* no
Style guide: own
Preferred length: 8,000 wds
Copies: 2
Notes: endnotes
Tables, graphs, maps, line drawings
Foreign languages accepted: no
• REVIEWS
Materials reviewed: books

The Russian Review: An American Quarterly Devoted to Russia Past and Present

Russian history, literature, social sciences, art, and other humanistic studies
Ed: Allan Wildman
  History Department
  Ohio State University
  230 West 17th Avenue
  Columbus, OH 43210
Bk Rev Ed: same
4/yr, 144 pp; subs $28
Circ: 1,600
Readership: academics
Indexed/Abstracted: ABC, AHCI, BRI, CCAH, HI, IMB, MLA, PAIS, WAH
• MANUSCRIPTS
Query: no; *Abstract:* no
Style guide: Chicago
Preferred length: 10,000 wds max
Copies: 3
Notes: endnotes
Blind referee: yes
Acceptance rate: 1/3
Time to consider ms: 2-4 mos
Charts, pictures, tables, graphs, maps
Foreign languages accepted: Russian (translated), some passages in Cyrillic and other languages
• REVIEWS
Seeking reviewers: yes
Unsolicited reviews accepted: no
Materials reviewed: books
Review length: 500-800 wds
How to apply: letter

Include in application: professional degrees, institutional affiliation, areas of expertise, published works, foreign languages, current research
- ADDITIONAL NOTES

The editors are also interested in analytic review articles of several books. It is expected that all contributions and reviews are by trained scholars or specialists on Russia in some discipline and conform to the highest standards of scholarship in the field.

Sage: A Scholarly Journal on Black Women

Black women, feminist scholarship
Affiliation: Spelman College
Ed: Patricia Bell-Scott
   P.O. Box 42741
   Atlanta, GA 30311-0741
Bk Rev Ed: Miriam DeCosta-Willis
2/yr; subs $15
Circ: 2,000
Readership: academics, general public
Indexed/Abstracted: ABC, AHI, MLA
- MANUSCRIPTS

Query: preferred; *Abstract:* no
Style guide: MLA
Preferred length: 25 pp max
Copies: 3
Notes: endnotes
Blind referee: yes
Acceptance rate: 1/2
Time to consider ms: 6–12 mos
Charts, pictures, tables
Foreign languages accepted: no
- REVIEWS

Seeking reviewers: yes
Unsolicited reviews accepted: yes
Materials reviewed: books, films
Review length: 8 pp max
How to apply: letter

Saguenayensia

Saguenay-Lac-Saint-Jean
Affiliation: Société d'histoire du Lac-St.-Jean and the Société Historique du Saguenay
Ed: Société Historique du Saguenay
   930 Jacques Cartier est
   C.P. 456
   Chicoutimi, PQ G7H 5C8
   CANADA
Bk Rev Ed: same
4/yr, 44 pp; subs $25
Readership: general public
Indexed/Abstracted: ABC
- MANUSCRIPTS

Query: no; *Abstract:* no
Preferred length: 15 pp
Copies: 1
Notes: footnotes
Acceptance rate: 3/4
Time to consider ms: 1 mo
Charts, pictures, tables, graphs, maps
Foreign languages accepted: French
- REVIEWS

Seeking reviewers: yes
Unsolicited reviews accepted: yes
How to apply: letter
Include in application: foreign languages

St. Joseph Valley Record

Local history of the St. Joseph Valley River region
Affiliation: Northern Indiana Historical Society
Eds: Kathleen Stiso Mullins and Diane Barts
   808 West Washington
   South Bend, IN 46601
2/yr, 8–30 pp; subs $35 library rate
Circ: 5,000
Readership: general public, society members
- MANUSCRIPTS

Query: preferred; *Abstract:* no
Preferred length: 20–50 pp
Copies: 1
Notes: endnotes
Blind referee: no
Acceptance rate: 3/5
Time to consider ms: 6 mos

All illustrations accepted
Foreign languages accepted: no
• ADDITIONAL NOTES
The Northern Indiana Historical Society is in the process of expanding. The editors may at a future date be interested in reviewers.

San Jose Studies

Interdisciplinary; primarily humanities and social sciences
Affiliation: San Jose State University
Ed: Fauneil J. Rinn
  San Jose State University
  San Jose, CA 95192
3/yr, 126 pp; subs $12
Circ: 400
Readership: academics, general public
Indexed/Abstracted: ABC, AHI, MLA
• MANUSCRIPTS
Query: no; *Abstract:* no
Style guide: any
Preferred length: 10–30
Copies: 2
Notes: endnotes (as few as possible)
Blind referee: yes

The San Luis Valley Historian

Historical information and stories concerning six southern Colorado counties—Alamosa, Rio Grande, Mineral, Saguache, Conejos, and Costilla
Affiliation: Adams State College
Ed: Frances McCullough
  5522 East Road 5 North
  Monte Vista, CO 81144
Bk Rev Ed: same
4/yr, 44 pp; subs $12
Circ: 375
Readership: academics, general public, local history buffs
• MANUSCRIPTS
Query: no; *Abstract:* preferred
Style guide: none
Preferred length: 50 pp max
Copies: 2

Notes: whatever is necessary
Blind referee: no
Acceptance rate: 4/5
Time to consider ms: varies
Charts, pictures, tables, graphs, maps
Foreign languages accepted: no
• REVIEWS
Seeking reviewers: no
Unsolicited reviews accepted: yes
Materials reviewed: books
Review length: ½ pp
• ADDITIONAL NOTES
The editors have published local history manuscripts, theses, articles, high school papers, college studies, and parts of books. They will consider anything which applies to their local history.

Saskatchewan History

History of Saskatchewan
Affiliation: Saskatchewan Archives Board
Ed: Kathlyn R. M. Szalasznij
  Saskatchewan Archives Board
  University of Saskatchewan
  Saskatoon, SK S7N 0W0
  CANADA
Bk Rev Ed: same
3/yr, 40 pp; subs $15
Circ: 650
Indexed/Abstracted: ABC
• MANUSCRIPTS
Query: preferred; *Abstract:* preferred
Preferred length: 12–14 pp
Copies: 1
Notes: endnotes
Blind referee: yes
Time to consider ms: 1–4 wks
Charts, pictures, tables, graphs, maps
Foreign languages accepted: no
• REVIEWS
Seeking reviewers: no
Unsolicited reviews accepted: no
Materials reviewed: books

Scandinavian Studies

Interdisciplinary Scandinavian studies
Affiliation: American Association for

the Advancement of Scandinavian
Study
Ed: Steven P. Sondrup
   3003 JKHB
   Brigham Young University
   Provo, UT 84602
Bk Rev Ed: same
4/yr, 175 pp; subs $35
Readership: academics, general public
Indexed/Abstracted: ABC, AHCI,
   CCAH, HI, IMB, MLA
• MANUSCRIPTS
Query: no; *Abstract:* no
Style guide: varies with discipline
Preferred length: open
Copies: 2
Notes: endnotes
Blind referee: yes
Time to consider ms: 2-3 mos
Charts, pictures, tables, graphs, maps
Foreign languages accepted: quotations only with translations
• REVIEWS
Seeking reviewers: yes
Unsolicited reviews accepted: no
Materials reviewed: books, art exhibitions
Review length: 750-1,000 wds
How to apply: letter
Include in application: professional
   degrees, institutional affiliation,
   areas of expertise, published
   works, foreign languages, current
   research

Scandinavica

Scandinavian literature, language and
   history
Affiliation: University of East Anglia
Ed: Janet Garton
   Norvik Press
   University of East Anglia
   Norwich NR4 7TJ
   U.K.
Bk Rev Ed: W. G. Jones
2/yr, 150 pp; subs £17.50
Circ: 550
Readership: academics

Indexed/Abstracted: ABC, AHCI,
   CCAH, IMB, MLA
• MANUSCRIPTS
Query: preferred; *Abstract:* preferred
Style guide: MLA
Preferred length: 10,000 wds max
Copies: 2
Notes: endnotes
Blind referee: yes
Acceptance rate: 3/10
Time to consider ms: 6 mos
Charts, tables, graphs, maps
Foreign languages accepted: French,
   German; will translate Danish,
   Norwegian, and Swedish
• REVIEWS
Seeking reviewers: yes
Unsolicited reviews accepted: no
Materials reviewed: books
Review length: 500-800 wds
How to apply: letter
Include in application: institutional
   affiliation, areas of expertise, published works, foreign languages,
   current research

Schoharie County Historical Review

History of Schoharie county
Affiliation: Schoharie County Historical Society and Old Stone Fort
   Museum
Ed: Edward A. Hagan
   134 Cliff Street
   Middleburgh, NY 12122
Bk Rev Ed: same
2/yr, 36 pp; subs $12.50
Circ: 1,000
Readership: academics, general public, membership
• MANUSCRIPTS
Query: yes; *Abstract:* no
Style guide: none
Preferred length: 5-10 pp
Copies: 1
Notes: footnotes or none
Blind referee: no
Charts, pictures, tables, graphs, maps
Foreign languages accepted: no

• REVIEWS
Seeking reviewers: no
Materials reviewed: any related to
  Schoharie County

Schuyler County Historical Society Journal

Schuyler County history
Affiliation: Schuyler County Histori-
  cal Society
Ed: Barbara H. Bell
  3460 Co. Rd. 28
  Watkins Glen, NY 14891
4/yr, 16 pp; subs $7
Circ: 300
Readership: general public
• MANUSCRIPTS
Query: yes; *Abstract:* preferred
Preferred length: 2–3 pp
Copies: 1
Notes: bibliography
Blind referee: no
Acceptance rate: 1/3
Time to consider ms: 3–4 mos
No illustrations accepted
Foreign languages accepted: no

The Scottish Historical Review

Scottish history
Affiliation: The Company of Scottish
  History; Aberdeen University Press
Eds: A. Grant
  Department of History
  University of Lancaster
  Lancaster LA1 4YG
  U.K.
      or
  I. G. C. Hutchison
  Department of History
  University of Stirling
  Stirling FK9 4LA
  U.K.
Bk Rev Ed: I. G. C. Hutchison
2/yr; subs £15
Readership: academics
Indexed/Abstracted: ABC, AHCI,
  BHI, CCAH, IMB

• MANUSCRIPTS
Query: no; *Abstract:* no
Style guide: own
Preferred length: varies
• REVIEWS
Materials reviewed: books

Scottish Tradition

Scottish history, literature, culture,
  Scots abroad, especially in Canada
Affiliation: University of Guelph
Ed: E. Ewan
  History Department
  University of Guelph
  Guelph, ON N1G 2W1
  CANADA
Bk Rev Ed: A. McDonald
1/yr, 175 pp; subs $20
Circ: 150–200
Readership: academics, general public
• MANUSCRIPTS
Query: no; *Abstract:* no
Preferred length: 20–40 pp
Copies: 1
Notes: endnotes
Blind referee: yes
Acceptance rate: 1/2
Time to consider ms: 2–3 mos
Charts, tables, graphs, maps
Foreign languages accepted: no
• REVIEWS
Seeking reviewers: yes
Unsolicited reviews accepted: no
Materials reviewed: books
Review length: 300–500 wds
How to apply: letter
Include in application: professional
  degrees, institutional affiliation,
  areas of expertise, published
  works, current research

Scripta Mediterranea

All aspects of Mediterranean culture
  and civilization, past and present,
  especially interdisciplinary and
  cross-cultural studies
Affiliation: University of Toronto
Ed: Anthony Percival

Society for Mediterranean Studies
c/o Department of Spanish and
Portuguese
University of Toronto
Toronto, ON M5S 1A1
CANADA
Bk Rev Ed: same
1/yr, 100 pp; subs $20
Readership: academics, general public
• MANUSCRIPTS
Query: preferred; *Abstract:* yes, 1 in
English and 1 in French
Style guide: MLA
Preferred length: 30 pp max
Copies: 1
Notes: endnotes
Charts, pictures, tables, graphs, maps
Foreign languages accepted: French
• REVIEWS
Seeking reviewers: no
Unsolicited reviews accepted: no

Seaport

New York city history, especially the
city's history as a port in the 19th
century
Affiliation: South St. Seaport Museum
Ed: Madeline Rogers
South St. Seaport Museum
207 Front Street
New York, NY 10038
Bk Rev Ed: James Keller
c/o The New Yorker
20 W. 43 St.
New York, NY 10036-7441
4/yr, 52 pp; subs $36
Circ: 10,000
Readership: museum members
• MANUSCRIPTS
Query: yes; *Abstract:* yes
Preferred length: 1,500–2,500 wds
Copies: 2
Notes: none
Blind referee: yes
Acceptance rate: 19/20
Time to consider ms: 1–8 wks
Pictures, maps
Foreign languages accepted: no

• REVIEWS
Seeking reviewers: no
Unsolicited reviews accepted: no
• ADDITIONAL NOTES
Though *Seaport* is a popular
magazine for a non-academic audience, the editors pride themselves
on running well-written articles
based on primary research. They
are always looking for work by
scholars who can write for a
general audience. *Seaport* pays
$350–$500 per article.

The Settler

History of Bradford County, Penn-
sylvania
Affiliation: Bradford County Histori-
cal Society
Ed: Pat Parsons
21 Main Street
Towanda, PA 18848
4/yr, 44 pp; subs $10
Circ: 800
Readership: general public, society
members
• MANUSCRIPTS
Query: no; *Abstract:* no
Style guide: any
Preferred length: open
Copies: 1
Notes: any or none
Blind referee: no
Acceptance rate: 4/5
Time to consider ms: 3 mos
Charts, pictures, tables, graphs, maps
Foreign languages accepted: no

The Seventeenth Century

All aspects of 17th century studies
Affiliation: The Centre for Seven-
teenth-Century Studies, University
of Durham
Ed: Richard Maber
Centre for Seventeenth-Century
Studies
University Library
Palace Green

Durham DH1 3RN
U.K.
2/yr, 120 pp; subs £12
Circ: 450
Readership: academics, general public
Indexed/Abstracted: ABC, AHCI,
CCAH, MLA
• MANUSCRIPTS
Query: no; *Abstract:* no
Style guide: ModHum
Preferred length: 10,000 wds max
Copies: 2
Notes: endnotes
Blind referee: no
Acceptance rate: 1/3-2/5
Time to consider ms: 3 mos
Charts, pictures, tables, graphs, maps
Foreign languages accepted: no
• ADDITIONAL NOTES
Although there is no regular book
review feature, occasionally review
essays are published.

The Shaker Messenger

The American Shaker, past and
present
Ed: Diana Van Kolken
P.O. Box 1645
Holland, MI 49422-1645
Bk Rev Ed: same
4/yr, 28 pp; subs $14
Circ: 2,000
Readership: academics, others in-
terested in Shaker origins
• MANUSCRIPTS
Query: preferred; *Abstract:* no
Preferred length: 1,500 wds
Copies: 1
Notes: endnotes or footnotes
Blind referee: no
Pictures, maps
Foreign languages accepted: no
• REVIEWS
Seeking reviewers: no
Unsolicited reviews accepted: yes
Materials reviewed: books, films,
tapes, CDs
Review length: 250 wds

The Shaker Quarterly

Shaker history and artifacts
Affiliation: United Society of Shakers
Ed: Nancy E. Marcotte
R.R. 1 Box 640
Poland Spring, ME 04274
Bk Rev Ed: same
4/yr, 32 pp; subs $15
Circ: 300
Readership: academics, general public
• MANUSCRIPTS
Query: preferred; *Abstract:* preferred
Copies: 1
Notes: endnotes or footnotes
Blind referee: no
Time to consider ms: 1 yr
Charts, pictures, tables, graphs, maps
Foreign languages accepted: no
• REVIEWS
Seeking reviewers: no
Unsolicited reviews accepted: yes
Materials reviewed: books, films,
ephemera
Review length: 300 wds
How to apply: letter
Include in application: professional
degrees, institutional affiliation,
areas of expertise

Signs: Journal of Women in Culture and Society

Interdisciplinary scholarship on
women
Affiliation: University of Chicago
Press; University of Minnesota
Eds: Ruth-Ellen B. Joeres, Barbara
Laslett
c/o Center for Advanced Femi-
nist Studies
495 Ford Hall
224 Church Street, S.E.
University of Minnesota
Minneapolis, MN 55455
Bk Rev Ed: same
4/yr, 215 pp; subs $32.50
Circ: 5,800
Readership: academics, independent
feminist scholars

Indexed/Abstracted: ABC, AHCI,
AHI, BRI, CCSB, IMB, MLA,
SSCI, SSI, WAH
• MANUSCRIPTS
Query: no; *Abstract:* yes
Style guide: Chicago
Preferred length: 35 pp
Copies: 3
Notes: author-date system with
limited footnotes
Blind referee: yes
Acceptance rate: 1/10
Time to consider ms: 10 wks
Charts, pictures, tables, graphs, maps
Foreign languages accepted: no
• REVIEWS
Seeking reviewers: yes
Unsolicited reviews accepted: no
Materials reviewed: books
How to apply: letter
Include in application: professional
degrees, institutional affiliation,
areas of expertise, published
works, current research
• ADDITIONAL NOTES
Signs actively seeks and frequently
publishes historical articles,
reports, and archives pieces on a
wide range of subjects of interest
to feminist scholars. Contributors
are asked to keep in mind the interdisciplinary nature of the journal and also, where appropriate, to
address diversity issues involving
race, class, sexual preference, etc.

The Sixteenth Century Journal

Any human activity in any field be-
tween 1450 and 1600 A.D.
Affiliation: The Sixteenth Century
Studies Conference
Ed: Robert M. Kingdon
Institute for Research in the
Humanities
Old Observatory
University of Wisconsin
Madison, WI 53706
Bk Rev Ed: R. V. Schnucker

NMSU LB 115
Kirksville, MO 63501
4/yr, 225 pp; subs $35
Circ: 2,300
Readership: academics
Indexed/Abstracted: ABC, AHCI,
AHI, CCAH, HI, MLA
• MANUSCRIPTS
Query: preferred; *Abstract:* yes
Style guide: Chicago
Preferred length: 22 pp
Copies: 2
Notes: endnotes
Blind referee: yes
Acceptance rate: 1/7
Time to consider ms: 3 mos
Charts, pictures, tables, graphs, maps
Foreign languages accepted: no
• REVIEWS
Seeking reviewers: yes
Unsolicited reviews accepted: no
Materials reviewed: books
Review length: 600 wds
How to apply: letter or telephone call
Include in application: professional
degrees, institutional affiliation,
areas of expertise, current research

Skyways, the Journal of the Airplane 1920–1940

Building and restoring fullscale air-
craft of this period, plus relevant
historical material
Affiliation: World War I Aeroplanes,
Inc.
Ed: Kenn C. Rust
Box 3366
Glendale, CA 91221
Bk Rev Ed: same
4/yr, 82 pp; subs $25
Circ: 1,400
Readership: aviation historians and
builders
• MANUSCRIPTS
Query: preferred; *Abstract:* preferred
Preferred length: 300–400 wds
Copies: 1
Blind referee: no

Acceptance rate: 4/5
Charts, pictures, tables, graphs, maps
Foreign languages accepted: no
• REVIEWS
Seeking reviewers: yes
Unsolicited reviews accepted: yes
Materials reviewed: books, films
Review length: 300–400 wds
How to apply: letter
Include in application: areas of expertise, current research

Slavery and Abolition

Slave and post-slave societies
Eds: Gad Heuman and James Walvin
 c/o Frank Cass & Co. Ltd.
 11 Gainsborough Road
 London E11 1RS
 U.K.
Bk Rev Ed: same
3/yr; subs £30
Readership: academics
Indexed/Abstracted: ABC, BHI, WAH
• MANUSCRIPTS
Query: no; *Abstract:* no
Style guide: own
Preferred length: varies
Copies: 1
Notes: endnotes
• REVIEWS
Materials reviewed: books
Review length: varies

Slavic Review

Slavic studies, eastern Europe, Eurasia
Affiliation: University of Pennsylvania and the American Association for the Advancement of Slavic Studies
Ed: Elliott Mossman
 635 Williams Hall
 University of Pennsylvania
 Philadelphia, PA 19104-6305
Bk Rev Ed: Ben Eklof
4/yr, 240 pp; subs $45
Circ: 5,400

Readership: academics, Slavic specialists
Indexed/Abstracted: ABC, AHCI, BRI, CCAH, HI, IMB, MLA
• MANUSCRIPTS
Query: no; *Abstract:* no
Style guide: Chicago
Preferred length: 25 pp
Copies: 4
Notes: endnotes
Blind referee: yes
Acceptance rate: 1/10
Time to consider ms: 3 mos
Charts, pictures, tables, graphs, maps
Foreign languages accepted: for citations and quotations only
• REVIEWS
Seeking reviewers: yes
Unsolicited reviews accepted: no
Materials reviewed: books, films
Review length: 500–700 wds
How to apply: letter
Include in application: professional degrees, institutional affiliation, areas of expertise, published works, foreign languages, current research
• ADDITIONAL NOTES
All quotations of 50 words or less must be transliterated (Library of Congress). English translation must be provided for all quotations that are not merely grammatical illustrations.

Slavonic and East European Review

History, literature and language of East Europe
Affiliation: School of Slavonic and East European Studies, University of London; Modern Humanities Research Association
Ed: R. P. Bartlett
 c/o School of Slavonic and East European Studies
 University of London
 Senate House

Malet Street
London WC1E 7HU
U.K.
Bk Rev Ed: S. Safraz
4/yr, 200 pp; subs £54
Circ: 1,500
Readership: academics
Indexed/Abstracted: ABC, AHCI,
   BHI, CCAH, HI, IMB, MLA
• MANUSCRIPTS
Query: no; *Abstract:* no
Style guide: own
Preferred length: 8,000 wds
Copies: 2
Notes: footnotes
Blind referee: yes
Acceptance rate: 1/5–3/10
Time to consider ms: 4 mos
Charts, pictures, tables, graphs, maps
Foreign languages accepted: excep-
   tionally an East European language
• REVIEWS
Seeking reviewers: yes
Unsolicited reviews accepted: no
Materials reviewed: books
Review length: 700 wds max
How to apply: letter
Include in application: institutional
   affiliation, areas of expertise, pub-
   lished works, foreign languages,
   current research

Slovene Studies

Interdisciplinary studies of Slovenia
and Slovenes in diaspora
Affiliation: Indiana University; So-
   ciety for Slovene Studies
Ed: Tom M. S. Priestly
   Department of Slavic and East
      European Studies
   University of Alberta
   Edmonton, AB T6G 2E6
   CANADA
Bk Rev Ed: Rado L. Lencek
   Department of Slavic Languages
   Columbia University
   New York, NY 10027
2/yr, 125 pp; subs $20

Circ: 450
Readership: academics, society mem-
   bers
Indexed/Abstracted: ABC, MLA
• MANUSCRIPTS
Query: no; *Abstract:* yes
Style guide: MLA
Preferred length: 6,000 wds
Copies: 3
Notes: endnotes
Blind referee: yes
Acceptance rate: 2/5
Time to consider ms: 4–6 mos
Charts, pictures, tables, graphs, maps
Foreign languages accepted: no
• REVIEWS
Seeking reviewers: yes
Unsolicited reviews accepted: occa-
   sionally
Materials reviewed: books
Review length: 1,000–2,000 wds
How to apply: letter
Include in application: professional
   degrees, institutional affiliation,
   areas of expertise, foreign lan-
   guages, current research

Small Wars and Insurgencies

Contemporary and historical wars
   short of total war or coalition hos-
   tilities
Eds: Ian Beckett
   Department of War Studies
   RMA Sandhurst
   Camberley
   Surrey GU15 4PQ
   U.K.
      or
   Thomas-Durell Young
   Strategic Studies Institute
   U.S. Army War College
   Carlisle Barracks, PA 17013
Bk Rev Ed: Thomas R. Mockaitis
   Department of History
   DePaul University
   802 West Belden Avenue
   Chicago, IL 60614-3214
3/yr, 108 pp; subs £28

Circ: 400
Readership: academics, military
Indexed/Abstracted: ABC
• MANUSCRIPTS
Query: yes; *Abstract:* no
Style guide: own
Preferred length: 7,000-10,000 wds
Copies: 2
Notes: endnotes
Blind referee: yes
Time to consider ms: 1 yr max
Charts, tables, graphs, maps
Foreign languages accepted: no
• REVIEWS
Seeking reviewers: yes
Unsolicited reviews accepted: yes
Materials reviewed: books, videos
Review length: 500-1,000 wds
How to apply: letter
Include in application: professional
degrees, institutional affiliation,
areas of expertise, published
works, foreign languages, current
research

Snake River Echoes

Idaho history
Affiliation: Upper Snake River Valley
Historical Society
Ed: Louis Clements
102 W. 2000 N.
Rexburg, ID 83440
Bk Rev Ed: Jerry Glenn
594 Gemini Drive
Rexburg, ID 83440
4/yr, 24 pp; subs $10
Circ: 650
Readership: general public
• MANUSCRIPTS
Query: preferred; *Abstract:* no
Preferred length: varies
Copies: 1
Blind referee: no
Acceptance rate: 1/2
Time to consider ms: 1 mo
Pictures, maps
Foreign languages accepted: no

• REVIEWS
Seeking reviewers: no
Unsolicited reviews accepted: yes

Social Forces

General sociology, including histori-
cal sociology
Affiliation: Southern Sociological So-
ciety; University of North Carolina
at Chapel Hill
Ed: Richard L. Simpson
Department of Sociology
Hamilton Hall
University of North Carolina
Chapel Hill, NC 27599-3210
Bk Rev Ed: John Shelton Reed
4/yr, 300 pp; subs $28
Circ: 4,500
Readership: academics, government
researchers
Indexed/Abstracted: ABC, AHCI,
BRI, CCSB, PAIS, SSCI, SSI
• MANUSCRIPTS
Query: no; *Abstract:* yes
Style guide: own
Preferred length: 40 pp
Copies: 5 and $15 submission fee
Notes: endnotes
Blind referee: yes
Acceptance rate: 1/6
Time to consider ms: 60-79 days
Charts, tables, graphs, maps
Foreign languages accepted: no
• REVIEWS
Seeking reviewers: yes
Unsolicited reviews accepted: occa-
sionally
Materials reviewed: books
Review length: varies
How to apply: letter
Include in application: professional
degrees, institutional affiliation,
areas of expertise, vita

Social History

Social history
Ed: Janet Blackman
Department of Economics and
Social History

The University
Hull HU6 7RX
U.K.
Bk Rev Ed: John Seed
Rochampion Institute of Higher
Education
Whitelands College
West Hill
London SW15
U.K.
162 pp; subs $62 North America
Circ: 1,100
Readership: academics
Indexed/Abstracted: ABC, AHCI,
BHI, CCAH, HI, IMB, WAH
• MANUSCRIPTS
Abstract: yes
Style guide: own
Preferred length: 8,000 wds
Copies: 3
Notes: footnotes
Blind referee: yes
Tables, graphs, maps
Foreign languages accepted: no
• REVIEWS
Seeking reviewers: yes
Unsolicited reviews accepted: yes
Materials reviewed: books
Review length: varies
How to apply: letter
Include in application: professional
degrees, institutional affiliation,
areas of expertise, published
works, foreign languages, current
research

Social History/Histoire Sociale

Social history of Canada, USA, and
Europe
Affiliation: University of Ottawa;
York University
Ed: Jean-Pierre Gagnon
Université d'Ottawa
155 Seraphin-Marion
Ottawa, ON K1N 6N5
CANADA
Bk Rev Ed: Jean-Claude Dube
2/yr, 230 pp

Circ: 700
Readership: academics
Indexed/Abstracted: ABC, AHCI,
CCAH, CCSB, SSCI
• MANUSCRIPTS
Query: no; *Abstract:* yes
Preferred length: 25 pp
Copies: 3
Notes: endnotes
Blind referee: yes
Acceptance rate: 2/5
Time to consider ms: 3 mos
Charts, pictures, tables, graphs, maps
Foreign languages accepted: French
• REVIEWS
Seeking reviewers: yes
Unsolicited reviews accepted: yes
Materials reviewed: books
Review length: 750 wds
How to apply: letter
Include in application: professional
degrees, institutional affiliation,
areas of expertise, published
works, foreign languages, current
research
• ADDITIONAL NOTES
Although the emphasis is put on
Canadian history, the editors wel-
come manuscripts from other
countries, particularly Europe and
the USA, as well as manuscripts on
all aspects of social history.

Social History of Alcohol Review

International social history of alcohol
use
Affiliation: Alcohol and Temperance
History Group
Ed: Gregory Austin
4665 Lampson Avenue
Los Alamitos, CA 90720
Bk Rev Ed: same
2/yr, 50 pp; subs $10
Circ: 400
Readership: academics
• MANUSCRIPTS
Query: preferred; *Abstract:* yes

Style guide: Chicago
Preferred length: 20 pp
Copies: 2
Notes: endnotes or parenthetics
Blind referee: yes
Acceptance rate: 4/5
Time to consider ms: 3 mos
Will consider illustrations as necessary
Foreign languages accepted: no
• REVIEWS
Seeking reviewers: yes
Unsolicited reviews accepted: occasionally
Materials reviewed: books
Review length: 2–4 pp
How to apply: letter
Include in application: professional degrees, institutional affiliation, areas of expertise, published works, foreign languages, current research

Social History of Medicine

Social history of medicine
Affiliation: Society for the Social History of Medicine
Eds: Anne Digby
    Humanities Department
    Oxford Polytechnic
    Gypsy Lane
    Oxford OX3 0BP
    U.K.
        or
    Richard Smith
    All Souls College
    Oxford OX1 4AL
    U.K.
Bk Rev Ed: Roger Cooter
    Wellcome Unit for the History of Medicine
    Maths Tower
    The University
    Manchester M13 9PL
    U.K.
3/yr, 180 pp; subs £16
Readership: academics, physicians
Indexed/Abstracted: ABC, AHCI, CCSB, SSCI

• MANUSCRIPTS
Query: no; *Abstract:* yes
Style guide: own
Preferred length: 8,000 wds max
Copies: 2
Notes: endnotes
Blind referee: no
Time to consider ms: 8 wks
Tables, graphs, maps, diagrams
• REVIEWS
Materials reviewed: books
Review length: varies

Social Research

Social sciences
Affiliation: New School for Social Research
Ed: Arien Mack
    66 West 12th Street
    New York, NY 10010
4/yr, 236 pp; subs $24
Circ: 3,000
Readership: academics
Indexed/Abstracted: ABC, CCSB, PAIS, SSCI, SSI
• MANUSCRIPTS
Query: no; *Abstract:* no
Preferred length: 25 pp
Copies: 3
Notes: endnotes or footnotes
Blind referee: yes
Charts, tables
Foreign languages accepted: no

Social Science History

Social science approaches to historical study
Affiliation: Social Science History Association; Duke University Press
Ed: Russell Menard
    Department of History
    University of Minnesota
    614 Social Sciences
    267 19th Avenue South
    Minneapolis, MN 55455
4/yr, 150 pp; subs $30
Circ: 1,000
Readership: academics

Indexed/Abstracted: ABC, AHCI,
    CCAH, CCSB, SSCI, WAH
• MANUSCRIPTS
Query: no; *Abstract:* no
Style guide: own
Preferred length: varies
Copies: 3
Notes: endnotes

The Social Science Journal

Social sciences
Affiliation: JAI Press Inc.
Ed: Michael Katovich
    P.O. Box 30790
    Texas Christian University
    Fort Worth, TX 76129
Bk Rev Ed: same
4/yr; subs $55
Readership: academics
Indexed/Abstracted: ABC, AHCI,
    CCSB, PAIS, SSCI, SSI
• MANUSCRIPTS
Query: no; *Abstract:* no
Style guide: Chicago
Preferred length: 25 pp max
Copies: 4
Notes: endnotes
Blind referee: yes
Charts, tables, graphs, maps
Foreign languages accepted: no
• REVIEWS
Seeking reviewers: yes
Unsolicited reviews accepted: no
Materials reviewed: books
How to apply: letter
Include in application: professional
    degrees, institutional affiliation,
    areas of expertise, published
    works, current research

Social Science Quarterly

Social science research and/or theory;
    interdisciplinary
Affiliation: The University of Texas
    Press; Southwestern Social Science
    Association
Ed: Charles M. Bonjean
    310 Will C. Hogg Building

University of Texas at Austin
    Austin, TX 78712
Bk Rev Ed: Malcolm Macdonald
    Department of Government
    536 Burdine
    University of Texas at Austin
    Austin, TX 78712
4/yr, 240 pp; subs $25
Circ: 3,000
Readership: academics
Indexed/Abstracted: ABC, AHCI,
    BRI, CCSB, PAIS, SSCI, SSI,
    WAH
• MANUSCRIPTS
Query: no; *Abstract:* preferred
Style guide: own
Preferred length: 14–23 pp, 30 pp
    max
Copies: 4
Notes: endnotes
Blind referee: yes
Acceptance rate: 1/7
Time to consider ms: 2 mos
Charts, tables, graphs, maps
Foreign languages accepted: no
• REVIEWS
Seeking reviewers: yes
Unsolicited reviews accepted: no
Materials reviewed: books
Review length: varies
How to apply: letter
Include in application: professional
    degrees, institutional affiliation,
    areas of expertise, published
    works, foreign languages, current
    research

Social Science Research

Substantive issues in all social
    sciences areas; social science
    methods
Affiliation: Academic Press, Inc.
Ed: James D. Wright
    Department of Sociology
    Tulane University
    220 Newcomb Hall
    New Orleans, LA 70118
4/yr, 116 pp; subs $132

Readership: academics
Indexed/Abstracted: ABC, CCSB, SSCI, SSI
• MANUSCRIPTS
Query: no; *Abstract:* yes
Style guide: own
Preferred length: varies
Copies: 3
Notes: endnotes
Blind referee: yes
Charts, tables, graphs, maps
Foreign languages accepted: no

The Social Studies

Items of interest to social studies teachers at all levels
Affiliation: Heldref Publications
Ed: Helen S. Kress
 1319 Eighteenth Street, N.W.
 Washington, D.C. 20036-1802
Bk Rev Ed: same
6/yr, 48 pp; subs $28
Circ: 3,000
Readership: academics
Indexed/Abstracted: ABC, BRI, PAIS, WAH
• MANUSCRIPTS
Query: no; *Abstract:* no
Style guide: Chicago
Preferred length: 2,000–3,000 wds
Copies: 2
Notes: author-date system
Blind referee: no
Acceptance rate: 1/2
Time to consider ms: 3–5 mos
Charts, pictures, tables, graphs, maps
Foreign languages accepted: no
• REVIEWS
Seeking reviewers: no
Unsolicited reviews accepted: occasionally
Materials reviewed: books

Social Studies of Science

The study of science in its social dimension, encompassing history, philosophy, sociology, political science, and economics

Ed: David Edge
 Science Studies Unit
 University of Edinburgh
 25 Gilmour Road
 Edinburgh EH16 5NS
 U.K.
Bk Rev Ed: David Philip Miller
 Science and Technology Studies
 The University of New South Wales
 P.O. Box 1
 Kensington
 New South Wales 2033
 AUSTRALIA
4/yr, 220 pp; subs £35
Readership: academics
Indexed/Abstracted: ABC, AHCI, CCAH, CCSB, SSCI
• MANUSCRIPTS
Style guide: own
Preferred length: 6,000–18,000 wds
Copies: 5
• REVIEWS
Materials reviewed: books

Social Studies Review

Teaching history, social sciences, and social studies
Affiliation: California Council for the Social Studies
Eds: William Hanna and Damon Nalty
 One Washington Square
 San Jose State University
 San Jose, CA 95192
Bk Rev Ed: same
3/yr, 115 pp; subs $25
Circ: 3,000
Readership: academics, general public, K–12 social studies teachers
• MANUSCRIPTS
Query: preferred; *Abstract:* preferred
Style guide: MLA
Preferred length: 3–6 pp
Copies: 2
Notes: endnotes or footnotes
Blind referee: no
Time to consider ms: 1 mo

Charts, pictures, tables, maps
Foreign languages accepted: no
• REVIEWS
Seeking reviewers: yes
Unsolicited reviews accepted: yes
Materials reviewed: books, films,
    software, multimedia
How to apply: letter
Include in application: professional
    degrees, institutional affiliation,
    areas of expertise, published works

Society for Army Research Bulletin

History of the British army
Affiliation: Society for Army Research
Ed: M. A. Cane
    46 Galiworthy Road
    Kingston
    Surrey KT2 7BS   U.K.
Bk Rev Ed: same
4/yr, 64 pp; subs £18
Circ: 1,200
Readership: academics, military his-
    torians
Indexed/Abstracted: BHI
• MANUSCRIPTS
Query: yes; *Abstract:* no
Preferred length: 500–9,000 wds
Copies: 2
Notes: endnotes
Blind referee: no
Acceptance rate: 4/5
Time to consider ms: 2–3 wks
Charts, pictures, tables, maps
Foreign languages accepted: no
• REVIEWS
Seeking reviewers: no
Unsolicited reviews accepted: rarely
Materials reviewed: books
Review length: 500–1,000 wds
How to apply: letter
Include in application: areas of
    expertise

Source, Notes in the History of Art

Art history
Ed: Laurie Schneider

1 East 87th Street
Suite 7A
New York, NY 10128
4/yr, 36 pp; subs $20
Circ: 1,000
Readership: academics, collectors
Indexed/Abstracted: AHCI, CCAH
• MANUSCRIPTS
Query: no; *Abstract:* no
Style guide: Chicago
Preferred length: 1,000
Copies: 2
Notes: footnotes
Blind referee: no
Acceptance rate: 1/4
Time to consider ms: 6 mos
Charts, pictures, tables, graphs, maps
Foreign languages accepted: no

South Asia Bulletin

Socio-economic, political, cultural,
    historical, and contemporary
    aspects of South Asia
Affiliation: State University of New
    York, Albany
Ed: Vasant Kaiwar
    c/o Department of History
    State University of New York at
    Albany
    Albany, NY 12222
Bk Rev Ed: same
2/yr, 82 pp; subs $20
Circ: 700
Readership: academics
Indexed/Abstracted: ABC
• MANUSCRIPTS
Query: preferred; *Abstract:* yes
Style guide: own
Preferred length: 8,500–10,000 wds
Copies: 2
Notes: endnotes
Blind referee: yes
Time to consider ms: 4–6 mos
Tables
Foreign languages accepted: no
• REVIEWS
Seeking reviewers: yes
Unsolicited reviews accepted: no
Materials reviewed: books

Review length: 750–1,000 wds
How to apply: letter
Include in application: professional degrees, institutional affiliation, published works, current research

South Asia Research

Multi-disciplinary studies of South Asia including history, politics, anthropology, indology, etc.
Affiliation: School of Oriental and African Studies, University of London
Ed: David Arnold
  Department of History
  School of Oriental and African Studies
  Thornhaugh Street
  Russell Square
  London WC1H 0XG   U.K.
Bk Rev Ed: Michael Hutt
  Department of Indology
  School of Oriental and African Studies
  Thornhaugh Street
  Russell Square
  London WC1H 0XG   U.K.
2/yr, 100 pp; subs £7
Circ: 300
Readership: academics
Indexed/Abstracted: ABC
• MANUSCRIPTS
Query: preferred; *Abstract:* no
Preferred length: 8,000 wds
Copies: 2
Notes: endnotes
Blind referee: yes
Acceptance rate: 1/2
Time to consider ms: 2 mos
Charts, pictures, tables, graphs, maps
Foreign languages accepted: no
• REVIEWS
Seeking reviewers: yes
Unsolicited reviews accepted: no
Materials reviewed: books
Review length: 500 wds max
How to apply: letter
Include in application: professional

degrees, areas of expertise, published works, current research

South Carolina Historical Magazine

All aspects of the history of South Carolina
Affiliation: South Carolina Historical Society
Ed: Stephen Hoffius
  South Carolina Historical Society
  100 Meeting Street
  Charleston, SC 29401-2299
Bk Rev Ed: same
4/yr, 80 pp; subs membership
Circ: 4,250
Readership: academics, general public
Indexed/Abstracted: ABC, WAH
• MANUSCRIPTS
Query: no; *Abstract:* no
Style guide: Chicago
Preferred length: 25 pp
Copies: 3
Notes: endnotes or footnotes
Blind referee: no
Acceptance rate: 1/3
Time to consider ms: 3 mos
Charts, pictures, tables, graphs, maps
Foreign languages accepted: no
• REVIEWS
Seeking reviewers: yes
Unsolicited reviews accepted: occasionally
Materials reviewed: books
Review length: 700 wds
How to apply: letter
Include in application: professional degrees, institutional affiliation, areas of expertise, published works, current research

South Dakota History

Western and Great Plains history
Affiliation: South Dakota State Historical Society
Ed: Nancy Tystad Koupal
  Publications
  South Dakota State Historical Society

900 Governors Drive
Pierre, SD 57501-2217
Bk Rev Ed: Gerald W. Wolff
    Department of History
    University of South Dakota
    Vermillion, SD 57069
4/yr, 100 pp; subs $20
Circ: 2,300
Readership: academics, general public
Indexed/Abstracted: ABC, WAH
• MANUSCRIPTS
Query: no; *Abstract:* no
Style guide: Chicago
Preferred length: 30 pp max
Copies: 1
Notes: endnotes
Blind referee: yes
Acceptance rate: 7/10
Time to consider ms: 3–6 mos
Charts, pictures, tables, graphs, maps
Foreign languages accepted: no
• REVIEWS
Seeking reviewers: yes
Unsolicited reviews accepted: no
Materials reviewed: books
Review length: 500 wds
How to apply: letter
Include in application: professional
    degrees, institutional affiliation,
    areas of expertise, published works,
    foreign languages, current research

South of the Mountains

History of Rockland County, New
    York
Affiliation: Historical Society of
    Rockland County
Ed: Marianne B. Leese
    20 Zukor Road
    New City, NY 10956-4302
Bk Rev Ed: same
4/yr, 24 pp; subs $20
Circ: 2,000
Readership: society members
• MANUSCRIPTS
Query: preferred; *Abstract:* preferred
Preferred length: 18 pp max
Copies: 1
Notes: endnotes

Blind referee: no
Time to consider ms: 1 mo
Pictures, maps
Foreign languages accepted: no
• REVIEWS
Seeking reviewers: no
Unsolicited reviews accepted: no
Materials reviewed: books

Southern California Quarterly

California and American West
Affiliation: Historical Society of
    Southern California
Ed: Doyce B. Nunis, Jr.
    The Lummis House
    200 East Avenue 43
    Los Angeles, CA 90031-1399
Bk Rev Ed: same
4/yr, 112 pp; subs membership
Circ: 120
Readership: academics, general public
Indexed/Abstracted: ABC
• MANUSCRIPTS
Query: no; *Abstract:* no
Style guide: Chicago
Preferred length: open
Copies: 2
Notes: endnotes
Blind referee: yes
Acceptance rate: 3/5
Time to consider ms: 6 mos
Charts, pictures, tables, graphs, maps
Foreign languages accepted: no
• REVIEWS
Seeking reviewers: yes
Unsolicited reviews accepted: no
Materials reviewed: books
Review length: open
How to apply: letter
Include in application: professional
    degrees, institutional affiliation,
    areas of expertise, published works,
    foreign languages, current research

The Southern Friends Journal of the North Carolina Friends Historical Collection

Quaker history, especially of North
    Carolina and the Southeastern U.S.

Affiliation: North Carolina Friends
  Historical Society
Ed: Herbert Poole
  North Carolina Friends Histori-
  cal Society
  P.O. Box 8502
  Greensboro, NC 27419-0502
Bk Rev Ed: Carole Treadway
2/yr, 60 pp; subs $15
Circ: 450
Readership: academics, general public
Indexed/Abstracted: ABC
• MANUSCRIPTS
Query: no; *Abstract:* no
Style guide: Chicago
Preferred length: open
Copies: 1
Notes: endnotes
Blind referee: no
Acceptance rate: 8/10–9/10
Time to consider ms: 6 mos
Pictures, maps
Foreign languages accepted: no
• REVIEWS
Seeking reviewers: no
Unsolicited reviews accepted: occa-
  sionally
Materials reviewed: books

Southern Partisan Magazine

Southern politics, history, literature
Ed: Richard M. Quinn, Sr.
  P.O. Box 11708
  Columbia, SC 29211
Bk Rev Ed: Oran P. Smith
4/yr, 60 pp; subs $14
Circ: 10,000
Readership: academics, general public
• MANUSCRIPTS
Query: preferred; *Abstract:* preferred
Preferred length: 2,500 wds
Copies: 2
Notes: none
Blind referee: no
Charts, pictures, maps
Foreign languages accepted: no
• REVIEWS
Seeking reviewers: yes

Unsolicited reviews accepted: yes
Materials reviewed: books, films
Review length: 1,200 wds
How to apply: letter
Include in application: areas of ex-
  pertise, published works

The Southern Quarterly

Arts in the South
Affiliation: University of Southern
  Mississippi
Ed: Stephen Flinn Young
  Southern Station Box 5078
  Hattiesburg, MS 39406-5078
Bk Rev Ed: Noel Polk
4/yr, 120 pp; subs $9
Circ: 900
Readership: academics, general public
Indexed/Abstracted: ABC, AHI,
  MLA, WAH
• MANUSCRIPTS
Query: no; *Abstract:* no
Style guide: MLA
Preferred length: 16–20 pp
Copies: 1
Notes: endnotes
Blind referee: yes
Acceptance rate: 1/8
Time to consider ms: 3 mos
Charts, pictures, tables, graphs, maps
Foreign languages accepted: no
• REVIEWS
Seeking reviewers: no
Unsolicited reviews accepted: yes
Materials reviewed: books, films, ex-
  hibitions, performances
Review length: 500–750 wds
How to apply: letter
Include in application: professional
  degrees, institutional affiliation,
  areas of expertise, published
  works, current research
• ADDITIONAL NOTES
The audience of this journal is multi-
disciplinary. "Arts" is defined
broadly and includes the traditional
arts of high culture as well as pop-
ular arts. *Southern Quarterly* pub-

lishes articles based on original research or critical analysis.

The Southern Review

Southern letters and modernist literature
Affiliation: Louisiana State University
Eds: James Olney and Dave Smith
43 Allen Hall
Louisiana State University
Baton Rouge, LA 70803
Bk Rev Ed: same
4/yr, 245 pp; subs $15
Circ: 3,000
Readership: academics, general public
Indexed/Abstracted: ABC, BRI, HI, MLA
• MANUSCRIPTS
Query: no; *Abstract:* no
Preferred length: 5,000 wds
Copies: 1
Notes: none
Blind referee: no
Acceptance rate: 1/50
Time to consider ms: 2 mos
No illustrations accepted
Foreign languages accepted: no
• REVIEWS
Seeking reviewers: no
Unsolicited reviews accepted: no
Materials reviewed: books
Review length: 1,200–3,500 wds
How to apply: letter
Include in application: professional degrees, institutional affiliation, areas of expertise, published works, current research

Southern Social Studies Journal

The various areas within social studies at elementary, middle, high school, and higher education levels
Affiliation: Morehead State University and the Kentucky Council for the Social Studies
Eds: Charles Holt and Kent Freeland
UPO 738

Morehead State University
Morehead, KY 40351
Bk Rev Ed: same
2/yr, 80 pp; subs $10
Circ: 500
Readership: academics, general public
• MANUSCRIPTS
Query: no; *Abstract:* no
Style guide: MLA or *Publication Manual of the American Psychological Association*
Preferred length: 5–12 pp
Copies: 2
Notes: endnotes
Blind referee: yes
Acceptance rate: 3/4
Time to consider ms: 6–8 wks
Charts, pictures, tables, graphs, maps
Foreign languages accepted: no
• REVIEWS
Seeking reviewers: yes
Unsolicited reviews accepted: yes
Materials reviewed: books, films, video tapes
Review length: 2 pp
How to apply: letter, form
Include in application: professional degrees, institutional affiliation, areas of expertise, current research, teaching position

Southern Studies

Interdisciplinary studies of the South
Affiliation: Northwestern State University of Louisiana
Ed: Maxine Taylor
Department of Social Sciences
Northwestern State University
Natchitoches, LA 71497
Bk Rev Ed: same
4/yr, 125 pp; subs $20
Circ: 400
Readership: academics, general public
Indexed/Abstracted: ABC, MLA, WAH
• MANUSCRIPTS
Query: yes; *Abstract:* no
Style guide: MLA or Chicago

Preferred length: 20–25 pp
Copies: 2
Notes: endnotes
Blind referee: yes
Time to consider ms: 6 mos
No illustrations accepted
Foreign languages accepted: no
• REVIEWS
Seeking reviewers: yes
Unsolicited reviews accepted: occasionally
Materials reviewed: books
Review length: 300–400 wds min
How to apply: letter
Include in application: professional degrees, institutional affiliation, areas of expertise, published works, foreign languages

Southwest Review

General literary and intellectual quarterly
Affiliation: Southern Methodist University
Ed: Willard Spiegelman
   307 Fondren Library West
   Box 4374
   Southern Methodist University
   Dallas, TX 75275
4/yr, 160 pp; subs $20
Circ: 1,500
Readership: academics, general public
Indexed/Abstracted: ABC, AHI, BRI, HI, MLA
• MANUSCRIPTS
Query: no; *Abstract:* no
Style guide: Chicago
Preferred length: 3,500–7,000 wds
Copies: 1
Notes: none
Blind referee: no
Time to consider ms: 1 mo
No illustrations accepted

Southwestern Historical Quarterly

History of Texas and the Southwest
Affiliation: Texas State Historical Association

Ed: George B. Ward
   c/o Texas State Historical Association
   2/306 Richardson Hall
   University Station
   Austin, TX 78712
Bk Rev Ed: Norman Brown
4/yr, 200 pp; subs $25
Circ: 3,500
Readership: academics, general public
Indexed/Abstracted: ABC, AHCI, CCAH, HI, WAH
• MANUSCRIPTS
Query: no; *Abstract:* no
Style guide: Chicago
Preferred length: 40 pp max
Copies: 4
Notes: endnotes
Blind referee: yes
Charts, pictures, tables, graphs, maps
Foreign languages accepted: no
• REVIEWS
Materials reviewed: books
Review length: 400 wds
How to apply: letter
Include in application: professional degrees, institutional affiliation, areas of expertise, published works, current research

Southwestern Lore

Colorado archaeology and Rocky Mountain archaeology
Affiliation: Colorado Archaeological Society
Ed: Marcia J. Tate
   1390 S. Paris Ct.
   Aurora, CO 80012
Bk Rev Ed: Payson Sheets
   Colorado University
   Anthropology Department
   Boulder, CO 80309
4/yr, 36 pp; subs $10
Circ: 1,000
Readership: academics, general public, professional archaeologists
Indexed/Abstracted: ABC
• MANUSCRIPTS
Query: preferred; *Abstract:* preferred

Preferred length: 40 pp max
Copies: 2
Blind referee: no
Acceptance rate: 9/10
Time to consider ms: 3 mos
Charts, pictures, tables, graphs, maps
Foreign languages accepted: no
• REVIEWS
Seeking reviewers: no
Unsolicited reviews accepted: no
Materials reviewed: books

Speculum: A Journal of Medieval Studies

Medieval studies
Affiliation: Medieval Academy of America
Ed: Luke Wenger
1430 Massachusetts Avenue
Cambridge, MA 02138
Bk Rev Ed: Fredric L. Cheyette
4/yr, 250 pp; subs $20–45
Circ: 5,500
Readership: academics
Indexed/Abstracted: AHCI, BRI, CCAH, HI, IMB, MLA
• MANUSCRIPTS
Query: no; *Abstract:* no
Style guide: own
Preferred length: 15–50 pp
Copies: 2
Notes: endnotes
Blind referee: no
Acceptance rate: 1/10
Time to consider ms: 3–5 mos
Charts, pictures, tables, graphs, maps
Foreign languages accepted: no
• REVIEWS
Seeking reviewers: yes
Unsolicited reviews accepted: no
Materials reviewed: books
Review length: 1,200 wds
How to apply: letter
Include in application: professional degrees, institutional affiliation, areas of expertise, published works, foreign languages, current research

Studies in Dance History

The history of dance and related arts
Affiliation: Society of Dance History Scholars
Eds: John V. Chapman and Lynn Garafola
Division of Dance
University of California, Santa Barbara
Santa Barbara, CA 93106
2/yr, 128 pp; subs $30
Circ: 750
Readership: academics, general public
• MANUSCRIPTS
Query: yes; *Abstract:* no
Style guide: Chicago
Preferred length: 50,000 wds max
Copies: 2
Notes: endnotes
Blind referee: yes
Acceptance rate: 1/4
Time to consider ms: 6 mos
Charts, pictures
Foreign languages accepted: no

Studies in History and Philosophy of Science

Historical, philosophical and sociological studies of the sciences
Eds: Nicholas Jardine and Andrew Cunningham
University of Cambridge
Department of History and Philosophy of Science
Free School Lane
Cambridge CB2 3RH
U.K.
Bk Rev Ed: Perry Williams
4/yr, 175 pp; subs $255 institutional
Circ: 1,000
Readership: academics
Indexed/Abstracted: ABC, AHCI, CCAH, CCSB, HI, SSCI
• MANUSCRIPTS
Query: no; *Abstract:* no
Style guide: own
Preferred length: 10,000 wds max
Copies: 2

Notes: footnotes
Blind referee: upon request
Acceptance rate: 1/3
Time to consider ms: 6–8 wks
Charts, pictures, tables, graphs, maps
Foreign languages accepted: no
• REVIEWS
Seeking reviewers: yes
Unsolicited reviews accepted: no
Materials reviewed: books
Review length: essay length
How to apply: letter
Include in application: professional
　degrees, institutional affiliation,
　areas of expertise, published
　works, foreign languages

Studies in Popular Culture

Popular culture
Affiliation: Popular Culture Associa-
　tion in the South
Ed: Dennis R. Hall
　　c/o English Department
　　University of Louisville
　　Louisville, KY 40292
Bk Rev Ed: Jerome Stern
　　c/o English Department
　　Florida State University
　　Tallahassee, FL 32306
2/yr, 110 pp; subs $15
Circ: 350
Readership: academics
Indexed/Abstracted: MLA
• MANUSCRIPTS
Query: preferred; *Abstract:* no
Style guide: any approriate or MLA
Preferred length: 20 pp
Copies: 2
Notes: endnotes
Blind referee: no
Acceptance rate: 1/15–1/20
Time to consider ms: 6 mos
Charts, pictures, tables, graphs, maps
Foreign languages accepted: no
• REVIEWS
Seeking reviewers: no
Unsolicited reviews accepted: rarely
Materials reviewed: books
How to apply: letter

Studies in Romanticism

English, American, continental, and
　third-world parallels of literary,
　musical, and fine arts romanticism
Affiliation: Boston University
Ed: David Wagenknecht
　　236 Bay State Road
　　Boston, MA 02215
Bk Rev Ed: same
4/yr, 175 pp; subs $20
Circ: 1,800
Readership: academics
Indexed/Abstracted: ABC, AHCI,
　CCAH, HI, MLA
• MANUSCRIPTS
Query: no; *Abstract:* yes
Style guide: modified Chicago
Preferred length: 30–35 pp
Copies: 2
Notes: endnotes and footnotes
Blind referee: no
Acceptance rate: 1/10
Time to consider ms: 2–4 mos
Pictures, tables
Foreign languages accepted: no
• REVIEWS
Seeking reviewers: yes
Unsolicited reviews accepted: no
Materials reviewed: books
Review length: 6 pp max
How to apply: letter
Include in application: institutional
　affiliation, areas of expertise, pub-
　lished works, current research

Swedish-American Historical Quarterly

Swedish and Scandinavian immigra-
　tion and ethnic history
Affiliation: Swedish-American Histor-
　ical Society
Ed: Raymond Jarvi
　　North Park College
　　5125 N. Spaulding Avenue
　　Chicago, IL 60625
Bk Rev Ed: Byron Nordstrom
　　Gustavus Adolphus College
　　Saint Peter, MN 56082

4/yr, 64 pp; subs $25
Circ: 1,200
Readership: academics, general public
Indexed/Abstracted: ABC, MLA,
    WAH
• MANUSCRIPTS
Query: no; *Abstract:* no
Style guide: Chicago
Preferred length: 15–25 pp
Copies: 1
Notes: endnotes
Blind referee: sometimes
Acceptance rate: 1/2
Time to consider ms: 4–8 wks
Charts, pictures, tables, graphs, maps
Foreign languages accepted: no
• REVIEWS
Seeking reviewers: yes
Unsolicited reviews accepted: no
Materials reviewed: books
How to apply: letter or recommen-
    dation
Include in application: professional
    degrees, areas of expertise, pub-
    lished works, foreign languages,
    current research

Tampa Bay History

History of West, Central, and South-
    west Florida from Tampa to Fort
    Myers
Affiliation: University of South
    Florida
Ed: Robert P. Ingalls
    Department of History
    SOC 107
    University of South Florida
    Tampa, FL 33620
Bk Rev Ed: same
2/yr, 76 pp; subs $15
Circ: 700
Readership: academics, general public
Indexed/Abstracted: ABC, WAH
• MANUSCRIPTS
Query: no; *Abstract:* no
Preferred length: 15–30 pp
Copies: 1
Notes: endnotes

Blind referee: yes
Acceptance rate: 4/5
Time to consider ms: 1 mo
Charts, pictures, maps
Foreign languages accepted: no
• REVIEWS
Seeking reviewers: yes
Unsolicited reviews accepted: no
Materials reviewed: books
Review length: 500 wds
How to apply: letter
Include in application: professional
    degrees, institutional affiliation,
    areas of expertise, published works

Tar Heel Junior Historian

North Carolina history
Affiliation: North Carolina Museum
    of History
Ed: John Lee Bumgarner
    109 East Jones Street
    Raleigh, NC 27601-2801
2/yr, 48 pp; subs $4
Circ: 9,000
Readership: 4th–8th grades in public
    schools
• MANUSCRIPTS
Query: yes; *Abstract:* no
Style guide: Chicago
Preferred length: 750–1,500 wds
Copies: 1
Notes: none
Blind referee: yes
Time to consider ms: 6 mos
Charts, pictures, tables, graphs, maps
Foreign languages accepted: no

Teaching History

History instruction
Affiliation: The Historical Association
Eds: Richard Brown
    17 Sunbower Avenue
    Dunstable
    Bedfordshire LU6 1UQ
    U.K.
        or
    Hilary Cooper
    Goldsmiths' College

Lewisham Way
London SE14 6NW
U.K.
Bk Rev Ed: Richard Brown
50 pp; subs £38
Readership: history teachers
Indexed/Abstracted: ABC
• MANUSCRIPTS
Query: no; *Abstract:* no
Style guide: own
Preferred length: varies
Copies: 1
Foreign languages accepted: no
• REVIEWS
Materials reviewed: books, other
educational media
Review length: varies

Teaching History: A Journal of Methods

Classroom strategies and
methodologies at college and
secondary levels
Ed: Stephen Kneeshaw
College of the Ozarks
Point Lookout, MO 65726-0017
Bk Rev Ed: Bullitt Lowry
University of North Texas
P.O. Box 13735
Denton, TX 73203-3735
2/yr, 48 pp; subs $5
Circ: 750
Readership: academics
Indexed/Abstracted: ABC
• MANUSCRIPTS
Query: no; *Abstract:* no
Preferred length: 10–15 pp
Copies: 1
Notes: endnotes or footnotes
Blind referee: yes
Acceptance rate: 1/5
Time to consider ms: 4 mos
Charts, tables, graphs, maps
Foreign languages accepted: no
• REVIEWS
Seeking reviewers: yes
Unsolicited reviews accepted: no
Materials reviewed: books, films

Review length: 400–600 wds
How to apply: letter
Include in application: professional
degrees, institutional affiliation,
areas of expertise

Technology and Culture

History of technology and its inter-
actions
Affiliation: Smithsonian Institution
Ed: Robert C. Post
NMAH 5030
Smithsonian Institution
Washington, DC 20560
Bk Rev Ed: Jeffrey Stine
4/yr, 250 pp; subs $29
Circ: 3,000
Readership: academics, museum pro-
fessionals, engineers
Indexed/Abstracted: ABC, BRI,
CCAH, CCSB, SSCI, SSI, WAH
• MANUSCRIPTS
Query: no; *Abstract:* no
Style guide: Chicago
Preferred length: 30–40 pp
Copies: 3
Notes: footnotes
Blind referee: yes
Acceptance rate: 3/10
Time to consider ms: 4–6 mos
Pictures, tables, graphs, maps
Foreign languages accepted: no
• REVIEWS
Seeking reviewers: yes
Unsolicited reviews accepted: no
Materials reviewed: books, journals
Review length: 600–700 wds
How to apply: letter
Include in application: institutional
affiliation, areas of expertise, for-
eign languages

Tennessee Historical Quarterly

History of Tennessee
Affiliation: Tennessee Historical So-
ciety
Ed: Robert Jones
Box 444

Middle Tennessee State University
Murfreesboro, TN 37132
Bk Rev Ed: Margaret Ripley Wolfe
Department of History
Box 22660A
East Tennessee State University
Johnson City, TN 37614
4/yr, 68 pp; subs $25
Circ: 3,000
Readership: academics, general public, historical organizations
Indexed/Abstracted: ABC, WAH
• MANUSCRIPTS
Query: preferred; *Abstract:* no
Style guide: modified Chicago
Preferred length: 30 pp max
Copies: 2
Notes: endnotes
Blind referee: yes
Acceptance rate: 4/5
Time to consider ms: 6 wks
Charts, pictures, tables, graphs, maps
Foreign languages accepted: no
• REVIEWS
Seeking reviewers: yes
Unsolicited reviews accepted: no
Materials reviewed: books, films
Review length: 2–4 pp
How to apply: letter
Include in application: professional degrees, institutional affiliation, areas of expertise, current research

Tequesta

History of southern Florida and the Caribbean
Affiliation: Historical Association of Southern Florida
Ed: Arva Moore Parks
1601 South Miami Avenue
Miami, FL 33129
1/yr, 96 pp; subs $35
Circ: 3,500
Readership: academics, general public
Indexed/Abstracted: ABC
• MANUSCRIPTS
Query: preferred; *Abstract:* no
Style guide: Chicago

Copies: 2
Notes: endnotes
Blind referee: yes
Acceptance rate: 3/4
Time to consider ms: 8 mos
Charts, pictures, tables, graphs, maps
Foreign languages accepted: no

Theatre Research in Canada/ Récherches Théâtrales au Canada

Theatre research in Canada
Affiliation: Association of Canadian Theatre Research
Eds: Richard Plant and Leonard Doucette
c/o Graduate Centre for Drama
214 College Street
Toronto, ON M5T 2Z9
CANADA
Bk Rev Ed: James Noonan
2/yr, 200 pp; subs $15
Circ: 400
Readership: academics, theatre practitioners
• MANUSCRIPTS
Query: no; *Abstract:* yes
Style guide: own
Preferred length: 4,000 wds max
Copies: 1
Notes: endnotes
Blind referee: yes
Acceptance rate: a high rate with changes
Time to consider ms: 1 mo
Charts, pictures, tables, graphs, maps
Foreign languages accepted: French
• REVIEWS
Seeking reviewers: yes
Unsolicited reviews accepted: yes
Materials reviewed: books
Review length: 800 wds
How to apply: submit review
Include in application: professional degrees, institutional affiliation, areas of expertise, published works, current research, short biographical description

Theodore Roosevelt Association Journal

Life and times of Theodore Roosevelt
Affiliation: Theodore Roosevelt Association
Ed: John A. Gable
  Theodore Roosevelt Association
  P.O. Box 720
  Oyster Bay, NY 11771
Bk Rev Ed: same
4/yr, 26 pp; subs $25
Circ: 2,000
Readership: academics, general public
Indexed/Abstracted: ABC, WAH
• MANUSCRIPTS
Query: preferred; *Abstract:* no
Style guide: Turabian
Preferred length: varies
Copies: 2
Notes: endnotes
Blind referee: no
Acceptance rate: 4/5
Time to consider ms: 3 mos
Pictures
Foreign languages accepted: no
• REVIEWS
Seeking reviewers: yes
Unsolicited reviews accepted: yes
Materials reviewed: books, films
Review length: 1,000–1,200 wds
How to apply: letter
Include in application: professional degrees, institutional affiliation, areas of expertise

Timeline

History and prehistory of the Midwest
Affiliation: Ohio Historical Society
Ed: Christopher S. Duckworth
  1982 Velma Avenue
  Columbus, OH 43211
6/yr, 56 pp; subs $18
Circ: 17,000
Readership: general public
Indexed/Abstracted: ABC, WAH
• MANUSCRIPTS
Query: preferred; *Abstract:* no
Style guide: Chicago

Preferred length: 500–6,000 wds
Copies: 1
Notes: none
Blind referee: sometimes
Time to consider ms: 30 days
Pictures, graphs, maps
Foreign languages accepted: no
• ADDITIONAL NOTES
Timeline pays for manuscripts. Its articles are intended for the lay person, not the specialist.

The Tombstone Epitaph

19th century Western history
Ed: Wallace E. Clayton
  P.O. Box 1880
  Tombstone, AZ 85638
Bk Rev Ed: Don Bufkin
12/yr, 20 pp; subs $12.50
Circ: 7,700
Readership: general public, Western history buffs
• MANUSCRIPTS
Query: preferred; *Abstract:* no
Preferred length: varies
Copies: 1
Notes: none
Blind referee: no
Pictures, maps
Foreign languages accepted: no
• REVIEWS
Seeking reviewers: no
Unsolicited reviews accepted: no

Traces of Indiana and Midwestern History

History of Indiana and the Old Northwest
Affiliation: Indiana Historical Society
Ed: J. Kent Calder
  Indiana Historical Society
  315 W. Ohio Street
  Indianapolis, IN 46202
4/yr, 48 pp; subs $20
Circ: 10,000
Readership: academics, general public
• MANUSCRIPTS
Query: preferred; *Abstract:* no

Preferred length: 2,500–3,000 wds
Copies: 2
Notes: endnotes
Blind referee: yes
Acceptance rate: 1/5
Time to consider ms: 4 mos
Pictures, maps
Foreign languages accepted: no

The Tracker

19th century American organ
building, organs, musicians, etc.
Affiliation: Organ Historical Society
Ed: John K. Ogasapian
Durgin 217
University of Massachusetts-
Lowell
Lowell, MA 01854
Bk Rev Ed: Jerry D. Morton
c/o Organ Historical Society
P.O. Box 25811
Richmond, VA 23261
4/yr, 32 pp; subs $25
Circ: 3,200
Readership: academics, general pub-
lic, organists, organ builders
• MANUSCRIPTS
Query: preferred; *Abstract:* no
Copies: 1
Notes: endnotes
Blind referee: yes
Acceptance rate: 4/5
Time to consider ms: 3 mos
Charts, pictures, tables, graphs
Foreign languages accepted: no
• REVIEWS
Seeking reviewers: no
Unsolicited reviews accepted: no
Materials reviewed: books, CDs
How to apply: letter

True West

History of the trans–Mississippi West
from prehistory to about 1930
Ed: John Joerschke
P.O. Box 2107
Stillwater, OK 74076
Bk Rev Ed: same

12/yr, 68 pp; subs $19.95
Circ: 30,000
Readership: general public
• MANUSCRIPTS
Query: preferred; *Abstract:* no
Style guide: any
Preferred length: 3,000–4,000 wds
Copies: 1
Notes: endnotes or footnotes are
preferred
Blind referee: no
Acceptance rate: 1/6
Time to consider ms: 6–8 wks
Pictures, maps, documents
Foreign languages accepted: no
• REVIEWS
Seeking reviewers: yes
Unsolicited reviews accepted: occa-
sionally
Materials reviewed: books, films
Review length: 300 wds
How to apply: letter
Include in application: professional
degrees, areas of expertise, pub-
lished works, current research
• ADDITIONAL NOTES
The editors are very interested in
manuscripts written by professional
historians for a general readership.

The Turkish Studies Association Bulletin

Turkish and Ottoman Studies
Affiliation: Turkish Studies Associa-
tion
Ed: Madeline C. Zilfi
History Department
University of Maryland
College Park, MD 20742
Bk Rev Ed: Palmira Brummett
2/yr, 250 pp; subs $15
Circ: 400
Readership: academics, general pub-
lic, government officials, area spe-
cialists
• MANUSCRIPTS
Query: yes; *Abstract:* preferred
Style guide: Turabian or Chicago

Copies: 1
Notes: endnotes
Blind referee: yes
Acceptance rate: 1/3
Time to consider ms: 3 mos
Charts, tables, graphs
Foreign languages accepted: French,
German, Turkish
● REVIEWS
Seeking reviewers: yes
Unsolicited reviews accepted: no
Materials reviewed: books
Review length: 500–700 wds
How to apply: letter
Include in application: professional
degrees, institutional affiliation,
areas of expertise, published
works, foreign languages

Twentieth Century British History

Contemporary British history; comparative history with Britain
Eds: R. I. McKibbin
St. John's College
Oxford OX1 3JP
U.K.
or
J. S. Rowett
Brasenose College
Oxford OX1 4AJ
U.K.
Bk Rev Ed: Ewen Green
Department of History
University of Reading
Reading RG6 2AA
U.K.
3/yr, 120 pp; subs £33
Circ: 400
Readership: academics
Indexed/Abstracted: ABC
● MANUSCRIPTS
Query: no; *Abstract:* no
Preferred length: 5,000–10,000
wds
Copies: 3
Notes: footnotes
Blind referee: sometimes

Charts, pictures, tables, graphs,
maps
Foreign languages accepted: no
● REVIEWS
Seeking reviewers: no
Unsolicited reviews accepted: occasionally
Materials reviewed: books, films,
fiches, etc.
Review length: 1,000–3,000 wds

Ufahamu

African studies
Affiliation: James S. Coleman African Studies Center, University of
California, Los Angeles
Ed: Angaluki Muaka
James S. Coleman African Studies Center
10244 Bunche Hall
University of California, Los
Angeles
405 Hilgard Avenue
Los Angeles, CA 90024-1310
Bk Rev Ed: Mary Lederer
4/yr, 110 pp; subs $14
Circ: 300
Readership: academics
Indexed/Abstracted: ABC, MLA
● MANUSCRIPTS
Query: no; *Abstract:* no
Style guide: MLA
Preferred length: 15–25 pp
Copies: 2
Notes: endnotes
Blind referee: no
Acceptance rate: 1/2–2/3
Time to consider ms: 6 mos
Charts, tables, graphs, maps
Foreign languages accepted: no
● REVIEWS
Seeking reviewers: no
Unsolicited reviews accepted: yes
Materials reviewed: books
Review length: 5 pp
How to apply: letter
Include in application: professional
degrees, institutional affiliation,

areas of expertise, published
works, current research

The Ukrainian Quarterly

Ukrainian, East European, and Asian
affairs
Affiliation: Ukrainian Congress Com-
mittee of America, Inc.
Ed: Nicholas Chirovsky
203 Second Avenue
New York, NY 10003
Bk Rev Ed: Petro Matiaszek
4/yr, 120 pp; subs $25
Circ: 1,500
Readership: academics, general public
Indexed/Abstracted: ABC, IMB,
MLA
• MANUSCRIPTS
Query: preferred; *Abstract:* no
Style guide: MLA
Preferred length: 3,000–6,000 wds
Copies: 2
Notes: endnotes
Blind referee: no
Acceptance rate: 1/8
Time to consider ms: 6–8 wks
Charts, tables
Foreign languages accepted: no
• REVIEWS
Seeking reviewers: yes
Unsolicited reviews accepted: no
Materials reviewed: books
Review length: 1,500–2,500 wds
How to apply: letter
Include in application: professional
degrees, institutional affiliation,
areas of expertise, published works

Utah Historical Quarterly

Utah history and prehistory
Affiliation: Utah State Historical
Society
Ed: Max J. Evans
300 Rio Grande
Salt Lake City, UT 84101
Bk Rev Ed: Stanford J. Layton
4/yr, 100 pp; subs $15
Circ: 3,200

Readership: academics, general public
Indexed/Abstracted: ABC, WAH
• MANUSCRIPTS
Query: no; *Abstract:* no
Style guide: Chicago
Preferred length: 20 pp max
Copies: 1
Notes: endnotes
Blind referee: yes
Acceptance rate: 1/4
Time to consider ms: 8 wks
Charts, pictures, tables, graphs,
maps
Foreign languages accepted: no
• REVIEWS
Seeking reviewers: yes
Unsolicited reviews accepted: no
Materials reviewed: books
Review length: 500–600 wds
How to apply: letter
Include in application: professional
degrees, institutional affiliation,
areas of expertise, published
works, current research

Valley Forge Journal

American Revolution
Affiliation: Valley Forge Historical
Society
Ed: Lawrence H. Curry
250 Wyncote Road
Jenkintown, PA 19046
2/yr, 90 pp
Circ: 1,100
Readership: academics, society mem-
bers
Indexed/Abstracted: ABC
• MANUSCRIPTS
Query: no; *Abstract:* no
Preferred length: 10–50 pp
Copies: 1
Notes: endnotes or footnotes
Blind referee: no
Acceptance rate: 9/10
Time to consider ms: 3–4 mos
Charts, pictures, maps
Foreign languages accepted: no

Ventura County Historical Society Quarterly

Ventura County history from origins to present
Affiliation: Ventura County Museum of History and Art
Ed: Charles Johnson
  100 E. Main Street
  Ventura, CA 93001
4/yr, 40 pp; subs $35
Circ: 2,000
Readership: academics, general public
• MANUSCRIPTS
Query: preferred; *Abstract:* preferred
Style guide: Chicago
Preferred length: 6,000–8,000 wds
Copies: 1
Notes: endnotes
Acceptance rate: majority
Pictures, maps
Foreign languages accepted: no

Vermont History

Vermont social, economic, political, and intellectual history; New England history with Vermont focus
Affiliation: Vermont Historical Society
Ed: Gene Session
  Vermont Historical Society
  109 State Street
  Montpelier, VT 05609-0901
Bk Rev Ed: same
4/yr, 64 pp; subs $25
Circ: 2,700
Readership: academics, general public
Indexed/Abstracted: ABC, WAH
• MANUSCRIPTS
Query: preferred; *Abstract:* no
Style guide: Chicago
Preferred length: 4,000–10,000 wds
Copies: 2
Notes: endnotes
Blind referee: no
Acceptance rate: 1/2
Time to consider ms: 6–8 wks
Charts, pictures, tables, graphs, maps
Foreign languages accepted: no

• REVIEWS
Seeking reviewers: yes
Unsolicited reviews accepted: no
Materials reviewed: books
Review length: 750–800 wds
How to apply: letter
Include in application: professional degrees, institutional affiliation, areas of expertise, published works, current research

Victorian Periodicals Review

Newspapers, magazines, reviews, and other serial publications of Victorian Britain
Affiliation: Southern Illinois University-Edwardsville
Ed: Barbara Quinn Schmidt
  English Department
  Southern Illinois University-Edwardsville
  Edwardsville, IL 62026-1436
Bk Rev Ed: same
4/yr, 52 pp; subs $15
Circ: 650
Readership: academics
Indexed/Abstracted: ABC, AHI, MLA
• MANUSCRIPTS
Query: no; *Abstract:* no
Style guide: MLA
Preferred length: 10–20 pp
Copies: 2
Notes: endnotes
Blind referee: yes
Acceptance rate: 1/2
Time to consider ms: 6–12 mos
Charts, pictures, tables, graphs, maps
Foreign languages accepted: no
• REVIEWS
Seeking reviewers: yes
Unsolicited reviews accepted: yes
Materials reviewed: books
Review length: 800–1,200 wds
How to apply: letter
Include in application: professional degrees, institutional affiliation, areas of expertise, published works, current research

Victorian Studies

The study of English culture of the
Victorian period, c. 1830–1914;
interdisciplinary
Affiliation: Indiana University
Ed: Donald Gray
   Ballantine Hall 338
   Indiana University
   Bloomington, IN 47405
Bk Rev Ed: Jean Kowaleski
4/yr, 130 pp; subs $16
Circ: 2,700
Readership: academics
Indexed/Abstracted: ABC, AHCI,
   BRI, CCAH, HI, MLA
• MANUSCRIPTS
Query: no; *Abstract:* no
Style guide: MLA
Preferred length: 25–35 pp
Copies: 2
Notes: parenthetical documentation,
   works cited
Blind referee: yes
Acceptance rate: 1/10
Time to consider ms: 4 mos
Charts, pictures, tables, graphs, maps
Foreign languages accepted: no
• REVIEWS
Seeking reviewers: no
Unsolicited reviews accepted: no
Materials reviewed: books
Review length: 800–2,000 wds
How to apply: letter
Include in application: professional
   degrees, institutional affiliation,
   areas of expertise, published
   works, foreign languages, current
   research

Vietnam

All aspects of the Vietnam War
Affiliation: Empire Press
Ed: Col. Harry J. Summers, Jr.
   602 S. King Street
   Suite 300
   Leesburg, VA 22075
Bk Rev Ed: varies
6/yr, 72 pp; subs $16.95

Circ: 166,000
Readership: academics, general public
• MANUSCRIPTS
Query: yes; *Abstract:* no
Style guide: own
Copies: 1
Notes: endnotes
Blind referee: no
Acceptance rate: 1/10
Time to consider ms: 4–6 mos
Charts, pictures, tables, graphs, maps
Foreign languages accepted: no
• REVIEWS
Seeking reviewers: no
Unsolicited reviews accepted: no
Materials reviewed: books, films
How to apply: letter
Include in application: institutional
   affiliation, areas of expertise

Vietnam Generation

Interdisciplinary look at the Vietnam
   War, Vietnam War generation, and
   the 1960s
Affiliation: Vietnam Generation, Inc.
Ed: Kali Tal
   2921 Terrace Drive
   Chevy Chase, MD 20815
Bk Rev Ed: Dan Scripture
4/yr, 120 pp; subs $40
Circ: 500
Readership: academics, general pub-
   lic, activists
Indexed/Abstracted: ABC
• MANUSCRIPTS
Query: no; *Abstract:* no
Style guide: MLA or Chicago
Preferred length: 10,000 wds max
Copies: 2
Notes: endnotes
Blind referee: yes
Acceptance rate: 3/10
Time to consider ms: 6–8 wks
Charts, pictures, tables, graphs, maps
Foreign languages accepted: no
• REVIEWS
Seeking reviewers: yes
Unsolicited reviews accepted: yes

Materials reviewed: books, films,
videos, software
Review length: 500–1,000 wds
How to apply: letter
Include in application: professional
degrees, institutional affiliation,
areas of expertise, published
works, current research
• ADDITIONAL NOTES
The editors are interested in oral
history, personal narratives and
memoirs in addition to traditional
historical subjects.

Virginia Cavalcade

Virginia history and culture
Affiliation: Virginia State Library and
Archives
Ed: Edward D. C. Campbell, Jr.
Division of Publications and Cul-
tural Affairs
Virginia State Library and Ar-
chives
Eleventh Street at Capitol Square
Richmond, VA 23219-3491
4/yr, 48 pp; subs $6
Circ: 8,500
Readership: general public
Indexed/Abstracted: ABC, MLA,
WAH
• MANUSCRIPTS
Query: preferred; *Abstract:* no
Style guide: Chicago
Preferred length: 15–20 pp
Copies: 1
Notes: endnotes
Blind referee: yes
Acceptance rate: 1/6
Time to consider ms: 4 wks
Charts, pictures, maps, transparencies
Foreign languages accepted: no
• ADDITIONAL NOTES
Virginia Cavalcade seeks essays writ-
ten in a narrative, anecdotal style
for a general readership on the
history and culture of Virginia
from the age of exploration to
1945.

Virginia Magazine of History and Biography

Virginia history, all periods
Affiliation: Virginia Historical Society
Ed: Nelson D. Lankford
P.O. Box 7311
Richmond, VA 23221-0311
Bk Rev Ed: same
4/yr, 144 pp; subs $35
Circ: 4,700
Readership: academics, general public
Indexed/Abstracted: ABC, AHCI,
CCAH, HI, WAH
• MANUSCRIPTS
Query: no; *Abstract:* no
Style guide: modified Chicago
Preferred length: 30–35 pp
Copies: 3
Notes: endnotes
Blind referee: yes
Acceptance rate: 1/4
Time to consider ms: 2 mos
Charts, pictures, tables, graphs,
maps
Foreign languages accepted: no
• REVIEWS
Seeking reviewers: yes
Unsolicited reviews accepted: no
Materials reviewed: books
Review length: 600 wds
How to apply: form
Include in application: professional
degrees, institutional affiliation,
areas of expertise, published works

Virginia Quarterly Review

Literature and discussion
Affiliation: University of Virginia
Ed: Staige D. Blackford
One West Range
Charlottesville, VA 22903
Bk Rev Ed: same
4/yr, 288 pp; subs $15
Circ: 4,000
Readership: academics, general public
Indexed/Abstracted: ABC, AHCI,
BRD, BRI, CCAH, HI, MLA,
WAH

• MANUSCRIPTS
Query: no; *Abstract:* no
Style guide: any
Preferred length: 20–25 pp
Copies: 1
Notes: none
Blind referee: no
Acceptance rate: 1/10
Time to consider ms: 1 mo
No illustrations accepted
Foreign languages accepted: no
• REVIEWS
Seeking reviewers: yes
Unsolicited reviews accepted: yes
Materials reviewed: books
Review length: 5–10 pp
How to apply: letter
Include in application: professional
degrees, institutional affiliation,
areas of expertise, published works

WWI Aero, The Journal of the Early Aeroplane

Building or restoring fullscale air-
craft, 1900–1920
Affiliation: World War I Aeroplanes,
Inc.
Ed: Leonard E. Opdycke
15 Crescent Road
Poughkeepsie, NY 12601
Bk Rev Ed: same
4/yr, 130 pp; subs $25
Circ: 2,100
Readership: aviation historians,
builders
• MANUSCRIPTS
Query: preferred; *Abstract:* preferred
Style guide: own
Preferred length: 1,500–3,000 wds
Copies: 1
Blind referee: no
Acceptance rate: 4/5
Charts, pictures, tables, graphs,
maps
Foreign languages accepted: no
• REVIEWS
Seeking reviewers: no
Unsolicited reviews accepted: yes

Materials reviewed: books, films,
drawings, catalogs
Review length: 300–400 wds
How to apply: letter
Include in application: areas of ex-
pertise, current research

Washington History: The Magazine of the Historical Society of Washington, D.C.

Local urban, social and cultural
history of Washington, D.C.
Affiliation: The Historical Society of
Washington, D.C.
Ed: Howard F. Gillette, Jr.
The Historical Society of Wash-
ington, D.C.
1307 New Hampshire Avenue,
N.W.
Washington, D.C. 20036-1507
Bk Rev Ed: Ronald M. Johnson
2/yr, 96 pp; subs $35
Circ: 3,000
Readership: academics, general pub-
lic, society members
Indexed/Abstracted: ABC, WAH
• MANUSCRIPTS
Query: preferred; *Abstract:* no
Style guide: modified Chicago
Preferred length: 30 pp
Copies: 3
Notes: endnotes
Blind referee: yes
Acceptance rate: 4/5
Time to consider ms: 2 mos
Pictures, maps
Foreign languages accepted: no
• REVIEWS
Seeking reviewers: yes
Unsolicited reviews accepted: no
Materials reviewed: books, films,
exhibits
Review length: 1,000 wds
How to apply: letter
Include in application: professional
degrees, institutional affiliation,
areas of expertise, published
works, current research

- ADDITIONAL NOTES

The editors are especially interested in articles comparing Washington to other urban areas. A heavily illustrated journal, *Washington History* requires illustrations for all contributions. Because the journal is read by the general public as well as scholars, a premium is placed on clear and lively writing.

Welsh History Review

Welsh history
Affiliation: University of Wales
Ed: Kenneth O. Morgan
Plas Penglais
Aberystwyth
Dyfed SY23 3DF
U.K.
Bk Rev Ed: same
2/yr, 150 pp; subs £10
Circ: 1,000
Readership: academics, general public
Indexed/Abstracted: ABC, AHCI, BHI, CCAH
- MANUSCRIPTS
Query: preferred; *Abstract:* no
Style guide: own
Preferred length: 10,000 wds
Copies: 2
Notes: footnotes
Blind referee: sometimes
Acceptance rate: 2/5
Time to consider ms: 3 mos
Charts, pictures, tables, graphs, maps
Foreign languages accepted: Welsh
- REVIEWS
Seeking reviewers: no
Unsolicited reviews accepted: no
Materials reviewed: books, microfiche, computerized data
Review length: 700 wds
How to apply: letter or personal contact
Include in application: professional degrees, institutional affiliation, areas of expertise, published works, foreign languages, current research

West Virginia History

History, biography, genealogy and bibliography of West Virginia
Affiliation: State of West Virginia Division of Culture and History
Ed: Frederick H. Armstrong
The Cultural Center
Capitol Complex
Charleston, WV 25305
Bk Rev Ed: same
subs $12
Readership: academics, general public
Indexed/Abstracted: ABC, WAH
- MANUSCRIPTS
Query: no; *Abstract:* no
Style guide: Chicago
Preferred length: varies
Copies: 2
Notes: endnotes
Foreign languages accepted: no
- REVIEWS
Materials reviewed: books

The Westchester Historian

History of Westchester County, New York
Affiliation: Westchester County Historical Society
Eds: Barbara Davis and Elizabeth Fuller
Westchester County Historical Society
2199 Saw Mill River Road
Elmsford, NY 10523
Bk Rev Ed: same
4/yr, 24 pp; subs $25
Circ: 1,000
Readership: academics, general public
- MANUSCRIPTS
Query: preferred; *Abstract:* preferred
Preferred length: 10 pp
Copies: 1
Notes: endnotes
Blind referee: no
Pictures, maps
Foreign languages accepted: no
- REVIEWS
Seeking reviewers: no

Unsolicited reviews accepted: yes
Materials reviewed: books
Review length: 1 pp

Western Historical Quarterly

The westward movement from the
Atlantic to the Pacific; twentieth
century regional studies; the Span-
ish borderlands; developments in
Western Canada, Northern Mex-
ico, Alaska, and Hawaii
Affiliation: Utah State University and
the University of New Mexico
Ed: Clyde A. Milner II
c/o Western Historical Quarterly
Utah State University
Department of History
Logan, UT 84322-0740
Bk Rev Ed: Anne M. Butler
4/yr, 144 pp; subs $30
Circ: 2,800
Readership: academics, general pub-
lic, public historians
Indexed/Abstracted: ABC, AHCI,
BRI, CCAH, HI, WAH
• MANUSCRIPTS
Query: no; *Abstract:* no
Style guide: Turabian
Preferred length: 35 pp
Copies: 2
Notes: endnotes
Blind referee: yes
Acceptance rate: 1/10
Time to consider ms: 2–8 wks
Charts, pictures, tables, graphs, maps
Foreign languages accepted: no
• REVIEWS
Seeking reviewers: yes
Unsolicited reviews accepted: no
Materials reviewed: books
Review length: 500 wds
How to apply: letter, form
Include in application: vita

Western Legal History

Legal history of the American West
Affiliation: Ninth Circuit Historical
Society

Ed: Bradley Williams
125 South Grand Avenue
Pasadena, CA 91105
Bk Rev Ed: same
2/yr, 150 pp; subs $25
Circ: 2,000
Readership: members of the western
bench and bar
Indexed/Abstracted: ABC, WAH
• MANUSCRIPTS
Query: yes; *Abstract:* no
Style guide: Chicago
Preferred length: 20–35 pp
Copies: 2
Notes: endnotes
Blind referee: yes
Acceptance rate: 4/5
Time to consider ms: 3 mos
Charts, pictures, tables, graphs, maps
Foreign languages accepted: no
• REVIEWS
Seeking reviewers: yes
Unsolicited reviews accepted: yes
Materials reviewed: books, films
Review length: 1,000 wds
How to apply: letter
Include in application: professional
degrees, areas of expertise

Western States Jewish History

Trans–Mississippi/Pacific Rim Jewish
history
Affiliation: Western State Jewish His-
tory Association
Ed: William M. Kramer
3111 Kelton Avenue
Los Angeles, CA 90034
Bk Rev Ed: same
4/yr, 96 pp; subs $20
Circ: 800
Readership: academics, old families
Indexed/Abstracted: ABC, WAH
• MANUSCRIPTS
Query: preferred; *Abstract:* no
Style guide: Chicago
Preferred length: open
Copies: 2
Notes: endnotes

Blind referee: sometimes
Acceptance rate: 1/2
Time to consider ms: 3 mos
Pictures
Foreign languages accepted: no
• REVIEWS
Seeking reviewers: yes
Unsolicited reviews accepted: yes
Materials reviewed: books
Review length: 300 wds
How to apply: letter
Include in application: professional
  degrees, institutional affiliation,
  published works

The Wicazo SA Review

Native American studies
Affiliation: Eastern Washington
  University and University of
  California, Davis
Ed: Elizabeth Cook-Lynn
  Rte #8 Box 510
  Dakotah Meadows
  Rapid City, SD 57702
Bk Rev Ed: same
2/yr, 80 pp; subs $20
Circ: 680
Readership: academics, general pub-
  lic, Indian communities
Indexed/Abstracted: ABC, MLA
• MANUSCRIPTS
Query: no; *Abstract:* no
Preferred length: 10–40 pp
Copies: 1
Time to consider ms: 3–4 mos
Foreign languages accepted: Indian
  languages
• REVIEWS
Seeking reviewers: yes
Unsolicited reviews accepted: yes
Materials reviewed: books

Wild West

All aspects of the American West
Affiliation: Empire Press
Ed: William M. Vogt
  602 S. King Street

Suite 300
Leesburg, VA 22075
Bk Rev Ed: varies
6/yr, 72 pp; subs $16.95
Circ: 140,000
Readership: academics, general public
• MANUSCRIPTS
Query: yes; *Abstract:* no
Style guide: own
Copies: 1
Notes: endnotes
Blind referee: no
Acceptance rate: 1/10
Time to consider ms: 4–6 mos
Charts, pictures, tables, graphs,
  maps
Foreign languages accepted: no
• REVIEWS
Seeking reviewers: no
Unsolicited reviews accepted: no
Materials reviewed: books, films
How to apply: letter
Include in application: institutional
  affiliation, areas of expertise

The William and Mary Quarterly: A Magazine of Early American History and Culture

The history and culture of colonial
  America and the early Republic;
  related history of the British Isles,
  the European continent, Africa and
  other areas of the New World to
  approximately 1820
Affiliation: College of William and
  Mary; Colonial Williamsburg
  Foundation
Ed: Michael McGiffert
  Box 220
  Williamsburg, VA 23187
Bk Rev Ed: John E. Selby
4/yr, 190 pp; subs $25
Circ: 3,800
Readership: academics, general pub-
  lic, historical organizations
Indexed/Abstracted: ABC, AHCI,
  BRI, CCAH, HI, MLA, WAH

- MANUSCRIPTS
Query: no; *Abstract:* no
Style guide: Chicago
Preferred length: 40 pp max
Copies: 3
Notes: endnotes
Blind referee: yes
Acceptance rate: 1/6
Time to consider ms: 30–90 days
Charts, pictures, tables, graphs, maps
Foreign languages accepted: no
- REVIEWS
Seeking reviewers: yes
Unsolicited reviews accepted: no
Materials reviewed: books, exhibitions
Review length: varies
How to apply: letter
Include in application: professional
degrees, institutional affiliation,
areas of expertise, published works,
foreign languages, current research

Winterthur Portfolio

Interdisciplinary study of the arts in
America and the historical context
in which they developed
Affiliation: University of Chicago
Press; Winterthur Museum,
Garden, and Library
Ed: Catherine E. Hutchins
Winterthur Museum
Winterthur, DE 19735
Bk Rev Ed: Shirley Wajda
Boston University
American and New England
Studies Program
226 Bay State Road
Boston, MA 02215
3/yr, 110 pp
Circ: 1,800
Readership: academics, general public
Indexed/Abstracted: ABC, AHCI,
CCAH, MLA, WAH
- MANUSCRIPTS
Query: no; *Abstract:* preferred
Style guide: modified Chicago
Preferred length: varies
Copies: 2

Notes: endnotes
Blind referee: no
Charts, pictures, tables, maps
Foreign languages accepted: no
- REVIEWS
Seeking reviewers: yes
Unsolicited reviews accepted: occa-
sionally
Materials reviewed: books
Review length: varies
How to apply: letter
Include in application: professional
degrees, institutional affiliation,
areas of expertise, published
works, current research

Wisconsin Magazine of History

History of Wisconsin and the Upper
Midwest
Affiliation: The State Historical So-
ciety of Wisconsin
Ed: Paul Hass
816 State Street
Madison, WI 53706
Bk Rev Ed: William C. Marten
4/yr, 80 pp; subs $25
Circ: 6,500
Readership: academics, general pub-
lic, society members
Indexed/Abstracted: ABC, WAH
- MANUSCRIPTS
Query: preferred; *Abstract:* no
Style guide: Words Into Type
Preferred length: 30–40 pp
Copies: 1
Notes: endnotes
Blind referee: occasionally
Acceptance rate: 1/4
Time to consider ms: 1 mo
Charts, pictures, tables
- REVIEWS
Seeking reviewers: no
Unsolicited reviews accepted: rarely
Materials reviewed: books
Review length: 3 pp
How to apply: letter
Include in application: professional
degrees, institutional affiliation,
areas of expertise, published works

Women's History Review

Women's history
Ed: June Purvis
   School of Social and Historical
      Studies
   Portsmouth Polytechnic
   Bunaby Road
   Portsmouth PO1 3AS
   U.K.
Bk Rev Ed: June Hannam
   Humanities Department
   Bristol Polytechnic
   Fishponds
   Bristol BS16 2JP
   U.K.
3/yr; subs $49 U.S.
Circ: 900
Readership: academics, general public
• MANUSCRIPTS
Query: no; *Abstract:* yes
Copies: 3
Blind referee: yes
Acceptance rate: 7/20
Time to consider ms: 2 mos
Pictures
Foreign languages accepted: no
• REVIEWS
Seeking reviewers: yes
Unsolicited reviews accepted: yes
Materials reviewed: books
Review length: 500–700 wds
How to apply: letter
Include in application: areas of
   expertise

Works and Days: Essays in the Socio-Historical Dimensions of Literature and the Arts

Multi-disciplinary approaches to the
   relations between the arts and their
   socio-historical and socio-cultural
   contexts
Affiliation: Indiana University of
   Pennsylvania
Ed: David B. Downing
   English Department
   110 Leonard Hall
Indiana University of Pennsyl-
   vania
Indiana, PA 15701
Bk Rev Ed: same
2/yr, 120 pp; subs $12
Circ: 300
Readership: academics
Indexed/Abstracted: AHI, MLA
• MANUSCRIPTS
Query: no; *Abstract:* no
Style guide: MLA
Preferred length: 20–30 pp
Copies: 2
Notes: endnotes
Blind referee: no
Acceptance rate: 1/4
Time to consider ms: 3 mos
Charts, pictures, tables, graphs, maps
Foreign languages accepted: no
• REVIEWS
Seeking reviewers: no
Unsolicited reviews accepted: yes
Materials reviewed: books, films
Review length: 10 pp
How to apply: letter

World Affairs

International relations, law, foreign
   policy
Affiliation: American Peace Society
Ed: Mark Falcoff
   1319 18th Street, N.W.
   Washington, DC 20036
4/yr, 48 pp; subs $30
Circ: 1,000
Readership: academics
Indexed/Abstracted: ABC, CCSB,
   PAIS, SSCI, SSI, WAH
• MANUSCRIPTS
Query: no; *Abstract:* no
Style guide: Chicago
Preferred length: 25–40 pp
Copies: 2
Notes: endnotes
Blind referee: no
Acceptance rate: 1/5
Charts, tables, graphs, maps
Foreign languages accepted: no

World War II

All aspects of World War II
Affiliation: Empire Press
Ed: Michael E. Haskew
  602 S. King Street
  Suite 300
  Leesburg, VA 22075
Bk Rev Ed: varies
6/yr, 88 pp; subs $16.95
Circ: 200,000
Readership: academics, general public
• MANUSCRIPTS
Query: yes; *Abstract:* no
Style guide: own
Copies: 1
Notes: endnotes
Blind referee: no
Acceptance rate: 1/5
Time to consider ms: 4–6 mos
Charts, pictures, tables, graphs, maps
Foreign languages accepted: no
• REVIEWS
Seeking reviewers: no
Unsolicited reviews accepted: no
Materials reviewed: books, films
How to apply: letter
Include in application: institutional
  affiliation, areas of expertise

World War II Journal

World War II history
Affiliation: Merriam Press
Ed: Ray Merriam
  218 Beech Street
  Bennington, VT 05201
4/yr, 60 pp; subs $20
Circ: 200
Readership: academics, general pub-
  lic, collectors, modelers, veterans,
  wargames, historians, buffs
• MANUSCRIPTS
Query: yes; *Abstract:* yes
Preferred length: open
Copies: 1
Notes: endnotes
Blind referee: no
Acceptance rate: 9/10
Time to consider ms: 1 mo

Charts, pictures, tables, graphs, maps
Foreign languages accepted: no

World War II Notes

Reviews and news about WWII
  books, magazines, articles, and
  other items of interest
Affiliation: Merriam Press
Ed: Ray Merriam
  218 Beech Street
  Bennington, VT 05201
Bk Rev Ed: same
4/yr, 50 pp; subs $20
Circ: 300
Readership: academics, general pub-
  lic, collectors, veterans, modelers,
  wargames, historians, buffs
• REVIEWS
Seeking reviewers: yes
Unsolicited reviews accepted: yes
Materials reviewed: books, films,
  articles
Review length: 500 wds max
How to apply: letter
Include in application: professional
  degrees, institutional affiliation,
  areas of expertise, published
  works, foreign languages, current
  research

Yesteryears

New York state history and gen-
  ealogy
Ed: Malcolm O. Goodelle
  3 Seymour Street
  Auburn, NY 13021
Bk Rev Ed: same
4/yr, 36 pp; subs $9
Circ: 200
Readership: academics, general public
• MANUSCRIPTS
Query: no; *Abstract:* no
Preferred length: 30 pp max
Copies: 1
Notes: footnotes
Blind referee: no
Charts, pictures, tables, maps
Foreign languages accepted: no

• REVIEWS
Seeking reviewers: no
Unsolicited reviews accepted: yes
Materials reviewed: books
Review length: 100 wds

The York Pioneer

Ontario history, especially in the
  Toronto region
Affiliation: The York Pioneer and
  Historical Society
Ed: Jeanine C. Avigdor
  61 Thorncrest Road

Etobicoke, ON M9A 1S8
CANADA
1/yr, 68 pp; subs $11
Circ: 600
Readership: general public
• MANUSCRIPTS
Query: preferred; *Abstract:* no
Preferred length: 4,000–8,000 wds
Copies: 1
Notes: footnotes
Blind referee: no
Acceptance rate: 9/10
Pictures, maps
Foreign languages accepted: no

Subject Index

Acadia 21, 54
Accounting 21
Administration 136
African-Americans 22, 35, 45, 131, 144, 228
Africans/Africa 22, 121, 126, 131, 148, 155, 168, 174, 175, 255
Agriculture 23
Airplanes 234, 260
Alabama 24, 116, 210
Alaska 24, 262
Alberta 25
Alchemy 25
Alcohol 238
American Indians 29, 196, 263
Amish 180, 209
Anabaptists 180
Ancient *see* Classical/ancient
Anglicans 36
Angola 174
Anthropology/archaeology 26, 27, 85, 103, 117, 162, 167, 247
Appalachia 38, 135, 199
Arab studies *see* Middle East
Archaeology *see* Anthropology/archaeology
Architecture 40, 41, 155, 166
Archives/libraries 27, 39, 69, 74, 116, 156, 169, 170, 214, 216, 217
Arizona 40, 129
Arkansas 40, 89, 153
Army *see* Military
The Arts 40, 41, 75, 79, 95, 101, 106, 111, 118, 131, 133, 134, 155, 166, 195, 214, 222, 227, 242, 245, 248, 252, 254, 264
Asia 49, 50, 63, 73, 79, 82, 86, 99, 129, 130, 140, 144, 147, 155, 163, 186, 187, 204, 211, 243
Astronomy 126
Austria 94
Aviation 43, 151, 234, 260

Baja, California 146
Balkans 143
Baltic states 130, 170
Baptists 43, 44
Baseball 44, 194
Benedictines 28
Bible 61
Biography 45, 101, 170, 179, 209, 253, 259
Biology 107
Blacks 22, 35, 45
Brazil 174
British Columbia 43, 46
Bus transportation 52
Business 21, 53

California 54, 55, 76, 146, 229, 244, 257
Canada—General 33, 44, 47, 56, 57, 73, 132, 173, 210, 212, 213, 224; *see also* Canada—Local/provincial/regional
Canada—Local/provincial/regional 21, 25, 42, 43, 46, 54, 60, 89, 103, 125, 188, 193, 199, 201, 218, 223, 228, 229, 267; *see also* Canada—General
Caribbean 34, 132, 252

Catholic church 61, 150, 219
Caves 149
Celtic 55
Central Europe 62, 74
Chemistry 25
Chesapeake Bay 177
Children 96
China 50, 63, 69, 99, 144, 187; *see also* Asia
Christians *see* Religion
Church and state 132
Cities 22, 63, 159, 211, 267
Civil War (U.S.) 26, 41, 65, 70, 118, 133; *see also* United States—General; United States—Local; United States—State and regional; The South (U.S.); The Southwest (U.S.); *and names of individual states*
Classical/ancient 30, 51, 61, 66, 67, 101
Coast Guard *see* Maritime; Military
Colorado 68, 212, 229, 247
Columbia University 69
Commonwealth (British) 104, 139
Computers 108, 109, 117
Confederates (American) 70, 133
Congress (U.S.) 70
Connecticut 70, 71
Cornwall 76
Czechoslovakia 74

Dalhousie University 75
Dance 75, 248
Decorative arts 134
Delaware 75
Dentistry 51
Design 40, 133
Developing areas 134
Devon 76
Diplomacy/international affairs 74, 77, 86, 96, 115, 120, 121, 123, 124, 127, 133, 223, 236, 265
District of Columbia 260
Dorset 198
Durham University 78

Eastern Europe 80, 86, 235
Economics 81, 87, 111, 135, 208
Education 110, 136
Eighteenth century 51, 81, 82, 222
Emblems 83
England *see* Great Britain
Environment 84
Episcopalians 36
Eskimos 86
Estonia 130
Ethiopia 155
Ethnic 26, 29, 56, 61, 85, 86, 102, 127, 151, 249, 263; *see also* African-Americans *and* Jewish
Europe 52, 58, 60, 62, 71, 74, 80, 82, 86, 87, 91, 94, 95, 100, 106, 115, 117, 125, 130, 136, 142, 143, 158, 170, 174, 186, 187, 212, 223, 227, 229, 230, 231, 235, 236, 256; *see also individual countries*

Family 110, 137
Film 40, 88, 104, 129
Finland 130
Florida 85, 89, 210, 250, 252
Folklore 89, 90, 96, 128, 137, 208
French/France 71, 73, 91, 186, 224
Frontier *see* The West/frontier (U.S.)

Garden history 92, 137
General history 28, 57, 67, 72, 74, 81, 82, 83, 103, 104, 107, 114, 133, 138, 139, 143, 145, 158, 159, 171, 176, 191, 208, 227
Georgia 41, 93, 148, 226
Germans/Germany 61, 94, 95, 151, 161
Great Britain—General 25, 46, 71, 83, 104, 106, 119, 131, 139, 187, 207, 231, 255, 258, 261; *see also* Great Britain—Local/regional
Great Britain—Local/regional 46, 54,

63, 68, 76, 198; *see also* Great
  Britain — General
Great Lakes 119, 165, 181
Great Plains (American) 97, 161, 183,
  190, 196, 213, 243
Greece 142
Greek Orthodox 98
Gulf Coast (U.S.) 98, 114

Ireland 57, 83, 207, 219
Islam 31, 39, 48, 147, 175
Italians/Italy 58, 125

Japan 99, 140; *see also* Asia
Jewish 30, 77, 125, 140, 262

Hawaii 100, 262
Hayes, Rutherford B. 100
Hemingway, Ernest 101
Hispanics (American) 102
Holocaust 77
Human rights 96, 115
Humanities 33, 38, 40, 48, 58, 62,
  69, 75, 78, 81, 82, 97, 101, 116, 127,
  132, 136, 145, 165, 169, 175, 182,
  185, 191, 195, 196, 198, 199, 206,
  214, 215, 218, 227, 232, 234, 245,
  247, 249, 259, 265; *see also*
  Interdisciplinary
Hungary 115
Hutterites 180

Kansas 161, 162
Kent (U.K.) 54
Kentucky 88, 220
Korea 99, 163; *see also* Asia

Labor 48, 163, 164, 165
Lake Superior 165
Landscape 166
Latin America 35, 36, 49, 102, 132,
  140, 167, 174, 181, 252
Latvia 130
Legal 31, 72, 141, 168, 262
Liberia 168
Library *see* Archives/libraries
Lincoln, Abraham 118, 170
Linguistics *see* Philology/linguistics
Literature/language 26, 29, 31, 32,
  34, 35, 38, 67, 129, 167, 174, 192,
  198, 224, 226, 227, 245, 246, 259,
  265; *see also* Philology/linguistics
Lithuania 130, 170
Local history 146, 171
Logic 108
Long Island (N.Y.) 172, 173
Louisiana 42, 173, 197
Lutherans 69

Iberia 117
Idaho 166, 237
Illinois 63, 101, 118
Indiana 92, 119, 228, 253
Industrial Age 117
Intellectual 38, 62, 67, 106, 108, 111,
  112, 113, 153, 154, 189
Intelligence/security 120
Interdisciplinary 48, 59, 70, 77, 83,
  113, 115, 122, 123, 124, 132, 133,
  134, 139, 145, 146, 150, 154, 169,
  172, 177, 189, 204, 205, 206, 207,
  213, 215, 216, 218, 219, 229, 235,
  258; *see also* Humanities *and*
  Social sciences
Inuit 86
Iowa 36, 96, 206

Maghreb 175
Maine 175
Marine Corps *see* Maritime; Military
Maritime: 32, 36, 176, 189, 190, 232
Martha's Vineyard 78

Maryland 95, 176, 177
Massachusetts 78, 85, 105
Mathematics 102
Media 88, 104, 144, 160, 178, 214, 217, 219, 257
Medicine 52, 55, 110, 153, 178, 239
Medieval 37, 55, 95, 106, 142, 178, 179, 221, 225, 234, 248; *see also* Reformation *and* Renaissance
Mediterranean 231
Mennonites 180, 209
Mesoamerica 36
Mesopotamia 51
Methodists 180, 215
Methodology/theory 67, 105, 108, 109, 240; *see also* Teaching
Mexico 156, 162, 181, 262
Michigan 97, 181
Micronesia 157
Middle East 31, 39, 48, 50, 51, 121, 147, 161, 175, 182, 254
The Midwest (U.S.) 36, 119, 182, 183, 197, 200, 201, 253, 264
Migration 123
Military 23, 51, 120, 133, 141, 149, 150, 161, 174, 183, 184, 190, 236, 242, 258, 266; *see also* Civil War (U.S.)
Mills 200
Minnesota 165, 185, 227
Mississippi 142, 185, 194
Missouri 93, 186
Model building 189
Montana 187
Mormons 143
Mozambique 174
Museums 51, 74, 219, 264
Music 79, 106, 212, 254

National Archives (U.S.) 216
Native Americans 29, 196, 263
Nautical *see* Maritime
Naval *see* Maritime
Nebraska 190
Netherlands 58

Nevada 191, 197
New Brunswick 199
New England 70, 85, 105, 191
New Hampshire 105
New Jersey 50, 192, 213
New Mexico 193
The New World *see* Western Hemisphere
New York 22, 63, 98, 115, 172, 173, 193, 226, 230, 231, 232, 244, 261, 266
Newfoundland 193
Newspapers 144, 160; *see also* Media
Nineteenth century 195
North Carolina 195, 244, 250
North Dakota 196
Nova Scotia 199
Nursing 110

Ohio 45, 197, 200, 211
Oklahoma 64
Ontario 103, 201, 212, 267
Oral history 202
The Organ 254
Oregon 203
Oregon Trail 203
Ottoman studies 254

Pacific 100, 204, 205, 262
Pacific Northwest 68, 203, 204, 205
Parliaments 207
Peace studies 122, 133; *see also* Diplomacy
Peasant studies 145
Pennsylvania 95, 155, 208, 209, 211, 232
Periodicals 144, 160, 257; *see also* Media
Pharmacy 210
Philippines 211
Philology/linguistics 29, 34, 36, 50, 51, 58, 67, 113, 224, 230
Philosophy 38, 67, 108, 111, 154, 215

Photography 23, 111, 184, 210
Poland 212
Polynesia 100
Popular culture 145, 249
Portugal 117, 174
Presbyterians 32
Preservation 73, 103, 177, 200
Presidency (U.S.) 70, 100, 213, 253
Prince Edward Island 125
Princeton University 214
Printing 214
Prints 118, 214
Psychohistory 216
Public history *see* Archives/
  libraries

Quakers 58, 217, 244
Quebec 42, 218, 224
Queen's University 218

Radicalism 158, 218, 219
Radio 104
Railroads 188, 219
Reenactment 171
Reformation 219, 221; *see also*
  Medieval
Refugees 123
Religion 28, 32, 36, 41, 43, 44, 58,
  61, 64, 65, 69, 88, 98, 99, 112, 119,
  132, 135, 143, 150, 152, 160, 180,
  209, 215, 217, 219, 220, 233, 244
Renaissance 221; *see also* Medieval
Rhode Island 194, 225
Richard III 225
Roman Catholics *see* Catholic church
Romanticism 249
Roosevelt, Theodore 253
Rural life 227
Russians/Russia 149, 151, 223, 227;
  see also Slavs *and* Soviet Union

St. Lawrence 21
Saskatchewan 229
Scandinavia 229, 230, 249

Science and technology 25, 37, 38,
  39, 47, 51, 52, 55, 80, 102, 107, 110,
  112, 117, 124, 126, 149, 153, 178,
  189, 210, 239, 248, 251
Scotland 119, 231
Seventeenth century 232
Sexuality 154
Shakers 233
Sixteenth century 234
Slavery/abolition 235
Slavs 60, 74, 80, 100, 149, 151, 158,
  212, 223, 227, 235, 236, 256
Slovakia 74
Slovenia 236
Social history 69, 72, 79, 147, 154,
  208, 237, 238, 239, 241
Social sciences 31, 48, 113, 123, 138,
  139, 154, 166, 237, 239, 240
Somerset 198
The South (U.S.) 24, 40, 89, 93, 98,
  133, 134, 142, 148, 173, 185, 195,
  243, 245, 246, 251, 259
South Carolina 243
South Dakota 243
The Southwest (U.S.) 90, 129, 150,
  156, 162, 193, 247
Soviet Union 86, 149; *see also*
  Russians/Russia
Space travel 43
Spanish/Spain 52, 117
Sports 44, 122, 149, 194
Swedes/Swedish 249

Teaching 60, 108, 109, 113, 241, 246,
  251, 252
Television 104
Tennessee 72, 99, 135, 251
Texas 81, 114, 150, 168, 206, 247
The Theatre 106, 195, 222, 252
Third World 134, 157
Transportation 52, 158, 188, 219
Turkey 254

Ukraine 100, 158, 256
United States—General 28, 33, 34,

35, 59, 70, 79, 100, 127, 128, 129, 152, 181, 199, 215, 216, 223, 256, 263; *see also* United States – Local; United States – State and regional; Civil War (U.S.); The South (U.S.); The Southwest (U.S.); The West/frontier (U.S.); *and names of individual states*

United States – Local 41, 42, 45, 50, 63, 72, 76, 78, 81, 85, 89, 92, 95, 97, 98, 99, 101, 114, 115, 116, 135, 146, 148, 153, 155, 165, 166, 168, 172, 173, 174, 185, 194, 197, 206, 210, 211, 213, 226, 228, 229, 230, 231, 232, 244, 250, 252, 257, 260, 261; *see also* United States – General; United States – State and regional; Civil War (U.S.); The South (U.S.); The Southwest (U.S.); The West/frontier (U.S.); *and names of individual states*

United States – State and regional 24, 36, 37, 38, 40, 54, 55, 64, 68, 70, 71, 75, 88, 89, 90, 93, 96, 97, 98, 100, 105, 118, 119, 129, 142, 148, 156, 157, 161, 162, 166, 173, 175, 177, 181, 183, 185, 186, 187, 190, 191, 192, 193, 195, 196, 200, 201, 203, 204, 205, 206, 208, 209, 220, 225, 227, 237, 243, 247, 250, 251, 253, 256, 257, 259, 261, 262, 264, 266; *see also* United States – General; United States – Local; Civil War (U.S.); The South (U.S.); The Southwest (U.S.); The West/frontier (U.S.); *and names of individual states*

Utah 256

Valley Forge 256
Vermont 257
Victorian era 257, 258
Vietnam war (U.S.) 258
Virginia 42, 174, 226, 259

Wales 261
War *see* Military
Washington, D.C. 260
Washington State 68
The West/frontier (U.S.) 37, 43, 54, 55, 68, 129, 156, 157, 162, 184, 187, 188, 191, 201, 203, 204, 205, 212, 253, 254, 256, 262, 263; *see also* United States – General; United States – Local; United States – State and regional; The South (U.S.); The Southwest (U.S.); *and names of individual states*
West Virginia 96, 211, 261
Western Hemisphere 27, 28, 35
William and Mary, College of 263
Wisconsin 185, 264
Women 41, 88, 92, 93, 114, 159, 218, 222, 228, 233, 265
World War II 266
Wyoming 37

Yorkshire 46